Angola under the Portuguese

Angola
under the Portuguese
The Myth and the Reality

Gerald J. Bender

UNIVERSITY OF CALIFORNIA PRESS
BERKELEY AND LOS ANGELES

University of California Press
Berkeley and Los Angeles, California

© Gerald J. Bender 1978
First published 1978

First California Paperback Printing 1980
ISBN 0-520-04274-3
Library of Congress Catalog Card Number 76-7751

Printed in the United States of America

1 2 3 4 5 6 7 8 9

To Tammy

Contents

BIBLIOGRAPHY

INDEX

List of Tables

List of Illustrations

Acknowledgements

During the course of the ten years of research and writing which have transpired since I first journeyed to Portugal and Angola, I have incurred a considerable number of debts: to friends and family for their emotional support and encouragement, to professors and colleagues for their intellectual encouragement and supportive criticisms, and to the many individuals here and abroad who, whether or not they agreed with my premises or conclusions, generously opened doors to information and sources otherwise impossible to reach. It is frustrating for me to know that in these few pages of acknowledgement I will not be able to thank by name all those who have assisted me in one way or another and that I will inevitably, but inadvertently, omit some deserving individuals. Finally, I would like to pass on the exasperation I have felt, while writing these pages, with the apparently limited number of ways to say 'thank you'.

As I approached the completion of this work, I realized how importantly I had been influenced by certain individuals whom I knew prior to beginning the study. My basic understanding of the general patterns and nuances of race relations was decisively formed by James Tillman, Jr. and Mary Tillman, to both of whom I will always be intellectually indebted. I am also indebted to Professor Robert T. Holt for his excellent teaching and skilful guidance during my undergraduate studies and for talking me out of attending law school and suggesting that I pursue graduate studies in African politics at UCLA.

The potential value of conducting research on Angola was first suggested by Professors C. S. Whitaker, Jr. and James S. Coleman and was reinforced by the encouragement of Professors James Duffy, William Gerberding, and Daniel Biebuyck. Michael A. Samuels opened valuable doors and graciously put at my disposal his knowledge and understanding of the problems and logistics of conducting research on contemporary Angola.

I am also grateful for the assistance and hospitality offered in Lisbon by Professors Ilídio do Amaral, Abilio Lima de Carvalho, Narana Coissoro, Raquel Soeiro de Brito, João Baptista Pereira Neto, Oscar Soares Barata, and Antonio de Silva Rego. Drs. Luís Polanah and Mario Antonio Fernandes de Oliveira deserve special thanks for their insights and strong support during many difficult months in Lisbon. I would not have been able to enter Angola without the intervention of Narana

Coissoro, Antonio de Silva Rego, and Carlos Texeira da Mota, who yielded vital assistance during my five-month battle with the PIDE, Ministry of Overseas Affairs, and especially then Foreign Minister Franco Nogueira, all of whom objected to issuing me a visa to Angola.

My fieldwork in Angola could not have been nearly as fruitful as it was nor could I have gained a fraction of my understanding of rural Angola without the help, support, hospitality, and insightful advice of Eduardo Cruz de Carvalho whose collaboration I was fortunate to have enjoyed during most of the period this study was written. In addition, I owe a great debt to all those people in the Missão de Inqueritos Agrícolas de Angola who were invaluable teachers and friends, especially Julio Morais, Francisco Sá Pereira, José Almeida, Jaime Almeida, Manual Dias, Manuel de Oliveira, Elias Candeias, and Duarte Candeias. I also benefited from the penetrating observations and valuable assistance of João David de Morais and Luisa Maria Simões-Raposo. All of these individuals risked their personal and professional security to provide me with data and/or documents which contradicted the official government line and without which this study would probably not have exceeded the level of polemicism.

I am grateful to Fernando Borges Mouzinho and Fernando Couto e Silva, the former president and vice-president of the Junta Provincial de Povoamento de Angola (JPP), who generously allowed me access to data within the JPP. It would not have been possible for me to travel outside Luanda without the assistance of Major José Monroy who, while holding views contrary to my own, intervened with the PIDE/DGS and accepted responsibility for my travel in the interior. Michael Chapman and Martim Cabral also intervened with the PIDE/DGS on my behalf and helped me to obtain logistical support.

My research and writing after the fieldwork in Portugal and Angola greatly benefited from the many meaningful, intellectual exchanges with friends such as Franz-Wilhelm Heimer, Gerard Chaliand, Juliette Minces, Basil Davidson, Douglas Wheeler, Jorge Vieira da Silva, Ismael Gaspar-Martins, Shimshon Zelniker, and Lawrence Henderson. All were continual sources of stimulation and moral encouragement and none of them ever 'lost the faith'.

I would like to thank Tamar Zelniker, Ricardo Klorman, and Clarence and Charlotte Levine for their assistance in the preparation and interpretation of the data and tables found in Chapter 4. I am also very grateful for the encouragement and assistance so generously extended by Patricia Tsien and Gilberto Schlittler of the United Nations. The Foreign Area Fellowship Program provided the financial assistance which enabled me to spend two years in Portugal and Angola. I would also like to express my thanks to the Ford Foundation and especially Wayne Fredericks and Haskell Ward, who were responsible for the Foundation's establishment within the UCLA African Studies Center of the Interdisciplinary Research Program on Angola, Mozambique, and Guinea-Bissau which I directed between 1971 and 1974. It was during this period that much of the research and writing of this study were accomplished. To Colleen Hughes Trujillo I am particularly grateful for her many forms of assistance, including research, editing, translating, moral support, and expert typing.

A few friends and colleagues gave generously of their time to read either large portions or the entire manuscript and contributed many helpful comments and suggestions. Among them I would like to mention, in particular, Professors Leo Kuper and Michael Lofchie. Allen Isaacman has been a constant source of intellectual inspiration and strong emotional support throughout the entire course of this study. I have benefited greatly from my long association with John Marcum whose works have profoundly shaped the study of contemporary Angola. John's friendship, willingness to share knowledge, and expert advice over the years are deeply appreciated.

To an inspiring and stimulating teacher and friend, Richard L. Sklar, I owe special gratitude. His wise counsel, constant encouragement, penetrating insights and criticisms, and careful reading of the manuscript immensely improved the quality of my work. He has been a perfect adviser and an ideal friend throughout. I owe my deepest debt of gratitude to my wife, Tammy. The dedication of this study to her is but a token acknowledgement of her share in the effort, from her help in the research, translations, typing, and editing to her effective nudging during the course of the writing. Those friends who are familiar with her vital role know that in many ways this is really our study and also know why I dedicate it to her with so much love.

Needless to say, the final product is probably not written as any of these friends and acquaintances would have preferred, nor do they necessarily agree with all that I have said. As comforting as it might be to find a scapegoat, all errors of fact and interpretation are, unfortunately, my sole responsibility.

Introduction

I have repeatedly dealt with this theme—the reason why we defend the Overseas with arms. And I showed that we must continue to protect populations whose desire is to remain Portuguese and continue to preserve a work of civilization built and maintained through the labour and grace of Portugal and which will endure only with Portugal.

Specifically, south of the equator, the two great provinces of Angola and Mozambique, which Portugal created out of a mosaic of poor and generally decadent tribes scattered over inhospitable lands, Angola and Mozambique are populated by blacks, whites, and Asians who love their motherland. There races are blended, cultures are altered, relationships are more intimate, efforts are united to continue and perfect a type of society in which men are limited only by their abilities, their merits or their work.

We therefore consider it our duty to defend those who trusting in Portugal are loyal to its flag; and we understand it to be our duty to safeguard a work which represents a positive contribution to the progress of Humanity and Civilization.[1]

Marcello Caetano
Speech to National Assembly
5 March 1974

It is difficult to find a single decade during the five centuries of Portugal's presence in Angola when a king or prime minister did not feel compelled to defend the country's colonial policies against foreign and domestic censure. Seldom could the colonial expenditure and efforts be defended on the basis of large profits for the metropolitan treasury or by visible material progress in the African colonies. Portugal was too poor and lacking in manpower to develop the colonies or even to effectively exploit their resources for her own benefit. Despite these objective economic realities, however, Portuguese leaders were never in want of a reasoned reply to the foreign and domestic critics of Portugal's colonial vocation. Marcello Caetano's defence, quoted above, was one of the last efforts by a Portuguese statesman to uphold colonialism in Africa. His words, images and arguments are strikingly similar to those his predecessors had used for more than a century. The characteristic emphasis is on the human and spiritual rather than material 'virtues' of Portuguese colonialism which, it was argued, engendered harmonious multiracial societies in Angola, Mozambique and Guinea-Bissau.

Since the early fifteenth century Portuguese explorers, authors and

---

[1] Caetano, 1974a, pp. 4–5 (of supplement).

statesmen have extolled the grandeur of their colonial mission to discover, conquer, settle and proselytize within distant lands. For centuries Portuguese scholarship, literature and political discourse have eulogized the bravery of the soldiers, the tenacity of the settlers and, most of all, Portugal's divinely inspired responsibility to transmit Christian values and western civilization to the native inhabitants of Africa, the Americas, India and Asia. Before the mid-twentieth century most of this self-adulation was directed inward, mainly to inspire pride among the Portuguese people. Since national prestige could not be sustained with reference to Portugal's internal condition, it was sought in the Portuguese record of exploits 'beyond the seas'. Thus the glorification of the colonizing mission principally served the psychological rather than the political needs of successive Portuguese regimes.

Beginning with the intensification of anti-colonial criticism in the United Nations in 1951, Portugal began to shift the emphasis of her 'mission' from exaltation of the overseas settler to aggrandizement of the emergent and racially mixed societies in Angola and Mozambique. Henceforth, the quality of her racial policy in Africa would constitute Portugal's first line of defence against international criticism. In addition, the legal term 'colony' was abandoned in favour of 'overseas provinces', which enabled António de Oliveira Salazar to reject foreign criticism resentfully as unwarranted interference in the internal affairs of his country.[2]

The decolonization of British, French and Belgian Africa during the late 1950s and early 1960s, India's incorporation of Goa, the outbreak of rebellions in Angola (1961), Guinea-Bissau (1963) and Mozambique (1964) heightened international pressures against Portugal. The Portuguese Government responded by asserting that its continued presence in Africa was necessary for the preservation of the vaunted multiracial

---

[2] Since the sixteenth century Portugal varied the designations for its overseas possessions, alternatively calling them colonies, overseas territories, overseas provinces, and states. In 1576 the historian João de Barros referred to the 'province' of Brazil and in 1663 the expression 'overseas provinces' appeared for the first time. However, 'colonies' was the primary designation until 1822, when the first written constitution (which established the principle of the indivisibility of all Portuguese territories and the citizenship of all their inhabitants) referred to 'overseas provinces'. For the next century both designations were employed officially, although most writers seemed to prefer 'colonies'. 'Overseas provinces' appeared once again in the Republican constitution of 1911, but usage varied as frequently as regimes changed during the Republic. The end of the Republic in 1926 brought 'colonies' back into favour until 1951 when, under intense international criticism, Salazar insisted upon returning to 'overseas provinces' as he reminded all concerned of the 1822 principle of the indivisibility of all Portuguese territories. As part of Caetano's (symbolic) 'overseas reforms' in 1972, the designation of 'state' was adopted for Angola and Mozambique. After 25 April 1974, 'colonies' once again appeared in all official and most non-official references to Angola, Mozambique and Guinea-Bissau. With independence, 'nation' finally replaced all previous appellations.

For a discussion of the Portuguese view of the U.N. censure of colonialism during the 1950s and early 1960s, see Nogueira, 1963, pp. 39–76.

societies. Only days before the coup of April 1974, Caetano proclaimed: 'We are fighting to defend the right of all men to live together in Africa and, above all, to defend the multiracial society we formed there.'[3] In fact, Portugal pointed to her multiracial societies as proof that she was not engaged in exploitative colonialism and was therefore morally entitled to remain in Africa. This position is epitomized in the words of Franco Nogueira, who was Portuguese Foreign Minister throughout most of the 1960s:

> We alone, before anyone else, brought to Africa the notion of human rights and racial equality. We alone practised the principle of multi-racialism, which all now consider to be the most perfect and daring expression of human brotherhood and sociological progress. Throughout the world no one questions the validity of the principle; but hesitation is shown in admitting that it is a Portuguese invention and in recognizing that the Portuguese nation practises it, for this would be to grant us moral authority and would impose a feeling of respect which would be incompatible with the designs aimed at us.[4]

Such declarations were made for domestic as well as foreign consumption—especially during the wars in Africa, when it became increasingly necessary to provide Portuguese citizens with a rationale for the great hardships they were forced to bear. During the thirteen years of warfare against the nationalists, almost half of every annual budget was allocated to military expenditure, the metropolitan economy remained backward and stagnant, and thousands of young men lost their lives in battle, while more than a million metropolitan Portuguese emigrated to seek better fortunes. It was not likely that the populace would be content to view the protection of Portuguese and foreign capital investments in the colonies as an adequate justification for their tribulations. Not surprisingly, the Salazar and Caetano regimes appealed to the Portuguese pride in the 'Overseas' in order to unite the country behind the war effort. Pride in the overseas provinces had become as vital a part of the Portuguese 'national character' as codfish was to the Portuguese diet or *fado* music to the country's proverbial soul. The regime sought to nurture this pride by inundating the country with pamphlets, books, movies, posters, and speeches in praise of the congenial multiracial societies in the African 'provinces'—Portugal's unique 'contribution to the progress of Humanity and Civilization'.

Naturally these efforts to gain political support for Portugal's African

[3] These remarks were made in an interview with the French magazine *Le Point* (1974c, p. 11). Excerpts of over forty addresses and interviews in which Marcello Caetano invoked a similar defence of Portuguese colonialism can be found in Caetano, 1973c, pp.7–102; 1974, p. 5 (of supplement). Also see 1951b, pp. 41–2.

[4] Nogueira, 1967, pp. 148–9. Nogueira resigned as Foreign Minister in 1969, when he found the Caetano regime to be too liberal, in order to become a spokesman for the ultra-conservative members of Parliament. He was briefly imprisoned in the fall of 1974 for activities contrary to the peace and stability of the country and later emigrated to Brazil.

policy rested on the assumption that harmonious multiracial societies really existed in Africa and were in a process of maturation. It was not especially difficult to persuade metropolitan Portuguese that multi-racialism was alive and well in the overseas provinces. Adages such as 'God created the Portuguese and the Portuguese created the mestiço' were probably as familiar to metropolitan Portuguese as were the words of their national anthem or stanzas from Camões' *Os Lusíadas*. After all, was not Brazil a living testimonial to the absence of racism among the Portuguese and to their ability to create societies in which individuals were judged by their actions, not their colour? Brazil not only provided Portugal with evidence for a plea of 'innocence by association' but with the ideology of 'lusotropicalism', which explained Portuguese attitudes towards race relations.

It was far more difficult to persuade the international community to accept both the validity of lusotropicalism and the political corollaries that justified Portuguese colonial rule. Nevertheless, many foreigners— apart from conservative or racist whites—were convinced of the absence of racism in Portuguese theory and practice. Shortly after his visit to Lisbon in 1923 to attend the Third Pan-African Congress, W. E. B. DuBois wrote: 'Between the Portuguese and the African and near-African there is naturally no "racial" antipathy—no accumulated historical hatreds, dislikes, despisings.'[5] Half a century later (1973), Kenya's Foreign Minister Njoroge Mungai noted in an address before the United Nations General Assembly, 'Portugal is a nation where there is no racism'.[6] It must be added, however, that neither DuBois nor Mungai drew the conclusion that Portugal's apparent national aptitude for racial toleration justified her pretension to determine the destinies of some thirteen million colonial Africans. This was Portugal's most difficult problem: to convince people to accept her claim that she had the right to remain in Africa in order to protect and maintain these 'paradigms of racial democracy'.

Portugal's African vocation was supported most often by her military allies. Political leaders in the United States, Britain, France, Germany and other European countries frequently rationalized their overt and covert support of Portuguese colonial policies with references to Portugal's presumed history of racial toleration in Africa. The views of such influen-tial American statesmen as Dean Acheson, George Kennan and George Ball as well as Admiral George Anderson (former Ambassador to Portugal and Chairman of the Foreign Intelligence Advisory Board) illustrate the political dividends that Portugal realized from this emphasis on its multiracial image.[7] In 1970 Secretary of State William

[5] DuBois, 1925, p. 424; also see pp. 425–6.

[6] Cited in Angola Comité, 1973, p. 9. For a summary of Mungai's entire speech (which was very critical of Portuguese colonialism) to the General Assembly on 10 October 1973, see *U.N. Monthly Chronicle*, 1973, p. 145.

Rogers advised President Nixon that 'the declared Portuguese policy of racial toleration is an important factor in this equation [of progress toward self-determination]. We think that this holds genuine hope for the future.'[8] Whereas most Portuguese and many American and European statesmen accepted the validity of the lusotropical assertions of racial toleration in the colonies, a number of prominent black, mestiço, and white Angolans condemned lusotropicalism as a cruel myth perpetrated to blind the world to the realities of racial oppression and exploitation.[9] They particularly attacked the doctrines of Brazilian sociologist Gilberto Freyre—the 'father' of lusotropicalism—and those who endorsed his theories, for dwelling on interracial sexual liaisons while ignoring basic economic and political facts. In the mid-1950s Mario Pinto de Andrade declared: 'Lusotropicalism, not valid for explaining the formation of Brazil, is entirely false for the colonial circumstances in Africa.'[10]

These critics urged that it was necessary to go beyond the goals and aspirations of the Portuguese ideology on race relations and look at the daily lives of blacks in the colonies. They pointed to the fact that after five hundred years of colonialism less than 1 per cent of the Africans in Angola were considered 'civilized' or 'assimilated' under Portuguese (pre-1961) law, and asked if this could be reconciled with Portugal's claims for the success of her 'civilizing mission'? They stressed the absence of Africans and mestiços in all important positions in both the private and public sectors of colonial society, as well as their minuscule representation in the upper levels of the educational system, and asked what hope this held for the future of those who were not white? Furthermore, they produced evidence documenting the continued use of forced labour, wide-

---

[7] For examples of these men citing the lack of Portuguese racism as part of the basis of their support for Portugal in the late 1960s and early 1970s, see: Ball, 1968, pp. 245–52; Kennan, 1971, pp. 230–5; and Dean Acheson's exceptionally vindicatory foreword to *The Third World* by Franco Nogueira (Acheson, 1967, pp. 11–17). Admiral Anderson believed so strongly in the correctness of the Portuguese cause that he told the House Sub-Committee on Africa: 'I think again that if we could stop the guerrilla warfare being waged against the Portuguese, the Portuguese would then have more of their own funds available to spend in accelerating the introduction of new schools, facilities, work projects and so forth for their African citizens.' U.S. Congress, House Sub-Committee on Foreign Affairs, 1970, p. 124.

[8] Rogers, 1971, p. 458.

[9] Virtually every prominent nationalist leader and most of their supporters within and outside the liberation movements who wrote about race relations in Angola adopted this position. Excerpts from relevant speeches and articles by Agostinho Neto, Holden Roberto, Jonas Savimbi, Mario Pinto de Andrade, Viriato da Cruz, and others can be found in the valuable collection of nationalist documents published in Chilcote, 1972a, *passim*. Also see Boavida, 1967, p. 13 and *passim*. One of the most cogent attacks on the mythology of lusotropicalism can be found in the late Amílcar Cabral's foreword to Basil Davidson's *The Liberation of Guiné* (1969a, pp. 9–15).

[10] Andrade, 1955, p. 29 and *passim*, especially pp. 27–8. This article is a strong attack on Gilberto Freyre which Andrade continued a few years later in the preface to the landmark anthology of poems he edited (1958, pp. vii–xv).

spread expropriation of African lands, arbitrary arrests and torture, and even massacres of entire villages, and inquired if this was part of the 'civilization' they were expected to assimilate? In short, while the liberation movements engaged the Portuguese army on the battlefield, they and their supporters challenged the Portuguese people and all concerned foreigners to measure the claims of lusotropicalism against the social, economic, and political realities of the more than 95 per cent of the population who were not white. These partisans were no less confident than the Portuguese themselves that candid observers and historians would vindicate their claims.[11]

While the Portuguese and the nationalists rarely agreed about basic facts, the major differences in their historical perspectives transcended questions of fact. These differences reflected antithetical sets of values, beliefs, cognitions, and attitudes which each side used in its analysis and interpretation of Portuguese race relations. In turn, these analyses and interpretations largely determined the nature of the evidence which was gathered and presented as well as the questions that were derived from this evidence. Thus for many Portuguese (and their supporters) lusotropicalism was an accurate explanation of Portuguese racial egalitarianism—viewed as unique in the modern world—while for others it gave expression to a myth that ignored the realities of racial arrogance, cultural genocide, human degradation, and exploitation.

This study of Angola under the Portuguese is an examination of the role of lusotropicalism in the formulation of policies and legislation affecting racial interaction, the goals of these policies, and the manner in which they were implemented by local Portuguese from the time of their initial arrival in the colony at the end of the fifteenth century until Angola's attainment of independence in 1975. I adduce evidence about the number, background, economic activities, and settlement patterns of the Portuguese in Angola, and show how these factors are related to the reality of race relations. My selection of particular historical epochs and events reflects my view of their importance to a critical examination of the theory of lusotropicalism and to an understanding of the develop-

[11] Following his claims of Portuguese non-racism and superiority cited in note 4, Franco Nogueira manifested extreme confidence when he wrote: 'We invite others to visit us and compare, but many, some of them highly responsible people, refuse to do this because they prefer to attack us rather than to have to confess that in Angola or in Mozambique they saw what they were unable to see anywhere else in Africa.' Nogueira, 1967, p. 149.

My own experience with the former Foreign Minister (and university professor) the following year (1968) was in direct contradiction to his statement. After my refusal to grant him complete censorship rights over any of my published and unpublished materials on Angola, as a condition for withdrawing his refusal to approve my visa to Angola, Nogueira demanded a guarantee that my studies would be favourable to the Portuguese. When I explained that all I could guarantee was that my studies would be as objective as possible, he replied: 'To be objective is to be favourable to the Portuguese.' Interview with Franco Nogueira, Lisbon, 8 March 1968.

ment of white settlement in Angola. I have also endeavoured to present new data and little-known evidence. Above all, I have tried to feature materials and analyses that appear to illuminate the potential problems of race relations in an independent Angola and her sister states of Portuguese expression in Africa and elsewhere in the Third World.

Part I of this study is an attempt to answer a simple question: did the formation of Portuguese society and culture uniquely prepare those Europeans who have lived in the colonies to pursue and/or maintain amicable and egalitarian relations with non-European peoples? Because a basic tenet of lusotropicalism is that the formation of Portuguese culture and society was uniquely non-racial, it is necessary to probe the characteristics of the Portuguese before as well as during their first interactions with Africans. Following a discussion of the development and role of lusotropicalism in Brazil and Portugal, two important historical epochs are analysed in Chapter 1: (a) the centuries prior to the consolidation of the Portuguese nation during which successive foreign civilizations influenced and shaped the culture of the Portuguese people, (b) the first century of Portuguese contacts with Africans—especially with the Bakongo in northern Angola—when the unique racial egalitarianism was not only said to have been manifested, but routinized for all times.

Brazil has been acclaimed widely as a paradigm of racial assimilation and the most perfect example of a racial democracy in the world. Indeed, Freyre, Salazar, Caetano and many others have offered Brazil as proof that there is something unique in Portuguese attitudes towards race which, it is argued, is also apparent in Angola since it, too, was colonized by the Portuguese. This deceptively simple syllogism (i.e. Portuguese colonizers in Brazil created racial harmony; the Portuguese were the colonizers in Angola; therefore, racial harmony prevails in Angola) is not only a product of lusotropical theory but an argument which has fundamentally influenced Portuguese and non-Portuguese perceptions of Angolan race relations. Usually the resultant assertion is that Angola is on the way to becoming another Brazil or has already reached this plateau. Occasionally, however, the syllogism is swallowed whole and regurgitated, as in the following example:

> The general attitude toward miscegenation is an important factor in the nature of racial tensions in society. A critical difference exists on this issue between most Portuguese and peoples from certain other societies . . . The Portuguese racial contact in Africa has much in common with similar [non-racist] contacts in Brazil . . . Prejudice based on appearance is perhaps not even as prevalent in Portuguese Africa as in Brazil, since the percentage of *mestiços* among the top social strata is higher in Angola than in Brazil. Nowhere in Portuguese Africa are the kinds of black and white stereotypes and categories found in the form so common in other parts of the world.[12]

[12] Abshire and Bailey, 1969, pp. 202–4. Both Abshire and Bailey spent over a month conducting research in Angola in the late 1960s.

These and other assertions are examined in the second chapter, in which Portuguese miscegenation patterns throughout the world are compared in an attempt to discover whether they were similar to one another and whether, as the syllogism assumes, the sole factor of the nationality of the white (Portuguese) population can explain the character of the race relationships in question. Other explanatory variables are considered in a comparison of Portuguese miscegenation patterns and attitudes towards mestiços with those of other European colonizers in the New World and Africa. In addition, the question of whether Brazilian and Angolan societies are sufficiently similar to generalize from one to the other is considered in an analysis of the component racial groups in each country. I have also assessed the extent to which race relations in both Brazil and Angola conform to the precepts of lusotropical ideology.

Since lusotropicologists have claimed that the Portuguese colonizers' special characteristics created racial harmony in the Portuguese colonies, Part II is a discussion of the number and background, economic activities, settlement patterns, and racial attitudes of the white settlers in Angola. Once again Brazil played an important, although indirect, role in influencing Angolan history; for in the popular mind in Portugal, the South American colony connoted the proverbial 'pot of gold' at the rainbow's end, in contrast to Angola, which represented hardship and even death. As a result, Brazil attracted the overwhelming majority of Portuguese emigrants, even after its declaration of independence in 1822. In fact, by the final quarter of the nineteenth century, when over half a million Portuguese were in Brazil, only three thousand were in Angola and even fewer in all the other African colonies combined (São Tomé, Cape Verde, Guinea and Mozambique).[13]

Because free men were usually unwilling to become soldiers, administrators, priests or, especially, settlers in Angola, nearly all the Portuguese in the colony until the early decades of the present century were exiled convicts, or *degredados*. For over four centuries the dungeons of Portugal were the most important source of white settlers for Angola. The role of the degredados in Angolan history is analysed in Chapter 3.

In spite of the reluctance of metropolitan Portuguese to view Angola as a desirable place to settle, Portuguese colonial theorists continued to insist that the best means of guaranteeing Portuguese sovereignty, of 'civilizing' the indigenous populations, and of developing the colonial economies was by the settlement of Portugal's farmers in the hinterlands of the overseas empire. If we restrict the term 'white settler' to include only those who left Europe with the intention of permanently living in the colony—as distinguished from soldiers, degredados, or members of the

---

[13] These numbers were compiled by Oliveira Martins from censuses conducted between 1869 and 1879 (1887, p. 181, chart 1, and p. 189, note 1).

colonial service—then white settlement did not begin in Angola until the middle of the nineteenth century (1849–51), when almost five hundred Brazilians arrived at the southern Angolan port of Moçamedes. Their arrival, however, proved to be an anomaly and when it was clear that Angola was not attracting substantially more settlers, either from the metropole or Brazil, the Government decided to turn its attention to methods of direct intervention in the settlement process. This intervention meant that the Government selected prospective settlers for Angola, provided them with free transportation to the colony and, once they had arrived, with land, housing, animals, seeds and subsidies. In the Portuguese colonial lexicon this was referred to as directed or planned settlement. The objectives of planned settlement in rural Angola, its results, and its impact on the lives of the Africans are analysed in Chapter 4 in three distinct periods: (a) 1900–50; (b) 1951–60; and (c) 1961–72.

Patterns and mechanisms of white domination in Angola since the end of slavery are emphasized in Part III. It was the hope of humanitarian statesmen, such as the Marques de Sá da Bandeira, that the decrees to abolish the transatlantic slave trade in 1836 and domestic slavery in 1878 would engender a new era when Africans would no longer be abused by the Portuguese. These good intentions, however, collided with the avarice of local Portuguese, whose behaviour motivated a Governor General to warn the King in 1873 to abandon forever any illusions that the whites would cease to exploit the Africans.[14] The political, economic, and social policies and practices of the Portuguese in Angola subsequent to that Governor's warning until 1961, when African nationalists took their struggle against Portuguese domination to the battlefield, are considered in Chapter 5.

When the war of independence began in Angola in February–March 1961, the Portuguese Government was forced to reassess some of its colonial policies. A number of reforms intended to equalize the races before the law were initiated. Thus overt manifestations of racial prejudice were legally discouraged; however, white domination continued and was even expanded until the middle of the 1970s. The long history of abuses against the African population now became a military problem and many soldiers, along with many in the civil service, recognized that the system had to be radically restructured in order to eliminate or at least manage the problem of African alienation; but the question was how? Three broad clusters of opinions emerged among civilian and military officials. One group believed that the Africans could be won over to the Portuguese side if the Government implemented economic and educational programmes which would provide them with meaningful opportunities to improve their social and economic positions. A second group argued

---

[14] The confidential letter from the Governor General to the King, sent 4 June 1873, is quoted in Sá da Bandeira, 1873, p. 68.

that there was not enough time for Portugal to implement the reforms that could mitigate the alienation of the Africans. Therefore the problem was how best to control the African people and prevent their collaboration with the nationalists. Finally, a minority maintained that the Government should help rural Africans improve their traditional economic systems because any attempt to effectuate major structural changes (whether for 'modernization' or control) would simply exacerbate the grave social and economic problems already plaguing millions of Africans and could, therefore, boomerang.

The first two groups ('developmentistas' and 'controlistas') differed strongly on preferred goals but shared the belief that the best means for achieving their ends was the concentration of rural Africans into large villages near roads. The latter argued that strategic hamlets were necessary for effective surveillance and control of the millions of dispersed Africans in rural Angola, while the former maintained (not unlike those who support *ujamaa* in Tanzania) that this was a requisite first step for the Government to be able to provide increased services and assistance necessary for the social and economic advancement of the African peasantry. The third group ('Africanistas') was highly critical of any programme which involved massive resettlement of African herdsmen and local farmers. The debates among these officials over the wartime policies directed at the rural peasantry and the Angolan economy in general are analysed in Chapter 6.

The fourth and final part of this study consists of a concluding chapter in which the historical and contemporary realities of race in Angola are appraised in the light of future prospects.

PART I

Lusotropicalism

CHAPTER ONE

Lusotropicalism: Theory and Early Practice

Introduction

To understand Angola under the Portuguese one must first understand lusotropicalism, the ideology which was used to explain and justify the Portuguese presence in Africa. The proponents of lusotropicalism maintained that because of the (asserted) historically unique absence of racism among the Portuguese people, their colonization of tropical, non-European territories was characterized by racially egalitarian legislation and human interaction.[1]

To most non-Portuguese, lusotropicalism is a romantic myth (at best) or an invidious lie (at worst) used to obscure the realities of Portuguese colonialism. Foreigners have rarely assumed that the Portuguese people actually believed in lusotropicalism or that it inspired Portuguese policy and action in Africa. Yet, for the overwhelming majority of the Portuguese people prior to the military coup of April 1974, lusotropicalism truly represented Portuguese policies, practices and goals. It is doubtful whether any other ideology has been more widely and fervently believed by the Portuguese or has generated as much written attention within Portugal.[2] Even today, some years after the downfall of the Salazar/Caetano dictatorship, many of the Portuguese who now consider themselves 'anti-colonial' continue to believe in a number of the basic tenets of lusotropicalism.

The most persistent themes in the abundant literature expounding lusotropicalism can be synthesized as follows:

Given the unique cultural and racial background of metropolitan Portugal, Portuguese explorers and colonizers demonstrated a special ability—found among no other people in the world—to adapt to tropical lands and peoples. The Portuguese colonizer, basically poor and humble, did not have the exploitative motivations of his counterpart from the more industrialized countries in Europe. Consequently, he immediately entered into cordial relations with the non-European

---

[1] See Chilcote, 1972a, pp. xxii–xxiii; Hammond, 1967, 205–6; and Gaspar, M. da C., 1966, pp. 125–44.

[2] Duffy, 1962b, pp. 10–11; and Boxer, 1963, p. 2.

populations he met in the tropics. This is clearly demonstrated through Portugal's initial contacts with the Bakongo Kingdom in the latter part of the fifteenth century. The ultimate proof of the absence of racism among the Portuguese, however, is found in Brazil, whose large and socially prominent mestiço population is living testimony to the freedom of social and sexual intercourse between Portuguese and non-Europeans. Portuguese non-racism is also evidenced by the absence in Portuguese law of the racist legislation in South Africa and until recently in the United States barring non-whites from specific occupations, facilities, etc. Finally, any prejudice or discrimination in territories formerly or presently governed by Portugal can be traced to class, but never colour, prejudice.

While lusotropicalism has been most commonly associated with Portugal's presence in Africa, its origins are deeply rooted in the Brazilian experience during the early decades of the twentieth century. Until this time, Brazilian elites had almost unquestioningly accepted European cultural and intellectual values and traditions as the only civilized measures by which to judge any society; by those measures Brazil was condemned to congenital inferiority. A deep pessimism pervaded the thinking of the Brazilian elites, who readily proclaimed their own 'bankruptcy' and accepted 'the teachings which humiliate and lower us in our own eyes, including the doctrine of racial inferiority'.[3] Many Brazilians assumed that their country's lack of development was a direct consequence of the 'debilitating' influence of the large black and mestiço population.[4]

The decade of the 1920s in Brazil was marked by intense cultural and political unrest which started with the Modernist movement in 1922 and was climaxed by the revolution that brought Getúlio Vargas to power in 1930.[5] During this decade the new generation of Brazilian artists and scholars (who formed the Modernist movement) caused a profound intellectual and psychological upheaval by giving national values and themes precedence over foreign values. One of the most prominent aristocratic canons which drew the fire of these rebellious intellectuals was that concerning the black's role and contribution to Brazilian society. By the 1930s an entirely new socio-anthropological literature had appeared which emphasized that blacks were an integral element in Brazilian society through their significant contributions to Brazilian history and development.[6]

The leading light of this new school was Gilberto Freyre, who had

[3] Sodré, 1942, pp. 1–11.

[4] A stark example of the official Brazilian belief in the racial inferiority of Indians and blacks is Oliveira Vianna's introduction to the 1920 Brazilian census. His essay is replete with references to the superiority of the white race and to the inferiority of blacks and Indians. Vianna, 1922, pp. 281–400, especially pp. 325–44.

[5] Burns, 1970, pp. 272–90; Skidmore, 1964, 492–3.

[6] Burns, 1970, p. 276.

returned to Brazil in 1925 after completing his education in the United States. He was strongly influenced at Columbia University by the noted anthropologist Franz Boas, who made Freyre aware of the distinction between race and culture, between genetics and environment. During his graduate studies, Freyre concluded that miscegenation had been a positive force in Brazil and he incorporated this revolutionary idea into his Master's thesis. Encouraged by H. L. Mencken, he re-worked his thesis into a full-length book, *Casa grande e senzala*, whose appearance in 1933 acted as a shock treatment on the Brazilian psyche.[7]

Freyre turned the country's inferiority complex inside out and converted Brazil's multiracial past from a liability into an asset. Combining eclectic research with a strong streak of romanticism, he offered Brazilians the first documented description of their national character which was unabashedly optimistic.[8] They no longer needed to see scandal and shame in their racial mixture; instead they could look to their art, literature, music, dance, in short to their culture to discover a richness and a vitality that were a result of the fusion of races and civilizations. Always central to Freyre's discussion of this fusion was his view of the uniqueness of the Portuguese who settled in the tropics of the New World, and it was he who coined the term lusotropicalism.

As the decades of the 1920s and 1930s ushered in a new self-awareness, pride and nationalism in Brazil, Portugal was laying the foundation for her own regeneration. The naming of António de Oliveira Salazar as Prime Minister in 1932 marked the beginning of an indefatigable effort to recapture the national pride which had eluded the Portuguese since the mid-seventeenth century. Neither the Bragança dynasty during its long reign (1640–1910) nor the First Republic (1910–1926) had been able to resuscitate the glory which Portugal knew during the age of discoveries. Power and prestige in Europe had come to be measured in material terms following the industrial revolution—a revolution which had only barely touched the western flank of the Iberian peninsula by the time Salazar took power. By material standards Portugal was a dwarf among giants in Europe and her African colonies were among the poorest and most neglected on the African continent. By the end of the First Republic, Portugal was both materially and spiritually sick and it was left to António de Oliveira Salazar, suitably

[7] Freyre, 1964. Reference to Mencken's influence on Freyre is found in Crawford, 1961, p. 205. For his discussion of Freyre in general, see pp. 203–16.

[8] Skidmore, 1974, pp. 173, 190–2. While Skidmore is quite critical of Freyre's scholarship, he acknowledges Freyre as the most influential figure in Brazilian intellectual history for over three decades. Frank Tannenbaum goes so far as to argue that Brazilian intellectual history can be divided into two periods: before and after the publication of *Casa grande e senzala*. Tannenbaum, 1964, pp. 124–5.

For a critical view of Freyre's contribution to the general literature on Brazilian race relations, see Bastide, 1974, pp. 111–23.

educated in economics and theology, to nurse the nation back to health.

During Salazar's initial years in power, Portugal's poverty, exacerbated by the world depression, precluded significant economic development. Development required natural resources, skills, technology and capital, all of which Portugal lacked. In order to restore Portuguese self-confidence and national pride, Salazar rejected material criteria for measuring power and prestige and substituted in their place such intangibles as the spirit, temperament and history of a people. In short, Salazar revived the imperial consciousness of the Portuguese, seeking in the great expanses of Portuguese-controlled Africa the prestige which was absent at home.[9]

National pride was therefore manufactured not by machines but with the tip of the pen, for words were cheap and authors abundant and the country was soon inundated with books, pamphlets, journals, speeches and conferences which glorified the imperial past and the importance of Portugal's accomplishments and 'mission' in Africa. It is difficult to find a more explicit statement of the objective of this campaign than that which appeared in a 1935 lead editorial of a new journal, *O mundo português*, founded specifically to disseminate knowledge of and rekindle pride in the colonies:

> We must always keep alive in the Portuguese people the dream of beyond-the-seas and the pride and consciousness of the Empire. Africa is more than agricultural land and it is capable of producing what a metropole needs. Africa is for us a moral justification and a reason for being as a power. Without it we would be a small country, with it we are a great nation.[10]

Thus Portugal, after more than seven centuries of existence as a nation-state, and her former colony Brazil, independent only one century, found themselves in a similar crisis condition in the decade of the twenties. Neither could measure up to the North American-European standards of excellence by which they had been judging themselves: they were desperately clinging to the bottom rungs of the ladder of the western civilization they so ardently apotheosized. But western civilization was a racist civilization which considered as inferior not only black men but also any white man who socially and/or sexually mixed with blacks. This struck at the very core of Brazilian society and, especially, at the Portuguese settler 'responsible' for creating Brazil's multiracial population. It was difficult to maintain self-esteem

[9] For a penetrating discussion of the imperial revival during the early years of Salazar's Estado Novo (New State), see Duffy, 1959, pp. 268–79. It is interesting to recall here the words of Salazar's first Colonial Minister, Armindo Monteiro, who noted that during his generation the colonies had been almost totally ignored by men of importance in Portugal. Cited in Soares, V. H. V., 1935, p. 386.

[10] 'Editorial' in *O mundo português* 2, 1935, p. 218. The entire editorial is found on pp. 217–19.

when countries such as England considered the impoverished Portuguese settler 'on the zoological scale between the monkey and black'.[11]

Both Portugal and Brazil in the early 1930s sought to establish their grandeur through lusotropicalism, emphasizing the positive nature of Portuguese racial mixing in the tropics. However, while each country asserted a unique absence of racism among the Portuguese settlers, there was a major difference between the way they viewed blacks. Led by Freyre, the Brazilians stressed the symbiotic nature of the racial contact between the Portuguese and African civilizations, whereby each borrowed and profited from the other's culture. Observable differences between the races in Brazil were attributed to cultural and educational factors rather than to genetic or racial characteristics.[12]

Portugal, on the other hand, characterized Africans as intrinsically inferior; in fact, Portugal's self-adulation over her 'civilizing mission' was dependent upon that inferiority. In 1933 both Salazar and his Colonial Minister Monteiro were explicit in this regard: Monteiro argued that colonization required 'boundless tolerance and pity for the inferiority of the blacks in the bush', while Salazar held that it was imperative for Portugal to safeguard 'the interests of those inferior races whose inclusion under the influences of Christianity is one of the greatest and most daring achievements of Portuguese colonization'.[13]

Some Portuguese officials, such as Vicente Ferreira, the former Portuguese High Commissioner and Governor General of Angola, believed Africans were so backward that they were incapable of being civilized even by the Portuguese. He argued:

These so-called civilized Africans, as all colonial sociologists have recognized, are generally no more than grotesque imitations of white men. With rare exceptions ... the 'civilized African' maintains a primitive mentality, poorly concealed by the speech, gestures and dress copied from Europeans.[14]

Even Norton de Matos, twice Governor General of Angola and an

---

[11] Galvão, 1937, p. 221. An eighteenth-century English historian of Jamaica warned that if blacks were admitted into England the result would be a contaminated mixture ''til the whole nation resembles the *Portuguese* and *moriscos* in complexion of skin and baseness of mind'. Quoted in Jordan, 1968, pp. 254–5.

[12] See Freyre's introduction to *Masters and Slaves*, 1964, pp. 3–11.

[13] Monteiro, A., 1936, p. 8; Salazar, A. de O., 1939, p. 177.
Two years after Monteiro's speech cited above, he wrote:
To colonize is essentially to deal with the Negro. At least for now the white is destined to be the director, the technician, the responsible [individual]. In the tropics he would make a sad figure working with his own muscle, alongside the native. The latter is the great force of production, the abundant and docile consumer element which Africa offers. (Monteiro, 1935, p. 43)

[14] Ferreira, 1954d, p. 40. He was the High Commissioner and Governor General in Angola from 1926 to 1928. The exceptions he refers to involve cases where miscegenation has occurred.

outspoken critic of Portugal's African policies and practices, feared that the inferiority of Africans could dilute or even ruin the effectiveness of Portuguese colonization if the government did not put 'for at least a century, the greatest obstacles to the fusion of the white race with the native races of Angola'.[15]

While the Portuguese strain of lustropicalism retained much of the paternalism and attitudes of racial and cultural superiority found in the 1930s, most of the overt racism had been eliminated from the ideology before the 1974 coup. It fell to Gilberto Freyre to provide the necessary corrective for the Portuguese theorists. Until 1940, when he published *O mundo que o português criou* (The World the Portuguese Created), Freyre had primarily concentrated on Brazilian society.[16] In this work, however, he began to include the Portuguese in all parts of the tropics, although he was somewhat guarded about the Portuguese in africa. It was not until the early 1950s, when the Portuguese government sponsored his first trip to all of Portugal's colonies, that Freyre universalized, with conviction, lusotropicalism.

In the book he wrote following this trip (*Um brasileiro em terras portuguesas*), Freyre concluded that the Portuguese he encountered in India, Timor and Africa manifested the same lusotropical qualities as the Portuguese who settled Brazil. He argued that the Portuguese appreciation of tropical (non-European) values and peoples distinguished them as pioneers of modern tropical civilizations.[17] His emphasis on Portuguese tolerance and assimilation of tropical values added a new dimension to the Portuguese ideology which, until then, had almost exclusively viewed the assimilation process in a unilinear fashion; that is assimilation had connoted the Europeanization of the Africans, not the reverse! Whenever African values and living patterns influenced the Portuguese, it was viewed as a setback.[18]

Nevertheless, despite the similarities and differences between the

---

[15] Norton de Matos, 1926, pp. 42–3 and p. 231. For a similar position advocating sexual separation of the races, see Barreiros, 1929, p. 57.

[16] Freyre, 1940.
For an excellent critique of this book and of Freyre's lusotropicalism in general, see the article published by Andrade, 1955, pp. 24–35.

[17] Freyre, 1953, especially pp. 176–9. Also see 1958, *passim* (this edition contains an English translation following the Portuguese text); 1961.

[18] For a landmark study of the Africanization of the Portuguese in Africa, see Isaacman and Isaacman, 1972, *passim*. In this study, which was accorded the Herskovits Award by the African Studies Association in 1973, the Isaacmans trace the evolution of the Portuguese and their descendants who in the middle of the eighteenth century established crown estates, *prazos*, in the lower Zambesi valley. The 'Africanization' of these *prazeros* was so complete after one and a half centuries that, prior to the Berlin Conference of 1885, they formed alliances with Zambesi chiefs to drive the Portuguese from the region. One *prazero* wrote at the time: 'We must expel all the Portuguese and make an alliance with the British who are sympathetic to the aspirations of the Africans.' Isaacman and Isaacman, 1975, p. 35. Also see Isaacman's latest book, 1976.

Portuguese and Brazilian strains of lusotropicalism, the focal point of the ideology for each country has been the assertion of a uniquely non-racial Portuguese colonizer.

Since lusotropicalism was considered a major justification for Portugal's attempt to maintain its hegemony in Africa, its assertions must be carefully examined in the light of historical and contemporary realities. For example, was the formation of the Portuguese nation such that it produced a different type of colonizer from the rest of Europe and, if so, what was the nature of early Portuguese contacts in Africa? Does Brazil really represent a paradigm of racial assimilation in the world today and to what extent are the Portuguese responsible for the character of contemporary Brazil? Are Brazilian and Angolan societies sufficiently similar to generalize from one to the other? Did the Portuguese colonizer manifest similar racial attitudes and behaviour in all parts of the world colonized by Portugal? Did the treatment of blacks in the Portuguese colonies conform to the non-racist tenets of the lusotropical ideology? These and other question s are answered throughout the remainder of Part I.

Portugal before the Explorations

Central to lusotropicalism is the belief that the varied and intensive cultural contacts of the early inhabitants of Portugal gave rise to a unique civilization capable of existing amicably with all other civilizations. The proponents of this thesis point with pride to the fact that over the roughly twenty centuries prior to consolidation in 1267 of the area constituting modern Portugal, the native inhabitants of Portugal were influenced and shaped by a variety of cultural, ethnic, racial and religious groups. From the arrival of the Phoenicians in the eighth century BC until the final expulsion of the Moors in the thirteenth century AD, the Iberian tribes absorbed at least seven major civilizations including the Greeks, Celts, Carthaginians, Romans, Visigoths and Moors. Each left an indelible mark on the emerging Portuguese society.[19]

We should consider two important questions in determining the relevance to lusotropical assertions of these centuries of foreign occupations and contact: (1) Are adaptability to and assimilation of foreign traits unique to the Portuguese? (2) Does the assimilation of foreign traits necessarily lead to lusotropical behaviour?

In many ways lusotropicalism implicitly assumes that the Portuguese are *sui generis* among world cultures in their cultural and material adaptation. What we see from Portugal's early history, however, are

---

[19] For a detailed discussion of the impact of each of these civilizations on the native inhabitants of Portugal, see Bender, 1975b, pp. 36–44; references to (and brief discussions of) two dozen sources which are useful in understanding this period of Portuguese history are found on pp. 67–70.

merely examples of cultural and material diffusion which characterize the history of practically every culture and nation in the world. The cultures in contact have varied but the process has been as ubiquitous as man's belief in a being or force outside himself. In his classical *Study of Man*, Ralph Linton states, 'There is probably no culture extant today which owes more than 10 per cent of its total elements to inventions made by members of its own society.'[20] In general, where social structures and value and belief systems permit, a culture will assimilate or absorb those foreign elements which enable it to more effectively exploit its material and cultural environment. Furthermore, the intricate process of diffusion probably remains below the level of historic consciousness.[21] That is to say, the members of the society are either not aware of or soon forget the foreign origin of assimilated elements which often become 'as American' as the hot dog (which originated in Germany).

Lusotropicalism further assumes that the Portuguese adoption of material or cultural traits from one group of non-Europeans *ipso facto* created a basis for amicable behaviour with all non-Europeans. The American colonists fighting against the British often sustained themselves on the Indian staples of corn, maple, buffalo meat, and tobacco and utilized Indian weapons such as the tomahawk. Yet, these borrowed elements did not influence the American colonists to treat the Indians amicably when the pioneers started across the plains. The desire for land and profits overshadowed all cultural and material assimilation. In Nigeria the Ibos and Yorubas assimilated infinitely more of English culture than did the Hausa-Fulani, but it was the former groups who constituted the vanguard of the independence movement, while for a time the Hausa-Fulani leadership urged the British to remain. The assimilation of European culture traits by the Ibos and Yorubas brought them into direct conflict with the British for control over their institutions and political advancement. In neither the American nor the Nigerian cases did the process of assimilation or cultural/material diffusion bring about amicable relations between the groups involved. Similarly, one cannot look to pre-fifteenth-century patterns of material and cultural diffusion and assimilation in Portugal to find the explanation for post-fifteenth-century Portuguese behaviour towards the non-European peoples they encountered in Africa, India, Asia and Latin America.

Were Portuguese relations with non-Europeans within the metropole and elsewhere truly amicable? For example, what was the nature of Portuguese relations with the Jews and Moors (the two groups considered

---

[20] Linton, 1936, p. 325. Linton (pp. 326–27) follows this assertion with a long example which takes the 'solid American' through his average day that poignantly illustrates how few of the elements which enter into his day actually originated in the United States.

[21] Kroeber, 1937, pp. 139–42.

non-European in Portugal) before intensive Portuguese colonization began?[22]

Freyre and others maintain that there was considerable miscegenation between the Portuguese and the Moors and Jews which reputedly resulted in a Portuguese tolerance of, even preference for, dark-complexioned women.[23] This miscegenation, however, may have been more common during the Moorish occupation. Unquestionably the most peaceful and tolerant relations between the Portuguese, Moors, and Jews transpired under the Moorish rule of Portugal.

The period following the establishment of the Portuguese state in the middle of the twelfth century was marked by increasing intolerance, culminating in the Inquisition, which initially was intended to expel Jews and Moors who refused to accept Christianity.[24] Before the Inquisition both peoples were heavily taxed and forced to live in separate quarters, segregated from the Christian population by walls.[25] In some parts of Portugal they were proscribed from holding public office, practising certain professions, or owning land.

After the initial expulsion of the Moors and Jews in 1492, the Inquisition, which continued for nearly three centuries, was aimed principally at New Christians (Jews and Moslems who had converted to Christianity) and their descendants, since few Jews or Moslems remained who had not ostensibly converted. A remote Jewish ancestor, however, sufficed for the leaders of the Inquisition to imprison a New

[22] Freyre and others maintain that the long Portuguese contact with the Jews and the Moors resulted in a 'de-Europeanization' of Portuguese economic, social and political life (1964, p. 208). However, it is questionable whether or not the Jews in Portugal should be considered 'non-Europeans'. The Jews in Iberia (before the Inquisition) included both the descendants of Semites who migrated from the Middle East as well as those who were physically European. Furthermore, many of the traits which Freyre argues were brought to Portugal by the Jews could be considered as being more 'European' than the Portuguese traits they displaced (ibid., pp. 211–12). The same could be said of many Moorish innovations in Portugal.

It is difficult to know how many Jews were in Portugal before the Inquisition, but the importance of their contribution to the growth of science, culture and commerce in Portugal is unquestioned. One estimate of the number of Jews around the end of the fifteenth century is 200,000, which is undoubtedly exaggerated but, if true, would mean they constituted approximately one-fifth of the Portuguese population. Jorge, 1940, pp. 41–2. Also see: Marques, A. H. de O., 1972, vol. I, p. 167; Livermore, 1966, pp. 126–7; Correa, 1943, p. 97.

[23] Freyre, 1964, pp. 208–11 and Dias, J., 1960, p. 22. Not all Portuguese agree with Freyre that mixing with the Moors and Jews was fortunate. Lucio d'Azevedo and Pires da Lima maintained that Portuguese miscegenation with Jews and blacks caused the decadence of Portugal. Azevedo, L. d', 1913, pp. 76–93; and Lima, J. A. P. da, 1940, pp. 41–2.

[24] For a truly excellent study of the Inquisition in Portugal, see Saraiva, 1969, especially pp. 11–12, 47–73. Perhaps the most complete documentation and interpretation of the Inquisition is found in António Baião's classic three-volume study (1972).

[25] During the fourteenth and fifteenth centuries there were three walled areas in Lisbon where the Jews were segregated, covering about 1·4 per cent of the city area. Marques, A. H. de O., 1972, vol. I, pp. 80, 167–8.

Christian, expel him, send him into exile in Africa, or burn him at the stake.[26]

Ironically, Portugal manifested its most intolerant and brutal behaviour towards its own 'infidels' at the very time the Portuguese were meeting and colonizing the African and Indian 'infidels'. In fact, prior to the end of the Inquisition in 1769, Jews, Moors and Negroes were frequently referred to in official documents as *raças infectadas* (infected races).[27]

If there was a legacy of amicability among the Portuguese towards the Moors after seven centuries of contact in Iberia, it was not apparent in their relations with the Moors they encountered in Africa. Beginning with the conquest of the Moroccan coastal town of Ceuta in 1415 and until the middle of the eighteenth century, Portugal was engaged in almost constant warfare with the Moors. At times these battles reached the proportion of a holy crusade; personal accounts of some of the battles reveal that the Portuguese soldiers often made no distinction between combatants and civilians since none of the 'infidels' was deemed worthy of human consideration.

Initial African Contacts

After the capture of Ceuta Portuguese sailors, under the tutelage of Prince Henry the Navigator, gradually made their way down the coast of Africa.[28] By 1460, the year of Prince Henry's death, Portuguese ships had reached as far as Sierra Leone. Contacts with Africans during Prince Henry's lifetime could not have been more antithetical to lusotropicalism. A richly detailed narration of these voyages by Henry's personal chroni-

---

[26] Oliveira Marques argues that many of the New Christians who were persecuted were 'good Portuguese', while only a minority continued to practise Judaism clandestinely. Ibid., p. 208.

Nowell, among others, has argued that the Inquisition had a disastrous impact on Portuguese colonization because it eliminated 'the one class which could have given the empire some financial organization and solidarity'. Nowell, 1973, p. 53.

A number of Portuguese scholars, such as Sá da Bandeira, have argued that expulsion of Jews from Portugal during the Inquisition 'made the Portuguese nation one of the most ignorant in Europe'. Sá da Bandeira, 1873, p. 133. Also see Saraiva, 1969, pp. 27–46.

For a breakdown of the average number of Jews, New Christians and other 'heretics' sentenced and executed during the entire Inquisition, see Marques, A. H. de O., 1972, vol. I, pp. 399–400.

[27] Boxer, 1965, p. 148.

[28] Prince Henry, the youngest son of the Portuguese king, João I, established a school of navigation and ship design in the coastal town of Sagres in the Algarve, where he trained most of the ship captains during the first half-century of Portuguese explorations. See von Hapsburg and Marjay, 1965, pp. 11–20. For an account in English of Prince Henry's motivations for the conquests and discoveries in Africa, see the translation of the Prince's personal biographer, Azurara, 1896, vol. 1, pp. 27–30; 1899, vol. 2, p. vi.

For a highly distorted perspective on Prince Henry, see Freyre, 1961, pp. 237–8.

cler, Gomes Eanes de Azurara, recounts the initiation of the African slave trade with the expeditions of Antão Gonçalvez and Nuno Tristão to Senegal in 1441 and 1443 respectively.[29] By 1446 there were nearly a thousand African slaves in Portugal. Azurara, who witnessed the return of many of the early slave ships, described the anguish which overcame the Africans as families and friends were separated indiscriminately, 'faces bathed in tears ... [while] others struck their faces with the palms of their hands, throwing themselves upon the ground'.[30] However, neither Prince Henry nor many Portuguese through the centuries viewed such scenes as indicative of Portuguese cruelty. On the contrary, slaves were considered fortunate for, according to Azurara, they would receive the light of the holy faith and gain knowledge of bread, wine and clothes instead of living their lives in 'bestial sloth'.[31]

Slavery, however, was not the only objective of the Portuguese explorations. They also sought minerals, ivory, spices, and souls as they searched for a land or sea route to the fabled riches of the Orient. Their experience in the Maghreb provided them with important knowledge which fed these ambitions: they learned of gold on the Guinea coast which was beyond the control of their Muslim enemies, and of Arab navigation on the East African coast, confirming that the continent was surrounded by water.[32] By 1471 Portuguese sailors had arrived in Ghana and found it so rich in gold that a decade later they built their first fort in West Africa (Elmina), in order to deter other European explorers following in their wake.[33] Another fort was built at Benin (Nigeria), where Portugal found not only more wealth, but a well-developed kingdom which greatly impressed the crown. The Portuguese and Benin kings exchanged gifts and diplomatic missions and the latter's son even adopted Christianity.[34] Further down the coast, along the northern frontiers of

[29] Azurara, 1896, vol. 1, pp. 39–50. Also see Oliveira Martins, 1887, p. 53.

[30] Azurara, 1896, vol. 1, pp. 81–2.

[31] Ibid., vol. 1, p. 51 and pp. 84–5.

[32] Oliver and Fage, 1962, p. 113.

[33] Davidson, 1961, p. 9. It is of interest to note the report of one of the Portuguese in Elmina who observed that while there was much miscegenation between the African women and the Portuguese (especially the *degredados*, Portuguese prisoners who worked on the ships), no mestiços were found in the area. He speculated that the African women must have aborted or practised infanticide in order not to have children from the Portuguese. Cited in Brásio, 1953, vol.III, p. 90.

[34] Crowder, 1962, pp. 60–2. The Portuguese were extremely impressed with the Benin people's ability to quickly acquire the skill of reading, a skill which few of the Portuguese sailors possessed. In 1516 the Portuguese representative at Benin, Duarte Pires, wrote to King Manuel, 'your highness will be pleased to know that they are very good learners'. Quoted in Crowder, p. 61. After 1520 no Portuguese lived for any length of time in the Niger region (p. 62).

William Bosman, a Dutchman who wrote at the turn of the seventeenth century, commenting on the relations between European men and the women of Benin, observed that 'the women of Benin behave themselves very obligingly to all; but more especially to the Europeans, except the Portuguese which they don't like very well'. Bosman, 1963, p. 12.

Angola, the Portuguese encountered in 1482 the undisputed leader among the coastal states of Central Africa—the vast Kongo Kingdom.[35]

In many ways the African kingdoms such as Benin and Kongo closely resembled the small kingdom of Portugal (whose population was approximately one million), while in other respects (e.g. degree of centralization, political control, manufacture of cloth and artifacts) they probably surpassed medieval Portugal.[36] Consequently, Portugal's first diplomatic initiatives with these African kingdoms were motivated less by magnanimity than by respect and the kingdom most respected in Lisbon was that of Kongo, located on both sides of the Congo (Zaïre) river. It is perhaps because early Portuguese contacts with the Bakongo were the most egalitarian in Portugal's five centuries in Africa that this period is frequently cited by lusotropical writers as epitomizing the nature of Portugal's racial and cultural relations in Africa.[37]

Thanks to a fortuitous accident during Diogo Cão's first journey to Angola in 1483, four of his men were left behind in the court of the Manikongo (the Kongo king), which prompted Cão to take four Bakongo hostages back to Lisbon. King João II viewed the arrival of these hostages as an excellent opportunity to impress their king and accordingly he provided them with the finest royal hospitality, including the best food, clothes, housing, education and, of course, religion. At the same time, Cão's four men received an equally hospitable reception from the Manikongo during the two years they spent in his royal court in Mbanza Kongo. Thus, both Portugal and Kongo were able to observe one another from the heart of each other's kingdom.

Clearly impressed by reports received from their respective emissaries during the initial decade of contact, the two kings exchanged ambassadors as well as gifts. Nzinga Nkuwu (the Manikongo) sent members of the royal clan to Lisbon to request missionaries and technicians. João II (King of Portugal) complied with this request, adding teachers and explorers to the group. Shortly after their arrival in Kongo in 1491, the Manikongo, many of the royal family, and most of the noblemen were baptized in the Catholic Church.[38] Nzinga Nkuwu and one son, however,

[35] Vansina, 1966, p. 37. For a detailed account of the Bakongo and their neighbours at the time of the Portuguese arrival, see pp. 38–45.

[36] Wheeler and Pelissier, 1971, p. 28; July, 1970, pp. 151–2; Davidson, 1961, p. 29; Marques, A. H. de O., 1964, p. 1.

[37] There is considerable agreement among historians of Angola on the underlying motivations and facts concerning the nature of early Portuguese-Bakongo relations. This agreement is no doubt accounted for largely by the fact that most historians have relied on the same scanty sets of documents which are available on this period. Some of the more useful accounts of the period can be found in Ralph Delgado, n.d., vol. 1, pp. 61–194 (originally published in 1948); Vansina, 1966, pp. 37–69; Felner, 1933, pp. 17–85; Farinha, 1969, passim; Davidson, 1961, pp. 117–62; Duffy, 1959, pp. 5–23; Wheeler in Wheeler and Pelissier, 1971, pp. 28–31; Birmingham, 1965, pp. 6–10; July, 1970, pp. 152–5; Boxer, 1969, pp. 28–31; and Collins, 1971, pp. 8–11.

[38] Delgado, n.d. vol. 1, pp. 79–88.

returned to their traditional religious beliefs and practices several years after their 'conversion', but another son, Mbemba Nzinga or Afonso I, received more than ten years of clerical instruction in Lisbon before he succeeded his father in 1505. Afonso's succession to the throne was a major triumph for Portuguese policy; after only two decades of contact with the Kongo Kingdom, the Bakongo were ruled by a king who not only believed in the superiority of Portuguese civilization and religion, but was determined to propagate them vigorously throughout his kingdom.[39]

Unfortunately for Afonso, his good intentions and convictions were not matched by the Portuguese. The crown began to lose interest in Kongo as Vasco da Gama and Bartholomeu Dias finally discovered the passage to India at the turn of the century. Increasingly the Kongo Kingdom was viewed as a repository for slaves, especially by the Portuguese in São Tomé, who officially (through decrees) dominated the slave trade on the coast.[40]

The slave trade was already a fact of life by the time Afonso came to power in 1505, but it intensified greatly during his almost four decades as king. Whereas approximately 60,000 slaves were taken out of Kongo within the first two decades of contact, 345,000 slaves were exported from 1506 to 1575.[41] Even many of the priests who had been sent to evangelize at Afonso's request took up the lucrative practice of buying and selling slaves, which further disillusioned Afonso, who may have been the most sincere and faithful Christian in Kongo.[42]

Afonso's frequent complaints to King Manuel (who succeeded João II in 1495) about the degrading behaviour of the Portuguese in his kingdom were basically ignored until 1512, when Manuel issued a *regimento*, or statute, governing relations between Portugal and Kongo. His *regimento*, consisting of thirty-four points which incorporated Afonso's demands and Manuel's responses, was a master plan for the acculturation of the Bakongo.[43] Manuel, who referred to his Catholic counterpart in Mbanza Kongo as his 'brother', manifested an extremely egalitarian and

[39] Ibid., pp. 91–9; Duffy, 1959, pp. 12–19; Boxer, 1963, p. 20; and Cuvelier, in Vansina, 1966, p. 47.

[40] Felner, 1933, pp. 61–2; and Vansina, 1966, p. 46.

[41] Delgado, n.d., vol. 3, p. 455 (Appendix 6). These figures refer only to the area of Kongo, not the territory in Angola south of the Kongo Kingdom which, in fact, provided the bulk of the slaves taken from Angola. Also see Davidson, 1961, pp. 144–51.

[42] The attitude of the clergy toward Africans during the latter part of the sixteenth century became increasingly less empathic. See, for example, the view expressed by Padre Garcia Simões in a letter sent to the Jesuit Provincial, 20 October 1575: 'Almost all have verified that the conversion of these barbarians will not be achieved through love, unless they have first been made subjects and vassals of the King Our Lord through arms.' Quoted in Brásio, 1953, vol. 3, p. 142.

[43] A copy of this *regimento* (excluding a few paragraphs which are unintelligible in the original) can be found in Felner, 1933, Appendix 5, pp. 383–90. For a discussion of this *regimento*, see Delgado, n.d., vol. 1, pp. 110–15.

peaceful attitude towards Afonso in the *regimento*. This attitude was clearly an anomaly in Portuguese-Bakongo relations and not indicative of the peacefulness of the times, as some Portuguese scholars have asserted.

While the egalitarian tone of the *regimento* may have been unparalleled in early European relations with African kingdoms, the fact is that the spirit and intentions of the document were never effectuated, principally due to the avarice of the local Portuguese, who had no intention of compromising their commercial interests. This early instance of Lisbon's 'good intentions' and 'magnanimity' being undermined by insubordinate nationals in Africa is illustrative of an important reality which plagued practically every Portuguese regime from King D. João II at the end of the fifteenth century to the government of Marcello Caetano and, in some instances, the Armed Forces Movement which overthrew him.

By 1526 preoccupation with the slave trade eclipsed any Portuguese intentions of good will. Afonso was so distraught he banned all trade and issued an order to expel every white with the exception of teachers and missionaries; however, he was forced to revoke this order a few months later. In a letter directed to João III (1526) Afonso wrote, 'there are many traders in all corners of the country. They bring ruin to the country. Every day people are enslaved and kidnapped, even nobles, even members of the King's own family.'[44]

By this time proselytizing activity was practically moribund. Only four priests remained in the entire kingdom. Nowhere was the demise of the missionary work more evident than in the treatment of Afonso's son, Henrique, who had been consecrated as the first African bishop in the Roman Catholic Church. After thirteen years of clerical study in Lisbon and Rome, D. Henrique returned to Kongo in the capacity of bishop only to be ridiculed and ignored by the white clergy in his father's court. Incensed by this mistreatment of his son, Afonso complained in 1526 to João III that it had caused D. Henrique to become seriously depressed and sick.[45]

Afonso and his son Henrique were caught between two worlds and, unfortunately, suffered the worst of both. Each was the object of Portuguese scorn and intrigue, occasionally encouraged by Lisbon, while at the same time their 'Portuguesization' estranged them from their own people, who sought to escape the pernicious effects of the slave trade perpetrated by Afonso's Portuguese 'allies.' Eventually Afonso lost nearly complete control over his kingdom as the Portuguese expanded the slave trade at all costs. Relations degenerated so far that one Friar Alvaro ordered eight Portuguese to try to kill the Manikongo during the Easter

[44] Paiva Manso, *História do Congo*, p. 54, cited by Vansina, 1966, pp. 52–3.

[45] Felner, 1933, p. 394, Document No. 9. D. Henrique returned to Europe around 1529 where he remained until his death on his return voyage to Kongo some time before 1539. Also see Delgado, n.d., vol. 1, pp. 140 and 418, note 10.

church service in 1540. The cannonball fired into the church missed Afonso but wounded many innocent people. Afonso died shortly after this attempt on his life, marking the end of even the most symbolic manifestations of friendship and equality between the Bakongo and the Portuguese.[46]

The confusion following Afonso's death and the decimating effects of the slave trade so weakened the Bakongo that they were unable to resist the 'Jaga' invasions in 1569, which expelled both the Manikongo and the Portuguese from the Kongo capital.[47] With Portuguese aid the new Manikongo was eventually restored in Mbanza Kongo, but by this time Portuguese (slave) interests had shifted southward. By the end of the sixteenth century practically all signs of Portuguese culture and religion had disappeared among the Bakongo, and the initial period of amicable relations between the two kingdoms was followed by an enmity which persisted into the mid-1970s.[48]

The death and destruction which the Portuguese traders visited on the African populations in the interior assumed such magnitude that by 1611 the crown had to bar whites from the interior.[49] Whites ignored the 1611 decree and continued trading in the interior (the decree was rescinded in 1758). A letter sent to the King by the Bishop of Luanda in 1617 indicates that the governors were as culpable as the traders in this human destruction.[50] By the latter part of the century the famous soldier/historian, Cadornega, summarized the first two centuries of Portuguese-Bakongo relations with the observation that 'we will say how our lord punished this kingdom which was so Catholic ... [It] is a pity and heartache to see how this new Christianity of the Kongo Kingdom was retarded.'[51]

[46] Felner (1933, p. 65) argues that Afonso died sometime in 1540–1, while Delgado (n.d., vol. 1, p. 193) and Boxer (1969, p. 20) mark 1543 as the year of his death.

[47] Wheeler notes that approximately 8,000 to 10,000 slaves were transported annually from Angola around 1550. Wheeler and Pelissier, 1971, pp. 30–1.
Most accounts of this invasion are taken from the notes of Duarte Lopez which were incorporated into a book by Filippo Pigafetta in 1591. See Pigafetta, 1970, pp. 96–8. Joseph Miller, (1973, pp. 121–49) however, has assembled a considerable amount of evidence to suggest that the invaders were not the Jagas from the east but were perhaps more local enemies such as the Nsundi and Mbata aided by the Tyo.

[48] For further information on late nineteenth- and early twentieth-century anti-Portuguese attitudes and activities among the Bakongo, see Marcum, 1969, vol. 1, pp. 49–56; Wheeler, 1968, pp. 40–59. For a contrary position and an excellent example of how lusotropical interpretations can distort the historical record, see Cardoso, 1968.

[49] This *regimento* can be found in Felner, 1933, Document No. 36, pp. 442–9, especially p. 445. Also see Dias, G. S., 1959, pp. 234–5.

[50] The Bishop of Luanda warned the King in 1617 that based on his long experience in Angola which covered the period of five governors, '[the governors] risk everything, molesting and robbing the natives and residents, often making unjust wars, capturing, killing and oppressing innocents, and causing all types of vexations which can't be stated'. A copy of this letter can be found in Felner, 1933, Document No. 38, pp. 452–6.

[51] Cadornega, 1942, vol. 3, pp. 283–4. (This book was first published in 1681.)

During the Salazar and Caetano regimes, officials and scholars frequently cited the five hundred years of Portuguese contact with African peoples as proof that the Portuguese were able to treat Africans as equals. Time, however, means nothing by itself; it is what transpires during the passage of time that is important. Extensive contact can breed contempt as well as respect and compassion; it can be destructive or constructive. On the one hand, Portuguese contact with the Bakongo reached its luso-tropical peak in practically every respect during the reign of Afonso I. On the other hand, the demise of the Kongo Kingdom as a leader in Central Africa was guaranteed by the nature of Portuguese intervention in the area, including the obviously debilitating effects of the slave trade. No Manikongo after Afonso I ever received the same respect and recognition from a Portuguese regime. Nevertheless, he died a broken man, rejected by the Bakongo and scorned by the local Portuguese. His son, D. Henrique, consecrated as a bishop, died in similar circumstances; four and a half centuries passed before another African from Angola was appointed a bishop in the Catholic Church.[52]

The fundamental importance for lusotropical theory of Portugal's initial contacts in Angola rests almost solely upon the decrees and statutes which emanated from Lisbon. However, while legislation may afford a reasonable means for ascertaining what a society believes its behaviour *ought to be*, it does not record the actual behaviour of that society's members. The lacuna between ideals and practices is even greater when the ideals of one society are applied within the context of another. Portuguese legislation reflected the ideals of sixteenth-century Portuguese society whose norms and expectations were considerably different from those of the Portuguese in Angola. With rare exceptions, whenever European social ideals conflicted with local Portuguese avarice, whether in Mbanza Kongo or Bahia, those ideals were compromised. While it may be true that Lisbon's pronouncements and statutes covering relations with Africans in the sixteenth century were more egalitarian than those promulgated in London, Paris, Amsterdam, or Brussels, the behaviour of Portuguese nationals in direct contact with Africans was not appreciably better or worse than their counterparts from the other European colonizing nations.

[52] On 11 March 1970, Pope Paul VI nominated Eduardo André Muaca as acting Bishop of Isola. *Boletim Geral do Ultramar*, 1970, p. 217. The announcement of this nomination is followed by a lengthy statement on D. Henrique, in classical lusotropical wording, which draws a clear parallel between the two Angolan bishops as though nothing to the contrary occurred during the intervening centuries. We are reminded that it was the Portuguese 'who were the first to think of creating an indigenous hierarchy in the middle of the fifteenth century, and more than think, they made it into a reality with the election of D. Henrique as Bishop of Utica. History repeats itself, but with much stronger antecedents, given the level of evangelization of the Portuguese Overseas Territories' (p. 219). On 4 October 1973, the Vatican appointed Muaca to the Catholic bishopric of Malange. *The Times* (London), 5 October 1973.

CHAPTER TWO

The Dynamics of Miscegenation

Proof that a multi-racial society is possible is forthcoming from Brazil, the greatest Latin-American power and a nation of Portuguese roots. It would, therefore, be necessary to deny this fact, as well as many others, to sustain the impossibility of a social constitution of this type on African territory.

António de Oliveira Salazar (1966)[1]

Brazil can serve as an example. But, unfortunately, little is known in Europe about its particulars or its history. A policy of racial equality was also carried out in the political and social spheres there—just as is happening in our African territories. If the world will give us time, we could also finish the building of multiracial societies in which, as in the case of Brazil, distinctions according to ethnic groups do not exist.

Marcello Caetano (1973)[2]

Introduction

The Portuguese, lacking substantial evidence of racial harmony in Asia and Africa, sought to validate their lusotropical claims of non-racism through the example of Brazil. Brazil served Portugal by providing a cloak of innocence by association which, in part, counteracted the guilt by association Portugal suffered for her close ties with the avowedly racist regimes of South Africa and Rhodesia.

Brazil has been widely acclaimed as a paradigm of racial assimilation and the most perfect example of a racial democracy to be found in the contemporary world.[3] The Portuguese accepted this acclamation as an article of faith for, as both Salazar and Caetano suggest above, it was

[1] Salazar, A de O., 1966, p. 6.
[2] Marcello Caetano, 1973b.
[3] Charles Wagley argued that:
Brazil is renowned in the world for its racial democracy ... Today, it may be said that Brazil has no 'race problem' in the same sense that it exists in many other parts of the world; people of three racial stocks, and mixtures of all varieties of these stocks, live in what are essentially peaceful relations. (Wagley, 1952, p. 7)
Interesting recent examinations of this claim can be found in: Donald, 1972, pp. 23–4 and *passim*; and Dzidzienyo, 1971, pp. 3–22.

Portugal's *raison d'être* in Africa. They assumed that the key factor in the Brazilian racial equation has been the presence of Portuguese culture and, furthermore, that the 'Portuguese factor' has held such overriding importance that the Brazilian experience would inevitably be repeated in Angola.

Central to this belief that race relations in Angola would emulate those in Brazil is the premise that the nature of race relations in any racially mixed society is determined by the nationality of the white population.[4] In this chapter the importance of nationality will be measured against other variables which may have influenced European patterns of mis-

TABLE I

Racial Composition of Angolan Population (1777–1970)[a]

YEAR	WHITE		MESTIÇO		BLACK		TOTAL[b]	
	Number	Per cent	Number	Per cent	Number	Per cent	Number	Per cent
1777	1,581	—	4,043	—	—	—	—	—
1845	1,832	0·03	5,770	0·10	5,378,923	99·9	5,386,525	100
1900	9,198	0·20	3,112	0·06	4,777,636	99·7	4,789,946	100
1920	20,700	0·48	7,500	0·18	4,250,000	99·3	4,278,200	100
1940	44,083	1·20	28,035	0·75	3,665,829	98·1	3,737,947	100
1950	78,826	1·90	29,648	0·72	4,036,687	97·4	4,145,161	100
1960	172,529	3·60	53,392	1·10	4,604,362	95·3	4,830,283	100
1970	(290,000)	(5·10)	—	—	—	—	5,673,046	100

[a]The population statistics cited before 1940 (when the first official census was conducted) are generally accurate for whites and mestiços, most of whom lived in or near coastal settlements and were therefore relatively easy to identify and count. The statistics on Africans, however, were based on poorly informed estimates and crude guesses which usually underestimated the actual size of the African population. I include them in this table nevertheless since they are the only statistics available and because if they are in error it is on the side of exaggerating the proportion of whites in Angola.

The estimate of 1777 was prepared by Governor D. António de Lencastre, found in Lemos, 1941, vol. I, pp. 3–5. The statistics for 1845 are taken from Lima, J. J. L. de, 1846, vol. III, p. 4–A, Table 1. It should be noted that he grossly underestimated the African population (378,923), which Lemos tried to correct by adding 5 million to Lima's estimate. (The Lemos figure for Africans in 1845 is used in this table since it is clearly more accurate despite the fact that it overestimates the population.) The statistics for 1900 and 1920 are found in Lemos, ibid., p. 33. The statistics for 1940–60 are taken from the official censuses: 1940, vol. I, pp. 78–9; 1950, vol. I, p. 15; 1960, vol. I, p. 35. The total population figure for 1970 is preliminary and can be found in U.N., 1972, p. 2. The justification for the 1970 estimate of the white population can be found in Bender and Yoder, 1974, pp. 26–31.

[b]The totals for 1940, 1950 and 1960 do not include the 'Others' in the census which are respectively: 63, 105, 166. Most if not all of the 'Others' are Goans.

[4] For a critique of explanations based on 'national character' see Bender, 1967, pp. 394–6.

cegenation in the New World and in Africa such as: the nature of the non-white societies; the level of assimilation of the component racial groups; types of economic activities pursued; the availability of slave, free and skilled labour; the availability of land and jobs; and the demographic composition of the population, especially the proportion of non-

TABLE 2

Racial Composition of Brazilian Population (1818–1970) [a]

YEAR	WHITE		MESTIÇO		BLACK		OTHER		TOTAL	
	Number	Per cent	Number	Per cent	Number	Per cent	Number	Per cent	Number	Per cent
1818	1,000,000	27	500,000	13	2,000,000	53	250,000 (Indian)	7·0	3,750,000	100
1872	3,787,289	38	4,188,737	42	1,954,543	20	—	—	9,930,569	100
1890	6,302,198	44	5,934,291	41	2,097,426	15	—	—	14,333,915	100
1940	26,171,778	63·5	8,744,365	21	6,035,869	15	242,320 (Oriental)	0·6	41,194,332	100
1950	32,027,661	61·8	13,786,742	26·6	5,692,657	11	329,082 (Oriental)	0·6	51,836,142	100
1970	—	—	—	—	—	—	—	—	92,237,570	100

[a] The population statistics for 1818 are estimates derived from figures found in E. Bradford Burns, *A History of Brazil* (New York: Columbia University Press, 1970), p. 43 and p. 103. It is not possible to be precise because the statistics were collected according to the following categories: white, slave, freed man, or Indian. The population statistics for 1872 and 1890 represent the first two official Brazilian censuses and can be found in Rodrigues, 1965, pp. 72–3 and Nascimento, 1968, p. 31. The total population for some years does not equal the actual total population of Brazil since those who were not identified under any colour classification were excluded. In 1940, for example, 41,893 were counted but not classified according to colour. The number of Indians is a rough estimate which unfortunately cannot be measured against later censuses since Indians were included under the mestiço category after 1940. (The actual designation in the census is *pardos*, a term which loosely includes all brown people. In addition to Indians, it includes any combination of mixture among whites, mestiços, blacks and Indians.) See Governo do Brasil, vol. 1, 1956, p. xvii. The population for 1940 is found in Rodrigues, pp. 72–3 and for 1950 in Governo do Brasil, 1956, p. 69. The population for 1970 is found in *U.N. Demographic Yearbook 1970*, Table 2 as quoted in Ruddle and Hamour, 1971, p. 57, Table 6. No racial breakdowns can be found after the 1950 census since the question of colour was dropped from the census after the passage of the Afonso Arinos Law in 1951, which was intended to officially end all discrimination. See Eduardo Pinto, 'Preconceito de classe atinge negros 80 anos apos abolição' (1968).

One should note that these racial designations have been employed most imprecisely by Brazilians up to 1950. Census enumerators varied in utilizing social and physical criteria for determining race, thus a wealthy mestiço could be counted as white while another who is extremely poor could have been counted as black. For more on this point see *infra*, p. 31, note 35.

whites and the ratio of white women to white men. Following a comparison of the component racial groups in Brazil and Angola, Portuguese patterns of miscegenation and attitudes towards mestiços will be contrasted with those of the English, French, Spanish and Dutch in North, Central and South America, the West Indies and Africa. It is only through this comparative analysis that the importance of nationality and the uniqueness of the Portuguese experience of miscegenation and race relations can be adequately evaluated in order to assess the validity of generalizing the Brazilian pattern of race relations to Angola.

A striking contrast can be seen in the historical and contemporary racial compositions of Brazil and Angola. (See Tables 1 and 2.) More than a quarter of Brazil's population was white by the beginning of the nineteenth century, while the proportion of whites in Brazil today is approximately two-thirds of the entire population. In Angola, on the other hand, whites did not account for even 1 per cent of the population until the 1920s, and never composed more than 5 per cent of the inhabitants. Viewed in another way, the number of whites in Brazil today is greater than the entire population of either France or Germany, while the total white population of Angola was no larger at its peak than 4 per cent of the inhabitants of Rio de Janeiro.

Blacks have never constituted less than 95 per cent of the Angolan populace whereas, by the middle of the nineteenth century, blacks comprised about a fifth of Brazil's population and their proportion has steadily declined to approximately 10 per cent today. Finally, mestiços make up about a quarter of the Brazilian population, outnumbering blacks by more than two to one, while in Angola mestiços barely represent 1 per cent of the entire population. Clearly, in terms of racial composition, Brazil and Angola have very little in common.

Whites in Brazil and Angola

Almost from the time of Pedro Alvares Cabral's accidental 'discovery' of Brazil on his way to India in 1500, Portugal directed its imperial ambitions and its population towards Brazil rather than Africa.[5] The first colonists arrived in 1530 and by 1549 approximately 3,500 Portuguese were in Brazil. By the end of the century their numbers had expanded tenfold, or approximately the size of the white population in Angola at the outbreak of the Second World War. In the popular mind in Portugal, Brazil connoted the proverbial 'pot of gold' at the rainbow's end, whereas Angola represented hardship, even death, from counterattacking African armies or the harsh elements. Until the nineteenth century, Angola served

---

[5] Bettencourt, 1961, pp. 35–7; Burns, 1970, pp. 20–32; and Rodrigues, 1965, pp. 15–16.

as little more than a provider of black slaves for the plantations of Brazil; in point of fact, Angola was practically a colony of Brazil until the latter declared its independence from Portugal in 1822.[6] By 1818 more than one million whites were living in Brazil and by 1880 their number had increased over sixfold. By the latter year, the population of Metropolitan Portugal was only three-quarters of the number of whites in Brazil.[7]

Whereas most of the initial colonization was carried out by Portuguese settlers, a large number of whom were sent as degredados or exiled criminals, many nationals of other European countries also emigrated to Brazil. When it was apparent that the task of settling Brazil was well beyond Portugal's capacity, a royal decree, issued in 1808, opened Brazil's doors by permitting foreign nationals to become property owners and citizens.[8]

The acute need for immigrants was greatly exacerbated by the termination of the slave trade in 1850 and the abolition of slavery itself in 1888. Before 1850 the annual number of immigrants rarely exceeded 1,000, while an annual average of 31,000 slaves were imported (during the first half of the nineteenth century). From 1853 to 1856, the year the slave traffic ceased altogether, only 512 slaves were imported.[9] Brazil desperately needed new sources of labour. This vast country, larger than the continental U.S.A., had a population of only seven million by the end of the slave trade. Fortunately for Brazil, her greatest need for new immigrants coincided with the political turmoil in Europe which drove millions of Europeans to the New World in search of a better life. Over the next century Brazil's reputation for prosperity and opportunity encouraged almost five million of these emigrants to choose Brazil as their new home. The variety of their nationalities can be seen in Table 3.

[6] The Portuguese Naval Minister, Martinho de Melo e Castro, wrote in 1781 that it certainly

cannot be seen without great pain that our domains of Brazil have absorbed all of the commerce and navigation from the coast of Africa, *to the total exclusion of Portugal*, and that part which the Brazilians don't dominate is in the hands of foreign nations. (Quoted in Dias, G. S., 1959, p. 235.)

Sousa Dias concurs with Melo e Castro, stating that 'Angola was, in fact, a colony of Brazil' (p. 238). Lopes de Lima shows that the situation had not significantly altered a half century later. He noted that during the years 1830–2, ninety boats arrived in Luanda from Brazil while only eleven came from Portugal. Lima, J. J. L. de, 1846, p. 74. Also see Knapic, 1964, p. 25.

[7] In 1890 the population of Metropolitan Portugal was 4,660,095. Government of Portugal, *Boletim da Junta da Emigração*, 1965, p. 13.

[8] Bettencourt, 1961, p. 49; Poppino, 1968, p. 184; and Smith, T. L., 1972.

[9] Burns's (1970) conservative estimate of the number of slaves who survived the Atlantic crossing to Brazil is 1,600,000 (p. 128). During the six-year period preceding the official end of the slave trade, an average of 43,825 were annually imported; for the yearly importations, see Rodrigues, 1965, p. 159 and Poppino, 1968, p. 166.

TABLE 3

Immigration to Brazil by Nationality 1850–1950[10]

Nationality	Number	Per cent
Italian[11]	1,540,000	32·0
Portuguese	1,480,000	30·8
Spanish	600,000	12·5
German	230,000	4·7
Japanese	190,000	4·0
Other	760,000	16·0
Total	4,800,000	100·0

Like her northern neighbour in the New World, Brazil is comprised of immigrants of practically all nationalities, no single nation (including Portugal) contributing more than a third of the total number of immigrants.[12] This variety in the ethnic and national backgrounds of Brazil's white population in conjunction with the equally varied cultural backgrounds of Brazil's non-white inhabitants underscores the fallacy of conceiving the Brazilian 'national character' as almost exclusively derived from Portuguese antecedents.

Clearly, the major catalyst for the unprecedented wave of white emigration to Brazil was the radical change in the economy from slave to salaried labour.[13] More than half of all European immigrants between 1870 and 1920 went to the coffee farms and plantations in São Paulo.[14] By the end of the nineteenth century, Brazil possessed the essential con-

[10] The data used in compiling this table are found in Rodrigues, 1965, p. 82. Over thirty nations are encompassed by the category 'other' including, in order of numerical importance: Russia (about 110,000), Austria (90,000), Turkey (80,000), Poland (55,000), France (42,000), Romania (40,000), and the United States (30,000). For brief discussions on the background of each nationality group, see Poppino, 1968, pp. 182–99 and Smith, T. L., 1972, pp. 118–43.

[11] The importance of Italian emigration to Brazil is even greater during the period 1820 to 1930, when 34·1 per cent of the immigrants were Italians, compared with 30·0 per cent for the Portuguese. The most intense period of immigration occurred in the last quarter of the nineteenth century, when approximately 40 per cent of all immigrants arrived. The annual average between 1891 and 1900 was 112,500 (Burns, 1970, pp. 263–4). It is interesting to contrast this latter average with the annual average Portuguese emigration of 27,000 to all parts of the world during the same decade. *Boletim da Junta de Emigração* 1967, p. 14. Also see Villas, 1929, p. 100.

[12] In 1790, 61–6 per cent of white Americans were of English origin but their proportion has generally declined since then, especially during the latter part of the nineteenth and early twentieth centuries, when the largest emigration to the United States occurred. Jordan, 1968, p. 339; and Morris, 1953, p. 448.

[13] For further information see Fernandes, 1969, pp. 8–21. This book was originally published in Portuguese under the title *A integração do negro na sociedade de classes*.

[14] Poppino, 1968, p. 188.

ditions to stimulate large-scale immigration: an expanding economic infrastructure which required large labour inputs, a commitment to pay living wages, and an open attitude towards non-Portuguese immigrants.[15]

The absence of these conditions in Angola explains to a considerable degree why Angola attracted far fewer white immigrants than Brazil.[16] While coffee and sugar plantations date back to the 1830s, the importance of plantation agriculture in Angola is essentially a post-World War II phenomenon.[17] Trade, not agriculture, was the main economic preoccupation of the Portuguese in Angola. They therefore preferred exporting slaves to enrich the Brazilian plantations to developing large-scale plantation farming in Angola itself.[18] The economic changeover from slave or forced labour to free salaried labour is a recent occurrence in Angola, resulting from the revocation of the *indigenato* statute in 1961. Finally, the Portuguese were reluctant to open Angola's doors to non-Portuguese immigration.

The largest foreign groups to settle in Angola were the Boers and the Germans, but most of them had left by the end of the 1920s. The Boers reached their population peak of approximately 2,000 in 1928, when they began their trek back to South Africa.[19] After the departure of the Boers, the non-Portuguese white settlers in Angola never exceeded more than 2 per cent of the total white population.[20] This is a marked contrast with

[15] Many Brazilian industrialists believed that the substitution of a free work force for slaves was the solution to Brazil's labour problem. This attitude led a number of them to actively recruit European labourers to replace slaves even before emancipation. See Graham, 1970, p. 58.

[16] More whites emigrated to Brazil during the year of abolition than Angola's total white population in the mid-1950s. (In 1955 the white Angolan population was estimated to be 134,690.) Morgado, 1958, p. 248.

[17] One index of the expansion of coffee plantations after World War II is the increase in tons of coffee exported: 1926 = 10,014 tons; 1941 = 14,184 tons; 1962 = 156,887 tons; 1972–73 'coffee year' (October 1972–September 1973) = 193,407 tons. See Marques, W., 1964, pp. 174–9; and *A Província de Angola* (Luanda), 9 November 1973. Also see Wheeler and Pelissier, 1971, pp. 54 and 64.

[18] Peirre Gourou discusses some of the factors which motivated the Portuguese to export slaves from Angola rather than use them as agricultural labourers in Angola. He believes that not only was it easier for the Portuguese to conquer the Indians in Brazil than the Africans in Angola but also that to have used the slaves in their country of origin would have been impractical because of the ease of escape. 'Etude comparée de l'Amazonie et du Congo Central' (1959, cited by Rodrigues, 1965, p. 17).

[19] The number of Boers in Angola grew from about 300 in 1879 to approximately 2,000 at the time of the trek out of Angola in 1928. In 1958, there were 58 Boer families, consisting of 500 individuals, living in Angola. See Wheeler in Wheeler and Pelissier, 1971, pp. 71–6; Guerreiro, 1958, pp. 12–16; Rosental, 1934, pp. 1–14 and Paxeco, 1916, pp. 71–8. For a comparison of the Angola Boers with those in Mozambique, see Camacho, 1930, *passim*.

[20] The number of foreign residents in Angola from 1942 to 1956 is found in Ponce, 1960, p. 74. The 1960 census (vol. 2, p. 47) lists 3,103 'foreign residents' in Angola but 1,046 of this number came from what were then known as Congo-Leopoldville and Congo-Brazzaville and were most probably Africans.

Brazil, where over two-thirds of the white population is non-Portuguese.

Another major contrast between the white populations in Brazil and Angola is the proportion of 'native born'. The overwhelming majority of Brazilian whites have roots in the country extending over many generations. In 1920 only about one of every ten whites was not native born, and by 1950 the ratio had decreased to one of every forty-four. In Angola, on the other hand, more than two out of three whites in 1960 were not native born.[21] Therefore, the roots of over 70 per cent of Angola's whites, prior to their exodus in 1975, did not extend back even one generation.

In short, relatively few similarities existed between the white populations of Brazil and Angola, either in terms of absolute numbers, percentage of total population, national origins, past and present economic activities, or percentage of native born. The economic conditions which stimulated large-scale white emigration to Brazil in the late nineteenth and early twentieth centuries were never repeated in Angola.

Contrast between Blacks in Brazil and Angola[22]

One of the most radical differences between the Brazilian and Angolan racial mosaics is the degree of black assimilation, influenced over time by significant interacting variables such as settlement patterns, cultural adaptation, economic integration and proportion of blacks in the total population. The absolute number of blacks in each country is relatively equal, but there the similarity ends. The proportion of blacks in Brazil has steadily declined from over half of the population in the eighteenth and nineteenth centuries to approximately 10 per cent today. Black 'emigration' to Brazil effectively ended with the termination of the slave trade, in part because Brazil established ethnic quotas on immigration— similar to those enacted in the United States—which 'guaranteed

[21] In 1960, 70·5 per cent of the whites in Angola were born outside the colony. Província de Angola, 1967, p. 13. In the capital of Luanda, only 21·5 per cent of the whites were born in Angola.

It is interesting to note that this proportion of 'native-born' whites in Angola is less than Rhodesia, where in 1961 35 per cent of the white population was born in Rhodesia. Kay, 1970, p. 30.

[22] It is difficult to find a single term for members of the Negroid race in all parts of the world which is both inoffensive and corresponds to local usage. For example, a quarter of a century ago the direct descendants of Africans in Brazil were as offended by the term *negro* as American Negroes were by the term black. Today, the opposite is true in both countries. An additional problem arises because the term black in Brazil does not include mestiços, while in the United States it does. Throughout this study, when the term black is applied outside the United States, it will refer only to those who are presumed to be direct descendants from Africans, with no Caucasian or other racial mixture.

[Brazil's] ethnic integrity'.[23] In Angola, on the other hand, blacks have never constituted less than 95 per cent of the population. If we look at the population figures in terms of the white component, we see that in Brazil not only did whites outnumber blacks before the end of the nineteenth century, but their numbers have increased to the extent of approximately six hundred whites for every one hundred blacks today; in Angola there were only four whites for every one hundred blacks.

Black settlement patterns vary considerably between Brazil and Angola, strongly affecting the degree of contact between blacks and whites in each country. Brazilian blacks have never been a landed class, and after abolition they migrated to the cities in such proportions that the majority now live in Brazil's large urban centres.[24] Thus, throughout their history in Brazil, blacks have been in close contact with the white population. Precisely the opposite is true in Angola, where the overwhelming majority of Africans have always lived on their own or communally-held lands in the rural areas. In 1970 only 10 per cent of Africans lived in urban centres—a little more than half of them in Angola's capital, Luanda— whereas over 50 per cent of whites lived in Angola's five major cities.[25] Until recent decades, then, most Africans have had little or no association with whites.

The difference in the degree of black assimilation in Brazil and Angola has not only been affected by the amount of interracial contact but by the type of dominant culture blacks have been expected to assimilate. Brazilian culture underwent considerable 'Africanization' for centuries. Rodrigues notes that while the Portuguese exerted their greatest influence on the Brazilian class structure, the socio-economic structure was primarily influenced by the blacks and Indians 'so that from the beginning Brazil

---

[23] Brazil enacted legislation in 1890 which prohibited Africans and Asians from entering the country without special congressional approval. Burns, 1970, p. 264. For twentieth-century Brazilian legislation restricting non-European immigration similar to the U.S. Immigration Act of 1921 and the McCarran-Walter Act of 1952, see Rodrigues, 1965, pp. 89–91.

[24] Graham, 1970, p. 68; Fernandes, 1969, pp. 7–8, pp. 29–30 and p. 191; Smith, 1971, pp. 639–41.

[25] According to a provisory analysis of the 1970 Angolan census there were twenty-four cities and towns in Angola with at least 2,500 inhabitants. These urban centres contained 568,499 Africans, 62,248 mestiços and 216,078 whites. The capital city of Luanda accounted for 55 per cent of the African, 57 per cent of the white and 61 per cent of the mestiço urban residents in Angola. In 1970 the white population in Angola's five largest cities was the following: Luanda (124,814), Nova Lisboa (14,694); Lobito (14,152), Benguela (10,175) and Sá da Bandeira (13,429). Estado de Angola, 1972, p. 8.

One measure of interracial contact in Brazil and Angola can be inferred from the overall index of urbanization in both countries. In 1960, 45 per cent of Brazilians lived in urban centres (towns or cities with 2,000 or more inhabitants), compared with 15 per cent of Angolans who, in 1970, were living in towns or cities with 2,500 or more inhabitants. For further information on urbanization in Brazil see Rios, 1971, pp. 269–88; and Smith, T. L., 1971, pp. 62–70. (All future citations of T. Lynn Smith refer to the fourth edition of his *Brazil: People and Institutions*.)

was more a Negro and Tupi product than a Western, Portuguese one'.[26] Once again, Angola is at the opposite end of the spectrum, since prior to independence Africans had little influence on either the class or socio-economic structures. With the exception of occasional *sertanejos* (frontiers-men) and bush traders, the Portuguese in Angola have been largely impervious to African influences, even in such aspects as music, food and language, which have been so noticeably influenced in Brazil.[27] In short, Africans in colonial Angola were expected to assimilate an almost pure, unmitigated Portuguese culture, barely modified by the slightest trace of their own numerically dominant cultures. This cultural rigidity and the exaggerated standards demanded of Africans (prior to 1961) before they could be officially considered assimilated help explain why less than 1 per cent of Africans in 1950 were legally classified as *assimilados*.[28]

On the other side of the coin, the intensive deculturalization process which was ubiquitous among slave societies in the Americas also aided black assimilation in Brazil. Torn from their homelands, families and cultures, Africans brought to Brazil were subjected to the Portuguese language, values, foods, rules of behaviour and gods almost before their arrival. Unlike Africans who were enslaved in Africa or Indians in the New World, black slaves in the Americas were unable to draw strength from their own cultures and social groups and consequently were more

[26] Rodrigues, 1965, p. xiv. There have been many studies of the influence of African cultures in Brazil. An excellent discussion of this phenomenon, as well as references to most of the important studies on this subject, can be found in Rodrigues, 1965, chapter 2, pp. 36–51. Also see Smith, T. L., 1971, p. 58, notes 11–13; pp. 528–46, and pp. 723–5. It should be noted that the remnants of African cultural patterns are not found uniformly throughout Brazil. Marvin Harris, in his 1950 study of a community in the mountain region of central Brazil, (1952: pp. 50–1) reported that 'throughout the area remnants of African patterns are few and incidental'. He further observed that 'in Minas Velhas and in the satellite villages there is no sub-culture which sets the Negroes apart from the members of the community'.

[27] For further information on the *sertanejos* in Angola, see Wheeler and Pelissier, 1971, pp. 44–5 and Dias, G. S., 1971, pp. 7–78.

Until the end of the 1960s, because practically no African music was played on Angolan radio stations, many Africans saved their money to purchase short-wave radios in order to hear African music broadcast from Zaïre and the Congo. In addition to the music, however, these radios picked up the broadcasts of the Angolan nationalist organiza-tions, which caused enough concern among Portuguese officials to open a radio station (run by the army) aimed principally at African listeners and called 'The Voice of Angola'. It was even agreed, for the first time, to intermittently use some of the African languages on the radio station. Ironically, many of the African announcers selected were so 'assimilated' they could not properly speak their traditional languages and con-sequently became the brunt of many African jokes, particularly among the Kimbundus of Luanda and the Ovambos in the south.

[28] *Assimilados* were Africans and mestiços considered to have fully assimilated Portuguese culture. Before 1961 all assimilados were legally classified as 'civilized' along with all whites, while the remaining 99 per cent of (non-assimilado) Africans were classified as 'uncivilized'. For a more complete discussion of assimilados see Chapter 5.

easily assimilated. While Brazil may be somewhat unique in the number of African traditions which have survived in the New World, by the end of the nineteenth century the culture of most Brazilian blacks—not unlike their counterparts in the rest of the Americas—more closely approximated that of the dominant white society than their African ancestors.[29]

The changing nature of the Brazilian economy which reduced the demand for slave labour had a profound effect on the assimilation and incorporation of blacks into Brazilian society. The most lucrative phase of the sugar-plantation economy ended by the close of the seventeenth century—almost two hundred years before slavery was legally abolished. Whereas abolition in the American South came when the slave-based economy was in its prime, the production of slave-worked plantations in Brazil was either stagnant or actually declining at the time of abolition. Thus, the freeing of slaves did not represent the same loss to the owner in Brazil as it did in the United States. On the contrary, slaves represented a capital investment and had to be fed during good and bad times, which was not true for the share-cropping or wage-labour systems that replaced slavery and in which the worker shared the risk with the land-owner.[30] Not unexpectedly, there was a higher rate of manumission in Brazil than in the United States, Angola and other countries where slavery remained profitable. By the end of the eighteenth century there were already 406,000 'free' blacks in Brazil; by the time of abolition it is estimated that black freemen outnumbered slaves by three to one.[31] In

[29] Blacks were assimilated rapidly throughout most of Latin America. Beltran notes that while there were some differences between the world view of whites and Negroes (blacks and mestiços),

these differences were not as radically divergent from each other as they were from the concepts of the Indians who preserved a set of ideas derived directly from the ancient Meso-American thought and barely modified by acculturation. Basically the conditions for the integration of the Negro and mulatto were as favourable as they were un-favourable for the Indian (Beltran, 1970, p. 25).

A discussion of the rapid assimilation of blacks in Uruguay can be found in Rama, 1970, pp. 32–3. Also see Wagley and Harris, 1958, p. 89; Fernandes, p. 564.

[30] For an examination of the major features of the sugar cycle in Bahia (Brazil), see Schwartz, 1973, pp. 147–98. Also see Wagley and Harris, 1958, p. 99 and pp. 127–8.

[31] Ramos, A., 1952, p. 143; and Wagley and Harris, 1958, p. 91.

For a penetrating statistical analysis of the economic and non-economic factors in Brazilian manumission, see Schwartz, 1974, pp. 603–35. Based on a random sample of the records of 1,160 slaves who were manumitted in Bahia (1684–1745), Schwartz examines the influence on manumission of: the economy, motivations of slave owners, value of slaves, self-purchase, agricultural seasons and the age, sex, colour, origin, health and residence (urban-rural) of the manumitted slaves themselves. He suggests that, since almost 20 per cent of the manumissions were conditional and almost half of the former slaves in his sample purchased their own manumission (or had someone else purchase it for them), his data undercut 'the traditional humanitarian interpretation of Brazilian manumission' (p. 42). For the variations in the proportion of 'free Negroes' in the American coastal slave states in 1790 and 1810, see Jordan, 1968, pp. 406–7. In the latter year they ranged from 75·9 per cent of all blacks in Delaware to 1·7 per cent in Georgia.

other words, approximately 75 per cent (1,500,000) of Brazilian blacks were generally integrated into the non-slave economy by 1888.

At the time of abolition there was approximately one slave for every eleven whites in Brazil, while there were about fifteen slaves for every white in Angola. Nevertheless, the actual number of slaves in Angola represented less than 2 per cent of the African population. In 1873, five years before slavery was 'legally' abolished in Angola, there were 58,061 slaves and 31,768 freemen (manumitted slaves and/or their descendants).[32] Unlike Brazil, the remaining blacks in Angola were neither slaves nor freemen. On the contrary, the vast majority of Africans, deeply rooted in their indigenous cultures, were almost completely removed from the influence of Portuguese culture and society in Angola.

In sum, there is little similarity between the black populations of Brazil and Angola. In addition to the obvious contrast of blacks being a minority in Brazil but a majority in Angola, they differ widely with respect to urban/rural living patterns, sustained contact with whites, ties with indigenous African cultures, level of assimilation, land tenure and integration into the non-agricultural economy. The economic forces which shaped the colonization of Brazil and influenced the formation, development and character of Brazil's black population were not nor will they ever be substantially present in Angola.

Mestiços[33]

Fundamental to the image of non-racism among the Portuguese has been the large number of Brazilian mestiços. Miscegenation with Indians and, later, Africans began immediately upon the arrival of the Portuguese in

[32] Pery, 1875, p. 357. It is not clear how Pery arrived at this breakdown of slaves and *libertos* (freemen) in 1873 since, as part of Portugal's gradual abolition of slavery, all slaves became *libertos* in 1869. In many cases, according to Duffy (1959, pp. 77, 151–2, 158), these *libertos* were still slaves but were just given a new name.

Wheeler notes that most of the *libertos* who were actually free tended to drift beyond the frontiers into vagabondage instead of working within the European sector. Wheeler and Pelissier, 1971, p. 63.

[33] Unfortunately, there is scanty information concerning miscegenation in Portugal during the period when blacks formed a part of its population. In fact, most histories of Portugal contain little more than passing references to the presence of African slaves. Yet, African slaves constituted an important segment of Portuguese society, being an integral part of the labour force, for more than three centuries—longer than the period of slavery in the United States.

In a 1535 letter written from Evora, a Flemish priest wrote, undoubtedly exaggerating, that 'slaves were swarming all over. All the work is done by captive blacks and Moors. Portugal is being glutted with this race. I'm beginning to believe that the slaves in Lisbon outnumber the Portuguese.' Actually, from about the middle of the sixteenth century until at least 1620, approximately 10 per cent of Lisbon's 100,000 inhabitants were Africans. Oliveira Marques doubts that slaves ever constituted more than 10 per cent of the Portuguese population in the early seventeenth century, but adds that there is no reliable source for evaluating the impact of slavery on the growth of the Portuguese population. Brásio maintains that 'numerous blacks' were in Portugal from the sixteenth to the eighteenth century. Although slavery was abolished in Portugal (not in the

Brazil.[34] In the last quarter of the nineteenth century, over 40 per cent of the Brazilian population was classified as mestiço and, while their proportion has gradually declined, they still represented more than 25 per cent of the population in 1950 (see Tables 2 and 4).[35] The assertion that a large percentage of mestiços in Brazil is proof, *ipso facto*, of the absence of Portuguese racism presupposes that racial attitudes and behaviour can be deduced from the historical incidence of miscegenation and that the Brazilian pattern of miscegenation is both unique and representative of Portuguese relations with non-whites in all parts of the world.[36] These suppositions will be examined through three perspectives: (1) Portuguese colonization in South America, Africa and Asia; (2) European colonization in the New World; and (3) European colonization in Africa.

---

colonies) in 1761, as late as the mid-nineteenth century Lichnowsky reported seeing 'thousands of blacks on the streets in Lisbon', noting that they were not treated as men by the Portuguese 'but as an inferior race of domestic animals'.

Interestingly enough, there appears to be little trace today of the documented presence of Africans in Portugal, i.e. where are the indigenous blacks or mestiços in modern Metropolitan Portugal? Their absence implies that there was little or no miscegenation between Africans and Portuguese in the metropole, despite the claims in the sixteenth century that it was difficult 'to find a house without at least one female slave', which further minimizes the relevance of the Portuguese national character in the miscegenation process.

Quotes by Flemish priest and Lichnowsky and from Brásio found in Brásio, 1944, pp. 12–13, 94, 114. Also see Duffy, 1959, pp. 133–4; Atkinson, 1960, p. 151; Marques, A H de O., 1972, pp. 167, 295.

[34] Wagley, 1952, p. 143; Burns, 1970, p. 33; and Smith, 1972, pp. 63–5.

[35] Considerable scepticism over the reliability of data on mestiços was expressed in the long notes to Tables 2 and 3, but it cannot be overemphasized. This is especially true for practically all societies outside the United States where mestiços have constituted a distinct class. In these societies colour is often a question of culture and thus the adage that 'every rich Negro is a mulatto and every poor mulatto is a Negro' has almost universally affected the accuracy of data on mestiços. Skin pigmentation, hair texture, facial structure, wealth, education and family background are used with differential emphasis, varying sometimes from census taker to census taker and from respondent to respondent. Nevertheless, the data can be relied upon to give us a reasonably accurate picture of the racial composition of the countries which are considered here. For example, even if we assume (which I don't) that the census data on mestiços in Brazil and Angola are exaggerated or underestimated by as much as one hundred per cent, it does not change the basic fact that the proportion of mestiços in Brazil is infinitely greater than in Angola. In other words, it makes little difference whether the proportion is ten or fifty times greater in Brazil.

For more on the reliability of data on mestiços see: Wagley, 1952, pp. 14 and 148–9; Harris, 1970, pp. 63 and 72–3; Beltran, 1970, p. 27; Rodrigues, 1965, p. 75; Patch, 1960, pp. 112–13; Lowenthal, 1969, pp. 293–312, especially, pp. 305–6; Bastide, 1974, p. 111; Pitt-Rivers, 1967, pp. 542–59; and Smith, 1972, p. 69.

[36] Mendes Corrêa, who was one of Portugal's most famous anthropologists in recent decades, argues that the examples of miscegenation found in the Portuguese colonies testify to the absence of racial prejudice among the Portuguese. Corrêa, 1953, p. 48; also see Freyre, 1964, pp. 161–2. The assertion also presupposes an absence of racism in Brazil which will be explored at the end of this section on mestiços.

TABLE 4

Number and Per Cent of Mestiços and Ratio to Whites in Former Portuguese Colonies

Territory	Official Census	Total Population	Mestiço Population	Per cent Mestiço	Number of Mestiços per 100 Whites
Cape Verde	1950	148,331	103,251	69·60	4,600
Brazil	1950	51,836,142	13,786,742	26·60	43
São Tomé and Principe	1950	60,159	4,300	7·15	400
Angola	1960	4,830,449	53,392	1·10	31
Guinea	1950	510,777	4,568[a]	0·90	200
Mozambique	1960	6,578,604	31,465	0·48	32
Macau	1950	187,778	122	0·06	4
Goa and Dimão	1950	637,591	200	0·03	22
Timor	1950	442,378	48	0·01	8

[a] A large number of the mestiços in Guinea were actually born in Cape Verde. The 1950 census notes that there were at least 1,703 Cape Verdians in Guinea. If they are deducted from the total number of mestiços (4,568), the percentage of mestiços in Guinea would drop to 0·56%, or almost the same as Mozambique. Província da Guiné, 1959, vol. 1, Table 5.

If it is true that a large percentage of mestiços is indicative of the absence of racism, then Brazil stands—with the exception of three small and relatively insignificant islands—as a singular example of Portuguese non-racism in all of the territories they colonized.

The exceptions noted are the small islands of Cape Verde, São Tomé, and Principe, which were all uninhabited when first discovered and whose combined population today of less than 350,000 is a product of the mixture of African slaves, exiled convicts and Jews expelled during the Inquisition. These islands were also atypical of Portugal's colonies in that they did not attract virtually any white settlers after the end of the slave trade.[37] With this caveat, it can be seen in Table 4 that the percentage of mestiços in Portugal's African colonies was relatively insignificant, while in the Portuguese Indian and Asian colonies the percentage of mestiços was barely negligible. Thus, in terms of percentages of mestiços, Brazil is unquestionably a racial anomaly among the territories colonized by Portugal.

While the proportion of mestiços provides some insight into the racial composition and character of a given country, and may even be a key to the understanding of its race relations, it may not be an accurate index

[37] For further information on early settlement in the islands of Cape Verde, São Tomé, and Principe see: Tenreiro, 1961; 1953, pp. 219–28; Brito, 1967, pp. 2–19; Amaral, 1964, 1967; Silva Rego, 1967; Duffy, 1959, p. 135; and Newitt, 1973, p. 9.

of the actual dynamics of miscegenation. The size of the indigenous population, for example, and its ratio to the white population could mask intensive miscegenation if the whites constitute a very small proportion of the total population. Therefore, another index of miscegenation—the number of mestiços per one hundred whites—has been included in Table 4 in order to eliminate the influence of the size of the indigenous population. This perspective not only highlights the differential patterns of Portuguese miscegenation but shows that by the middle of the twentieth century there was almost no difference between the two large African colonies of Angola and Mozambique and little difference between both colonies and Brazil.

Utilizing this index of miscegenation, it would appear that, with the exception of Cape Verde, considerably less miscegenation occurred in the Portuguese colonies than in certain areas colonized by other Europeans. In Jamaica, for example, there are approximately 1,600 mestiços for every one hundred whites, while the ratio in Guyana is 1,100/100, and 850/100 in Trinidad-Tobago. While this measure does avoid some potential problems affecting the analysis of the dynamics of miscegenation, it must be used cautiously in comparative interpretations. For example, the ratio is affected considerably by the level of white immigration: an historical period of considerable miscegenation can be eclipsed when followed by massive white immigration (e.g. Brazil); or, a period of intensive miscegenation can be accentuated if followed by little or no white immigration (e.g. Cape Verde, Jamaica, Trinidad, or Guyana).[38] Despite these qualifications, however, the vast differences in the number and per cent of mestiços and their ratio to whites in the former Portuguese colonies clearly underscore the fact that Portuguese reactions to non-whites were not the same everywhere. Portuguese men bearing essentially the same cultural baggage reacted differently throughout the world.

If the differences in Portuguese patterns of miscegenation cannot be explained by the singular factor of Portuguese culture or the Portuguese national character, it is necessary to examine other factors which influenced and shaped sexual and human relations in the European colonies in the New World and Africa.

Miscegenation in the New World

A study of the racial composition of Latin America reveals that Brazil—with slightly over one-quarter of its population considered mestiço—has

---

[38] Before the massive European immigration which accompanied the abolition of slavery in Brazil there were approximately the same number of whites and mestiços, but this fact is masked by the white immigration which is included in the present ratio of about 2·5 whites for each mestiço. Precisely the opposite has occurred in Jamaica, where white emigration (rather than immigration) has kept the absolute number of whites stationary since 1844. See Bell, W., 1964, pp. 7–8.

a smaller proportion of mestiços than all but five countries in South and Central America and the Caribbean. Mestiços comprise over half the population in ten of the eighteen former Spanish colonies, constituting over two-thirds of the inhabitants in seven of these countries.[39] Even in the non-Iberian West Indies—colonized by England, France and Holland —approximately one-third of the twelve million inhabitants are classified as mestiço.[40]

The experience of European colonization shows that white attitudes towards miscegenation and mestiços were strongly influenced, if not actually determined, by the interplay of two demographic factors: ratio of European men to women and the proportion of whites in relation to non-whites. Whenever Indians and/or blacks comprised a majority of the population and most of the whites were single males, a significant mestiço group developed (usually equal to the size of the European population) which was racially and socially distinguished from both blacks and whites. It is almost axiomatic that where these demographic conditions obtained there was a noticeable absence of any stigma against sexual intercourse between white men and non-white women; on the contrary, it was normal and expected. This was as true for the English in the Caribbean, the Spanish from Chile to Mexico, the French in Martinique, the Dutch in Brazil and the West Indies, as it was for the Portuguese and other Europeans in Brazil. Even the Chinese, who are often reputed to be socially endogamous in the diaspora, mixed with other groups, when males outnumbered females. In Jamaica, for example, there was considerable Chinese miscegenation with blacks; by 1960 there were as many Afro-Chinese as pure Chinese.[41]

For Portuguese or other European men to have acted differently in their sexual behaviour would have been extraordinary. Clearly no one in Europe from the sixteenth to the nineteenth centuries expected white men to remain chaste in the New World. The sexual activities of European men were rarely inhibited by the fact that the women were of different races and cultures. In fact, there is considerable evidence indicating that these differences stimulated the Europeans' sexual fantasies

[39] Mestiços include mixtures of European-Indian, European-African and Indian-African. Most of the miscegenation in Spanish America resulted from mixtures of Spanish and Indians while the pattern in Brazil, the West Indies and the Caribbean usually consisted of unions between Europeans and Africans.

Argentina, Uruguay, Costa Rica, Cuba and Haiti have a smaller proportion of mestiços than Brazil. The following countries have larger proportions of mestiços than Brazil: Honduras (90%), El Salvador (75%), Colombia (74%), Venezuela (70%), Nicaragua (68%), Panama (65%), Chile (65%), Mexico (60%), Dominican Republic (60%), Ecuador (about 50%), Guatemala, Peru, and Bolivia (about 33%). The sources used in compiling these estimates can be found in Bender, 1975b, p. 146, note 46.

[40] See Lowenthal, 1969, pp. 296–7; and Mintz, 1974, pp. 46–7, 51–2; for a penetrating discussion of miscegenation among the British, French and Dutch, respectively, in Latin America, see Degler, 1971, pp. 228–9, 239.

[41] Bell, W., 1964, p. 9.

and drives. The human biological sex drive removes the barriers which human groups utilize to differentiate themselves; at times, it has even overcome the boundaries by which humans differentiate themselves from animals. Thus, to assume that the readiness of Portuguese and other European men to mate with non-white women was indicative of European egalitarian attitudes, rather than lust, is a gross distortion of reality.

Whether lascivious European attitudes towards non-whites predate the initial contacts with Indians and Africans, as Freyre and Jordan maintain for the Portuguese and English, respectively, or they developed immediately after the first contacts, by the dawn of the sixteenth century dark-skinned people were associated throughout Europe with great passion and potent sexuality. From Shakespeare's *Othello* to Camões' *Os Lusíadas*, non-whites were lustfully depicted in the literature of Europe.[42] White preoccupation with black sexuality throughout the colonial period in Brazil is well documented by Freyre in his numerous references to the 'undisguised animality' which marked sexual relations between the Brazilian colonialists and black women who 'merely represented an outlet for sexual feelings'.[43] While sensual fantasies still excite western attitudes towards interracial sex, few today misperceive lust for respect or confuse eroticism with egalitarianism.

The importance of the demographic variables of sex and race in the development of attitudes towards miscegenation can be seen by contrasting the English colonies in the Americas. It is significant that in Jamaica, the English colony where whites constituted the smallest proportion of the population and where the imbalance between white males and females was the greatest, there were five mestiços for every four whites near the end of the eighteenth century. The shortage of white women and the abundance of black and mestiço slave women led to considerable miscegenation, which scandalized some of the residents. There were, for example, the familiar admonitions by some Jamaicans that the colony would be better off if the white men had less sexual attraction and 'attachment to black women', but they were lost voices, as can be seen in Edward Long's observation on Jamaican miscegenation in 1774:

He who should presume to shew any displeasure against such a thing as simple as fornication, would for his pains be accounted a simple blockhead; since not one in twenty can be persuaded that there is either sin; [*sic*] or shame in cohabiting with his slave.[44]

[42] The association of sexuality and race in Shakespeare's *Othello* is analysed by Jordan, 1968, pp. 37–8; also see pp. 32–6. For Camões, see Saraiva, 1963, pp. 61–9 and Gilberto Freyre, 'Camões, Lusist and Tropicalist', 1961, pp. 111–28. Camões is more explicit in attributing eroticism to non-whites in his lyrical works, especially those about India.

[43] See for example the following works by Freyre: 1964, pp. 350, 377; 1963, pp. 386–7; and 1953, pp. 181–3. Also see Duffy, 1959, p. 74.

[44] Long, 1968, p. 140. Also see Brathwaite, 1971, pp. 176–7, 193; Wagley and Harris, 1958, pp. 102–4.

The English also cohabited' with their slaves in the North American colonies but nowhere as frequently or as openly as in South Carolina, the one American colony where blacks outnumbered whites.[45] A traveller from Boston reported after his trip through the Carolinas in 1773 that 'the enjoyment of a negro or mulatto woman is spoken of as quite a common thing: no reluctance, delicacy or shame is made about the matter'.[46] The capital of Charleston was the only English city in America where it was possible to publicly jest over miscegenation and the *South Carolina Gazette* may have been the only newspaper in the colonies to publish articles concerned with interracial sex.[47] In short, there appears to have been a correlation in South Carolina between the high percentage of blacks (about 60 per cent) and white attitudes towards miscegenation— attitudes which more closely approximated those in Jamaica than elsewhere in the North American colonies.

The demographic composition of the population in the New World colonies was a determinant not only in the formation of attitudes towards miscegenation but, by extension, in the formation of attitudes towards mestiços. Wherever there was a relative absence of white women and the percentage of non-whites was much larger than that of whites, mestiços constituted a distinct social stratum, often legally recognized, between whites and blacks and/or Indians. This phenomenon occurred in all of the New World colonies, irrespective of the national and cultural backgrounds of the European colonizers, as long as the demographic imbalances were operative.

In Jamaica mestiços were differentiated from blacks as early as the eighteenth century, when many had already attained middle-class status.[48] While most mestiços were illegitimate, many of the French and English fathers in the West Indies recognized their mestiço children, often educated them in Europe, and left them large properties.[49] Throughout the West Indies whites recognized free mestiços as superior to slaves and free blacks, and gave them privileges according to their shade; within the mestiço group itself, rank and privilege depended largely on proximity

[45] For variations in the proportion of blacks in the North American colonies during the eighteenth century, see Jordan, 1968, pp. 102–3. For a higher estimate of the proportion of blacks in Virginia and South Carolina, see Stampp, 1956, p. 24.

[46] Cited by Jordan, 1968, p. 145.

[47] Jordan, 1968, pp. 140–1, 145–9, 170–3.

[48] As early as 1797 official documents recognized four classes in Jamaica: 'Whites, free people of colour having special privileges granted by private acts, free people of colour not possessing such privileges and slaves.' Brathwaite, 1971, p. 105. Also see Bell, W., 1964, p. 10 and Wagley, 1952, p. 143.

[49] Brathwaite, 1971, p. 193; Lowenthal, 1969, p. 300; and Degler, 1971, p. 232. The same pattern occurred among the French in Martinique. By 1790 mestiços owned one-quarter of all slaves and one-third of all property in Martinique. Wagley and Harris, 1958, pp. 103, 106.

to European features.[50] It is striking that essentially the same Englishmen who never socially or legally distinguished mestiços from blacks in North America—even when they were almost white—found it necessary to countenance the social assent of mestiços in Jamaica as early as 1733 with legislation that declared:

> no one shall be deemed a Mulatto after the Third Generation, as aforesaid, but that they shall have all the Privileges and Immunities of His Majesty's white Subjects of this Island, provided they are brought up in the Christian Religion.[51]

Thus, with the stroke of a pen, the English in Jamaica transformed all mestiços beyond the third generation into whites—the same mestiços whom their kith and kin continued to enslave and consider 'Negroes' in the North American colonies.

The differentiation of mestiços from blacks and Indians was motivated more by self-interest than magnanimity, for it proved to be as beneficial to whites as it was for mestiços. Throughout the Americas, wherever whites were greatly outnumbered, mestiços not only came to occupy an intermediate position in the social structure but, from early times, collaborated with the white power structure against blacks and Indians in order to preserve the social and political order. Mestiços constituted important elements in the colonial service, especially in the armies which conquered the Indians in Brazil, Mexico, Uruguay, Chile and other former Spanish colonies. Furthermore, in most of these countries the early alliance they formed with whites has endured socially, if not politically, to the present time.[52]

In the United States the failure to develop a separate social status for mestiços, or what Degler has aptly termed the 'mulatto escape hatch', stems directly from the relative absence of the demographic factors which

[50] Lowenthal, 1969, p. 299. Brathwaite notes how the mestiço servants were treated with more respect than other slaves as it was 'considered inhuman that the child of a white man should be reduced to the same state as that of a negro'. M. G. Lewis, *Journal of a West India Proprietor, Kept During a Residence in the Island of Jamaica* (London, 1834), cited by Brathwaite, 1971, p. 175.

In studies of race in the Caribbean in the early part of the nineteenth century, no less than 126 different names were utilized for identifying and describing the different gradations of mestiços. (Wagley and Harris, 1958, pp. 106–7.) It is unlikely that Brazilians have any equal in the world in differentiating types of mestiços. In a study carried out by Marvin Harris (1970, pp. 75–86) a hundred Brazilians were shown facial drawings of mestiços which varied in terms of skin tone, hair form, lips and nose types and sex (yielding 72 possible discrete combinations). The sample responded with *492* different categorizations!

[51] *Actas Jamaicas* (1738), pp. 260–1, cited by Jordan, 1968, p. 176. Also see Degler, 1971, p. 250.

[52] Brathwaite, 1971, pp. 193–4; Degler, 1971, pp. 239–40; Wagley and Harris, 1958, pp. 106, 115–16; Beltran, 1970, pp. 18–19; Rama, 1970, p. 45; Hoetink, 1970, p. 120; and Steward and Faron, 1959, pp. 272–3.

prevailed throughout most of Latin America.[53] There was clearly little necessity for whites to seek mestiço collaboration in the North American colonies where the combined proportion of blacks and mestiços declined from an apex of 19 per cent in the eighteenth century to approximately 10 per cent of the population over the past one hundred years. Moreover, the North American colonies differed from the rest of the New World not only in the high proportion of whites but in the early balance between white men and women. After the seventeenth century, a large percentage of the English immigrants came in families. By 1750, with the exception of the frontier (where blacks were even more scarce than women), there were probably no more than 110 men for every 100 women and in most places even less (the ratio in Jamaica at this time was 200/100).[54]

The early balance between white males and females, coupled with the overwhelmingly large proportion of whites, precluded the development of a special stratum for mestiços in the North American social structure. There is little evidence to show that mestiços were ever accorded higher status than blacks or even preferred as house servants or concubines.[55]

[53] Degler, 1971, pp. 227–30. Degler argues that the mulatto escape hatch is:
The key that unlocks the puzzle of the differences in race relations in Brazil and the United States ... the presence of a separate place for the mulatto in Brazil and its absence in the United States ... define remarkably well the heart of the difference. (p. 224)
He later adds:
the significant point is that the mulatto escape hatch, which in the past has done so much to make prejudice and discrimination milder and the opportunities for colored people greater in Brazil than in the United States, has also had the effect of inhibiting the advancement of the Negroes as a group ... Even as economic opportunities open up in an expanding Brazilian economy, the tendency will be for the rising mulattoes and educated Negroes to be drawn off from the mass, for that is the genius of the Brazilian pattern of race relations: individual, rather than group mobility ... The ordinary Brazilian Negro sees some mulattoes rising and thus is led to believe that if he can marry lighter at least his children may be able to rise and improve their lot. (pp. 275–6)
[54] Jordan, W. D., 1968, pp. 175–6.
[55] That mestiços were occasionally distinguished from blacks—as in the case of the 1860 Federal Census, which indicated over 500,000 mestiços in the South, or approximately 12 per cent of the 'coloured' population in the slave states—does not imply that they were singled out for special treatment. On the contrary, Georgia was the only colony in North America where, for a time, mestiços were juridically differentiated from blacks. Stampp, 1956, pp. 194–6, 351.
Historians concerned with the American colonies have commonly made a distinction between the Portuguese (and Spanish) attitudes toward illegitimate mestiços and those of the English and Dutch. They point to the fact that the former often recognized the paternity of their illegitimate mestiço children and educated and willed them money and property, while the latter did not. In fact, the difference between North and South America in this respect is one of *degree*, not *kind*. We have already seen that this acknowledgment did occur in North America and to an even greater extent among the English, French and Dutch in the Caribbean. At the same time it should not be forgotten that well under half of the white Brazilian fathers of illegitimate mestiços directly or indirectly acknowledged them.

However, there is some indication that at least in South Carolina mestiços thought of themselves as superior to blacks, mistakenly believing that white blood was a source of social elevation—a proposition which the numerically dominant whites and blacks categorically denied. White blood carried status in America only when it was unadulterated.[56]

It was suggested above that the assertion that the large percentage of mestiços in Brazil proved the absence of Portuguese racism rested on two presuppositions: (1) Brazil epitomized the pattern of miscegenation in all Portuguese colonies and this pattern was unique to the Portuguese; (2) racial attitudes and behaviour can be deduced from the frequency of miscegenation. The first supposition was shown to be fallacious because the Brazilian pattern of miscegenation was neither unique in the New World nor typical of other Portuguese colonies. The second supposition is equally false.

While the demographic conditions in the United States were not conducive to the development of a separate status for mestiços, a brief drive through the centre of most American cities reveals that interracial sex may have been proscribed by custom or even law but it was by no means unknown among the early European settlers and their descendants. In fact, the very Europeans to whom Freyre invidiously attributes 'the incapacity, equally characteristic of the homosexual, to pleasingly impregnate coloured women ... to perpetuate themselves in multi-coloured offspring ... [like the] Portuguese in the tropics' somehow managed to create a proportionately greater number of 'multicoloured offspring' than the Portuguese in any part of the world outside Brazil and Cape Verde.[57] Herskovits and others estimate that 72 to 83 per cent of American blacks are mestiços, which means that approximately 8 per cent of all Americans

---

[56] An anonymously written article in the *South Carolina Gazette*, 23 March 1735, is one of the few examples where the subject of mestiços was publicly discussed during the colonial period:

It is observed concerning the Generation of *Molattoes*, that they are seldom well beloved either by the Whites or the Blacks. Their Approach towards Whiteness, makes them look back with some kind of Scorn upon the Colour they seem to have left, while the Negroes, who do not think them better than themselves, return their Contempt with Interest: And the Whites, who respect them no Whit the more for the nearer Affinity in Colour, are apt to regard their Behaviour as too bold and assuming, and bordering upon Impudence. As they are next to Negroes, and but just above 'em, they are terribly afraid of being thought Negroes, and therefore avoid as much as possible their Company or Commerce: and Whitefolks are as little fond of the Company of *Molattoes*. (Quoted in Jordan, W. D., 1968, p. 170. Also see Stampp, 1956, p. 339.)

[57] Freyre, 1953, p. 182. In this passage Freyre attempts to distinguish Northern European patterns from Portuguese patterns of miscegenation. The historical reality of interracial sex in the United States, however, bears little similarity to Freyre's characterization. In fact, illicit sexual relations in the American South between young white boys and black women were often expected at an early phase of the boy's sexual experience. See Dollard, 1937, p. 134; and Stampp, 1956, pp. 350–5.

today could be classified as mestiços.[58] Yet no one has ever suggested that this proportion of mestiços proves that American whites are not racists. The noncorrelation between the percentage of mestiços and racial attitudes is even more apparent in South Africa, where nearly 10 per cent of the population is mestiço (coloured).

The lack of relationship between interracial sex and general race relations in the New World is exemplified by the history of the Indians in Brazil. During the first two centuries of Brazilian colonization, the Portuguese openly fornicated with Indians but they rarely manifested tolerance for Indians in general, referring to them as savages, barbarians and animals. The Indians were exploited, enslaved, driven from their land, ravaged by foreign diseases and massacred. In the early sixteenth century, when the Portuguese first arrived, there were an estimated 1·5 million Indians in Brazil; by 1750 few remained along the coastal fringe. Today, the approximately 100,000 to 150,000 Indians who have survived in Brazil, mainly on reserves, are still occasionally terrorized and murdered.[59]

Until the expulsion of the Jesuits from Brazil in 1759, the Church and the Crown did provide some protection for the Indians against the settlers and *vaqueiros*. Africans, however, although expected to worship a Catholic God, were considered beyond the pale of His countenance and protection. Academics and others occasionally become so involved in debates about the comparative treatment of slaves, the number of Africans who survived the Atlantic crossing, the collaboration of African chiefs, the relative humanity or cruelty in certain manumission processes, etc., that one can

[58] Using a sample of 1,500 American blacks in 1930, Herskovits calculated that 28·3 per cent had no known white ancestor, 14·8 per cent had more white than black ancestors, 25·2 per cent had about the same number of white and black ancestors, and 31·7 per cent had more black than white ancestors. Wirth and Goldhamer argued in 1944 that their study of the same question revealed that between 72 per cent and 83 per cent of American blacks had at least one known white forebear. Herskovits, 1930; and Wirth and Goldhamer, 1964, pp. 68, 214, 234.

[59] An observation by Herring (1961, p. 239) epitomizes the self-image which many Portuguese have concerning their early relations with the Indians in Brazil: 'The Englishman, in the name of his God, shot his Indians; the Portuguese, with a slight nod to his God, slept with his Indians.'

In fact, however, Europeans in Brazil killed considerably more Indians than they slept with. The image of Portuguese benevolent treatment of the Indians in Brazil no doubt stems from the plethora of decrees and legislation which were ostensibly intended to guard the Indians' life, freedom and property; but like so much of Portuguese legislation, good intentions were not matched by actual practice. Simonsen, among others, even questions the 'good intentions' when he shows that Jesuit attempts to protect the Indians from slavery were motivated by economic interests rather than altruism. Indians have benefited very little from protective policies adopted either by the Jesuits or by the Indian Service (initiated in 1910). Whenever attempts to guarantee Indians land or honest wages were counter to the economic interests of the Brazilian frontiersmen, the result was disastrous for most Indians. The present construction of the Transamazonian highway is only the latest example of this sad phenomenon. Simonsen, 1937, vol. 1, pp. 200–1.

THE DYNAMICS OF MISCEGENATION 41

lose sight of what a pitiless business slavery was everywhere. Regardless of how many African chiefs collaborated in the slave trade or whether more slaves survived the Atlantic crossing in English than French ships, everyone, including the Portuguese, treated the slaves as less than human.

Throughout most of the colonial period, laws promulgated by the Portuguese Crown prohibited whites from marrying blacks or Indians and forbade slaves, free blacks, Indians and mestiços from voting, holding public office, occupying certain positions in the Church, bearing arms, dancing, singing or holding festivals in the streets, wearing jewels or expensive clothes (symbols of the upper class) and practising non-Catholic religions.[60] Local conditions and social reality rendered many of these laws as meaningless and unenforceable as King Manual's 1512 *regimento* governing relations between Portugal and the Kongo Kingdom. Nevertheless, discrimination against free blacks, mestiços and Indians did exist during and after the colonial period, and has not disappeared with the removal of the discriminatory legislation. The elimination of slavery did not appreciably alter the racial composition of Brazil's social structure; even today whites almost exclusively dominate the elite while blacks are still concentrated at the bottom of the social and economic sectors.

It is not possible to give the racial breakdowns of education and occupational status beyond 1951, when all racial designations were dropped from official statistics. However, a brief look at the situation in 1950 suffices for a dramatic illustration of the low position of blacks in Brazilian society. For example, of the total population ten years of age or more, only 34 per cent of the whites were classified as illiterate, compared with 69 per cent of the mestiços and 73 per cent of the blacks.[61]

TABLE 5

Brazilians 10 Years or More by Colour and Highest Educational Course Completed in 1950[62]

Race	None	Elementary	Secondary	University
White	58·2%	33·7%	6·9%	1·2%
Mestiço	79·7%	18·8%	1·4%	0·2%
Black	78·6%	20·8%	0·6%	less than 0·1%

[60] Further information on discriminatory legislation against non-whites in Brazil can be found in Degler, 1971, pp. 213–19 and p. 271; Smith, T. L., 1972, p. 63; Burns, 1970, p. 269; Freyre, 1963, pp. 260–7 and p. 399; Marques, A. H. de O., 1964, vol. 1, p. 267; and in the following works by Boxer: 1963, p. 125; 1965, pp. 147–8; and 1962, pp. 17–18 and p. 166.

[61] Smith, T. L., 1972, pp. 490–1.

[62] Adapted from Smith, T. L., 1972, Table 65, p. 493. In support of his assertion that blacks are grossly under-represented in the schools and universities, Degler (1971, p. 143) notes that in 1950, in the state of Bahia, whites constituted only 30 per cent of the population, but made up 83 per cent of the secondary school graduates and 88 per cent of those who completed the university or other higher educational courses.

This gap is also evident in the amount of formal education attained by each group in 1950, as seen in Table 5.

The disparities in the educational background of Brazilian whites and non-whites extend throughout the economic sectors, thereby reinforcing white domination. An analysis of Brazilian employers by colour in all economic sectors reveals the extent of control which whites exercise over the economy.[63] In 1950 whites comprised 62 per cent of the total population; yet they constituted 84 per cent of all employers and over 91 per cent of all employers outside the agricultural, forestry and fishing sectors. The predominance of whites in the upper levels of the economy and educational system has engendered predictable consequences for the advancement of non-whites, especially blacks, into positions of power and responsibility in Brazil.

In 1968 the influential newspaper *O Jornal do Brasil* published an important study on the position of blacks in Brazil eighty years after abolition.[64] According to the study, less than 2 per cent of federal civil service employees in 1968 were black and most of them were in the lower echelons. No blacks occupied positions on the Supreme Court; black officers with the rank of general or admiral were practically non-existent, as were black politicians at all levels of government. In the Senate, for example, there were no blacks and only one mestiço. At the time of the study, no black had ever entered the foreign service training institute, the only black ambassador (appointed to Ghana in 1961) having been selected from outside the foreign service ranks. The study asserted that it was extremely rare to encounter a black in direct contact with the general public in either commercial or government services. Finally, in 1968 less than 1 per cent of Brazil's engineers, doctors, lawyers, teachers, and economists were black.

These data not only illustrate the relative absence of non-whites in the Brazilian power elite but also underscore the presence of prejudice and discrimination in Brazilian society. Despite contemporary government decrees against references to discrimination in Brazil, few Brazilians deny its existence. The only argument concerns the nature of the discrimination, i.e. whether it stems from racial, colour, or class prejudice among whites.

The difficulty of making categorical assertions about the nature of prejudice in any society is compounded in a large and heterogeneous country like Brazil where prejudice has clearly varied from time period to time period as well as within each region, city, neighbourhood and

[63] For a table of Brazilian employers classified according to colour, see Bender, 1975b, p. 115, Table 6.

[64] Pinto, E., 1968. Also see Azevedo, T. de, 1959, pp. 107–19, especially the figure on p. 114; Pierson, 1967, p. 349; Fernandes, 1970, pp. 122, 125–9 and 134–5; Degler, 1971, pp. 140 and 271; Smith, 1972, p. 66; and Dzidzienyo, 1971, pp. 5–11.

among individuals. Most Brazilians and students of Brazil, however, have argued that prejudice against blacks and mestiços cannot be considered racial because the definition of race in Brazil is based on social criteria and colour. Thus, they attribute discrimination to class, with class being determined by income, culture, occupation, education, family history and colour.[65] In other words, according to this argument, prejudice against non-whites in Brazil, unlike the United States, is not rationalized on the basis of innate genetic inferiority.

Most Brazilians do not consider white domination of the upper class as an indication of racial prejudice. Instead, they point to the significant mestiço representation in the middle class as proof that prejudice and discrimination are not racial. They argue that mestiços have almost always occupied an intermediate position in the class structure, seldom treated like blacks, who are overwhelmingly found in the lower class; *ergo*, any discrimination against blacks and mestiços is based on class.

Two problems with this argument immediately arise. The first concerns the utility of distinguishing between the congruent categories of race and class in the Brazilian context.[66] In fact, many characteristics of class, such as family background and appearance, are ascribed directly from an individual's racial background. The second problem arises from the fact that Brazilians rarely consider blacks and mestiços as part of the same racial group—unlike the United States, where they are thought of as constituting a single race.

The absence of a satisfactory and universally accepted definition of race or precise criteria for differentiating races complicates any discussion of racial discrimination in Brazil. The principal difficulty is how to categorize the mestiço. Since mestiços are only rarely classified as either white or black, it is possible to residually consider them as a distinct race. From this perspective one could conceive of most prejudice against non-whites in Brazil in racial terms. Because there are exceptions, however, most scholars prefer to avoid racial classifications of prejudice in order to account for those who do not conform to the general Brazilian pattern of a high correlation between race and class.

Fernandes and others have attempted to circumvent this definitional problem with the notion of colour rather than racial prejudice. Fernandes argues that colour serves as both a racial mark and a symbol of social

---

[65] Some of the many discussions on class versus racial prejudice in Brazil can be found in Pierson, 1967, p. 349; Harris, 1958, p. 62 and pp. 72–3; Wagley, 1963, p. 100 and 1965, pp. 531–45; and Burns, 1970, p. 269.

[66] For more on the congruence between race and class in Brazil, see Wagley, 1963, pp. 138–9 and 1952, p. 145 and pp. 148–54; Degler, 1971, pp. 104, 110–11, 141 and 199; Willems, 1953, p. 244; and Dias, J., 1960, p. 21.

position, with the former often qualifying or negating the latter.[67] He notes that while most whites extend more opportunities to lighter mestiços, the thrust of the system 'is to maintain a close connection between colour and the lowest social positions'; in other words, 'to put the Negro in his place'.[68]

Just as individual exceptions to the general pattern of congruence between colour and social status do not indicate an absence of colour prejudice in Brazil, neither have they helped to advance the status of blacks and mestiços in general nor have they modified the low conception of blacks which permeates Brazilian society.[69] The abundance of adages and stereotypes demonstrating this conception in Brazil are clearly reflected in both the attitudes and behaviour of most Brazilians.[70]

In sum, the debate may continue over whether the manifest discrimination against non-whites in Brazilian society is indicative of race, colour, or class prejudice, or some combination of these; yet this epistemological

[67] Fernandes, 1969, p. 324 and Degler, 1971, pp. 110–11. Nogueira (1959, pp. 166–75) has suggested that 'prejudice of mark' should be used for Brazil rather than colour in order to incorporate non-colour characteristics such as hair texture, shape of lips and nose and even educational background. He distinguishes this from a prejudice of origin found in the United States and South Africa.

The experience of famous black entertainers and sports stars such as the singer Wilson Simonal and the world-famous soccer player Pele poignantly demonstrates how class can be eclipsed by colour. Pele once walked over two hours with two black teammates after his car broke down near a small town where their team was playing one evening. When asked by his coach why they didn't hitchhike instead of walk, Pele responded, 'Who would give a lift to three Negroes at night on a lonely road?' Quoted in the Los Angeles Times, 20 November 1969.

[68] Fernandes, 1969, pp. 320, 324, and 347–8. Until now there has been little need for overt discrimination to keep blacks out of the middle or upper class because blacks have only recently started to compete with whites for jobs; therefore, one can anticipate more prejudice in the future. Harris suspects that the greatest tension will occur in the middle rather than upper class, while Wagley predicts that it will be found most often in competition for upper-class positions. See Harris, 1958, p. 78; Wagley, 1952, pp. 149 and 155; Degler, 1971, p. 283; and Bastide, 1967, p. 312.

[69] Degler, 1971, pp. 115–16 and 198.

[70] Harris notes that in the community he studied in the state of Bahia the superiority of whites over blacks was considered a scientific fact which even permeated school textbooks. For example, none of the six (white) teachers in the town took exception to the following passage in one of the standard textbooks: 'Of all races the white race is the most intelligent, persevering, and the most enterprising ... The Negro race is much more retarded than the others.' Gaspar de Freitas, Geografia e história do Brasil, quoted in Harris, 1958, p. 52. Harris cites numerous pejorative anecdotes and stereotypes of blacks and mestiços which were generally accepted as facts; see especially pp. 52–6. For further examples see Pierson, 1967, Appendix B, pp. 362–5; Fernandes, 1969, pp. 325–8 and pp. 392–3; and Degler, 1971, p. 113.

It should be noted that many of the derogatory anecdotes and stereotypes of blacks can be traced to Portugal, where they have been a part of the culture for centuries. See Brásio, 1944, pp. 19, 21, 31, 33–4, and 37–53.

For a number of examples of how these stereotypes and attitudes have been translated into discriminatory behaviour, see Kalili and Mattos, 1967, pp. 35–60, especially 35–8 and 40, 43 and 45.

question must strike blacks, mestiços and Indians as abstrusely academic and highly irrelevant given the reality that prejudice, regardless of its origin, has kept them on or near the bottom of Brazilian society.

Miscegenation in Africa

Since the pattern of miscegenation in Brazil was neither typical of the Portuguese colonies in general nor unique in the New World, one might inquire if at least the Portuguese were unique among the European colonizers in Africa. The Portuguese and many others believe that there has been no parallel to Portuguese miscegenation in Africa. In fact, however, the correlation between the demographic variables and frequency of miscegenation observed in the New World is equally discernible in Africa, once again irrespective of the nationality of the Europeans. The only apparent difference is that in Africa mestiços constitute a much smaller proportion of the populations and are therefore less noticeable politically, economically and socially.

Whereas a comparative analysis of mestiços in Latin America generally involves a quarter to three-quarters of the population of most countries, in Africa one can only compare fractions of 1 per cent. Since white settlement is a recent phenomenon in Africa (less than a century old in most countries), the number of Africans far exceeds the numerical presence of both the Europeans and the mestiços.[71] It was not until just prior to the Second World War that Angola became the second territory in Africa whose white population exceeded 1 per cent; by the middle of the twentieth century South Africa was still the only country where mestiços constituted over 1 per cent of the population.

Prior to the partition of Africa in 1885, few Europeans believed that it was ecologically feasible to settle whites in Africa.[72] Africa was con-

[71] In discussions of Europeans in Africa, the expressions 'white settlement' and 'white settlers' have had a wide range of interpretations, from inclusion of all whites present in Africa to only those who, having cut all ties to Europe, are permanently settled on the land as farmers. If we understand 'white settlers' to mean all Europeans who consider themselves permanent residents in Africa, regardless of their economic pursuits, then, excluding South Africa, there were probably less than two thousand white settlers in Africa by the end of the nineteenth century.

[72] The first British settlement scheme in Africa was initiated in 1820 in South Africa. However, the British did not try to settle whites outside South Africa until the twentieth century. Gann and Duigan, 1962, pp. 29 and 63.

The French made several attempts to establish white agricultural settlements in Senegal between 1817 and 1830, but the failure of these and other efforts finally led the government to conclude in 1859 that:

Nothing similar to Algeria could be undertaken in Senegal. The climate is against it. The land should therefore be left to the Africans ... at least as a general rule. The land cultivated by them will provide produce which will become the object of lucrative trade for the European, the only kind of work he can undertake in this climate. (Villard, 1972, p. 35; also see p. 34.)

sidered a graveyard for Europeans, who were in almost constant battle with Africans and/or the climate, animals, and insects such as the deadly malarial mosquito. Consequently, the great waves of European emigration in the late nineteenth and early twentieth centuries to the Americas, Australia, New Zealand, Algeria, Israel, etc., almost completely bypassed black Africa.

In the middle of the nineteenth century, Angola constituted the second largest European settler colony in Africa with fewer than two thousand whites, most of whom were soldiers, traders, administrators and degredados—not settlers! In 1887 only two Portuguese women were reported in Lourenço Marques (Maputo today), the capital of Mozambique, and it was not until 1890 that Rhodes arrived in Rhodesia with the first group of two hundred settlers from South Africa.[73] Finally, there was only one settler in the Kenyan Highlands by 1895 and seven years later the total white population of Nairobi barely exceeded thirty; at the same time a mere 125 Europeans were reported in the area of Dakar, Senegal.[74] Yet these are the very countries which, along with South Africa, came to be associated with intensive white settlement during the twentieth century.

Although the number of white settlers was quite small prior to the twentieth century, the majority of them were single males, which led to considerable miscegenation in all of the settler colonies. In the twentieth century, the differences found among the numbers of mestiços and their ratio to the number of whites are related to the period of time in which white males dominated the structure of the European population. A brief review of some of the colonies which attracted the most whites illustrates the determinative role which the absence of white women has had on the frequency of miscegenation in Africa.

The white population in South Africa in the mid-seventeenth century, when white settlement was initiated, consisted primarily of single males who manifested little colour consciousness in their choice of concubines or wives. In fact, during the early period of colonization interracial

---

[73] Duffy, 1959, pp. 79–81; Kay, G., 1970, p. 39; and Hoagland, 1972, pp. 227–8.

[74] It is interesting to note that when 'all classes of men of European origin' met in Nairobi in early 1902 to 'discuss the best means of promoting the colonization of this protectorate with European settlers', only twenty-two Europeans were present. Sorrenson, 1968, pp. 25, 42–3, 65. Also see 1967, p. 16; and Hill, 1960, pp. 639–42.

The white population of Dakar grew from 125 in 1900 to 2,500 by 1910. (See O'Brien, 1972, p. 54.) In 1970 the white population of Dakar was estimated at 27,500. O'Brien argues (p. 17) that:

Historically, Senegal was never a colony of European settlement ... Unlike white settlers elsewhere in Africa who became identified with the country as Algerians or Rhodesians, the French of Senegal never loosened their ties with metropolitan France. That they were never owners of the land or rooted from generation to generation to live, bear offspring and die on African soil made them expatriates rather than settlers.

marriages were actually encouraged.[75] While a large imbalance between white males and females still existed at the turn of the twentieth century, parity was almost achieved by 1918, when the ratio was 105/100. This white balance was undoubtedly an important factor (although not determinant) in the decision a decade later (1927) to prohibit legal unions between whites and blacks.[76]

The extent of South African miscegenation was clearly evident by 1911, when the more than 525,000 mestiços constituted just under 9 per cent of the total South African population. Today there are over two million mestiços in South Africa, representing almost 10 per cent of the total population and yielding a ratio of fifty-two mestiços for every hundred whites—greater than the ratios in Brazil, Angola, or Mozambique.[77]

South African mestiços have had virtually no ties with the African cultures; instead they traditionally identified with the white population. Until recent decades they enjoyed the most privileges among the non-white groups, but the extension of apartheid after 1948 has slowly chipped away these privileges, forcing the mestiços into a new (and unusual) position of having to co-operate increasingly with the Africans.[78] The example of South Africa underscores the fallacy of assuming amicable race relations from the presence of a large percentage of mestiços and/or from their treatment as a distinct, privileged group. South Africa also demonstrates

[75] Monica Wilson (1969b, p. 66) notes that the cleavage between whites and non-whites during the second half of the seventeenth century 'was between Christian and non-Christian, rather than on the ground of colour'.

For further information on early white settlement and miscegenation in South Africa, see Monica Wilson, 1969a, pp. 233–71; Katzen, 1969, pp. 183–232, especially pp. 196–213; Thompson, 1966, p. 20; Simons and Simons, 1969, p. 12; and Hoagland, 1972, pp. 104–5.

[76] Horrell, 1968, pp. 3–5.

The ratios of white males/females are taken from population statistics found in Union of South Africa, 1923, p. 143; and Republic of South Africa, 1966, p. A–26. The prohibition against whites marrying coloureds and Asians (i.e. all non-whites) was extended in 1950 in the wake of the Nationalist Party's assumption of power in 1948.

[77] Horrell, 1971, p. 24; and Thompson, 1966, p. 30.

The number of mestiços per one hundred whites was 43 in Brazil, 32 in Mozambique, and 31 in Angola. See *supra*, Table 4.

[78] In the mid-1960s Leo Kuper (1965, pp. 49–50) observed that while South African coloureds traditionally identified with whites and enjoyed more privileges than other non-white groups, they are changing their identification because of the increase in discrimination against them. 'The result has been a movement among Coloreds toward cooperation with Africans. This change so conflicts with their traditional attitudes that it is difficult to assess its significance.'

There have been sporadic statements by coloured leaders in recent years expressing support for black demands and protests but nothing as dramatic as what occurred during the demonstrations, strikes and riots in the summer of 1976. While these activities indicate that at least the younger generation of coloureds feels a solidarity with blacks, the main thrust of the protests was aimed at achieving equality for coloureds, not blacks. It is therefore unclear how the majority of coloureds would respond if the South African Government decided that the only way to maintain domination over blacks would be to grant full equality and some power to coloureds.

that historical attitudes among whites towards miscegenation and mestiços portend absolutely nothing for present or future race relations.

South Africans were responsible for initiating white settlement in other African territories around the turn of the twentieth century, e.g. in Namibia, Rhodesia, Zambia and Kenya. Sorrenson notes, for example, that until just prior to World War I, most of the whites in the Kenyan Highlands had come from South Africa with the intention of creating in Kenya a 'white man's country' modelled on South Africa.[79] The virtual absence of mestiços in Kenya today should not be interpreted as a sign that the South Africans brought racist ideas with them, but as a result of most of them (and other Europeans who came later) bringing their wives with them. Thus there has never been a serious imbalance in the number of white males and females in Kenya. In Namibia and Rhodesia, on the other hand, a large proportion of the South African immigrants were single males; consequently there was considerable miscegenation. In Namibia today, for example, the ratio of mestiços to whites is equal to that found in Angola and Mozambique prior to Independence.[80]

In Rhodesia before the twentieth century there were almost three times as many white males as females and, predictably, liaisons between European men and African women were quite common.[81] Interracial sex continued until the 1920s, when an influx of white women almost equalized the sex ratio. Thus the period of intensive miscegenation was comparatively short in Rhodesia.[82]

[79] Sorrenson, 1968, pp. 1 and 229. See pp. 4, 230-2, and 238 for more information on the English who settled in Kenya. Also see Gann and Duignan, 1962, pp. 71-2.

In Zambia whites have usually been temporary residents and only rarely permanent settlers. Nevertheless, it is interesting to note that South Africa has provided almost one-half of the Europeans in Zambia, compared with only a quarter who came from England. See Kaplan *et al.*, 1969, p. 96.

[80] There were 96,000 whites and 29,100 mestiços in Namibia in 1966 out of a total population of 610,000. Horrell, 1967, pp. 12 and 16-18; and First, 1963, pp. 41-5, 48.

[81] See Rogers and Frantz, 1962, pp. 14-15, 23, and 283; and Gann and Duignan, 1962, pp. 71-2.

[82] The drop in the sex ratio of whites in Rhodesia during the twentieth century can be seen in the following:

YEAR	M/F	YEAR	M/F	YEAR	M/F
1901	278/100	1926	126/100	1946	116/100
1904	246/100	1931	120/100	1951	111/100
1911	194/100	1936	116/100	1956	107/100
1921	130/100	1941	113/100	1961	102/100

These numbers were compiled from data found in Rogers and Frantz, 1962, p. 15 and Kay, G., 1970, p. 61.

It is interesting to note that legislation passed in Rhodesia in 1903 forbade intercourse between black men and white women; however, women's pressure groups failed in their attempt to secure the passage of a similar law prohibiting intercourse between white men and black women. Gann and Duignan, 1962, p. 72, note.

There was also a sharp drop in miscegenation in Madagascar with the arrival of a substantial number of European women. See Mannoni, 1964, p. 114. For a general description of the position of mestiços in Madagascar in the mid-1950s, see p. 118.

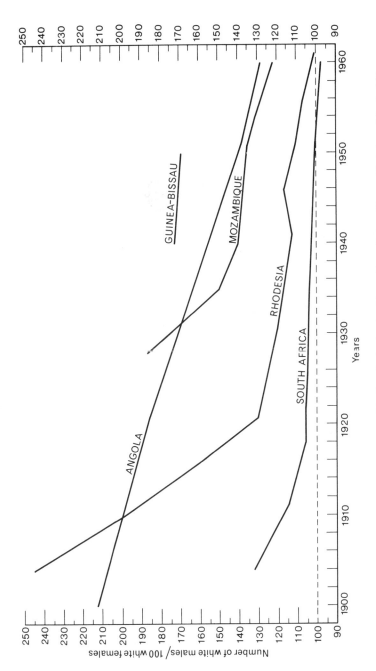

FIGURE 1: *Number of White Males/100 White Females in Angola, Mozambique, Guinea-Bissau, Rhodesia and South Africa*

As this study shows, the frequency of miscegenation is associated with a sexual imbalance among whites; furthermore, miscegenation will continue until that ratio is stabilized. Thus, one would expect to find a proportionately greater number of mestiços in South Africa, where a sexual imbalance among whites continued for centuries, than in Rhodesia, where single white males were preponderant for only a few decades. It is in this context that one must view miscegenation in the Portuguese African colonies, where the sexual imbalance among whites was greater in 1960 than that found in South Africa during the first decade of the twentieth century or in Rhodesia in the late 1920s. These differences are illustrated in Figure 1.[83]

In Senegal miscegenation began when the first French merchants arrived in the seventeenth century and continued throughout the eighteenth century, often with official encouragement. During the same period white women were virtually unknown. Most of the men invariably acknowledged the paternity of their mestiço offspring, often providing for their education and willing them properties and inheritances.[84] Although the mestiços identified with whites from the beginning, they often adopted independent political positions when their interests and privileges were threatened by the French. By the eighteenth century mestiços were already playing an integral part in the economic, social and political life of the colony, and at least until the twentieth century they were occasionally dominant politically. A measure of their strength and importance can be gauged by the fact that the first elected Senegalese representative to the French parliament (1848) was a mestiço. The first newspapers were founded by mestiços and they controlled many key sectors of the economy.[85] In fact, O'Brien reports that 'from 1900 to 1914, politics in Senegal was largely a struggle between rival *metisse* [mestiço] families, whose patriarchs had become company owners and powerful local businessmen'.[86]

The demise of the importance of mestiços during the present century paralleled the increase in white immigration, especially of white women. By 1926 there were approximately 1,500 white women in Senegal, which

[83] The data used for compiling this figure are found in: Rogers and Frantz, 1962, p. 15, and Kay G., 1970, p. 61 for Rhodesia; Union of South Africa, 1923, p. 143 and Republic of South Africa, 1966, p. A–26 for South Africa; and the official censuses for Angola, Mozambique and Guinea.

[84] Hargreaves, 1967, pp. 67 and 84; Roberts *et al.*, 1963, pp. 13–14; and O'Brian, 1972, p. 33.

[85] Hargreaves, 1967, pp. 86–7 and O'Brien, 1972, pp. 31 and 46–7. The extent of assimilation of mestiços can be seen in O'Brien's description (p. 264) of the old *metisse* families in St. Louis:

whose members identified so strongly with the French that their attitudes towards Africans seem to remain a caricature of certain negative premises of French colonial policy towards blacks. They have retained a kind of stilted French chauvinism preserved intact from the past, which seems to conclude in a denial of their partially African heritage.

[86] O'Brien, 1972, pp. 58 and 61.

not only reduced interracial liaisons for the first time, but injected more racist attitudes into the society.[87] As the ratio between white males and females equalized, the frequency of miscegenation attenuated until just after the Second World War, when a sudden and large influx of young Frenchmen immediately restored the earlier miscegenation pattern. This sudden imbalance in the sex ratio among whites was short-lived, however, dropping dramatically from 168 in 1946 to 100 by 1955. The drop in the frequency of miscegenation was equally dramatic.[88] In 1961 there were twenty-one mestiços for every hundred whites in Senegal, excluding the Cape Verdians.[89] In sum, the history of miscegenation in Senegal and of French attitudes towards mestiços illustrates once more the importance of demographic variables over the national background of the European population and further documents the fact that Portuguese miscegenation patterns have not been unique in Africa.

In 1594 the Portuguese Crown sent Angola twelve orphans and converted prostitutes—the first white women known in the colony—all of whom married but none of whom left any descendants. Half a century later fifteen more female orphans were sent to Angola, but few additional efforts were made to encourage female emigration. Although one of Angola's first governors brought his wife in 1615, it was not until 1773 that another governor was accompanied by his wife.[90] Until the middle

---

[87] Ibid., pp. 57 and 59.

[88] After World War II, the composition of the French community in Senegal changed; they were younger, generally from a lower socio-economic status, and their period of residence was relatively brief due to the types of employment opportunities. Furthermore, the influence of European women on sexual mores had engendered new attitudes among the French concerning the social acceptability of interracial affairs. The result was that during the period from 1945 to 1955 the number of liaisons between white men and black women increased but the relationships were generally casual and never acquired the legitimacy and status which had been attached to interracial relationships prior to the early part of the twentieth century. One consequence was that the accidental offspring of such liaisons were kept as well-guarded secrets. See O'Brien, 1972, pp. 63 and 93.

[89] According to Louis Verriere, (1963, pp. 1–5) there were approximately 7,000 mestiços and 38,000 Europeans in Senegal in 1961.

These figures do not include the approximately 30,000 Cape Verdians (or their descendants), virtually all of whom are also mestiços. Since World War II Senegal has been attracting large numbers of Cape Verdians who have settled in and around Dakar. They are generally artisans and, in an interesting contrast to Cape Verdians in the former Portuguese colonies, they live in the African areas in an African, rather than European, style. (See Roberts et al., 1963, pp. 62, 75.) If added to Senegal's indigenous mestiços, the Cape Verdians artificially inflate the ratio of mestiço/white in the same way in which the Cape Verdians have inflated the white/mestiço ratio in Guinea-Bissau. It is also interesting to note that Cape Verdians who emigrated to Africa chose Senegal over the former Portuguese colonies by more than ten to one!

[90] Discussions of the absence of white women in Angola before the twentieth century can be found in the following: Dias, G. S., 1947, pp. 5–25 and 1959, pp. 182–3; Amaral, 1960, p. 22; Boxer, 1965, p. 129; Capello, 1889a, p. 182; Cadornega, 1942, vol. 2, p. 514, and vol. 3, p. 30; Galvao and Selvagem, 1952, p. 46; Henrique Galvão, 1937, p. 194; Monteiro, J. J. 1875, vol. 2, p. 49; Hammond, 1966, pp. 38–9; Duffy, 1959, pp. 80–1; Ferreira, 1954c, p. 99; Lima, J. J. L. de, 1846, pp. 4–A, 83, 91 and 206.

of the nineteenth century, Angola was considered almost fatal for white women. In 1846, when Lopes de Lima observed that there was 'still no case of a white woman giving birth when it didn't cost the life of the mother and child', there were almost eleven white men for every white woman in Angola.[91] This overwhelming preponderance of white males naturally led to intensive miscegenation, and by the mid-nineteenth century there were more than three mestiços for every white in the colony.[92] The gap between the number of white men and women narrowed steadily after that time and, similar to the pattern in the New World, so did the frequency of miscegenation. The drop in the white male/female ratio can be seen in Table 6.

TABLE 6

White Male/Female Ratio in Angola[93]

YEAR	M/F RATIO
1846	1073/100
1900	213/100
1920	187/100
1940	154/100
1950	139/100
1960	127/100

The correlation between the sex ratio of whites and the frequency of miscegenation can be seen by comparing the figures from Table 6 with the annual increase in mestiços in two periods of twenty years before and after 1940. A conservative estimate of the annual natural increase of mestiços (i.e. among mestiços themselves) would be approximately two and a half per cent; therefore any increase greater than that could be attributed to miscegenation. The annual growth of mestiços from 1920 to 1940 was just under 7 per cent (6·8%). However, between 1940 and 1960 the growth rate declined by more than half (3·3%); that is, slightly above their natural increase.[94] The preliminary results of the 1970 census

[91] Lima, J. J. L., 1846, p. 206.

[92] Ibid., p. 4–A, Table 1.

[93] This table is based on population data found in ibid., and in the official Angolan censuses: 1940, vol. 8, p. 4; 1950, vol. 2, p. 1; 1960, vol. 1. p. 35; and in Carvalho, 1940, pp. 71–114.

[94] Discussions about the impact of increased numbers of white women on the decline of miscegenation in Angola can be found in: Villas, 1929, p. 10; Moreira, 1961a, pp. 178–80; Gaspar, 1966, p. 133; Carvalho, 1940, p. 111; and Wheeler, 1972b, p. 177. For a similar position concerning Mozambique, see Isaacman and Isaacman, 1975, pp. 9–10, 32–3.
Despite the claims of some over-zealous lusotropicologists, such as Pereira Monteiro, who maintains that marriages between whites and blacks are common occurrences in Angola, it is interesting to note that until 1961 when racial designations were dropped from the marriage registries, there were practically no recorded instances of whites marrying blacks in Angola. See Lemos, 1957, p. 451; and Monteiro, 1961, pp. 27–8.

indicate a significant increase in miscegenation during the 1960s. This decade, however, also saw a large influx of single white males who were sent to Angola as members of the armed forces.[95]

While the increase in the proportion of white women was a strong deterrent to miscegenation in Angola, the increase in the general white population slowly eclipsed the importance and privileges which mestiços enjoyed through the nineteenth century. It seems to be almost axiomatic in white settler colonies in the New World and Africa that once the white population is large and strong enough to rule by itself, its old allies— the mestiços—are relegated to an inferior role. Angola, especially, epitomized this axiom. Mestiços not only made an early identification with whites but performed important roles as middlemen during the slave trade. Following the end of the slave trade, mestiços continued to occupy key positions in commerce, the civil service, journalism, the military, and politics.[96] They seldom, if ever, identified with the Africans because for all practical purposes they were Portuguese in nearly every way except colour.

As soon as whites outnumbered mestiços at the end of the nineteenth century, they began to erect barriers in the path of further mestiço advancement. New laws and regulations were enacted which guaranteed that mestiços and assimilated Africans would never again enjoy the prominence they had experienced in the nineteenth century. In 1901 a law was passed which upgraded educational requirements for certain bureaucratic positions; a telegraphist, for example, was required to have certificates in geography and Latin, neither of which could be obtained in Angolan schools at that time. A government decree in 1911 raised educational requirements for entry into the lower ranks of the bureacracy to five years of secondary school; however, Angola did not have a secondary school until 1919.[97] With the division of the Angolan civil

---

[95] I have not seen any evidence confirming the claims by Wheeler and Hoagland that Portuguese military officers encouraged their troops, as part of the official policy, to leave mestiço children behind when they finished their tour of duty. However, it is true that the influx of hundreds of thousands of metropolitan troops who served in Angola during the 1960s did account for the increase of miscegenation. See Wheeler, 1967, p. 60; and Hoagland, 1972, p. 275.

Elsewhere, Wheeler (1972b, p.177) has averred that 'Miscegenation in the general settler population—as opposed to off-duty miscegenation by the Portuguese troops—by the late 1960s was decreasing and appeared to have little bearing on individual race attitudes'.

[96] Wheeler in Wheeler and Pelissier, 1971, pp. 93–7; and Duffy, 1959, p. 273. For an excellent discussion of mestiço and African radical journalism at the end of the nineteenth century, see Wheeler, Douglas L., 1970, pp. 854–76; 1972a, pp. 67–87; and Lopo, 1964a, pp. 75–83.

[97] Samuels (1972, pp. 62–3), points out that in 1907 the Overseas Ministry in Lisbon denied the request of a bishop in Angola to offer the five-year secondary school course (*lyceu*) in the Luanda seminary. This denial was vital, given the 1911 decree which required secondary education for entrance into the lower professional ranks of the administration. By the middle of 1913 the administrators, secretaries and clerks of local government in Angola were appointed in Lisbon, not Angola! Also see Wheeler in Wheeler and Pelissier, 1971, p. 97.

service into European and African branches in 1921, the demise of the mestiços and assimilated Africans was almost complete. The final nail in the coffin came in 1929, when statutes were passed which restricted the promotion of mestiços and assimilated Africans to the rank of first clerk in the bureaucracy, prevented competition between Europeans and non-Europeans for bureaucratic positions, and established different salary scales for Europeans and non-Europeans in the private and public sectors which endured until the outbreak of the Angolan war in 1961.[98] Once whites no longer needed or desired mestiço collaboration, the status of the mestiços fell. Even the independence war did not totally restore the position they once enjoyed in Angolan society; in fact, prior to the Portuguese coup in 1974, there were no mestiços (or Africans) in the upper echelons of the Angolan administration or army.

Just as the relatively egalitarian treatment accorded mestiços during the early phases of colonization in Brazil, Senegal and South Africa proved to be irrelevant to the understanding of the mestiços' demise in the twentieth century, the intensive miscegenation and former importance of mestiços in Angola are of little help in understanding Angolan race relations at the end of the colonial era.

Before the military coup of 25 April 1974 many, including almost all Portuguese leaders, appeared to be convinced that the force and spirit of lusotropicalism were so strong among the Portuguese settlers in Angola that it was only a matter of time before Angola would become the 'Brazil of Africa'. The asserted strength of lusotropicalism has been based on the frequency of miscegenation and the position which mestiços historically enjoyed in the Portuguese colonies. This chapter demonstrates that these two factors are a function of demographic variables, independent of the nationality of the European colonizers in either the New World or Africa. Furthermore, the economic, social and political inequality between whites and non-whites in Brazil must pose serious questions as to whether the Brazilian model of race relations is a desirable one for Angolans to attempt to emulate, even if it were possible to do so.[99] As it is, however, Brazil's history, ecology, economy, racial demography and pattern of black assimilation are so distant from the Angolan reality that the possibility of repeating the Brazilian racial experience in Angola can scarcely be contemplated.

[98] Ibid., pp. 97–8, and Samuels, 1972, pp. 61–5.
[99] President Neto is clearly not enamoured of the Brazilian model of race relations:
We don't want to be a Brazil, as some say. We don't have much confidence in the Brazilian solutions to its social problem. In Brazil the black is black and the white is white. We have no proof that in Brazil there has been a rise among the blacks who came from Angola, who are in Bahia and continue to sell their *doce de ginguba* and other specialities of Angolan cuisine, but who do not succeed in leaving the slums. This is not a solution. We have to have a better one. (Agostinho Neto: 'Quem é que vai resolver o problema de Angola são portuguese e angolanos ou os angolanos?', *Notícia*, 29 June 1974, p. 47)

PART II

White Settlement

Introduction

The pre-twentieth century history of the Portuguese in Angola is essentially the history of exiled criminals—*degredados*—who were dumped on Angola's shores like the garbage they were considered to be. In fact, Portugal was the first European nation to send the dregs from metropolitan dungeons and prisons to exile in overseas colonies, beginning in the early fifteenth century, long before Diogo Cão reached Angola. Portugal was also the last to realize the destructiveness and danger of such a policy and finally to abolish it.

The degredados were greatly responsible for the negative image of Angola held by the majority of the Portuguese people throughout the five centuries of a Portuguese presence in the territory. As early as the seventeenth century, an anonymously written poem described Angola as a 'turbulent land ... of bloody wars ... malignant and burning fever ... multitudes of mosquitoes ... snakes and strange animals of every type ... [a] hell in life ... the dunghill of Portugal where she purges her scum'.[2]

Portugal desired to maintain its hold on its largest and potentially wealthiest African colony and the obvious mechanism was white settlement; at the same time Portugal saw the colony as a convenient escape hatch for the rebellious and criminal elements of its metropolitan society. Chapter 3 is a general analysis of the degredados' role in the history of Angola.

The necessity for developing a stable white population in the hinterlands in order to secure Portuguese hegemony in Angola stimulated Lisbon to attempt a number of rural white settlement schemes after the

---

[1] Jesus, 1885, p. 1003.
[2] 'Descrição da cidade de Loanda e reyno de Angola', in Cadornega, 1942, pp. 383–6. This book was published originally in 1681.

latter part of the nineteenth century. Most of the early attempts used degredados. The bankruptcy of this policy, however, eventually led the government to try to encourage free whites to settle in Angola. This proved to be a difficult task, since many Portuguese still thought of Angola as merely an outpost for condemned exiles. While Angola's image had changed considerably by the early years of Salazar's New State, when the 'hair-raising phrase ... "He went to the coasts of Africa" was no longer used synonymously with "exile"', practically no Portuguese could be convinced to go to Angola to farm.[3] Furthermore, the government's agricultural settlement schemes, created to attract more Portuguese peasants, were, with rare exceptions, disastrous failures, socially and economically. The most recent and costly of these government planned settlement schemes, established in 1961 after the outbreak of the war, is analysed extensively in Chapter 4 in the context of the total impact of rural white settlement on race relations in Angola.

[3] Nascimento and Mattos, 1912, p. 21; and Lebre, 1934, p. 8.

CHAPTER 3

Degredados and the System of Penal Colonization

[We must] prohibit forever the sentences which burden this kingdom with prostitutes and degredados of the worst type, [for] the experience of more than two centuries shows that shuch shipments have been useless and often dangerous; ... their vices take root, they value idleness and lose their health and die quickly and through this excess of adversity their deaths become more useful than their lives.

Governor Sousa Coutinho (*1766*)[1]

Every Portuguese packet continues to bring from fifty to sixty emigrants sent to the west coast by the Portuguese government in order to deplete the prisons and get rid of dangerous and starving tramps. While rational colonization would be a blessing to the province and the home country, this kind of assisted emigration is a curse and a source of endless trouble.

Heli Chatelain (*1891*)[2]

... it is imperative that Angola be cleansed of elements prejudicial to its progress ... it is necessary that the people of Angola be free of the presence of the degredados.

Legislative Council of Luanda (*1926*)[3]

[1] Sousa Coutinho, Governor and Commander General in Angola from 1764–72, was perhaps the most enlightened Governor in the colony before the nineteenth century. He was strongly opposed to the degredado system, as indicated in this quote which is cited in Machado, 1940, p. 9.

[2] Heli Chatelain was a Swiss linguist who arrived in Angola in 1885 with a group of missionaries and who apparently served for a time as a commercial agent for the U.S. government. The quote is a dispatch which Chatelain sent from Luanda to William F. Wharton, Assistant Secretary of State, on 31 December 1891. 'Dispatches from U.S. Consuls in Saint Paul de Loanda, 1854–93', roll 5, vol. 5, no. 17. I would like to thank Michael A. Samuels for this reference.

[3] This quote is contained in a document sent to Lisbon by the Legislative Council, which strongly advocated 'dropping Angola from being a depository of degredados'. *Representação do 1° Conselho Legislativo aos poderes centrais* (Luanda: Empreza de Propaganda Colonial, Ltd., 1926), p. 12.

The sentence of maximum solitary confinement for eight years, followed by exile for twelve and the fixed sentence of exile for twenty-five years [is substituted in the criminal code] by the sentence of maximum imprisonment of sixteen to twenty years.

Decree Law No. 39 688 (1954)[4]
(Abolishing the Degredado System)

Early Penal Colonization in Angola

The first European nation to initiate—and the last to cease—the exploration and conquest of territories 'beyond the seas', the transatlantic slave trade, and the settlement of whites in tropical lands, Portugal was also the first and last European nation to use convicts in the colonization process. As early as the conquest of Ceuta, more than half a century before the first Portuguese ship arrived in Angola, Portugal deported convicts as sailors, soldiers, and settlers.[5] When it was not possible to persuade free men to join the *conquistas*, man the ships, or settle in the tropics, unwilling 'heroes' were recruited from the dungeons of Portugal. Nowhere in the Portuguese overseas empire was it more difficult to convince free men and women to settle than in Angola; consequently, between the arrival of Diogo Cao in 1484 and the first quarter of the twentieth century, the overwhelming majority of the Portuguese in Angola were exiled convicts, or *degredados*. In fact, degredados constituted the vanguard of the forces which attempted to penetrate the hinterland during the first century of Angolan colonization.

Until the late nineteenth century, the degredados in Angola were rarely imprisoned. Often free to enter commerce or government service, they were not only actively involved in the slave trade but were the major participants as soldiers in the discovery of Benguela. By the middle of

[4] The exile of degredados was stopped in 1954 when all sentences which required exile were abolished and replaced with imprisonment in the metropole. The quote refers to only one of a number of sentences which were changed. For a copy of the decree abolishing the degredado system see: Article 129 in *Diario do Governo* 1st Series, no. 122 (5 June 1954), pp. 652–3.

[5] With rare exceptions after the initial conquest of Ceuta in 1415, every Portuguese ship involved in the discoveries and conquests held a contingent of degredados. Moreover, the practice of stationing degredados in the conquered areas as an alternative sentence to death or imprisonment in Portugal began under King D. João I in the early decades of the fifteenth century. Laws governing the use of degredados in the conquests extend back to 1434. When the Portuguese armadas reached across North Africa to Tangiers, laws were enacted (e.g. 1474) to regulate the exile of degredados to these areas as well. By 1484 degredados were being sent to the islands of Principe, São Tomé and São Martinho. In the decades which followed they were shipped to Angola, Mozambique, India and Brazil as the empire expanded its horizons. See Melo, V. M. H. de, 1940, pp. 153–5; and Junior, F. B., 1916, p. 19.

For further references to the use of degredados during the fifteenth century see: Bacelar, 1924, p. 1 (of offprint); Amaral, 1960, p. 13; Patraquim, 1966, p. 25; and *Representação do 1° Conselho Legislativo*, p. 13.

the seventeenth century, practically all positions in the army, police, trading, skilled crafts, and wholesale and retail liquor businesses which were not filled by Africans were taken by degredados.[6] In 1662 the Municipal Council of Luanda requested and received permission from the Crown to send all degredados into the interior to serve their sentences, but this was never implemented because the dearth of personnel in civilian and military posts made the use of degredados essential.[7] The colony had so few whites that even the most incorrigible degredados had to be utilized—in the late seventeenth and early eighteenth centuries Luanda's white population consisted of fewer than 150 men, who themselves represented over half of Angola's entire white population.[8]

Before the end of the seventeenth century, Angola's reputation as a penal settlement and a white man's grave was both firmly established and well deserved. Periodically, the legions of regular degredados were augmented by campaigns to 'cleanse' Portugal and Brazil of Jews, Jesuits, and gypsies. The colony was caught in a vicious cycle: the alarmingly high death rate among whites in Angola discouraged virtually all Portuguese emigrants from choosing Angola (over Brazil *et al.*); the absence of free emigrants caused the Crown to resort to the use of degredados in order to maintain a Portuguese presence in the colony; and finally, the predominance of degredados among the Angolan white population reinforced the already strong reluctance of free Portuguese emigrants to go to Angola.

The degeneration of Angola's white population continued throughout the eighteenth century. Murderers, arsonists, rapists, and thieves were arriving with such regularity that the Portuguese Secretary of State, Melo e Castro, characterized the majority of Angola's European inhabitants near the end of the century as 'wicked and vicious people'.[9]

[6] See: Wheeler and Pelissier, 1971, p. 45; Felner, 1933, pp. 233-4; *Representação do 1° Conselho Legislativo*, p. 11; Silva Telles, 1903, pp. 10-11; Dias, G. S., 1959, p 173; Boxer, 1965, pp. 119, 133-4; and Serpa, 1972, p. 59.

[7] Boxer, 1965, p. 118.
When the Overseas Council met in 1675 to consider a means of increasing Angola's white population, they proposed (and the Crown accepted) that all people convicted of non-capital or civil offences could be pardoned if they went to Angola. The decree added that those who paid their own expenses could return to the metropole after two years and be paid on the basis of six years. See the annotated note of Cadornega, 1940, vol. 2, p. 552. This book was originally published in 1680.

[8] See Marques, A. H. de O., 1972, vol. 1, pp. 469 and 471; and Boxer, 1965, p. 136. Disease took a heavy toll on the Portuguese in Angola at this time. See, for example, Wheeler, 1964, pp. 351-62.

[9] Melo e Castro's observation on the low state of whites in Angola in approximately 1780 is quoted in Sousa Dias, *op. cit.*, p. 241. For further observations on the importance of degredados, their backgrounds and their miserable state during the eighteenth century see: Delgado, 1961, pp. 41, 47; Lima, 1846, p. 123; Galvão, 1937, pp. 194-6; Dias, G. S., 1959, p. 173; and Boxer, 1965, p. 119. For similar comments on Mozambique see: Hoppe, 1970, pp. 68-9, 160; and Isaacman, Allen F., 1972, p. 58.

In 1763 a degredado conspiracy to kill the governor and major officials and sack the capital was uncovered; yet even this did not lead to curbs on the flow of Portugal's scum. The frequent and cogent pleas against the degredado system from the highly respected Governor Sousa Coutinho (1764–72) fell on deaf ears in Lisbon. Cognizant that the degredados found the slave trade more attractive and profitable than farming or practising a trade, Sousa Coutinho warned his superiors in Portugal that the only way to avert total ruin in Angola was to replace degredados immediately with free Portuguese farmers. Frustrated and demoralized by his inability to change the policy, he offered Lisbon the heretical advice that foreigners would be preferable to degredados; but the Crown was not about to cease sending virtually its only representatives of Portuguese sovereignty in Angola.[10]

The apathy and indiscipline which epitomized the Portuguese presence in the interior spread to the coast, and the capital itself, by the beginning of the nineteenth century. Missionary activity, educational work, and the construction of buildings and roads in Luanda were nearly moribund as pressures increased to end the slave trade—still the colony's main source of revenue.[11] The behaviour of the degredados, who constituted a majority of the capital's white population, continued to scandalize the governors: 'I should like to be able to bring this colony

The Marques de Pombal (1750–77) was responsible for sending a large number of Jesuits to Angola as degredados during his crackdown on the religious order; many of them died before they ever reached their destinations in the interior. Jesuit detracters used their participation in the slave trade against them (e.g. in 1760 the Jesuits in Luanda owned 1,080 slaves, whose value represented 36 per cent of their holdings in Angola, as well as several ships engaged in the Angola-Brazil slave trade) but defenders argued that the Jesuits used these profits to provide whatever education there was in Angola. See: Duffy, 1959, pp. 53–4, 61, 118; Silva Rego, 1961, pp. 130–1, 275; Dias, G. S., 1959, pp. 242–3; Felner, 1933, document 42, pp. 467–8; and Hoppe, 1970, pp. 405–6, note 81. Boxer's survey of the documents covering degredados in Angola during 1714–77 revealed that approximately equal numbers came from Portugal and Brazil (1965, p. 208).

[10] An account of the degredado conspiracy of 1763 can be found in Lima, J. J. L. de, 1846, p. 119. Echoes of Sousa Coutinho's castigation of degredados in Angola were heard in Mozambique as well. Jerónimo José Nogueira de Andrade, for example, attributed part of the decadence of Portuguese commerce in Mozambique in 1790 'to the pernicious influence of degredados who were primarily involved in trade in the interior'. See: Silva Rego, 1970, pp. 207–9.

For more on Sousa Coutinho's government in Angola and his opposition to degredados, see: *supra*, note 1; G. S. Dias' excellent discussion 1959, pp. 203–4, 213–15, and *passim*; Duffy, 1959, pp. 71–2, 98; Lima, J. J. L. de, 1846, part 1, p. xxxiv; and Galvão and Selvagem, 1952, pp. 87–9.

[11] The overwhelming importance of the slave trade during this period can be seen in the fact that 84 per cent of the income earned in Angola between 1759 and 1803 came from the export of Angolan slaves to Brazil. Oliveira Martins (1887, p. 55), argued that 'from 1759 to 1803 the colonial registers give 642,000 Africans leaving from Angola for Brazil, or from 14,000 to 15,000 per year. The income from the exporting of Africans is reckoned at 160 contos and the total of the colony at 190 contos.' Duffy notes that between 1550 and 1850, slaves represented four-fifths of Angola's exports; 1959, p. 49. Also see Davidson, 1961, pp. 74–5.

to court so that your Royal Highness and his ministers could actually see the deplorable state it is in', reported Governor António de Melo at the turn of the nineteenth century, adding 'perhaps they will then believe that Angola is no Brazil'.[12]

Indeed, Angola was not Brazil, and never was this more clearly illustrated than in the dissimilar responses of the two colonies to the political turmoil which brought a constitutional monarchy to Portugal in 1822. Brazil declared its independence from Portugal without firing a shot, while the degredados and garrison troops staged a revolt in Luanda, which deposed the governor, who was replaced by a provisional junta presided over by the bishop.[13] The political instability in Portugal eventually resulted in civil war between the Absolutist and Liberal forces (1832–34), ending in a Liberal assumption of power in September 1835.[14] With the Liberal victory came a remarkable Portuguese statesman and humanitarian, the Marques de Sá da Bandeira, who had ruled the colonies as Naval Minister the previous two years. In one of his first acts as Premier in late 1836, Sá da Bandeira launched the first of many salvoes (extending over three decades) against the institution of slavery when he decreed an end to the transatlantic slave trade.[15] Governor Noronha, echoing the sentiments of most of his predecessors in Luanda that the end of the slave trade would bring ruin to the colony, complained to the Marques that he had cut off Angola's only branch of commerce, thereby causing a budget deficit and exposing all officials attempting to enforce the decree to the mortal hatred of the colony's white residents.[16]

[12] Quoted in Duffy, 1959, p. 97. Duffy maintains that António de Melo's frank report was sent in 1810, during his governorship of Angola, but it must have been earlier since Melo was governor from 1797 to 1802; see Lopo, 1964b, p. 37. For descriptions of Luanda at the turn of the century, see: Duffy, 1959, p. 73 and Silva Rego, 1969, pp. 13–14.

[13] For more on the Luanda revolt of 6 February 1822 see: Galvão and Selvagem, 1952, p. 96; Duffy, 1959, pp. 74–5 and Lima, 1846, part 1, pp. xxxvii–xxxviii.
The importance of degredados in the life of the colony at the time of the revolt can be inferred from the fact that during the first quarter of the nineteenth century—when the white population was approximately 1,000—about 100 degredados were sent annually to Angola. See Silva Rego, 1970, pp. 329–30.

[14] For further background on the political struggles in Portugal between the Absolutists and Liberals, as well as on the civil war (1820–36), see: Marques, A. H. de O., 1972, vol. 2, pp. 54–65, 105; Silva Rego, 1969, pp. 25–33; and Nowell, 1973, pp. 92–6.

[15] There is a wealth of literature on Sá da Bandeira, including a number of books which he wrote himself; for brief accounts of his initial attacks and decrees against slavery see: Marques, A. H. de O., 1972, vol. 2, p. 87; Wheeler and Pelissier, 1971, p. 52; Duffy, 1959, p. 76; and Duffy's sensitive and illuminating study of the issue of slavery (1967, pp. 7–10).

[16] Duffy, 1967, p. 7. Governor Noronha was merely the last in a long line of Governors before and after the decree of 1836 who believed that Angola could not financially survive without the slave trade. Even Governor António de Melo, who was quoted above as being so outraged by the deplorable state of the colony that he suggested to the Crown that he wanted to take it to court, argued in a report sent to the Crown in 1802:

During his tenure (1836-40) Sá da Bandeira's answer to those who were convinced that Angola could not survive without the slave trade was the promulgation of a series of laws designed to transform the slave-based economy through the introduction of widespread Portuguese settlement. He argued that Angola must no longer be a place of exile for degredados, but a home for honest and hardworking Portuguese citizens. In 1836 a settlement of free whites was founded along the Catumbella River (between Lobito and Benguela); but it failed, just as all previous attempts at white settlement had failed.[17] In addition, most of Sá da Bandeira's plans for the transformation of the Angolan economy were never implemented. By his final year as Premier, the lack of European agricultural production in Angola meant that anything not grown by Africans (e.g. coffee) but desired by the Portuguese had to be imported.[18] Furthermore, Lisbon was forced once again to turn to the degredados to provide an impetus for white settlement and in 1839 a royal edict granted free passage to Africa for the wives and children of degredados.[19]

White Society in the Mid-Nineteenth Century: Degredado Influence, Economic Impoverishment, and New Attempts at Settlement of Free Whites

There were only 1,830 whites in Angola in 1846 when Lopes de Lima

---

These domains of Your Majesty, in my opinion, are only worthwhile for the subsidies they provide the colonies of Brazil, which are the jewels in the Portuguese Crown, and, if one day we would be able to pass from the slaves we transport from Africa to America, we would immediately see ourselves obliged to abandon the establishments we have here; because they will not give us any other means to overcome the expenses of its maintenance, however small that might be! (Quoted in Dias, G. S., 1959, pp. 303-4.)

Sá da Bandeira's attempts to stop the slave trade during the 1830s were not immediately successful given the strong opposition in Angola and the fact that he lacked widespread support in Portugal itself. The slave trade persisted for decades after the initial decree, primarily carried out by degredados. H. Evans Lloyd maintained in 1845 that the Angolan slave trade was in the 'hands of a few individuals' who had been 'sent to those colonies as convicts, often for crimes of the deepest dye; that are not subject to any control or restriction, but are at liberty to direct every effort to one sole object—the rapid acquisition of wealth!' H. Evans Lloyd, 'Introduction' to Tams, 1969, pp. xiv-xv. Originally published in 1845 and translated from the German by H. Evans Lloyd.

[17] Galvão, 1932, p. 196; Lima, J. J. L. de, 1846, part 2, p. 40; and Guilherme Augusto de Brito Capello, 1889b, p. 182.

For Sá da Bandeira's programme to abolish slavery and encourage the development of European agriculture before becoming Premier (14 February 1836), see Silva Cunha, 1955, pp. 125-7.

[18] For accounts of the absence of European agriculture in Angola prior to 1840, see: Pery, 1875, p. 357; Lavradio, 1936, p. 8; Knapic, 1964, vol. 2, pp. 26-7. Also see Ralph Delgado's explanation of Portugal's failure to colonize southern Angola before the middle of the nineteenth century (1944, pp. 111-20), found in Oliveira, M. A. F. de, 1968, vol. 1, p. 259, note.

[19] Galvão, 1932, p. 196.

conducted his remarkable survey of the population (see Table 7). Outside the capital—where nine out of ten whites resided—it was not possible to find a European community which could instil hope in even the most optimistic of the Portuguese colonial planners. Benguela, Angola's second largest cluster of whites, could boast of only thirty-eight men and one woman almost two and a half centuries after the Portuguese conquest of this coastal city. Angola's reputation as a white man's grave was considerably nurtured by Lopes de Lima's description of Benguela:

> living in that country is a continual battle with disease and death: white men have contracted the incessant habit of always walking on the street with their hand on their wrist to observe their pulse, and when they see each other the usual question is—*has the fever gone* ... There are no white women, nor could there be any considering the certain death, especially if they are still of child-bearing age; because there is still no example until today of a white woman giving birth, that did not cost the life of the mother and child; this says everything.[20]

By 1848, only two years after this lugubrious account of living conditions in Benguela, twenty of the city's whites had died.[21]

TABLE 7

Size and Location of Angola's European Population in 1846[22]

Location	Men	Women	Total	
Luanda	1,466	135	1,601	
Benguela	38	1	39	
Pungo Andongo	25	8	33	
Massangano	20	2	22	
Mossamedes	20	—	20	
Other	105	10	115	
Total	1,674	156	1,830	

[20] Lima, 1846, part 1, p. 206. Emphasis followed by ellipsis in original. for further descriptions of the unhealthy conditions in Benguela at this time see: Tams, 1969, vol. 2, pp. 77–82; *Quarenta e cinco dias em Angola: apontamentos de viagem*, 1862, p. 87; and July, 1970, pp. 481–2.

[21] See Mario António Fernandes de Oliveira's excellent study of Luanda at the middle of the nineteenth century, 1964, p. 15 (of reprint). He further notes that during 1848 the following white deaths were reported: 98 in Luanda, 20 in 'the capital's zone of influence', 4 in Novo Redondo, and 6 in Mossamedes.

[22] Adapted from Lima, 1846, Table 1, p. 4–A.

Luanda's decadence, noted in the early 1800s, turned to decay by the middle of the nineteenth century. The end of the slave trade forced most of the degredados out of the interior, thereby eliminating almost the only tokens of Portuguese sovereignty in the hinterland. With few exceptions they migrated to Luanda, further reducing the already low moral state of the capital's white inhabitants.

Dozens of Portuguese and foreign travellers to Angola have left behind detailed memoirs documenting the 'scandalous' image which Luanda evoked at this time. Gambling, drinking, and debauchery were the Europeans' major preoccupations and many fortunes, wives, and lives were won and lost.[23] A German medical doctor who visited Angola in 1841–42 was astounded by the character of Luanda's elite:

> there were possibly some among them whose mind and understanding was rather more cultivated; but at all events, these were so few in number that they exerted no visible influence on the company. In one respect, however, they were all equal, for I doubt whether there was a single exception—they were all slave-dealers, who would not shrink from the commission of any crime, if it tended to promote their interests.
>
> Such are the elements of which society consists at Loanda [Luanda], and a stranger cannot for a moment forget by what company he is surrounded.[24]

Ironically, and despite the universal cultural and racial ethnocentrism which pervaded European attitudes in the nineteenth century, most travellers implicitly or explicitly acknowledged that Africans in Luanda manifested a high standard of morality and religiosity and were more reliable policemen, better soldiers, and perhaps even more skilled craftsmen than the Europeans.[25] Tams observed that all African girls, including slaves, had lovers before marriage, but

> the moment she marries, she is pledged to the strictest laws of honour and faithfulness.... It would be well if the European ladies in Loanda, even those of the highest rank, were to take a lesson from their sable sisters; they ought to be an example to the negresses [sic] in their married life, whereas, the very reverse is the case.[26]

[23] See: ibid., pp. 205–6; Tams, 1969, vol. 1, pp. 273–5 and *Quarenta e cinco dias em Angola*, 1862, p. 52.

[24] Tams, 1969, vol. 1, pp. 273–4. Also see *Quarenta e cinco dias em Angola*, 1862, p. 25.

[25] An absence of data on the skills possessed by Africans and Europeans in Luanda makes a precise comparison impossible. Oliveira's study of advertisements for slaves in 1851 reveals that many were highly skilled as locksmiths, cooks, masons, tailors, barbers, carpenters and cabinetmakers, shoemakers, blacksmiths, goldsmiths, painters and watchmakers (1964, p. 10).

A decade later, an anonymous traveller described a military company of artisans in the following terms: 'These artisans are generally degredados: there is not among them one good worker and almost all seemed to me not only old-timers but invalids. If artisan means—incapable—then the company of Loanda is perfectly organized.' *Quarenta e cinco dias em Angola*, 1862, p. 43.

[26] Tams, 1969, vol. 1, pp. 269–70. He further adds (pp. 270–1):

One Portuguese traveller who spent forty-five days in Angola (in 1862) and generally considered all Africans as being treacherous, liars, thieves, and drunks, nevertheless noted that there was 'in the blacks a greater predilection for ecclesiastics than in the whites'.[27] In addition, he observed that some of the 'parish priests ... instead of illuminating the people, are not ashamed of sordidly exercising the vile and hateful role of enlisters of white slavery'.[28]

About 1860 Winwood Reade described Luanda as

> ankle-deep in sand, the public buildings are either decaying or in 'status quo'; oxen are stalled in the college of the Jesuits. All that remains of the poetry and power is dying away in this colony. It is the Dark Ages in the interregnum between two civilizations. When will the second begin?[29]

Most visitors to Luanda were happy to leave the colony alive and few expressed a desire to return, as can be seen in the parting words of one Portuguese:

> We say goodbye, and goodbye forever, to that burning furnace called Loanda and to its cohort of mosquitoes, spiders, lizards and cockroaches —infernal scourge, which by day and night torment the misfortunate whom bad luck launches on those beaches of crocodiles. I leave with my stomach nauseated from the repugnant smell of cockroaches, which for a month and a half I felt in all the clothes I wore and in everything I ate and drank.[30]

The rage, the unbounded passion of the Portuguese of the coast to vie with each other in wealth, silences every other, nay, the most sacred feelings; so that even a husband's jealousy is appeased, if by the unfaithfulness of his wife, he may gain a few paultry pieces of gold. I myself witnessed the delight with which a Portuguese, high in office, received a head-dress of gold and pearls, the payment of another European, for having been permitted to enjoy his wife's company for a short time; although this circumstance was known to everybody, neither the man nor his wife evinced the slightest reserve in exhibiting to me their ill-gotten gnerdon [*sic*] and manifesting the liveliest joy.

[27] *Quarenta e cinco dias em Angola*, 1862, p. 9 (for negative view of Africans) and p. 25 for quote on African predilection for the ecclesiastics. It is interesting to note that this man, who considered Africans drunks and thieves, etc., later admitted that finding an African in a drunken state in Luanda was rare 'because on that point, with shame I admit, they are more civilized than the whites; they respect the law and submit with resignation to the punishment it imposes on them' (p. 77).

[28] Ibid., p. 116.

[29] Reade, W. Winwood, 1864, pp. 301–2, found in Duffy, 1959, p. 96. Also see *Quarenta e cinco dias em Angola*, 1862, p. 25.

[30] *Quarenta e cinco dias em Angola*, 1862, pp. 84–5. Elsewhere (p. 29) he castigates the devious methods which the government used to dupe Portuguese people into going to Angola and asks why it is done:

> To launch on the beaches of an inhospitable country hundreds of creatures who go to share the sad fate which our laws reserve for condemned criminals as the ultimate penalty, and which royal clemency or modern civilization commuted to perpetual exile. What a lovely picture of perversity!

Unhealthy conditions exacted a high death toll among the Europeans in Angola, especially among the degredados, for as difficult as it was for healthy Europeans to survive, the degredados often arrived already weak, malnourished, and diseased from Portuguese prisons. The first almanac published in Angola in 1851 lists 141 deaths among Luanda's European population of 830, or one of every six![31] During the next two decades the annual death rate dropped to approximately 7 to 10 per cent of the resident white community; among the degredado immigrants, however, it reached almost 50 per cent![32]

The degredados' life span was also dramatically shortened by their service in the army—they comprised the majority of the Portuguese troops in Angola. The precariousness of army life was aggravated, however, by the very behaviour of the degredados themselves, for, as all honest Portuguese officials and observers were quick to point out, they rarely amended the notorious behaviour which originally had gained them the ignominious status of 'degredado'. Official missions into the interior to foment or protect the slave trade, collect taxes, or procure forced labourers often gave the degredado troops an open licence to murder and plunder the African populations, frequently forcing them to move further inland to avoid the ravaging troops.[33] This pattern continued throughout the century, as can be seen in the 1887 annual report of Governor General Brito Capello:

> In order to demonstrate where the state of discipline of the garrison has arrived in this province, it is enough to expose here the numerous cases of extortion committed against the Africans by soldiers who serve in the interior; to remember the truly embarrassing fact ... of the desertion, by a great number of soldiers of the force which had

[31] See *Almanak statistico da Provincia d'Angola e suas dependencias para o anno de 1852*, pp. 8, 41.

[32] Wheeler's survey of the deaths among whites between 1861 and 1866 and 1870 and 1874 reveals that an average of 183 whites died annually. It is of interest to note that 58 per cent of all deaths occurred among civilians with the remainder being soldiers. Wheeler, 1963, Appendix 4, p. 405.

Oliveira Martins (1887, p. 228, note 1) calculated that 80 of the 193 degredados who entered Angola from 1870 to 1874 died.

[33] See: *Almanak statistico* (1851), p. 51; *Quarenta e cinco dias em Angola*, 1862, pp. 32–3, 74–5; and Duffy, 1959, p. 352, note 2. The degredado and non-degredado soldiers in the interior were no doubt encouraged in their excesses against the African population by many of the Governor Generals, such as José Rodrigues Coelho do Amaral who, in addressing the Overseas Council on 25 January 1856, asked the question: 'For what reason can't forced labour be regularly imposed on the Negro of Africa, who exercises no useful profession?' Quoted in Norton de Matos, 1926, p. 268. Joachim J. Monteiro is only one of many travellers who described the impact of the rural populations' devastation:

> We passed many places where towns. had formerly existed, but the inhabitants had been obligated to remove farther into the interior, or to the country about the River Dande, to escape the wholesale robbery and exactions of the Portuguese 'chefes'. (1875, vol. 2, p. 64.)

Monteiro's two volumes cover his fifteen years of travel in Angola, beginning in 1858.

gone to the aid of Lt. Artur de Paiva in Cubango; the premeditated freeing of prisoners, the insubordinations of the detachments in some concelhos, only because the chiefs did not satisfy their impertinent and illegal demands.

After noting that the police force was also composed of many degredados, he added:

> The police here are ignorant, they don't have any comprehension of their various duties, and it is not rare to see implicated in the cases of robbery and violence, the very soldiers to whom the government entrusted the security of the property and lives of the inhabitants of the capital.[34]

The end of the slave trade fulfilled the most dire predictions of the governors who had warned of economic doom. In February 1858, Monteiro observed that, with the exception of one Brazilian vessel carrying sugar and rum, no ship had arrived in Luanda for six months. One obvious reason for this dearth of ships was that Angola had no products to trade other than a little wax and ivory. Monteiro further noted that there were hardly any shops in Luanda 'so that provisions and other necessities were constantly exhausted and at famine prices'.[35] Too weak to transform its own feudal economy, Portugal lacked the industrial and capital bases to exploit its colonies' natural resources— a problem which continued to plague the Monarchy and later the Republic and New State regimes until the mid-1960s.

During the nineteenth century when the steam engine supplanted the ox, horse, and donkey and when guilds gave way to factories throughout Europe, Portugal continued to draw her economic inspiration from the Middle Ages. The metropole's economic backwardness had a profound impact on the colonies, most especially Angola, which became the 'jewel' of the Portuguese empire after the Brazilian declaration of independence in 1822. The new machinery and railroads in Britain and France required lubrication and the developing soap industry needed special vegetable oils which opened a market in their African colonies for such products as palm and peanut oils. This new trade more than offset the revenues lost from the cessation of the West African slave trade. The industrial revolution moved Britain, and later France, out of the monopolistic mercantile system into a system of free trade in which both countries viewed the entire world as their source of raw materials and as a market for their factory goods. This allowed these two industrial nations to 'magnanimously' forbid their citizens in the early 1800s to participate any further in the Atlantic slave trade and stimulated the penetration of

[34] Capello, 1889, pp. 90–2.
[35] Monteiro, 1875, vol. 2, p. 23.

the West African hinterlands in search of new opportunities for profit.[36]

Portugal, on the other hand, had little motivation to penetrate the interior of her African colonies in search of lubricants or other raw materials required for a machine-based economy. By 1850 Portugal had only forty-two miles of macadamized roads and in 1853 Portugal was the last country in Western Europe to start construction of a railroad. Figueiredo observed that the routes between Portugal's largest cities at this time were 'little more than beaten and stony tracks traversed painfully by two-wheeled chariots or litters', while river navigation was almost totally impeded by large deposits of sand in the beds and at the mouths of the rivers.[37] Portuguese steamships constituted only 2 per cent of all ships carrying goods to and from Portuguese ports in 1856; England accounted for 73 per cent and France 23 per cent of ships calling on Portugal that same year.[38] Unable to exploit its own resources, Portugal could scarcely contemplate exploiting those in the colonies.

The virtual non-existence of an economic infrastructure and the abjectly low technological development of Portuguese manufacturing prevented Portugal from imitating other European colonizing nations which were developing protected markets in their African colonies. Portugal exported few products, other than wine and rum, which its colonies could absorb. A comment by the Portuguese Industrial Association on the state of the Portuguese economy at the time of the 1865 O Porto exposition illustrates just how removed Portugal was from the industrial revolution transforming most of Europe:

> at the time [1865] we did not know how to weave raw cloth, neither for us nor for the blacks. In the cotton section, the factory of Rio Vizela ... was limited to the exporting of thread and other producers in Porto and Lisbon were almost reduced to the same thing. The cloth for dyeing and printing came from abroad, the wire nail was unknown, mechanical carpentry and locksmithery did not exist.[39]

---

[36] See: Rodney, 1968, pp. 61–2; Davidson, 1961, pp. 42–4, 74; and Minter, 1972, pp. 7–10. Robert L. Heilbroner notes that between 1900 and 1914 England exported about 7 per cent of its national income in the form of investments abroad, principally in its colonies (1963, pp. 108–9). In contrast, Portugal exported practically none of its national income during the same period.

[37] Figueiredo, 1966, pp. 2–3. Also see: Pery, 1875, pp. 189–91; Oliveira Marques, 1972, vol. 2, p. 8; and Hammond, 1966, p. 3. By contrast, England began her railroads in 1821 and France in 1823. Further information on the low level of Portuguese industrialization around the middle of the nineteenth century can be found in Oliveira Marques, 1972, vol. 2, pp. 6–16.

[38] The percentages were derived from the charts in Pery, 1875, found on pp. 186–7. Pery also noted that the life expectancy in Portugal in 1860 of 31 years was the lowest in Europe (p. 191).

[39] Associação Industrial Portuguesa, 1952, p. 43.

A decade after the Industrial Fair in Porto, Pery complained in his famous 1875 geography of Portugal:

This bleak economic picture provided little hope for those who clung to the illusion that Portugal could develop the post slave-trade Angolan economy. If any doubts remained they were dispelled in 1860, when King Dom Pedro V admonished one of his ministers (who informed him of a number of setbacks in Angola) that Portugal could only expand in Angola by 'weakening the metropolis in favour of the colonies'.[40] Consequently, Portugal further reduced its commitment to Angola and began a withdrawal from frontier garrisons to coastal settlements which, with sporadic exceptions, were still unable to attract free Portuguese men *and* women.

The only area outside Luanda which offered favourable prospects for white settlement was in Mossamedes and, given Brazil's historical importance in Angola, it is fitting that the first permanent white settlers in this area came from Brazil, not Portugal. An armed insurrection in the Brazilian city of Pernambuco in 1847–48 led a number of recent Portuguese immigrants and some Italians to petition Lisbon for assistance in settling in a salubrious zone in Africa.[41] Mossamedes, almost 200 miles south of Benguela along a stretch of desert coast, had been visited earlier by Portuguese traders and explorers who deemed the area healthy for European settlement. The Portuguese government, anxious not to miss this unique opportunity to attract European families, sent the petitioners a detailed memorandum on the area around the port of Mossamedes, along with an offer of financial assistance. Largely based on reports prepared by the former Governor (1784–90) and namesake of the town, the Baron of Mossamedes, the memorandum elated the Pernambucanos. The first contingent (170) arrived in Mossamedes in 1849, joined by 327 friends and relatives over the next two years.[42]

We do not have industrial statistics. The little that is done is due only to the zealous interest which Fradesso da Silveira has always shown for industry but this is no more than an isolated attempt with sparse data of general statistics only relevant to some industries and to some districts of the kingdom.

It is not possible to know for certain the number of industrial establishments, the number and salary of workers, the quantity and value of the products nor the raw material used ... (p. 145).

It is completely impossible to rigorously evaluate the total value of the transactions of internal commerce. (p. 175)

[40] Quoted in, and also see Wheeler in Wheeler and Pelissier, 1971, p. 56.

[41] For the background on the insurrection in Pernambuco which led to the emigration of Portuguese and Italians to Mossamedes, see: Haring, 1958, pp. 58–9. The former Angolan Governor General Brito Capello, noting that the troubles in Pernambuco were related to the downfall of the sugar industry which itself was connected to the abolition of slavery, suggests that the Pernambucans may have tried to transport to Angola what they lost in Brazil. The fact that the first group which arrived brought mills (*engenhos*) for fabricating sugar would appear to support this interpretation. Capello, 1889, pp. 182–5.

[42] Duffy, 1959, p. 98; and Carvalho, 1940, vol. 15, pp. 88–9.

Although for the most part Mossamedes was free of the dangerous mosquito and the debilitating humidity which had plagued all previously attempted white settlement along the northern and central coasts, it was too small and dry to support the new immigrants, who suffered crippling droughts and frequent crop failures. Some of the whites moved to Luanda and Huila, while the remainder discovered that the lack of fresh water was as perilous as disease-bearing insects.[43] By 1854, five years after the first settlers arrived, the number of whites in Mossamedes had fallen to 256. Their population fluctuated over the next three decades; in 1857 twenty-nine Germans arrived with assistance from Lisbon and during one period there was an influx of skilled degredados. By 1877 there were still only 508 Portuguese and 14 foreign whites in Mossamedes, of whom merely 29 were listed as farmers.[44] Nevertheless, the presence of almost two hundred women guaranteed that for the first time a European community outside the capital would be capable of reproducing itself enough to assure permanence. In addition, the white settlement in Mossamedes attracted other whites to settle in southern Angola, especially in the Huila Highlands, Porto Alexandre, and Bahia dos Tigres.

While the foundation for future white settlement grew out of the misery and arduous efforts of those early Mossamedes settlers, the number of whites actually settled in the Highlands and coastal fishing towns was a major disappointment to all who desired to protect Portuguese sovereignty against the almost continuous attacks of Africans whom they threatened and/or displaced, and against the real and imagined encroachments of the Germans, the English, the Boers, and the Protestant missionaries.[45] Only a decade before the European scramble for Africa was formalized in Berlin (1884–85), Portuguese settlement was still tenuous and confined to the littoral. Furthermore, there was little communication or intercourse among the major coastal cities, since overland travel remained dangerous and often fatal. More Portuguese colonists had to be found to open up the areas difficult to traverse along the coast and to penetrate the interior if Portugal hoped to maintain its sovereignty and control of the colony. Given Lisbon's weak financial capabilities and reduced commitment to assist in the colonization of Angola, a growing number of 'colonialistas' focused their attention once again on the one

[43] See Wheeler in Wheeler and Pelissier, 1971, p. 47 and Hammond, pp. 66–7.

[44] See: Capello, 1889, pp. 185–6; Pery, 1875, p. 357; *Quarenta e cinco dias em Angola*, p. 95; Hammond, 1967, pp. 66–7; and Amaral, 1960, p. 18. A census taken of the population of Mossamedes on 30 June 1877 showed that 57 of the 422 whites in Mossamedes were born in the colony. The census also reveals the following occupations of the settlers: sailors (40), fishermen (36), farmers (29), carpenters (18), journeymen (18), businessmen (16), bookkeepers (12), tailors (9), teachers (1), clergy (1), and many others. See Oliveira, 1968, vol. 1, p. 144 (chart opposite).

[45] See Urquhart, 1963, pp. 129–31 and Carvalho, 1940, pp. 90, 113. For the actual and imagined threats to Portuguese sovereignty see Wheeler in Wheeler and Pelissier, 1971, pp. 71–8.

element in Portuguese society capable of supplying the bodies for continu-ing Portuguese colonization in Angola—the degredado! Ignoring the previous four centuries of the abject failure of penal colonization in Angola, they pointed to the 'successful' use of degredado settlers in the United States and later Australia.

Although Portugal was the first nation to initiate the penalty of *degrêdo* (exile), other European colonizers (e.g. England, France, and Spain) incorporated this practice into their penal codes and colonization schemes.[46] In fact, the English use of degredados in settling the United States and Australia was considered to be a model by those Portuguese who supported the continued use of degredados to colonize Angola. Yet, while Portuguese penologists hailed the accomplishments of English penal colonization, they apparently overlooked the fact that the climate, quality of land, and sparse indigenous population of New South Wales or Van Diemen's Land in Australia could not have been more antithetical to the hot, humid, populous, and disease-infested regions of Angola, Goa, São Tomé, or Mozambique. Furthermore they failed to incorporate into their own programmes the very factors which accounted for England's success with penal colonization.

Whereas Portugal dredged up its degredados from among the murderers, rapists, arsonists, and perverts in its gaols, the vast majority (about 88 per cent) of English degredados were drawn from among the great unwashed of England's industrial slums, whose most serious crime was rarely more than the theft of an article of wearing apparel or some other petty larceny. The most common offence of the English degredados was to have been poor in a country where the rich had little tolerance for any transgressions by those less fortunate—a stark contrast to the vicious, morally bankrupt, and incorrigible criminals who were their Portuguese counterparts.

The English degredados further differed from those of Portugal in that they were considerably younger (average age was 26) and included significantly more women. In fact, one of every three degredados sent to Australia during the first two decades was female and one of six was female during the entire period of penal colonization. Overall, about 25,000 women were exiled to this colony, and it was essentially these women who became the mothers of Australia's first generation of native-born Europeans.[47]

As the number of free emigrants and respectable ex-convict settlers

[46] For a discussion of English, French and other Europeans' use of penal colonization, see Bender, 1975b, pp. 191–7 and pp. 237–41.

[47] Two books which are helpful in understanding English penal colonization in the United States and especially Australia are: Shaw, 1966 and Robson, 1965. An excellent account of attitudes and practices of European colonizers with respect to penal colonization is found in Junior, 1916, pp. 39–52. Also useful in Santos, B. dos, 1932, pp. 151–80. This excellent article was originally published in the *Boletim da Faculdade de Direito: Universidade de Coimbra* 12 (1930–1), pp. 161–201.

increased in Australia by the middle of the nineteenth century, so did local protests to ban further shipments of convicts. The 'Anti-Transportation League', formed in the 1840s, succeeded in halting all but a small amount of degredado immigration by 1853, and by 1867 penal transportation to Australia had ceased altogether.[48]

Portugal Returns to Penal Colonization

The lessons from the short history of Australian penal colonization were interpreted and applied differently throughout the Portuguese empire. In each colony the free settlers, often supported by local officials, tried to emulate Australia's Anti-Transportation League by demanding the immediate cessation of degredado imports to their respective colonies. India was spared the worst degredados after the 1852 penal reform and was finally free of them altogether when, in 1869, exile was limited to the African colonies.

Opposition was most effective in those African colonies which received the least degredados: from 1866 to 1874, Mozambique and São Tomé annually received about twenty-five degredados and Cape Verde five, while Angola annually acquired 130 degredados, or more than two-thirds of all degredados exiled.[49] The exile of degredados to Cape Verde and São Tomé was finally prohibited in the early 1880s and to Mozambique in 1885—leaving Angola as the sole repository for the metropole's outcasts.[50]

Penologists and the colonial administration in Lisbon viewed the colonies' protests against degredados as a logistical rather than substantive problem; i.e. debate principally concerned the location of exile, not the efficacy of the penalty itself, which was widely accepted as intrinsically

[48] For further information on the Anti-Transportation League, see Shaw, 1966, pp. 343–5, 348 and 353.

[49] The number of degredados sent to all the colonies between 1866 and 1869 can be found in Pery, 1875, p. 284. The number sent between 1870 and 1874 is given in Oliveira Martins, 1887, p. 192, note 1.

Portugal eliminated the death penalty in 1867, the same year in which the colonies were divided into first and second class zones for degredados—the zones distinguished on the basis of the gravity of crime committed (Melo, 1974, pp. 156–7). The immediate effect of these changes for Angola was that it received a significantly larger number of degredados convicted of murder. In 1869, for example, 100 degredados charged with homicide were sent to the colonies, principally to Angola, compared with 147 during the preceding three years (Pery, 1875, p. 284).

[50] There is some confusion in the literature over the exact dates when the *degrêdo* was prohibited in the Portuguese colonies. Melo, for example, argues that it was stopped in São Tomé and Principe in 1862, Mantero says 1881, while Nogueira avers 1882. Furthermore Melo argues that the shipment of degredados to Cape Verde was stopped in 1873 while Nogueira maintains that it ceased there in 1882. See: Melo, 1940, p. 159; Nogueira, António Francisco, 1963, pp. 37–8; and Mantero, 1969, p. 18. (Originally published in Portuguese in 1910.) Also see Silva Telles, p. 12 and Leitão, 1963, pp. 17–18.

sound. Australia proved this to all but a few doubters.[51] Portuguese penologists believed that neither the death penalty nor conventional imprisonment were effective deterrents to crime, therefore the country needed a drastic means to protect itself against a growing number of incorrigible criminals, the *degrêdo* appeared to present the best of all possible solutions, for even if it was not as 'intimidating' as some argued, at least it guaranteed the removal of these criminals from the metropole.[52]

It was argued further that removing the criminal from his or her criminal environment and providing new opportunities in a new land would make rehabilitation inevitable. A few dreamers, such as Professor Silva Ferrao in his 1856 treatise on the theory of penal law, went so far as to argue that the degredados could make a fortune in the colonies 'which either would bind them indissolubly to the country[s], or would cause them to return to the kingdom with their capital, completely rehabilitated, legally and morally'.[53] It was not important that only a tiny minority shared Silva Ferrao's delusions because for most, even Sá da Bandeira, what mattered above all was the cleansing of the metropole of its most pernicious elements, especially after 1867, when the death penalty was abolished.[54]

A secondary consideration for maintaining the *degrêdo* was the allegedly vital role it could play in the colonization efforts in Africa. Many defenders of the *degrêdo* claimed that 'we eliminate the debris and transport energies', and it was commonly agreed that nowhere were these energies needed more than in Angola.[55] In fact, the flow of Portugal's 'debris' constituted the bulwark of whites who could be persuaded to settle in the colony. The windfall of the few thousand Pernambucans who settled in Mossamedes and the Huila plateau at the middle of the century signalled the end, rather than initiation, of large waves of white settlers for the next three decades. A series of plans and decrees, designed to augment free white settlement (e.g. in 1852, 1856, 1857, 1862, and 1877), either atrophied on the drawing boards or failed for want of settlers.[56]

As Angola approached the final quarter of the nineteenth century, there was grave concern in Lisbon that the lack of effective Portuguese penetration into the interior and along the entire coast would fire the imperial ambitions of Britain, France, Germany, and Belgium.[57] (This

[51] See: Pinto, J. F., 1926, p. 156; and Silva Rego, 1969, p. 120.
[52] See Moreira, 1954, pp. 76–7; and Santos, Beleza dos, 1930–1, p. 152.
[53] Ferrão, 1856–57, p. 72. He was one of the most famous jurists in Portugal at this time.
[54] Sá da Bandeira, 1873, p. 154.
[55] Cited in Santos, Beleza dos, 1930–1, p. 169.
[56] For further information on some of the abortive plans for settlement between 1852 and 1877, see Galvão, 1937, pp. 197–8; Gaspar, 1961, pp. 19–20; and Duffy, 1959, p. 99.
[57] As late as 1873 Governor General José Baptista d'Andrade, in a letter to the Minister of the Navy and Colonies (28 October 1873), wrote: 'I am more and more convinced of the unsuitability of the military occupation at points which are long distances from the sea.' 'Relatório do Governador da Província de Angola—1873', *Relatórios dos Governadores*

concern proved to be more than justified in the 1880s, when treaties among the European colonial powers posited 'effective occupation' as the major criterion for colonial claims.)[58] One Governor General, Ponte e Horta (1870–73), did not assuage these concerns when he argued that Angola could not be considered a colony in the literal sense: 'Angola, which towers above the rest, and which is the jewel of our African domains, can be described as a political-military outpost ... however, a colony it isn't, because it lacks settlers. Everything there is precarious and unstable.'[59]

Lisbon appeared incapable of overcoming the lack of settlers without a heavy dependence on degredados. In 1869, Naval and Overseas Minister Rebelo da Silva promulgated the infamous decree which was intended to completely remodel penal colonization in Africa.[60] All degredados not employed in important positions in the public or private sectors, and all future degredados, were to be divided into groups according to the gravity of their crimes and were to be sent into the interior to establish 'model farms'.[61] It was envisioned that permanent white settlements would grow out of these farms. To help ensure this objective, Rebelo da Silva prohibited the degredados from having African or mestiça mistresses in the settlements and encouraged them to bring Portuguese wives, whose expenses would be paid by the state.[62] While the decree was meant to

---

das Provincias Ultramarinas (Lisbon, n.d.), p. 85. In his discussion of the lack of civilian or military penetration into Angola's interior until after the infamous treaty of Berlin in 1884, the Marques do Lavrádio noted that 'we called ourselves lords of a vast empire when, in reality we exercised a very fictitious dominion, a very small occupation' (1936, p. 183).

There is considerable literature on the lack of Portuguese occupation and penetration into the Angolan interior before the last quarter of the nineteenth century. The following are some of the sources which were helpful in understanding this phenomenon: Duffy, 1959, pp. 95–6; Amaral, 1960, p. 15; Hammond, 1966, p. 274; Pery, 1875, p. 357; Wheeler in Wheeler and Pelissier, 1971, pp. 51, 57; Monteiro, 1935, vol. 2, pp. 52–3, 63; Galvão and Selvagem, 1952, p. 106; Norton de Matos, 1926, p. 18; Maria Archer, 1936, p. 3; Boxer, 1963, pp. 39–40. Even Marcello Caetano (1951a, p. 1) argued that 'during almost all of the nineteenth century, the Portuguese colonial empire consisted, apart from the State of India, of islands and ports.'

[58] Lavrádio observed, after the Berlin Conference, that Portugal could no longer go to the conference table with a suitcase full of historical claims if she lacked the power to back them up (p. 88). Also see: Gann and Duignan, 1969, p. 117; Hammond, 1966, pp. 93, 98–100 and 106–7; and Cordeiro, 1934, pp. 590–632. Luciano Cordeiro founded the Portuguese Geographic Society in 1875 and a decade later he represented Portugal at the Berlin Conference.

[59] The speech of Ponte e Horta was delivered in 1877 and quoted in Oliveira Martins, 1887, p. 176. Oliveira Martins further notes that less than 16,000 hectares were cultivated in Angola at that time—principally in areas not under European control (p. 192).

[60] Sections of Rebelo da Silva's 1869 decree on penal colonization are quoted and analysed in: Silva Rego, 1969, pp. 19–20; Moreira, 1951, pp. 155–60; and Luciano Cordeiro, 1934, p. 532.

[61] Capello, 1889, p. 185. Also see Melo, 1940, p. 157.

[62] See Silva Rego, 1969, p. 122.

provide a blueprint for the occupation and settlement of the interior
through the forced labour of degredados, it proved in fact to be little
more than another piece of Portuguese legislation noted for its erudition
of language, good intentions, and poor implementation.

Portugal's plan to establish penal settlements in Angola's interior was
strongly endorsed by the free white population of Luanda. While Lisbon
was motivated by geo-political considerations, the free whites, concerned
for their own safety, were anxious to see the degredados removed to the
interior. Although most degredados had been sentenced to hard labour,
very few were made to work at all, and they generally participated in
the daily life of the capital, as can be seen in Monteiro's description of
Luanda in the early 1860s:

> the choicest specimens of ruffians and wholesale assassins are sent to
> Loanda to be treated with the greatest consideration by the authorities.
> On arriving on the coast, some are enlisted as soldiers, but the more
> important murderers generally come provided with money and letters
> of recommendation that ensure them their instant liberty, and they
> start grog-shops, etc., where they rob and cheat, and in a few years
> become rich and independent and even influential personages.[63]

Degredado transgressions in Angola were not confined to robbery and
cheating; they were convicted of almost every crime imaginable in the
colony, from murder and counterfeiting to raping young orphan girls.
'If permanent exile to Angola is the most severe punishment handed
down by Portuguese courts', Luanda's civilian whites asked, 'then how
can the criminals be stopped from returning to their nefarious ways once
they are in the colony?' The answer was ... they can't![64]

In 1876, in an attempt to control degredado behaviour and to use their
labour productively, the government decreed the establishment of four
degredado depositories in Angola. All convicts (male and female) were
to be confined in these depositories from which they would be assigned
to public work projects. Initially the depositories were intended as a stop-
gap measure until the implementation of the earlier decree on penal
settlements; however, indecision and inertia delayed their opening until

---

[63] Monteiro, 1875, vol. 2, p. 43.

[64] A number of crimes committed by degredados in Angola were recorded in the
Official Government Bulletin. For examples of degredados who were charged with counterfeiting and rape of an orphan, see respectively: *Boletim Official do Governo Geral da Província
d'Angola*, 1851, p. 2; and ibid., 1855, p. 3.

Monteiro notes that one method which the public exercised to control the behaviour
of degredados was to take the law into their own hands and beat or kill a degredado for
a crime he or she committed 'and no one would care to inquire how they came by their
death' (Monteiro, 1875, vol. 2, pp. 46–7).

1883.[65] The free whites' sense of urgency over the degredados was understandable in light of the fact that half of Luanda's European residents at this time were degredados, while only a quarter were free men and women outside the army![66]

Prior to 1883 the degredados were individual urban sores, but they became gaping wounds when they were herded together in depositories. The depositories were set up in Angola's most famous forts: São Filipe in Benguela and São Miguel in Luanda, the latter having reigned over the bay of Luanda since 1575 and which recently served as Command Headquarters for the Portuguese army during the Angolan Independence War.[67] The abysmal conditions in the depositories scandalized everyone, including the fort commanders! The commander in Benguela sent scores of letters to the Governor complaining about the lack of food, water, special facilities for female convicts, and space for the wives and families of the degredados. Without even the most basic necessities, such as shoes and clothing, the commander warned the Governor that the clothes he had requisitioned so often in the past had better be on the next ship because 'some of the degredados are barefoot and in a state of almost total nudity which is a manifest offence to public morality'.[68] Similar complaints emanated from the Luanda depository, especially over the scarcity of drinking water, which had to be transported in casks for more than fifteen miles.[69] The personnel in both depositories were overworked and understaffed (particularly when the officers and soldiers were assigned temporarily to units in the interior). The shortage of soldiers to maintain the depositories necessitated entrusting the positions of guards and turn-

[65] The 1876 decree called for the establishment of two depositories in Luanda and one each in Benguela and Mossamedes; however, plans for the latter were dropped in 1884 when shipment of degredados to Mossamedes was prohibited, while only one depository was opened in Luanda instead of two. See Oliveira and Couto, 1971, vol. 2, p. 484, note 1 and Junior, 1916, pp. 20–1.

[66] In 1881 there were 1,470 European residents in Luanda of whom 721 were civil and military criminals, 355 were in the army, and 394 were free Europeans. *Gazeta de Angola* (Luanda), 12 October 1881, found in Samuels, 1970, p. 10.

[67] For histories of the fort of São Miguel see: Bender, T. L., 1973, p. 5; Junior, 1916, pp. 29–37; and Oliveira and Couto, 1971, p. 484, note 1.

[68] Captain Commander António de Gravid to the Governor General, 9 April 1884 in *Benguela: Depósito de Degredados Registo do Ofícios, 1883–1895*, (972/132), Arquivo Histórico de Angola, Codice No. 2–3–21, p. 22.

[69] Major António Marianno Cesar d'Oliveira Ribeiro to Governor General, 13 April 1883 and 19 April 1883 in *Luanda: Copiador dos Ofícios Expedidos pela Secretária do Depósito dos Degredados, 1883–1885* (138/192), Arquivo Histórico de Angola, Codice No. 3–4–15, pp. 13, 18–9. The reference to the fact that water for the city of Luanda had to be carried in casks from a distance of 25 kilometres is found in 'Relatório da Associação Commercial de Luanda', *Boletim Oficial da Colónia de Angola*, no. 33 (suplemento), 1887, p. 82, cited by Amaral, 1960, p. 19.

keys to the degredados themselves which, predictably, led to an exceedingly high rate of escape.[70]

The Portuguese never resolved how to house or discipline the female convicts (degredadas) in Angola. Before the depositories opened, Luanda's governing council ordered degredadas to be placed under the care and discipline of the nursing sisters. According to Governor Ferreira do Amaral, however, the order was never carried out 'because there was neither a house nor sisters, and very little was known about the degredadas who were living in the city and given over to all types of debauchery without any kind of vigilance over their activities'.[71] The depositories were intended to remedy this situation, but condemning the degredadas to depositories was tantamount to abandoning them to the vagaries of the male convicts. For more than half a century during which the depositories functioned, every commander vainly lamented the state's contribution to the debasement of the degredadas and even the wives of degredados. Since the wives were seldom provided accommodations, a number were forced into prostitution in order to survive. Most degredadas, however, escaped the perils of the depositories by being requisitioned for jobs (primarily as domestics) or even marriage before their boats ever arrived in Luanda.[72] A large number of degredados also remained outside the depositories if they were employed by the government or private business. One convicted murderer, for example, did not become a depository inmate because he worked for the Luanda Municipal Council.[73]

[70] The commander of the Luanda depository informed the Governor General that, while he complied with the latter's order to dispatch his two assistant officers for other duty:

I must say to Your Excellency that it is with a serious prejudice to the service which is entrusted to me and to those officers: besides the amount of work of the deposit's organization, we have an immense daily routine, which we can barely finish and in order to accomplish anything one must actively work every day, not even taking off for holy days (Henrique d'Almeida Leite, 18 April 1884 in *Luanda: Copiador dos Ofícios*, pp. 159–60.)

The commander of the Benguela depository begged the District Governor to appoint a soldier as the prison turnkey instead of a degredado after having been informed that some degredados under guard had committed robberies. He pointed out that one of the reasons why such robberies occurred with such frequency was the fact that the guards were also convicts and were therefore most susceptible to bribery. João do Rosário Antão to Secretary of the Benguela government, 9 August 1906 in *Benguela Quartel: Depósito Subalterno de Degredados; Registo de Correspondência a Oficial Expedida, 1905–1907* (1494/305), Arquivo Histórico de Angola, Codice No. 3–5–64, pp. 78–9. (Ironically, one of two prisons in the U.S. which utilizes prisoners as guards is located in Angola, Louisiana.)

[71] 'Report of the Governor General of Angola', Francisco Joaquim Ferreira do Amaral (1 September 1882 to 1 September 1883), found in Oliveira and Couto, 1971, vol. 1, 675.

[72] See: Francisco José da Silva Marques' letter to District Governor, 19 November 1884; ibid., 4 September 1885 in *Benguela: Depósito de Degredados Registo dos Ofícios, 1883–1895* (972/132), Codice No. 2–3–21, pp. 35, 72; Vicente Lopes, 'Angola, 1906–1910', *O mundo português* 2 (August–September 1936), pp. 348–9; and Junior, p. 56.

[73] Letters sent by depository commanders provide considerable information on the movements of degredados in and out of the depositories. During March and April 1883 (chosen because they were the first two months of correspondence on file in the Angolan

Agricultural Penal Settlements

While the government was establishing the depositories, the first of the agricultural penal settlements was founded in Malange—fourteen years after they were decreed. Its name, *Esperança* (hope), was appropriate since the convicts were provided little more than that. True to Portuguese tradition in Angola, Esperança suffered the same handicaps which had decimated every attempt since 1593 to establish agricultural penal settlements. It lacked planning, land preparation, a hospitable climate, fertile soil, competent supervision, medical aid and, most importantly, degredado settlers.[74] The shockingly high death rate forced the closure of Esperança in 1886; in the short period of fourteen months, 44 of its degredado settlers had died (33 in Esperança and 11 in Luanda hospitals). Demoralized by the disaster in Esperança, the chief of the Angolan Health Service proclaimed that Europeans simply were not able to reproduce east of Luanda.[75] A second penal settlement, Rebelo da Silva, was set up in Benguela in 1885. While it outlived Esperança by a few years, it ultimately failed for essentially the same reasons, with one additional handicap. At a time when life expectancy for men in the metropole was only 31 years, the *youngest* man in Rebelo da Silva was 40 years old![76]

Despite the abject failure of the initial attempts at agrarian penal colonization, intense pressure to occupy and garrison the frontiers, com-

archives), the commander requested that 77 degredados be allowed to leave the depository to take positions in both the public and private sectors. He also inquired about 14 degredados who were 'unaccountably missing'. The numbers of degredados who left the depository noted here does not include those who were temporarily or permanently attached to a military company. *Luanda: Copiador dos Ofícios*, pp. 1–27.

Information on the convicted murderer working in the Municipal Council can be found in Henrique d'Almeida Leite's letter to the Administrator of the Luanda Concelho, 13 May 1884 in ibid., p. 171.

[74] For a comprehensive background on the penal settlement of Esperança, see Patraquim, 1966, pp. 71–94. The first attempt to establish a penal settlement with degredados occurred in 1593 in the area of Quissama, just south of the Cuanza river. Galvão, 1937, p. 194.

In the same year that Portugal undertook to locate military/agricultural penal settlements in the interior, João Bentes Castelo Branco observed that 'the treasury does not have the resources to permit even the thought of enlarging the army enough to garrison the very extensive frontiers of our colonies, to occupy and police the lands of all the chiefs who refused to submit'. 'Colónias militares', *Portugal em Africa* (Lisbon) 1 (1894), p. 122.

[75] Dr. Ramada Curto, Chief of Angolan Health Services, argued in the Governing Council of Angola:

that it was known that the Europeans do not reproduce east of Luanda; that of the 100 colonos with whom the penal colony [Esperança] was installed, 33 had died right there, 11 had come to their end in Luanda's hospital and some had to go to the south to convalesce, after having barely escaped the same fate. (*Acta da Reunião do Conselho do Governo de Angola*, to June 1886, Pasta 6, cited by Patraquim, 1966, p. 94. Also see Silva Telles, 1903, pp. 32–3.)

[76] For a detailed analysis of the failure of the agricultural penal colony, Rebelo da Silva, see Patraquim, 1966, pp. 97–118. also see Gaspar, 1958, pp. 39–42.

bined with the necessity to relieve Luanda and Benguela of the growing number of degredados, motivated yet another decree in 1894, which expanded the role of the settlements to include a military function. The degredados were to battle their way into the interior, defend the settlements against all attackers, plant food crops, and eventually send for their families.[77] The catastrophic fate of the degredados and officers who suffered the misfortune of being selected for this duty underscored not only the impossibility of using degredados to establish or maintain farm settlements in the interior, but also the poor relations between the Portuguese and Africans in the hinterland and thus the tenuous hold which Portugal exercised beyond the coast by the turn of the twentieth century.

With rare exceptions, all of the military agrarian penal settlements attempted in southern Angola were within a radius of one hundred and fifty miles from Benguela. Yet the commanders' descriptions of conditions in these settlements suggest that they could have been thousands of miles from the coast. A careful study of the correspondence sent by seven successive commanders to the Governor of Benguela between 1894 and 1900 reveals the blow which Portuguese prestige suffered from the folly of using degredados as settlers and soldiers in the interior of Angola.[78] This corres-

---

[77] Patraquim, 1966, p. 124.

[78] Correspondence from the commanders of the agricultural/military penal settlements in Benguela between 1894 and 1900 is found in two codices in the Arquivo Histórico de Angola. In order to expedite footnoting in this section, full references to the codices of the commanders' correspondence are presented here, thus allowing the reader to know where each of the abbreviated references in the text can be found. The correspondence is in chronological order, therefore little is lost by not footnoting the exact page references for each quote. For the period from 4 June 1894 to 15 July 1897 see: *Benguela Quartel: Colónia Penal Militar, Registo de Correspondência Expedida (1506/317)*, Codice 3–6–1. Commanders during this period whose correspondence is found here and the date they assumed their command are the following:

a)	Captain Frederico Cezar Trigo Teixeira	(4 June 1894)
b)	Alferes José Pedro de Macedo e Couto	(4 February 1896)
c)	Lieutenant João Moreira de Carmo	(15 July 1896)
d)	Lieutenant Jacinto Fialho d'Oliveira	(30 September 1896)
e)	Major Damião Augusto Ponte Ferreira	(29 May 1897)

Correspondence covering the period from 17 July 1897 to May 1900 is found in *Benguela Quartel: Colónia Penal Militar Agricola, Registo de Correspondência Expedida (1411/222)*, Codice No. 3–4–45. The Commanders were:
a) Major Damião Augusto Ponte Ferreira
b) Lieutenant Colonel António Julio Pinot Pizarro
c) Captain Joaquim Lopes Subtil
Finally, it should be recalled that the district of Benguela was considerably larger than the present district boundary. At the time of the period under study, it covered most of southern Angola and by 1911 included the areas of: Bie, Bailundo, Caconda, Dombe Grande, Egipto, Quilengues and Huambo. See *Grande enciclopedia portuguesa e brasileira* 4 (Lisbon and Rio de Janeiro: Editorial Enciclopedia, Ltd., n.d.), p. 529. This edition was published between 1940 and 1950.

pondence also clearly illustrates why the penal settlements were doomed to failure from the very beginning.

> Furthermore I am requesting Your Excellency to see fit to take measures for all personnel to leave this milieu as quickly as possible in order to avoid its total destruction, because there is no one who has escaped the malaria fevers. (Teixeira, 7 June 1894)

> It is my duty to inform Your Excellency for the information of His Excellency the Counsellor Governor General of the province that the colony can not be installed in this region because the terrain from the Quanza to here is worthless due to its sandiness, but also because the distance is quite great and the personnel who are capable of getting here come completely broken ... If perchance they insist that she, I mean the colony, is established in this region [near Caconda], it will cost a great deal without bringing in the least result, even if it were made up of free personnel. Of the condemned personnel, there is nothing good to hope for because in the prisons they completely lose the love of work and love for others; especially those who come from the Penitentiary, who do not see well and can make the marches only with difficulty ... From the Quanza to here the region is the poorest I know. If I had not promised to come to this region, I wouldn't have passed the Quanza because I already knew that I couldn't count on the element which was given me to command. (Teixeira, 3 April 1895)

> The detachment of Hunters No. 3 of the Garrison in the region of Lobale and the posts of the Zambeze, are without uniforms; the only military accoutrement which the majority have are hats which are already worn and ragged.
> This state of nudity, which gives the military force the appearance of common heathens, is very prejudicial to our prestige among these peoples. (Ferreira, 17 July 1897)

> Among the officials of the colony are found some who have been in this region for more than three years and they are anaemic and weak, not so much because of the climate as from the lack of nourishment to which all, without exception, are subjected ...
> While the official awaits the rations and clothes he requisitioned, he wastes away; at the same time his clothing and shoes wear so thin that within two years he doesn't have decent shoes or a uniform compatible with his official position. (Ferreira, 1 October 1897)

Rarely did a month pass during the six-year period under study when one of the commanders did not send a scathing letter to a government official castigating the degredados for their unwillingness to work, for the danger they presented to the officers and neighbouring Africans, and especially for the high incidence of desertion:

> I already had the occasion to inform Your Excellency that one cannot have nor should one have confidence in the criminals and in the meantime we do not hesitate to intern ourselves with such an element,

which at any given moment will certainly be our foremost enemy. We, unfortunately, have excessive practice in this and I am quite certain that the desertions will continue in such great numbers that one day it will not be surprising if the commanders of the posts find themselves completely abandoned. It is necessary to note that since the departure from Benguella to here, 35 desertions have been registered of whom 13 are still at large. (Teixeira, 29 June 1895)

The convicts flee constantly because there are no forces to guard them. The commander of the post of Chindumba has captured some but he doesn't have the military forces to escort them here. (Carmo, 22 July 1896)

The degredados cannot be counted on. When they work, twelve do the work of two; when they eat ... two consume the amount of twelve, and they are always ready to flee when they fear punishment; with such people whom can one count on in case of war? (d'Oliveira, 27 October 1896)

Lieutenant Fialho d'Oliveira's grave concern that he could not count on the degredados in battle was echoed by every other commander. When it was necessary to distribute weapons to degredados during times of war, they frequently used the arms to escape into the bush. Unable to count on its own (degredado) troops, Portugal was forced to rely on African troops to establish footholds in the interior. At the turn of the twentieth century the cold reality and irony for Portugal was that a European presence could only be established in most of Angola's interior with the military support of African troops conscripted from other parts of the territory.

Twice I was obliged to distribute cartridges to the criminals and they deserted in fives and sixes ... there can be no confidence in the criminal element and one cannot and should not put arms in their hands. Thus I am of the opinion that no more criminals should come here ... It is indispensable that a military command of 200 black troops be present in this area. (Teixeira, 4 March 1895)

It is not possible to sustain a colony [settlement] of Europeans in this region and much less so with degredados; the native force is indispensable but in numbers which can make them respected. (Teixeira, 20 March 1895)

No one can count or should count on the degredados in case of battle and the other troops, complaining that their salaries are months behind and that they have rendered service beyond which the law demands, almost deserve the same confidence. (Macedo, 23 June 1896)

The degredados were not only failures as soldiers, but also as farmers. Despite the fact that their primary purpose was to establish agrarian settlements in the interior, the degredados avoided farming and animal husbandry as though such activities were contaminated with leprosy.

The colony until today has lived in total passivity—being exclusively consuming, with agricultural activity reduced to the cultivation of little more than one hectare of land, and no cattle raising of any kind has been started. (d'Oliveira, 30 September 1896)

The state in which I found the penal colony upon taking over its command could not be sadder or more miserable. Agriculture does not exist, nor is winter the proper period for it. I found watermelons sowed in June, which is equivalent to sowing in the month of November in Portugal. Whoever did such a thing should be taken immediately to a mental hospital. The only remaining ox died on the day of our arrival ... I haven't a grain of rice for a sick man, everything was eaten before our arrival ... Unfortunate penal colony! Four years after installation, there was not a pig, goat or calf born here. The degredados are sustained on corn flour. (Pizarro, 10 August 1898)

Since the penal colonies were agricultural disasters they were almost totally dependent on the government for supplies. However, the requisitioned supplies often never arrived or, if they did arrive, were months late and rarely contained the essentials which had been ordered. Thus, the settlements were almost always on the brink of starvation. Eventually the lack of food led the degredados to assault the food stocks of neighbouring Africans and even motivated exchanges over the question of whether or not the degredados should be distributed among African villages which were better able to provide them with food and shelter than the Portuguese themselves.

I cannot assume the great responsibility of sustaining in this region such a high number of Europeans. Officially I have demonstrated that the element which *should be here is the native and not the European*, due to circumstances which I pointed out; however, the opposite is taking place which causes me to remind you once again that I cannot be responsible for what will occur in the future; I am therefore begging Your Excellency to see fit to request His Excellency the Counsellor Governor General of the Province to exonerate me from the command entrusted to me. (Teixeira, 29 June 1895)

The lack of meat completely discourages every convict because it is this food which gives him the energy to work. No cattle of any quality can be brought here and thus we only have cornmeal.(Carmo, 22 July 1896)

The storehouses of this settlement are entirely depleted of all goods and merchandise ... The commander is a simple fiction and a totally useless functionary due to the absolute lack of food or means of acquiring it to sustain the troops and degredados ... the same commander declares here and now that he desists from all the advantages and guarantees which were granted him to serve in Africa and requests permission to return to the metropole. (d'Oliveira, 18 December 1896)

Concerning the proposal for distributing the convicts throughout African huts, this may be the only possible solution [to avert starvation]

... but it would also aggravate a bad situation ... would the convicts, habituated to the European system, be able to sustain themselves? And, if during normal times this command needs constant prudence to maintain pacific relations between the natives and the convicts, how can conflicts be avoided when this vigilance is gone and they are dispersed through the villages, able to return to the ways which caused their ruin? Can one trust the instantaneous regeneration of individuals repudiated by the law as incapable of respecting the ties which maintain the equilibrium of the community? Would their being at the mercy of the native give them the practical notion of the necessary prudence of their situation? Would the native accept the intrusions with the altruism which is exclusive to the civilized races? The Governor of the District knows very well that the normal physiology of the bush native still obeys certain systems far withdrawn from the laws which cultured society is just beginning to modify ... All of them [degredados] constantly manifest their repugnance for staying here; 53 are absent and those present would be very pleased to leave the settlement: the Africans would certainly not regret their absence. (d'Oliveira, 14 April 1897)

The store, Ferreira Marques e Fonseca, in Benguela, which supplies the provisions for this settlement has lately sent provisions of very bad quality, some samples of which are enclosed with this note. The distribution of these materials to the soldiers as rations has led to assaults on the natives of Nan-Candundo who came here to sell dry fish and who rejected these supplies as payment for their trade. The commanders of the posts also complain about the quality of these supplies which all the natives reject. (Ferreira, 15 November 1897)

There is a terrible epidemic among the cattle on the plateau of Mossamedes which will easily spread to the Lobale region, which brings this command to contemplate a future of deprivation and misery which will annihilate the settlement and make the maintenance of the convicts in such a distant region impossible. Finally, this command proposes that the convicts be sent back to the coast, not only for the reasons mentioned above, but also for economic reasons. (Ferreira, 31 May 1898)

This command has the honour of communicating to the Government that the 64 shipments which left Benguella in August, with porters from Bailundo, still haven't arrived and their lack puts the colony in a *very* precarious state of nourishment because there is no fish nor rice nor beans; the only sustenance for the degredados are the potatoes which were destined for seed and which are now almost gone; if resources are not received in the next 15 days the command of this settlement will find himself in circumstances that he will not know how to resolve. (Pizarro, 16 January 1899)

[Commander Pizarro at this point sent letters complaining that, because the shipment of paper products ordered two years previously still had not arrived, there was no paper on which to write further letters, make charts, or collect information. See especially 30 January 1899.]

I request Your Excellency to attend to the pitiful state in which this and other posts are found with regard to materials; with the rations delayed the troops arriving have to live for months off the Africans which causes us to lose prestige, authority and the good name which we had among them, besides the break in discipline which such a state of affairs causes and for which I am responsible. (Subtil, 14 April 1900)

The troops are resigned to the lack of materials which have not arrived from headquarters but they should be closely watched to avoid their stealing from the Africans of this post (as has happened) which could cause serious difficulties for Your Excellency. (Subtil, 21 May 1900)

Degredados in the hinterland demonstrated such a profound aversion to agriculture, military service, self-help or anything remotely resembling discipline that settlement schemes proved to be completely counter-productive to all the objectives envisioned by the armchair colonial theorists.[79] In reality, degredados were nothing more than expensive para-sites and a constant menace for both the colonial administration *and* the local Africans. The abortive penal settlements further demonstrated Portugal's inability to supply or protect Europeans adequately beyond the coast. Clearly when the representatives of the crown became dependent on the altruism and magnanimity of African peasants for sus-tenance and survival, Portugal could only engender unmitigated disdain for its 'civilization' among those whom it considered congenitally inferior.

Degredados and the 'Civilizing Mission'

While available information on degredados before 1883—the year the Luanda and Benguela depositories were opened—is only sufficient to provide us with a general picture of their numbers and criminal activities, Silva Telles' empirical study yields enough statistical data on 4,114 convicts who entered Angola between 1883 and 1898 to support the characterization of the degredados presented thus far.[80] This average annual influx of 257 degredados during the sixteen-year period constituted, according to Silva Telles, just under two-thirds of all whites in the colony;

[79] At the end of the nineteenth century, Pinheiro Chagas, former Minister of the Navy and Overseas, commented on the results obtained under Rebelo da Silva's decrees on penal colonization, calling the decrees 'legislative monuments which honor the name of the minister who set them up, which fascinate by the elegance of their preambles and the sound ideas they embody, but which contributed very little to the development of the overseas territories'. *As colónias portuguezas no século XIX* (Lisbon, 1890), pp. 129–30, cited by Hammond, 1966, p. 68.

[80] Silva Telles, as Secretary General of the Lisbon Geographical Society, organized the First Colonial Congress in 1901, where he presented his study of the degredado system in Angola between 1883 and 1898. He gained his initial experience in Angola as a medical doctor before becoming a professor of tropical medicine in Lisbon. He later changed fields and became the Chairman of the Department of Economic Geography. In 1928 he was named Rector of the University of Lisbon and the following year he became Minister of Public Education.

while this figure may be slightly exaggerated, it does underscore the degredados' importance in the white population at the turn of the century.[81] Forty-five per cent of the degredados who arrived during this period had been convicted of 'crimes against persons', principally murder, while 39 per cent were guilty of 'crimes against property'—a sharp contrast with the pattern observed in Australia where only 3 per cent of the British degredados had been convicted of crimes against persons and 88 per cent against property.[82] Given their high death rate, very few of the degredados left the colony alive. Despite the fact that their average age upon arrival was the late twenties, their average life expectancy was only 13·6 years. Thus, for most degredados, their sentence was merely a disguised form of the death penalty. The small number who were able to return to the metropole were often 'so broken down by the sufferings endured' that their regeneration was viewed as impossible.[83]

During the early part of the twentieth century, the degredados' death rate improved but their quality worsened. Between 1902 and 1914, 57 per cent of the degredados had been convicted of crimes against persons, including: 921 for murder, 321 for assault causing bodily injury, and 177 for rape.[84] Less than 16 per cent of the degredados who entered Angola during this period were able to read, write or count![85] This high rate of illiteracy is undoubtedly a reflection of the degredados' class background for, as Table 8 clearly shows, the overwhelming majority of the degredados came from the bottom strata of society.

Degredados who entered Angola between 1902 and 1914 far outnumbered the free peasant immigrants—a pattern which persisted into the 1930s. Unlike Australia, however, the small number of female convicts —only 211—precluded the degredados from providing the nucleus of the colony's next generation of whites.[86] Not all degredados sent to Angola

---

[81] Silva Telles, 1903, pp. 15-16, 82.

[82] Because there was insufficient information on all degredados, Silva Telles's charts and tables only reflect that portion of degredados on whom information was available. In the case of the nature of the crimes for which the degredados were convicted, the sample included 2,540 of the 4,114 extant; see pp. 22-3. For more information on the crimes of degredados in Australia, see Hobson, 1965, p. 179 and p. 187 and Shaw, 1966, pp. 150-65.

[83] Silva Telles, 1903, pp. 53-5, p. 81.

[84] Junior, 1916, p. 73, table. This is 12 per cent greater than the period between 1883-98. The percentage of those convicted of crimes against property remained almost stable at 38 per cent, or 1 per cent less than the previous period.

[85] Ibid., p. 67, table.

[86] The number of female convicts is found in ibid., p. 64, table. While Portuguese statistics on white immigration in Angola do not specify whether the immigrant was a degredado or not, a comparison of the overall growth of the white population (e.g. 4,602 from 1900 to 1913) with the number of degredados recorded by the Luanda deposit as entering between 1902 and 1914 (2,638) indicates that degredados annually accounted for more than 60 per cent of all white immigrants. See ibid., p. 64 and Lemos, 1941, p. 33.

Wheeler's survey of the official bulletins of statistics (*Boletim Official*) indicates that degredados far outnumbered free peasant immigrants until after 1930. See Wheeler, 1963, pp. 351-2.

during this period were metropolitan Portuguese: 3 per cent were foreigners (the majority Spanish plus four Frenchmen and two Americans); and one of every five came from other Portuguese colonies (384 from Mozambique, 70 from Cape Verde, 46 from Goa, and 34 from Angola itself), a small number of whom were actually mestiços, Africans, or Indians.[86]

TABLE 8

Occupational Background of Degredados in Angola: 1902–14[88]

1) Salaried Workers		2,101
a) Factory Workers	(707)	
b) Agricultural Journeymen	(543)	
c) No Special Designation	(522)	
d) Domestics	(180)	
e) Fishermen	(94)	
f) Clerks	(55)	
2) Self-Employed		347
a) Farmers	(114)	
b) Businessmen	(97)	
c) Property Owners	(68)	
d) Female Servants	(59)	
e) Professionals	(6)	
f) Industrialists	(3)	
3) Military		101
4) No Profession		50
5) Civil Servants		32
6) Beggars		6
7) Prostitute		1
TOTAL		2,638

Since Angola's white population continued to be dominated by degredados through the early decades of the twentieth century, conditions were still not conducive to the establishment of permanent communities of stable white settlers who would carry out the Portuguese mission of 'civilizing' the Africans. Yet this was not always perceived by those responsible for the planning and execution of that mission. The lack of perception was partially determined by racial prejudice; for example, to Governor Calheiro de Menezes the 'simple presence of a European in the interior is conducive to the civilization' of Africans, even if that European is the most degenerate degredado.[89] Frequently the Lisbon

[87] Junior, 1916, p. 64, table.
[88] Ibid., pp. 70–1, table.
[89] Menezes, 1867, p. 23. Menezes wrote this in 1861. A decade later Governors Ponte

lawmakers shared Menezes' belief in the congenital inferiority of Africans and thus were incapable of perceiving the blatant incongruence of using degredados as 'civilizing' agents. On the other hand, those who had the misfortune of dealing directly with the degredados in Angola almost unanimously condemned the pernicious influence they exercised. Alexandre Sarsfield, for example, argued: 'It is hard to accept that such a scientific monstrosity is an actual fact of our penal legislation and that no one is raising his voice in this country to condemn it, to crush it, to annihilate it!'[90]

Oscar Lenz' observation in 1886 that the degredados had so 'completely corrupted' the population of Angola 'that the natives have lost all their respect' for the Portuguese was repeated annually by Portuguese officials over the next half century. As late as 1926 the Legislative Council in Luanda complained to Lisbon that the degredados gave 'everyone, especially the natives, such a lamentable idea of us and our civilization'.[91]

---

e Horta (1872) and Baptista d'Andrade (1873) presented perspectives diametrically opposed to those of Menezes. The former argued:

It is not unknown by anyone that even the scanty colonization which has made its way here is largely comprised of the scum of our Fatherland's citizens, of degredados or reprobates who in all conscience do not seem to be the most appropriate instrument for the education and morality of a people. (p. 5)

The following year Baptista d'Andrade wrote:

Our interests and civilization would profit a great deal if good missionary priests, educated to civilize the native, were sent to such concelhos instead of soldiers, the majority of whom are degredados convicted of all types of crimes. (pp. 85–6)

[90] Sarsfield, 1897, p. 136.

[91] Lenz, 1886, p. 50, cited by Patraquim, 1966, p. 39; and *Representação do 1° Conselho Legislativo aos poderes centrais*, p. 14. The Legislative Council added that the degredados 'are always bad elements which impede and prejudice our civilizing activity with these peoples' (ibid.).

For further comments and critique of the degredados' undermining the Portuguese civilizing mission, see: Silva Telles, 1903, pp. 27–8, 98–9; Jesus, 1894, p. 402; Leitão, 1963, p. 23; Gaspar, 1966, p. 23; and Couceiro, 1948, pp. 162–5.

Monteiro was also concerned about the impression of Portuguese civilization which Africans formed on the basis of their contact with the degredados, but he was more pre-occupied with the possibility that Africans would think even less of the Portuguese if they knew what conditions were like in the metropole. His comparison of the African civilizations he knew with metropolitan Portugal merits quoting at length:

It is impossible for anyone who has lived much amongst natives of tropical climates not to contrast the life led by them with that endured by a great portion of our own so highly civilized race—to compare their basically harmless, peaceful, healthy, and I may say sinless existence, with the grinding, despairing poverty, ignorance and vice underlying our civilization, with all its religions, wealth and luxury. We spend large sums in the fruitless attempt to reclaim and convert the negro [*sic*] from his so-called dark state, and we allow thousands of our innocent children at home to grow up as thieves and worse than savages.

It is lucky that the negro is unaware that those who are so anxious for his welfare and conversion from a comparatively innocent condition, come from a country where a state of ferocity, poverty and vice exists of which he has happily no conception, or it would make him look upon us with horror and surprise. (1875, vol. 2, pp. 311–12)

The noxious and corrupting influence of the degredados was by no means limited to Africans; in fact, most officials were more concerned about their impact on free whites than on Africans. Telles and Beleza dos Santos were only two of dozens to caution that not only was it utopian to hope that degredados would ever reform in Angola (since they normally used their time in the colony to 'perfect their trades') but furthermore that the degredados inevitably pulled the free white population down to their 'perverse level', rather than the reverse.[92]

In Benguela, especially after the depository closed in 1907, degredados were known to be behind almost all of the city's robberies and assaults, provoking strong outcries from many quarters.[93] The degredados were undoubtedly encouraged in their criminal ways by the knowledge that rarely would they be punished for their misdeeds. In 1897, for example, 88 per cent of the degredados in Angola escaped any form of discipline while 8 per cent were punished once and only 1 per cent more than once, principally for attempted escapes.[94]

As long as the metropole continued to export degredados, Angola was caught in a vicious cycle. The abysmal failure of the agricultural penal settlements at the end of the nineteenth century resulted in the removal of degredados from the interior back to Luanda and Benguela. Neither city, however, had enough prison space, staff, or money to keep more than a small portion under constant guard, and those who were confined were subjected to physical and moral conditions which shocked even some of the commanders responsible for their well-being. The majority were allowed to associate freely with the general population, responsible to practically no one other than themselves. The resultant high incidence of crime threatened and scandalized free whites and Africans alike. Yet, the human refuse continued to flow from Lisbon to Luanda, further threatening the security and development of the urban centres, while most

[92] See: Silva Telles, 1903, pp. 68, 74; Santos, B. dos, 1930–1, pp. 159–61; and Bacelar, 1924, p. 3.

[93] See the strong attack on crimes committed by degredados in the Holy Ghost periodical 'Os degredados e a ordem pública', *Portugal em África* 15 (22 May 1908), p. 160. Telles argued that 'the cities have schools of vice of which this province is unaware, where moral bankruptcy is easy and the road to crime even easier' (pp. 17, 74). One person who was aware was the commander of the Benguela deposit. In a letter to the District Governor in 1903, he pointed out that a number of crimes were being committed in the city by degredados assigned to the civilian and military hospitals and added that they should be forced to stay in the deposit at night in order to keep them off the streets. His advice, however, was never heeded. Letter sent by Lt. Joaquim da Silva Gonçalves to District Governor of Benguela, 8 October 1903 found in Benguela, *Depósito Subalterno de Degredados; Copiador de Ofícios, 1903–1904*, Arquivo Histórico de Angola, Codice No. 3–6–3, p. 25.

[94] Silva Telles, 1903, p. 82. The percentage of degredados 'punished' for crimes in Angola increased to about 22 per cent during the years 1912–14; however, this was still a small percentage of the number who actually committed crimes during that period. See Junior, 1916, p. 77.

of the interior continued to be uninhabited by Europeans.[95]

The protests of free whites in Luanda and Benguela, combined with grave concern over the lack of a stable Portuguese presence in the interior, led Republican lawmakers in Lisbon to issue a decree in 1919 which, once again, called for the establishment of agricultural penal settlements. The first (Capelongo) was located in Huila District and ostensibly was to hold four hundred male degredados; it was closed down only fourteen months after it opened. The climate—once having received ubiquitous praise—was (inexplicably) considered to be so precarious that an emergency evacuation of the staff and degredados had to be carried out. A few years later another attempt was made at the fort in Pedras Negras—where the Portuguese had conquered the famous Queen Jinga over three centuries earlier—but this also collapsed within months.[96]

Virtually no one in Angola entertained illusions about the high costs and dismal results of all attempts to establish permanent agricultural settlements with degredados; to some, however, it still represented the only possible solution until Lisbon ceased sending its unwanted convicts.[97] Consequently, more decrees were issued and more agricultural penal settlements were attempted, but none endured for more than a few years and none ever contributed to the colony's agricultural production![98] In the face of four and a half centuries of complete and total failure, it is natural to ask why the system was continued. Clearly the metropole was determined to cleanse itself of its worst criminals at any costs and, as long as few free Portuguese chose to emigrate to Africa, the policy was invariably rationalized as constituting a service for the cause of white settlement in Angola. Ferreira Pinto, on the other hand, argued in 1926 that Portugal continued to send its criminals to the colonies 'because we are prone to conserve all that is old and bad and destroy everything that is good in order to replace it with something worse'.[99]

---

[95] Willem Jaspert's description of the 21 male and 6 female degredados—all convicted of murder—with whom he had to 'spend four whole weeks in a floating hell' in 1926 on his way to Angola is sufficient to illustrate that the very dregs of Portuguese society were sent to Angola as degredados and to explain why they never contributed anything positive to the progress of the colony! (1929, pp. 37–42.)

The most extensive white settlement at this time was found in the Huila Highlands, yet by 1910 there were only about 3,275 Europeans found on the entire plateau. See Urquhart, 1963, p. 133.

[96] See: Patraquim, 1966, pp. 140–1 and *Representação do 1° Conselho Legislativo aos poderes centrais*, p. 17. In the latter it is argued that 'the history of these institutions [agricultural penal settlements] in Angola is the history of their failure'.

[97] See, for example, Pinto, J. P., 1926, pp. 157–8 and Bacelar, 1924, pp. 2–5.

[98] See: Patraquim, 1966, pp. 142–3, 160, 178, 184, 190; Silva Telles, 1916, p. 62; and Santos, B. dos, 1930–1, pp. 158, 195.

[99] Pinto, J. P., 1926, p. 156; also see p. 157.

Abolition

The outcry against the degredado system reached shrill proportions after the fall of the First Republic in 1926, but the major blow resulted from financial measures instituted by António de Oliveira Salazar.[100] As the dominant force in government from 1928, when he became Finance Minister, until his appointment as Prime Minister in 1932, Salazar attempted to curb any colonial expenditures from which the metropole did not directly profit. The transportation and maintenance of degredados in Angola were viewed as too costly under Salazar's tight fiscal policies, and it was further argued that the convict labour could be better utilized at home—a conclusion reached by the English in the middle of the previous century. In 1932, a decree was promulgated which abolished the exile of metropolitan convicts to Angola. The decree is interesting not only because of its emphasis on metropolitan economic considerations but also as a condemnation of the previous centuries of penal colonization in Angola:

> The old system of overseas penal colonization, carried out at random over successive decades and without a firm or well-defined plan, failed completely. The shipment of criminals to the overseas provinces, especially to Angola, which should [have] constituted an element of cheap and secure prosperity, was transformed over time into a dead weight which this possession [Angola] could hardly continue to endure....
> The hundreds of bodies which are annually exported to Angola without utility and the thousands of contos which are spent each year could well be applied in the utilization and exploration of such [uncultivated metropolitan] lands.
> Thus Angola will be freed from the nightmare of the disembarcation of successive levies of degredados, with their retinue of horrors, and a new and powerful work element will be mobilized for the benefit of the Metropole's economy.[101]

[100] Professor Beleza dos Santos' 1932 description of degredados in Angola characterizes the tone of the debate and the view of degredados held at the time of the first phase of abolition:

Many of them, the majority, lived a parasitic life, with resources obtained by the appropriation of that belonging to someone else, by all kinds of frauds or violence, by theft, trickery, at the cost of prostitution. Submerged in the lowest debauchery, deeply corrupted, saturated with alcohol, physically and morally ruined, they are generally rebellious against work by a congenital or acquired organic misery, by habit and even by a false self-love and rebellion. Either they never learned a profession, or they learned it badly or they don't want to exercise it. Economically [they have] low values, because they provide useful and persistent work only with difficulty, they are also morally inferior, which is very difficult and sometimes impossible to correct, at least in the present state of penal science. (p. 154)

[101] Decree No. 20 877 issued on 2 February can be found in *Colecção oficial de legislação portuguesa: publicado no ano de 1932*, first half (Lisbon: Imprensa Nacional, 1940), pp. 224–5. The decree was heavily influenced by the experiment in Sintra (a coastal city

This decree *did not*, however, include degredados from the other Portuguese colonies, nor did it alleviate the problem of degredados already in Luanda. Another decree was issued later that year (1932) which closed the Luanda depository and proposed the opening of another in the fort of Roçadas in the southwestern part of the colony (approximately 250 miles inland from the coast and 50 miles north of the Namibian border). The Roçadas depository was finally opened in 1936 with the intention of housing all male convicts condemned to exile by the courts of Angola, São Tomé, Cape Verde, and Guinea.[102] The convicts were supposed to work on military farms but the depository was closed two years later and the prisoners were transferred to various work projects in the interior or to Damba, an agricultural penal farm in the north (established in 1935).[103] In sum, although spared the unwanted metropolitan criminals, Angola continued to receive the scum of the other Portuguese colonies for nearly a quarter of a century; not until 5 June 1954 was the entire system of *degrêdo* finally and completely abolished.[104]

Conclusion

The history of penal colonization in Angola underscores why the Portuguese 'civilizing mission' was found wanting in almost every respect when the Portuguese dictatorship was overthrown on 25 April 1974.[105] It is a supreme irony and tragedy that the instruments employed by Portugal to carry out its civilizing mission had been drawn, until the past fifty years, from the dregs of Europe's most underdeveloped nation

---

about 18 miles west of Lisbon), where convicts were used as agricultural labourers. This experiment began within months after the overthrow of the Republic and the results were considered 'brilliant' by the famous law professor and Minister of Justice, Manuel Rodrigues, who drafted the decree; consequently, various glowing references to the experiment appear throughout the document. Also see Melo, 1940, pp. 175–7.

[102] For the decrees creating the depository at the Roçadas fort and a discussion of the necessity to remove the degredados from Luanda, see: *Colecção oficial de legislação portuguesa: publicado no ano de 1932*, second half (Lisbon: Imprensa Nacional, 1940), p. 640 and *Colecção oficial de legislação portuguesa: publicada no ano de 1936*, second half (Lisbon: Imprensa Nacional, 1947), pp. 310–11. An interesting provision in the first decree required all degredados to leave Angola within six months of the completion of their sentences and prohibited their return for two years after their departure.

[103] Ironically, in 1946 Damba was converted into a penal farm for African prisoners and in the early 1950s became an experimental scheme to 'modernize' African agriculture. The area was abandoned during the initial months of fighting in the north in 1961, then turned over to discharged metropolitan soldiers to farm under the direction of the Angolan Settlement Board. The former soldiers demonstrated that they were no more adept at farming or cattle-raising than the original convicts sent there in the mid-1930s!

[104] Decree No. 39 668 which abolished the degredado system in 1954 can be found in Correia, 1955, pp. 127–8.

[105] For a more comprehensive background on whites in Angola in late 1974, see Bender and Yoder, 1974, pp. 23–37, and Bender, 1974, pp. 150–5.

and were themselves considered beyond the pale of civilization. Further-more, there is practically no historical evidence that the degredados, the majority of whom were convicted murderers, ever reformed their criminal ways during their stay in the colony. Yet, they constituted the majority and vanguard of Portuguese contact with Africans for 450 of the 500 years of relations.

The Africans in Angola cannot be expected to have compartmentalized the nuances which differentiated free Portuguese from degredado soldiers who sacked the Bakongo capital of Mbanza Kongo in the sixteenth century; degredado soldiers who attacked Queen Jinga at Pedras Negras in the seventeenth century; degredados who overthrew the government and sacked Luanda in the eighteenth century; degredados in the late nineteenth-century agricultural penal settlements who plundered, and depended upon, local Africans for their sustenance; degredados who formed such an integral part of the slave trade during all of these centuries; or degredados who displaced African farmers in Damba and other areas during the twentieth century. These Portuguese, the degredados, have been perceived generally as part of a single civilization which engendered little envy, much fear, and even greater disdain. It is little wonder that degredados evoked these reactions from Africans since upstanding Portuguese in Angola feared and disdained them as well!

Finally, the degredado system laid the foundation for a lamentable pattern found among whites in Angola from 'discovery' until indepen-dence. Like the degredados before them, the free white immigrants of the twentieth century were drawn from among the lowest elements in Portuguese society. The majority of these immigrants, originating from essentially the same class as the degredados, lacked the same educational and occupational skills which could have contributed to, rather than exploited, the human and material development of the country.

CHAPTER 4

Directed White Settlement in Rural Angola: The Shattering of a Dream

Introduction

A fundamental tenet of Portuguese colonial policies over five centuries was that the best means of guaranteeing Portuguese sovereignty, 'civilizing' the indigenous populations, and developing the colonial economies was by the settlement of Portugal's farmers in the hinterlands of the Portuguese empire. The strongest efforts towards realizing these objectives were expended in Brazil, where grandiose and costly agricultural settlements were created as 'meccas' to attract white immigration to the Brazilian interior. By 1867, however, Brazil had only about 40,000 European farmers, or one out of every hundred European inhabitants.[1] The agricultural settlement schemes were generally not considered successful; in fact, only after Brazilian independence did rural settlement really develop to a significant extent in Brazil. In Angola, as pointed out in the previous chapter, the inability of successive Portuguese regimes to attract sufficient numbers of free white farmers engendered a series of futile attempts to use degredados to settle the Angolan hinterland.

These failures did not dissuade the Portuguese colonial theorists from their belief in widespread rural white settlement as the cornerstone of Portuguese colonization. While the efficacy of the policy was not questioned, there was much debate over the government's role in the settlement process. One group argued that the government should intervene directly by selecting the prospective settlers and providing them with free transportation, land, housing, animals, seeds, subsidies, and (occasionally) technical advice. In the Portuguese colonial lexicon, this was referred to as directed or planned settlement. Opponents to planned settlement argued for free or spontaneous settlement whereby prospective settlers would be responsible for themselves and would have to assume their own expenses. The theory of spontaneous settlement implied that the most efficacious use of government funds to encourage white rural settle-

---

[1] Poppino, 1968, pp. 185–7. In 1872 there were already 3,787,289 whites in Brazil (Poppino, Table 2).

ment would be to develop Angola's infrastructure and thereby attract the annual waves of Portuguese emigrants destined for other parts of Europe and the Americas.[2]

Despite the debates, successive regimes concentrated their efforts and expenditures on stimulating planned rather than spontaneous settlement; therefore it is the former which constitutes the focus of this chapter. The goals, objectives, and results of Portuguese planned settlement programmes in rural Angola during the twentieth century are analysed in three distinct periods: a) 1900–50, b) 1951–60, and c) 1961–72.

Although it was rarely stated explicitly during the final years of colonialism, the major underlying objective of every Portuguese attempt at white rural settlement was to secure Portuguese sovereignty in Angola by expanding their presence throughout the territory. White rural settlement was also viewed as an essential requisite for the 'civilization' of the African peoples in the interior of Angola and for rural economic development. Finally, 'civilizing the Africans' was the most important ideological justification—at times, rationalization—for pursuing the political objective of complete sovereignty.[3] The 1933 Colonial Act of Salazar's *Estado Novo* explicitly embodies this objective and justification in Article II: 'It is of the organic essence of the Portuguese Nation to carry out the function of possessing and colonizing overseas domains and of civilizing the indigenous populations.'[4]

In terms of these major objectives—expanding Portuguese hegemony, developing the rural economy, and 'civilizing' the African populations—white rural settlement schemes could be considered successful from the Portuguese point of view if the following questions could be answered affirmatively:

1. Did the settlement programmes attract sufficient numbers of long-term Portuguese settlers to the rural areas to establish a meaningful presence?

2. Did the settlers increase the economic productivity of the rural areas and, if so, were the expenditures for the settlement programme less than or equal to the costs of achieving similar development through

[2] For further discussion of the two types of settlement see Diogo, 1963, pp. 88–9; and Barata, 1966, p. 94.

Some authors distinguish a third type of colonization whereby the state pays the cost of transportation for the settler and his family and occasionally provides subsidies to help defray the costs of installation. This type, however, is most often associated with those who settle in the urban centres rather than the rural areas, which is the focus here. For example, see Gaspar, 1960, pp. 61–2.

[3] Silva Cunha, 1953, p. 106.

[4] Cited by Moreira, 1951, p. 17.

other means (i.e. various forms of assistance to the Africans in the same area)?[5]

3. Did the quality of the settlers enable Portugal to fulfil its 'civilizing mission' and lead to the development of multiracial communities?

It should be noted that before the military overthrow of the Caetano regime in 1974, most Portuguese officials did not empirically examine the question of success or failure of the white rural settlement schemes since they assumed that any white presence was *ipso facto* successful.[6] With this caveat we turn to an analysis of the planned settlement attempts during the first half of the twentieth century.

The Dream Versus the Reality: Planned Settlement, 1900–50

Before the twentieth century, the Portuguese in Angola rarely ventured beyond the coastal towns of Luanda, Mossamedes or Benguela. Consequently, by 1900 there were occasional traders, missionaries, and soldiers stationed in Angola's interior but almost no European agricultural settlers. Despite much propaganda to the contrary, some Portuguese argued in the early 1900s that Portugal still had not learned the secret of colonization.[7] While every Portuguese regime was motivated by the dream of transplanting Portuguese rural life to rural Angola, a number of factors militated against the fruition of that dream, and between 1900 and 1950 planned settlement was more of a complicated nightmare than a coherent reality.

The most important factor was the negative image which Angola conjured up among metropolitan Portuguese; i.e. Angola was ubiquitously viewed as a land infested with insects, wild animals, hostile Africans, and

---

[5] Given the paucity of data this is undoubtedly the most difficult question to answer. The first organized survey of European agriculture in Angola was conducted in 1950. It concentrated primarily on the major export crops which had low internal consumption, such as coffee and wheat. That survey has little utility for this study, however, since it presents the data for Angola as a whole, not on an individual or even regional basis. The first survey of African agricultural methods and production did not begin until 1960.

[6] This is essentially the position expressed by J. M. da Silva Cunha in an interview with this author in Lisbon, 19 June 1969. Silva Cunha served as Minister of the Overseas Territories for over a decade (including at the time of this interview) and was appointed Defence Minister a year before the Armed Forces Movement overthrew the Caetano regime. His appointment as a civilian angered most of the officers in the Portuguese military; furthermore, his reactionary views did not rest well with those officers committed to enlightened and egalitarian principles.

For additional examples, see Gaspar, 1961, p. 19; Soveral, 1952, p. 136; Sá Carneiro, 1949, p. 37; Ferreira, 1936, p. 147; and Abecasis, 1965, pp. 21–2.

[7] One of the most outspoken critics of the early twentieth century was Gomes dos Santos, who argued, 'we were a people of conquerers but we did not and still do not know how to colonize ... We are utopian dreamers, a people of sluggards and inepts always content with nominal sovereignty.' Gomes dos Santos, 1903, p. 5.

Francisco Xavier da Silva Telles maintained that 'after hundreds of years of domination, in spite of thousands of emigrants whom we have sent ... settlement was never demonstrated nor accomplished' (1903, p. 60).

degredados. The perennial pot of gold sought by Portuguese emigrants was to be found in the Americas, not in Africa. Brazil, the United States and Argentina attracted more than one million Portuguese from 1900 to the outbreak of World War II, while during the same period less than 35,000 Portuguese emigrants chose to make Angola their new home.[8]

The quality of the metropolitan who could be enticed to Angola was another important factor contributing to the difficulty of implementing successful planned settlement schemes. The Portuguese upper and middle class either remained in Portugal or had already left for better-known parts of North and South America. As a result, the government's appeals for prospective settlers were generally answered by rural peasants or the poor and unskilled in the urban areas. Furthermore, most rural Portuguese who did emigrate to Angola showed little or no interest in continuing agricultural pursuits once in the colony. Instead, they tended to settle in the cities, often displacing Africans from unskilled urban jobs.[9] On the other hand, many of the emigrants who actually became *colonos* (white agricultural settlers) in Angola were the metropolitan shoemakers, blacksmiths, tailors, doormen, and even some bankrupt businessmen.[10]

The colonos brought little with them to guarantee the success of their agricultural ventures. They lacked the most minimal education and were described in 1912 as 'generally poor, ignorant and illiterate and, for these very reasons, without much ambition, withdrawn and lacking initiative'.[11] Since the majority were from the poorest metropolitan classes, they arrived without any capital to invest in their farms. As one observer noted, 'you can't bring penniless people to a poor colony and expect settlement to be successful'.[12] They presented a sorry spectacle in the interior of Angola,

[8] *Boletin da Junta da Emigração*, 1965, p. 12, chart B. Also see Pereira, 1963, pp. 961–96; and Maurício, 1966, pp. 232–4.
During the nineteenth century, of the approximately 640,000 Portuguese emigrants, fewer than 10,000 went to Angola. Bettencourt, 1961, p. 55.
[9] See Amaral, 1960, p. 54 and Rebelo, 1961, pp. 114–16.
[10] Oliveira Santos, 1957–58, p. 76; and Barbosa, 1968, p. 156.
The term 'colono' is used in official demographic literature for any individual, excluding civil servants, who emigrated to Angola with a pass and (usually) a paid ticket issued by the Ministry of Overseas Territories. See Província de Angola, Direcção dos Serviços de Estatísticas, 1968, p. 64.
Colloquially, however, 'colono' referred only to those immigrants who settled as farmers in thr rural areas of Angola. In this study the term is employed in this latter sense, but does not refer to any dependents of the colono.
[11] Nascimento and Mattos, 1912, p. 20. Also see *1° Congresso Colonial Nacional, 1901: conferências preliminares e actas* (Lisbon, 1903), pp. 224–5; and Gabriel (Bishop of Malange), 1958, p. 188.
[12] Galvão, 1932, p. 23.
Eight years later João de Castro Osório made a similar point when he argued that 'agricultural colonization must not be done with poor farmers but with middle-class farmers who can enter on a cash crop basis in Angola'. 'Aspectos económicos do problema da colonização branca nas colónias portuguesas', presented to the Ninth Colonial Congress and reprinted in *Congresso do mundo portugues*, 1940, p. 265.

many living in total misery. A number were forced to beg for food from neighbouring Africans; the very Africans, former Governor General Norton de Matos noted, whom the colonos held in such low esteem yet who never refused to share their frugal supplies with the destitute whites.[13]

As noted previously, the majority of the colonos had never farmed before arriving in Angola. Yet even those who had been involved in agriculture in the metropole often failed in Angola either because they were the worst metropolitan farmers or because they were unable to adapt to the new crops and different farming methods required in Africa.[14] The successful Portuguese farmer in Angola was the exception, not the rule.

White rural settlement also suffered from the fact that many of the colonos demonstrated an aversion to agriculture and attempted to enter the field of commerce as soon as possible.[15] Since few fortunes were made in Angolan agriculture while many became wealthy through commercial activities, the colono's desire to avoid the physical demands of farming is quite understandable. Moreover, most colonos did not go to Angola with the intention of becoming permanent residents, but with the hope of making a quick fortune before their inevitable return to the metropole. Unfortunately, agriculture not only required more energy and capital than commerce, it also required a strong commitment of permanence.[16]

Considering all these factors, it is not surprising that by 1950 only 2,746 whites (less than 10 per cent of the active white male population)

[13] Norton de Matos, 1944, pp. 329-30. He argued that a better expenditure of government funds would be in buying the colonos clothes and sending them back to the metropole.

[14] Galvão argued that:

the metropolitan farmer, tied to his preconceptions and his metropolitan experience, failed lamentably in colonial agriculture—even when he was growing products which were familiar to him in the metropole ... the man who was a farmer in the metropole will not always be a good farmer colono in the colonies. (1937, p. 233)

This point was made even more strongly by a Portuguese army captain who argued that the Portuguese peasants in Angola:

are illiterate in everything, including agriculture, despite the fact that they have worked at it all of their lives. The methods they use are so antiquated they don't even come up to those used during the Roman Empire. Many of them have never heard of a plough, let alone use one. (Marcelino, 1930, pp. 19-20)

An exception to this general rule are the Madeirans who settled in the Huila highlands in 1884-5 (and to a lesser extent the Madeirans who arrived in 1889-91). Nevertheless, their agriculture, based primarily on the sweet potato, was subsistence and they contributed nothing to the economic development of the colony as a whole. I would like to thank W. G. Clarence-Smith for providing this information. Also see: Madeiros, 1976.

[15] Silva Rego, 1957, p. 224. Also see Nogueira, 1955, p. 117.

[16] Douglas Wheeler writes: 'The ordinary Portuguese inhabitant of Angola was not a farmer or industrialist, but a petty trader, a *sertanejo* (store-keeper), whose ambitions were limited to owning a *taberna* or store.' Wheeler and Pélissier, 1971, p. 64.

Some of these petty traders amassed small fortunes. Commerce required less capital because the traders in the interior received their goods on credit from large companies located in the major cities. These goods were then bartered with Africans for their agricultural products and cattle.

were working in Angolan agriculture.[17] While most serious scholars of the period agree that the poor selection of colonos was the primary cause for the failure of planned settlement during the first half of the twentieth century, all the blame cannot be attributed to the colono.[18]

Between 1900 and 1950, the government divised scores of programmes and passed innumerable laws designed to bring about the fruition of the planned settlement dream.[19] However, the government was seldom able to provide the technical and financial assistance required to carry out these programmes.[20] The lack of correspondence between legislation and execution led Galvão to remark,

> We have the most perfect and most copious legislation, synthesizing the best doctrines and holiest intentions—but we don't have, to correspond to such a flower of rhetoric arranged in articles and paragraphs, one example of the realization of European settlement.[21]

Even before leaving the metropole, a prospective emigrant faced inconsistencies in the circumstances governing his entering Angola. For example, while the government exhorted metropolitans to emigrate to Angola, it also passed laws requiring them to have passports and visas which, at times, were difficult to obtain. Furthermore, the shortage of ships often meant that the colono had to wait many months before he could finally depart.[22] Such problems prevented or dissuaded thousands of metropolitans from going to Angola.

Government technical and financial assistance, once the colono arrived in Angola, was equally problematical. For example, the government made almost no studies of the soil, water, or climate in the areas selected for prospective agricultural settlements.[23] Consequently, a number of the settlements failed because the location was found to be unsuitable for

---

[17] Direcção dos Serviços de Economia, 1953, p. 119, as cited in Amaral, 1960, p. 58.

[18] A partial list of the hundreds of authors who have emphasized the poor selection of colonos includes: Galvão, 1937, pp, 219–21, 232–4; Nogueira, 1955, pp. 109–10; Ponce, 1960, pp. 78–9, 221–2; Couto e Silva, 1968, pp. 153–6; Machado, A., 1935, pp. 230–1; Barbosa, 1948, p. 3; Torres Garcia, 1934, p. 167; and Edgerton, 1957, pp. 238–9.

[19] For excellent summaries of pre-1950 settlement schemes in Angola, see: Galvão, 1937, pp. 194–212, and United Nations, General Assembly, 18 November 1965, Document A/6000/Add.3, part 2, Appendix 2, pp. 36–40.

[20] Norton de Matos, 1926, pp. 120–1.

Also see Morgado, 1960b, p. 112; Gaspar, 1958, p. 37; and Nogueira, 1955, pp. 109–10.

[21] Galvão, 1932, p. 5. On page 6 Galvão quotes Salazar, frustrated with this lack of correspondence, calling Portugal's administrative life a 'colossal lie'. However, while Salazar was able to reform the colonial service (see Hugh Kay, 1970, p. 213), he was unable at least until the mid-twentieth century to improve significantly the correspondence between legislation and its execution in the area of white settlement in Angola.

[22] Santa Rita, 1940, p. 143; Alves, 1960, pp. 8–9.

This problem was infinitely more serious for those who desired to emigrate freely than for those who chose to enter one of the planned settlements.

[23] Galvão, 1932, p. 16; Barbosa, 1948, p. 3.

agriculture only *after* the settlement had been established.[24]

The poor colonos seldom brought capital to Angola, which made them totally dependent on the government for credit and financial assistance.[25] However, credit was often unavailable or insufficient for the colonos to sustain themselves and many were forced to abandon their farms.[26]

Unfortunately, the type of government assistance which did reach the colono often discouraged the individual's initiative to become a successfully independent farmer.[27] In order to tempt metropolitans into the settlement programmes, the government offered a prospective colono free passage to Angola, a house and elementary furnishings, cattle, seeds, land, and a pension for an initial period. Such dependence on the state made the colono more of a civil servant than an independent farmer with a strong feeling of ownership. In particular, the financial subsidies actually discouraged many colonos from devoting their full energies to their new farms.[28] These subsidies were usually equal to or greater than the income the colono had derived from his labours in the metropole, and occasionally were sufficient to pay for African labour on his farm. Whether or not the subsidies were intended for this latter expense, 'few were the colonos who did not unload the least physical effort on the native's shoulders'.[29] Norton de Matos was so repulsed by this pattern that he advocated prohibiting the use of African labour because as soon as the colono had blacks in his service, 'he stops working and becomes an employer, foreman, or overseer and moves down from producer to parasite'[30] Another official cited the colono attitude that 'only blacks should work in Africa' as one of the principal causes for the failures in white settlement through 1934.[31]

It is quite possible that had the government put its financial resources into making credit available to the colono or developing Angola's roads, markets, railways, etc. instead of providing subsidies, the settlement programme might have had some success. As it was, Angola lacked the requisite infrastructure, for most of the 1900–50 period, to execute the

[24] In 1934 the Director of Angola's Agricultural Services conducted a study which attempted to discover why the settlement of Quibala (founded in 1928) had failed. He noted that Quibala lacked fertile land, sufficient water for irrigation, buildings suited to the climate, and funds for the construction of new buildings. Cited by Galvão, 1937, pp. 206–8.

[25] The situation of the white farmers born in Angola was even worse, since no public assistance in any form was available to them. See Urquhart, 1963, p. 136.

[26] Couto e Silva, 1968, pp. 158–61. The most objective and comprehensive study of agricultural credit in colonial Angola is that by Cruz de Carvalho and Guimarães, 1968. Also see Lemos, 1936, pp. 3–4.

[27] One colono actually complained that since degredados received more assistance (food, lodging, medical aid, salaries, etc.) than the free colonos, he thought he'd be better off going to the metropole and returning as a degredado. Cited in Santos, B. dos, 1930–1, p. 189–90.

[28] Barbosa, 1948, p. 12.

[29] Mendes, 1957–8, p. 85.

[30] Norton de Matos, 1933, p. 95.

[31] Magalhães, 1934, p. 13.

settlement policies legislated.[32] Until the mid-1920s, for example, Angola had practically no roads or rail lines, which meant that settlers had to transport their agricultural produce from the interior by expensive Boer ox-carts or African porters.[33] The renowned Benguela Railway was completed only in 1929, after more than a quarter of a century of work at a cost of $40 million (over 80 per cent of which came from British sources).[34] Even by 1953, Angola had only fifty-three miles of asphalted roads.[35] Since the major aim of Salazar's *Estado Novo* was the stabilization of the metropolitan economy, the colonies were forced to pay their own way and Angola did not 'pay' enough to provide the type of infrastructure which could ensure the necessary base for the thousands of colonos envisioned in the settlement programmes.

In an attempt to shift part of the cost of financing planned settlement to the private sector, the government asked the Benguela Railway Company in 1935 to establish agricultural settlements along the rail lines in the Angolan Central Highlands. The Company was encouraged to avoid many of the pitfalls of previous government programmes, such as providing the colonos with financial subsidies, and was further directed to build an adequate infrastructure. In the first two years the Company spent $2·8 million.[36] Despite the better planning and larger expenditures, the results were as dismal as with the government's attempts; between 1935–49, the Company managed to attract a total of nineteen colonos, of whom only nine remained in 1949.[37]

The poor selection of colonos, conflicting policies, and inadequate or improper government assistance prevented the fulfilment of the government's dream of transplanting Portuguese rural life to rural Angola. After all the money and effort expended on the settlement programmes during the first half of the twentieth century, the colono population was very small, generally unstable, and impoverished. However, the directed settlement attempts did not occur in a vacuum. Hundreds of thousands of

---

[32] Carvalho, 1940, pp. 92–3; Baiao, 1966, pp. 12–13; José de Almeida Santos, 1966, pp. 50–1; and Monteiro, A., n.d., p. 11.

[33] Wheeler and Pelissier, 1971, pp. 67–8; Norton de Matos, 1926, p. 147.

[34] Duffy, 1959, pp. 347–8. W. G. Clarence-Smith notes that the completion of the railroad at Huambo in 1911 was an important step in opening the interior, despite the fact that the entire rail line was not completed until 1929. W. G. Clarence-Smith to Gerald J. Bender, 12 May 1974, personal letter.

[35] Niddrie, 1969, p. 5.

[36] Barbosa, 1948, pp. 18–19; and Norton de Matos, 1953, pp. 136–43; Fonseca, A. X. da, 1940, p. 570.

[37] Barbosa, 1948, p. 18. Barbosa maintains that the installations provided by the Benguela Railway Company were better than anything which had been attempted previously.

In light of the failure of the Company's settlement programme, Álvaro de Melo Machado argued in the 1942 annual report of the Benguela Railway Company that 'agriculture in Africa should be essentially left to the Africans ... and when Europeans have to work in agriculture, it should be as *fazendeiros* (large landowners) directing the work of Africans'. Quoted in Nogueira, 1963, p. 119.

rural Africans were affected—the Africans whom the Portuguese hoped to 'civilize' via these nuclei of Portuguese culture.

The Portuguese always prided themselves on their mission to 'civilize' Africans as well as their 'ability' to create multiracial communities in Africa. Theoretically all colonial policies were intended to foster these goals, including those policies related to white agricultural settlement. In fact, by the mid-twentieth century, if Portugal had any hope of developing a multiracial society where blacks and whites lived and worked together as equals, it had to occur in the rural, not the urban areas of Angola. In the cities there was little basis for racial harmony: Portuguese peasants displaced Africans from the lesser skilled positions they traditionally held; there were large disparities in wages paid to whites and blacks (including assimilados);[38] and the material and (presumed) cultural differences between Europeans and Africans were too great for meaningful social intercourse to occur.[39]

In the rural areas it was not possible to build widespread multiracial communities with fewer than 3,000 Portuguese farmers, 80 per cent of whom lived in the highlands south of the Cuanza River in 1950.[40] Not only were they too few in number, but government policies had actually tended to segregate the rural populations.[41] The 'settlement programmes' for Africans, distinct from the settlement policy for Europeans, usually implied the grouping together of dispersed African peoples, ostensibly for the purpose of improving their lives. In reality, these programmes generally had the effect of separating the two populations, reducing the quality and size of African-owned lands, and increasing social strain between Europeans and Africans as well as among Africans themselves.[42] Instead of receiving new houses, furniture, animals, and irrigated land,

---

[38] Before the legislative reforms of 1961, *assimilados* were those Africans and mestiços whom the Portuguese (legally) considered to have successfully assimilated Portuguese culture and language. However, both the private and public sectors paid Africans, including *assimilados*, lower wages than those paid to whites. The justification was that the salaries merely reflected the differential productivity of the two races. See Mendes, 1957–8, pp. 87–8.

[39] Practically the only kind of urban integration one found in colonial Angola occurred in the African slums, where some Portuguese were forced to live by economic circumstances. While some armchair theorists pointed to this phenomenon with pride, most Portuguese were embarrassed by this form of inverse integration in which the Portuguese assimilated himself to the African patterns at the bottom of the social scale rather than Africans being integrated into the upper echelons of Portuguese urban society.

[40] Amaral, 1960, p. 78.

[41] Vicente Ferreira was one of the principal advocates for removing Africans in Angola from the plateau areas and resettling them in the hot, humid zones. See 1954, pp. 48–50.

Also see Ferreira, 1933: 116; Barreiros, 1929, pp. 27, 34; Dias, M. da C., 1913, pp. 9–10, 22–9; and Faria e Maia, 1924 and 1930.

[42] For more detail on the pre-1961 settlement programmes for Africans, see Bender, 1972, pp. 334–7, 351; and Childs, 1944, pp. 2–4. Childs discusses some of the forced resettlement of Africans in the Central Highlands of Angola during 1941–4.

'settlement' for Africans was nearly synonymous with the loss of their best lands.[43]

If the settlement policies between 1900 and 1950 produced any inter-racial contact, it was largely on the basis of employer-employee relations and these contacts were the very antithesis of the Portuguese multiracial policy. Most of the 'employees' were 'forced labourers' whom the Portu-guese employers used, in the words of Marcello Caetano, 'like pieces of equipment without any concern for their yearnings, interests or desires'.[44]

Old Ideas, New Plans: The Decade of the Fifties

By the mid-twentieth century Portugal had had some success in convincing Portuguese peasants to emigrate to Angola. Contrary to government intentions, however, this peasant class settled in Angola's cities—especially Luanda—and not in the countryside.[45] The insignificant number of peasants who chose to become rural colonos offered no proof that Portugal had yet been able to establish a 'true continuation of the fatherland' in rural Angola.[46] Thus, in the early 1950s, while England introduced self-government in Nigeria, Portugal searched for new methods to further white agricultural settlement.

The failures of the past had increased the number of opponents to planned settlement but had not diminished the belief of government officials that the programme could be successful if some of the earlier problems were corrected. This time the government was determined to provide the infrastructure necessary for the settlements to be viable, to locate the settlements on land which would lend itself to agricultural pursuits, to make a more careful selection of colonos, and to prohibit the use of African labourers. Still anxious to pursue its dream, the government wanted to demonstrate that not only could the Portuguese colono survive in the interior but that he could become a successful farmer without entrusting all the work to Africans—as he had done in the past.[47]

In the early 1950s the government decided to create two large agricultural settlements (*colonatos*) in Angola: Cela in the Central High-lands and Matala (Capelongo) in the Cunene river valley. The plan for Cela called for the installation of 8,400 colono families (totalling 58,900

[43] In 1958, three years before war broke out in Angola, Oliveira Santos warned that many Africans in northern Angola were convinced that their lands had been stolen and suggested that trouble could result unless the practice were altered. Santos, O., 1957–8, p. 80.

[44] Caetano, 1946, p. 73.

[45] In 1955 just over half the entire white population of Angola lived in Luanda; two-thirds of the white population lived in Angola's eight largest cities. See Amorim, 1958–9: p. 109.

[46] Moreira, 1961, p. 9.

[47] See Afonso, 1961, p. 270; Neto, 1964, p. 210; Knapic, 1964, p. 50; and Caetano, 1946, p. 72.

individuals) by 1980.[48] A total of 1,700 families were to be settled in Cela during the Second National Development Plan (1959–64).[49] The idea for Matala grew out of the abandoned plans of the late 1940s which had anticipated the settlement of 15,000 Portuguese families throughout the Cunene river valley.[50] Matala was a modest version of this grandiose scheme, and it was hoped that the new colonato could attract about 1,000 families to settle in an area of approximately 1,150 square miles.[51]

In Cela each colono received approximately 45 acres of land, while each colono in Matala received between 12 and 15 acres, depending upon the size of his family. The government provided communal grazing fields for cattle in both colonatos.[52] In addition to the land, each colono also received a house and furniture, seeds, animals, farm implements, and a monthly subsidy of between $50 and $140. It appeared in the 1950s that the government was finally prepared to spend the sums of money which supporters of planned settlement had been urging for decades.

As had happened prior to 1950, however, the reality of the two colonatos did not approach expectations. Instead of the thousands of colono families anticipated, there were only a few hundred families actually living in Cela and Matala by 1960—approximately 300 in each.[53]

[48] Ventura, 1955, pp. 165–8. See especially Ventura's remarks on p. 343 in the record of the debates at the Congress.

[49] *Plano de Fomento para 1959–64: programa geral de execução de investimentos inscritos e estimativa de repartição dos encargos nos seis anos de vigência* (Lisbon: Imprensa Nacional, 1959), p. 225, cited by Neto, 1964, p. 211. It is of interest to note that an earlier draft (1958) of the Second Development Plan called for the settlement of 2,000 families in Cela. However, this number was reduced to 1,700 in the final version of the Plan. Neto, 1964, p. 211.

[50] Much of the inspiration for settlement programmes in the Cunene river valley came from Trigo de Morais. For further background on the role and thinking of Morais, see Barata, J. F. N., 1970, pp. 61–3; and United Nations, General Assembly, 18 November 1965, Document A/6000/Add. 3, part 2, Appendix 2, p. 40.

[51] In hectares, Cela was approximately 300,000 while Matala was 420,000. See Marques, W., 1965, pp. 573–4, 581–2.

[52] There were two types of farms in Cela. The most common farms had an average of 45 acres which were not always contiguous. The second type of farm was much larger and could have either 125 acres or 300 acres. (See Afonso, 1961, pp. 268, 276–8.) In Matala each colono received 12 acres of land if he had at least two children. Colonos with larger families could receive up to 25 acres. Barata, J. F. N., 1970, p. 62. In Cela approximately 2,500 acres of communal grazing land were established for each village of 24 to 30 families. The communal grazing land in Matala averaged 75 acres per family. In both colonatos the communal pastures had previously been used by Africans for grazing their cattle.

[53] A government agricultural survey of Cela, carried out in 1962–3, indicates that there were 270 colonos in Cela by the end of 1960, whereas Neto (1964, p. 215) puts the figure at 302. For the former figure, see Província de Angola, Missão de Inquéritos Agrícolas de Angola, *Recenseamento Agrícola de Angola: bacia leiteira Cela-Catofe (First Part), 1962–1963* (Luanda: M.I.A.A., 1964), Table 3.1. (The 270 figure is derived from this table by eliminating those who entered after 1960.)

There is also some confusion concerning the number of colonos in Matala by the end of 1960. Neto (1964, p. 220) includes 131 colono families who entered during 1960 in his total of 291, whereas Barata put the number who entered during 1960 at 66. See Nunes Barata, J. F. N., 1963, p. 48.

The quality of the colonos who settled in the two colonatos was as disappointing as their small numbers. Most were illiterate and many had never farmed before. By 1960, 122 colonos had left Cela, either on their own volition or by being expelled for offences ranging from alcoholism and refusal to work to theft and even rape.[54] Many of the Cela and Matala colonos who left on their own did so because of the poor preparation and/or quality of the land which had been given them.[55] Thus, despite the government's proclaimed intentions, the two major pre-1950 problems of poor selection and preparation of colonos and land continued to plague the planned settlement schemes in Angola.

The government's commitment to spend almost any amount necessary to develop the required infrastructure—by which it hoped to guarantee the viability of the new colonatos—came under severe attack by local critics, who charged that the expenditures were vastly in excess of what was needed. The exact figures cannot be determined since millions of dollars spent by various government departments on Cela's infrastructure are not explicitly listed in the budget as expenditures for Cela. My own estimate, based on a study of many budgets and consideration of a variety of estimates, indicates that it cost the Portuguese Government approximately $100,000 to settle each family in Cela and about $25,000 for each family settled in Matala.[56]

Everyone in Lisbon and Angola agreed that the two colonatos were expensive but the two questions which policy makers, interested in expanding the settlement schemes, had to face were: (1) Did the number and quality of colonos attracted to Cela and Matala justify the large expenditures? and (2) What impact did the colonatos have on race relations in Angola?

The responses to the first question were basically subjective. That is, what price tag (if any) did the policy maker put on the value of settling a Portuguese family in rural Angola?

The second question could be answered more objectively. From every perspective it can be argued that the colonatos had a negative impact on

[54] Neto, 1964, p. 215; Rebelo, 1961, p. 120; and records of the Junta Provincial de Povoamento de Angola (Provincial Settlement Board of Angola). Ponce (1960, p. 185) avers that 30 of the families who left Cela were expelled.

Some of the expulsions can be attributed more to the government than to the colonos themselves since the charges of 'rebelliousness' and 'refusal to co-operate' brought against expelled colonos really resulted from their complaints about the poor land and/or facilities which had been given them.

[55] One report indicated that 30–35 per cent of the soils in Matala were damaged from leaks in the drainage system. Oliveira Monteiro, 1968, pp. 2–3.

The late São Toméan geographer, Francisco Tenreiro, accused the government experts of not being able to tell the difference between good and poor soils in the case of Cela (1964, p. 58).

[56] For a more detailed discussion of how I arrived at these estimates, see Bender in Heimer (ed.), 1973c, p. 242 and p. 273.

race relations. The two populations were isolated from each other through the prohibition of African labour in Cela and through the removal of thousands of Africans from their traditional lands in order to make room for the two colonatos. These displaced individuals were often moved into areas already occupied by other Africans, thereby compounding the negative impact of the colonatos.[57] Furthermore, the restriction on African farm labour, according to some critics, prevented Portugal from fulfilling her 'civilizing mission'. For those who believed in such a mission, it was difficult to see how the Africans could be 'benefiting' from contact with the 'more advanced Portuguese civilization' when the law prevented the two races from working on the land together.[58]

Portugal never wavered from an indefatigable defence of the multiracial policy she claimed to pursue in Africa. Yet by 1960, with the exception of ten African assimilado farmers at Matala (none of whom was originally from the Matala area), Cela and Matala were really European colonatos.[59] Instead of contributing to the fulfilment of Portugal's 'civilizing mission', these colonatos had further segregated Angolan rural society and exacerbated the Africans' resentment of white settlers.

It is almost ironic that South Africa, following its invasion of Angola prior to independence, established its northern headquarters, supply base, and medical treatment centre at Cela. From November 1975 to 21 January 1976, when the MPLA captured Cela, the former colonato was the scene of some of the fiercest fighting in the war, which left most of the structures in the area destroyed.[60]

The Angolan Provincial Settlement Board, 1961–68

Before the outbreak of the Angolan war in March 1961, there had been discussions in the government concerning the integration of the colonatos, both in terms of bringing in substantial numbers of African farmers as

[57] For a detailed map of the large number of African villages affected in the area of Cela by the location of the colonato, see ibid., p. 243. For further information on this problem, see Ribeiro, 1975, p. 69; Tenreiro, 1964, pp. 57–8; and Oliveira Santos, 1957–8, p. 75. Many Africans were forced to move more than once, such as one African farmer I interviewed in the Cela area who complained that he and his relatives were forced to move seven times to make room for the expanding settlement.

[58] For an illuminating debate between Reis Ventura and Valdez dos Santos on the racial implications of prohibiting Africans from being farmers or workers in Cela, see *1.º Congresso dos Economistas Portugueses*, pp. 343–7. Also see Ponce, 1960, pp. 222–3.

[59] Neto, 1964, p. 220.

[60] It is also interesting to note that it was the capture of four South African soldiers at Cela (in mid-December, 1975), who were displayed in Nigeria before the international media, that prompted South Africa to admit that its alleged 'hot pursuit' along the southern Angolan border actually extended as far north as Cela (over 400 miles from the Namibian border).

well as permitting the employment of African labourers in Cela (which had been prohibited during the 1950s). The war, however, made it imperative that Portugal, determined as ever to remain in Angola, racially integrate the colonatos if it intended to expand the planned settlement programme.

The inclusion of Africans in the rural planned settlement programme had an economic as well as political rationale. African agricultural productivity had been in decline before the war for a variety of reasons attendant to their traditional patterns of shifting cultivation and aggravated by European confiscation of their lands in some areas. This decline, in addition to the extremely low prices paid for their agricultural products, forced many Africans, especially in the Central Highlands, to migrate in search of work as rural labourers. A number of Africans actually left Angola for more remunerative jobs in Zaïre, Namibia, and South Africa.[61] After 1961 a large majority of Africans from the combat areas north of the Cuanza river fled into Zaïre or went into hiding in the bush.[62]

The war provided the most serious challenge to hegemony in Angola that Portugal had ever faced and that challenge required the government to adopt new and imaginative policies, including in the field of rural settlement. After all, Portugal could hardly fight a war against a segment of the African population, continue to spend tens of millions of dollars on European planned settlement in the rural areas, and still maintain that she was pursuing policies aimed at the creation of a multiracial society in Angola for the equal benefit of Africans and Europeans.

The major policy changes came on 6 September 1961, six months after the outbreak of the war. Among the various laws decreed this day were five which were intended to:

(a) repeal the *indigenato* statute, thereby abolishing the distinction between 'non-civilized' non-citizens—more than 99 per cent of the African population—and 'civilized' citizens—which in 1950 included all whites, 89 per cent of the mestiços and 0·7 per cent of the Africans;[63]

(b) increase the regulation of land concessions and occupation;

[61] After a four-month trip to Angola and Mozambique in the mid-1940s while serving as António Salazar's Colonial Minister, Marcello Caetano argued that the depopulation of Angola's interior was attributable to two basic factors: (a) 'the blind selfishness of the Portuguese employers' and (b) the system of forced labour (1946, p. 72). Also see Neto, 1962, pp. 100–3 and Bender, 1972a, p. 349.

[62] The military commander of the Carmona region was quoted as conceding that approximately 500,000 Africans fled into Zaïre or went into hiding in 1961. United Nations, General Assembly, 17 October 1968, Document A/7200/Add. 3, p. 51.

[63] Província de Angola, 1953, pp. 68–9, 89, 109. This was the last year (1950) for which the official census divided the Angolan population into 'civilized' and 'non-civilized' categories.

(c) organize local African administrative bodies;
(d) co-ordinate 'general' and customary laws;
(e) create the Provincial Settlement Board of Angola (and Mozambique).[64]

The decision to establish the Angolan Provincial Settlement Board (*Junta Provincial de Povoamento de Angola*, referred to hereafter as the JPP) and empower it to spend millions of dollars at the very moment Portugal faced her greatest crisis in Angola underscores the overwhelming importance accorded rural planned settlement.[65] The JPP was given the responsibility to supervise and co-ordinate all settlement activities in rural Angola.[66] By rationalizing planned settlement organization and expenditures through the JPP, the government hoped to eradicate many of the problems encountered by earlier planned settlement programmes. Cela (but not Matala) was incorporated into the JPP and the selection process began for new settlement locations.

The JPP also began to look for new types of settlers. One month after the founding of the JPP, General Deslandes (Governor General of Angola during this period) emphasized in an address to the Angolan Legislative Council that the government intended to do everything possible to attract former soldiers to settle in the new colonatos; 'this youth who today defend the land, land which can be their own tomorrow if they want to farm it in peace with the same ardour with which they defend it in war'.[67] Some officials saw this as an excellent opportunity to establish para-military settlements in strategic parts of Angola while others simply viewed the former soldiers as a ready source from which to draw new colonos. While some 'soldier settlements' were established (e.g. Chitado along the southern border with Namibia), the para-military

[64] These decrees (Nos. 43.893, 43.894, 43.896, 43.897, and 43.895, respectively) can be found in the *Diário do Governo* (Lisbon), 1st series, no. 207, 6 September 1961. English translations of the decrees, with the exception of that for the Settlement Boards (No. 43.895), can be found in Coissoro, 1966, pp. 402–12.

[65] Adriano Moreira, 1962, p. 100; and 1961b, pp. 9–10. These are speeches which Moreira gave in Luanda and Porto, respectively, during the first weeks of the war. Also see the opening paragraphs of the Decree-Law No. 43.895 in *Diário do Governo*, 1st series, no. 207, 6 September, p. 1129. Moreira, Minister of the Overseas Territories at this time, was largely responsible for the 1961 colonial reforms.

[66] It must be noted that the JPP was also involved in activities not related to the settlement and maintenance of colonos. However, these activities consumed a minimal portion of the JPP's budget and because this discussion is related only to the settlement programmes, it will not treat any of the JPP's activities which extend beyond this scope. For a comprehensive review of all the activities and expenditures of the JPP, see Jordão, 1969.

[67] Quoted in Jordão, 1969, pp. 15–16. For a description of the colono programme for ex-soldiers, see Junta Provincial de Povoamento de Angola, 1967, pp. 99–103 and Jordão, 1969, pp. 42–4.

aspects were not incorporated into the settlements.[68]

The most important departure from previous planned settlement schemes was the emphasis on racial integration in the new colonatos. The decree which established the JPP called for the creation of fully integrated and stable multiracial communities which, it was argued, would be consistent with Portugal's unique historic mission in Africa. Portugal was determined once again to show the rest of the world, as well as herself, that she was capable of establishing multiracial communities in Angola.

A plan to bring Cape Verdians to Angola as colonos was one of the JPP's first innovations.[69] In part the inclusion of Cape Verdian colonos was intended to alleviate the demographic pressures on the Cape Verde Islands, where there were 826 inhabitants per square mile of arable land in 1960. More importantly, the Cape Verdians—three-quarters of whom are mestiços—had been among the most educated of all of Portugal's overseas subjects and therefore deemed 'civilized' under the native statutes of 1946 and 1954.[70] It was hoped that these individuals, whom the Portuguese considered perfect racial and cultural intermediaries between Africans and Europeans, would help stabilize the multiracial colonatos.[71]

While the new emphasis on racial integration of the colonatos was an important aspect of the JPP's plans, it must be remembered that an increased and stable European presence remained the major purpose of rural planned settlement. Before discussing the results of integrating the colonatos we must first examine the JPP's programmes in light of the number and quality of colonos, especially European colonos, attracted to the JPP colonatos. Prior to the JPP's creation there was a scarcity of concrete data on the individuals brought to settle in Angola's rural planned settlements. Fortunately, however, the JPP kept records on all colonos and ex-colonos in its settlement programme. Thus, the following discussion of the planned settlement schemes in rural Angola, guided by the three criteria for successful settlement set forth in the Introduction, is

[68] In early 1962 the Governor of Huila District, concerned with the possibility that South Africa might establish independent African states in Namibia, proposed a colonato to be built along the border at Chitado. The proposal was accepted and 43 colonos were sent to Chitado, of whom 35 were former soldiers (from the same battalion). By the end of 1963, only 27 of the 43 remained. See Junta Provincial de Povoamento de Angola, 1963, pp. 5, 165. South Africa used Chitado as a major base during its intervention into Angola in late 1975 and early 1976.

The para-military aspects of the soldier-colono programme were dropped principally because of the objection by the military, who viewed the programme as an encroachment on its authority and responsibility.

[69] The plan for bringing Cape Verdian colonos was presented in January 1962. That year 142 Cape Verdian colonos were settled in Angola.

[70] The Organic Law of 1946 (Article 246) exempted the inhabitants of Cape Verde, Macau and Goa from being classified as 'natives' or treated as 'natives' under the native statutes. See Wilensky, 1968, p. 169, note 30.

[71] Interview with Fernando Borges Mouzinho, President of the Junta Provincial de Povoamento de Angola, Luanda, 3 March 1969.

based on a careful analysis of JPP records up to 31 December 1968.[72]

From Table 9 we see that the JPP was faced with the same problem which had affected earlier government attempts to increase European planned settlement. In the period under study, the JPP was able to attract only 1,824 European colonos, of whom less than half remained by 31 December 1968.[73] Since 207 of the European colonos who remained had been admitted to Cela before the founding of the JPP, it can be said that only 633 colonos admitted after September 1961 remained in the colonatos. In fact, a significantly higher proportion of African and Cape Verdian colonos remained than did Europeans.

Among the ex-colonos the Europeans stayed the least amount of time: 64 per cent left within the first 18 months, compared with 43 per cent of the Cape Verdians and 38 per cent of the Africans for the same time period. Thus, with respect to the percentage of those who remained in the planned settlements and the length of time they stayed, the Europeans were the least stable settlers.

A partial view of the quality of those attracted to the planned settlements can be analysed with regard to age at time of admission, number of years of education, and number of dependants. These demographic variables,

[72] In 1968–9, the JPP headquarters in Luanda generously opened its records to me. These records, while not always complete, contained the following information for each colono and ex-colono in the JPP planned settlement programme: sex, birthplace, age, marital status, ethnic origin, education, number and type of dependants, date of entry into the programme, name of colonato in which he was settled, date and reason for departure of those who left the programme (i.e. the ex-colonos). The JPP records included 207 colonos who entered Cela before 1962 but did not include the 122 Europeans who left Cela prior to the founding of the JPP on 6 September 1961. Furthermore, I was unable to see the records of the Matala colonos, since Matala was not incorporated into the JPP.

It is unfortunate that the data on colonos only cover the period up to 31 December 1968. I received numerous promises that I could have all information needed after that date, but the promises and assurances were never fulfilled. It should be noted once again that in this discussion the term colono (or ex-colono) does not include any dependants.

[73] There are some major discrepancies between the figures gathered from the JPP records and those actually published by the JPP. Some of these differences are illustrated below:

	JPP	Author
European and Cape Verdian colonos to 1967	1,869	2,294
European and Cape Verdian ex-colonos to 1967	639	1,125

According to the JPP published figures, only 34 per cent of the European and Cape Verdian colonos left, whereas my figures, based on the same raw data, indicate that the percentage was actually 49 per cent.

The JPP figures can be found in Junta Provincial de Povoamento de Angola, 1967, Table XX, following p. 184; and Jordão, 1969, pp. 78–9. Elsewhere it is argued that the JPP admitted 2,224 colonos through 1967. See 'A batalha do povoamento é tão vasta e complexa como imperiosa', *Actualidade economica* (Luanda) 3 (30 May 1968).

TABLE 9

Number of JPP Colonos and Ex-Colonos (To 31 December 1968) [a]

Origin	Colono	Ex-Colono	Total
European [b]	840 (46%)	984 (54%)	1824 (100%)
Cape Verdian	428 (72%)	166 (28%)	594 (100%)
African [c]	528 (76%)	165 (24%)	693 (100%)
Total	1,796 (58%)	1,315 [d] (42%)	3,111 (100%)

Significant at the 0·001 level in the chi-square test.

Notes:

[a] All of the data presented in the tables and figures in this section cover the period from 6 September 1961 to 31 December 1968, with the exception of 207 (of the 840) European colonos, who entered Cela between 1953 and 1961.

[b] All but 14 of the Europeans are Portuguese.

[c] Although Africans are not emigrants to Angola, they are considered colonos in this discussion when they appear as such in the JPP records. It should be noted that although the JPP claimed to have more than 1,250 African colonos extant in 1968, it had records for only 693. Since the data presented here are taken exclusively from the JPP records, the latter sum is used. Most of the Africans for whom there were no records were located in the large African settlement of Caconda, in the northern part of Huila District.

[d] Of the 1,315 ex-colonos—i.e. those who left the settlements before 31 December 1968 —1,180 left voluntarily, 86 were expelled, and 49 died.

TABLE 10

Colono and Ex-Colono Age at Time of Admission

Age at time of admission	Colono	Ex-Colono	Total
30 or less	485 (28%)	628 (50%)	1,113 (37%)
31–40	578 (33%)	311 (25%)	889 (30%)
41–50	484 (27%)	206 (16%)	690 (23%)
51–60	177 (10%)	86 (7%)	263 (9%)
61 or more	37 (2%)	21 (2%)	58 (2%)
Total	1,761 (100%)	1,252 (100%	3,013 [a] (101%)

Significant at the 0·001 level in the chi-square test.

[a] Because those for whom there was no information have not been included in this and the following tables, the totals do not equal 3,111 as found in Table 9.

presented in Tables 10–12, respectively, underscore a number of distinct differences between colonos and ex-colonos. Table 10 shows that half of the ex-colonos were 30 years old or less at the time they were admitted by the JPP, whereas only 28 per cent of the colonos were in this age group. Moreover, Figure 2, which gives the per cent of colonos (of the total admitted) by each age group illustrates the fact that the per cent of colonos increases proportionately with their age at the time of admission.

FIGURE 2: *Per Cent of Colonos by Age at Time of Admission*

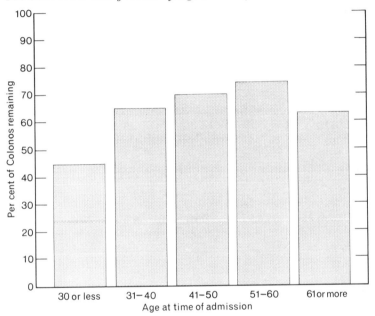

There is a strong relationship between the level of education of the settlers admitted and whether or not they remained in the planned settlements. While 66 per cent of those with no education remained in the planned settlements to 1968, only 43 per cent with one or more years of education remained. It is apparent from Table 11 that nearly three-quarters of those settled by the JPP had never attended school; futhermore these individuals were more likely to remain than those with one or more years of education. While 99 per cent of those with some education had not attended school beyond the fourth grade, simply being literate opened up many opportunities which most of them found more attractive than farming in a colonato. In fact, only one of every three Europeans up to forty years of age and with at least one year of education remained as a colono through 1968. The same trend occurred among Africans in this category, of whom only 46 per cent remained.

TABLE 11

Colonos and Ex-Colonos by Years of Education

Type of Settler	Years of Education		Total
	None	1 or more	
Colono	1,251 (73%)	464 (27%)	1,715 (100%)
Ex-colono	36 (51%)	621 (49%)	1,257 (100%)
Total	1,887 (63%)	1,085 (37%)	2,972 (100%)

Significant at the 0·001 level in the chi-square test.

The total number of dependants in a settler's household was a third factor strongly related to whether or not the colono remained. It can be seen in Table 12 that almost half (600 of 1,267) of the ex-colonos had no dependants. More importantly, of the 775 admitted without dependants, only 23 per cent remained as colonos! The table clearly shows that the probability of a colono remaining was directly proportional to the number of dependants in his household, a pattern which obtained for all three ethnic groups.

TABLE 12

Colonos and Ex-Colonos by Number of Dependants

Number of Dependants	Colono	Ex-Colono	Total
0	175 (23%)	600 (77%)	775 (100%)
1–3	574 (69%)	354 (31%)	828 (100%)
4–6	705 (75%)	231 (25%)	936 (100%)
7–9	276 (79%)	74 (21%)	350 (100%)
10 +	49 (86%)	8 (14%)	57 (100%)
Total	1,779 (58%)	1,267 (42%)	2,946 (100%)

Significant at the 0·001 level in the chi-square test.

Given this pattern and the fact that one of the JPP's goals was to settle stable families in the colonatos, one would assume that only those with dependants would be selected. This was not done, however, especially in the selection of Europeans. In Table 13 we see the percentage of European settlers selected by the number of children in their household. Nearly half of those selected had no children, despite the fact that they represented the smallest percentage who remained.

TABLE 13

European Colonos and Ex-Colonos by Number of Children

Number of Children	Colono	Ex-Colono	Total
0	227	585	812 (46%)
1–3	338	222	560 (32%)
4–6	195	112	307 (17%)
7–9	52	27	79 (4%)
10 +	8	2	10 (1%)
Total	820	948	1,768 (100%)

Significant at the 0·001 level in the chi-square test.

The data presented permit one to question whether planned rural white settlement in Angola was ever viable. We have seen that the Europeans were the least likely of the three ethnic types to stay in the colonatos— less than half of those admitted remained. Furthermore, those who chose to remain were frequently the least desirable as colonos. Irrespective of ethnicity or race, the most likely type to remain was the older, less educated colono who brought dependants with him. In fact, a further analysis of the data shows that 73 per cent of colonos admitted over the age of forty and with no education remained. Lacking the mobility and opportunities of the younger, more educated colonos, their economic and social circumstances left them few alternatives other than the colonatos. Nevertheless, while this group demonstrated a high degree of permanence, they (Europeans and Cape Verdians) experienced the most difficulty in adapting psychologically to the new environment they found in Angola.

On the other hand, those who were more psychologically flexible and physically better equipped to be good farmers in the planned settlements were precisely the individuals who demonstrated the least tendency to remain. Only 22 per cent of the colonos admitted under the age of forty, with some education and few or no dependants, remained in the colonatos. Actually, when viewed within a general perspective of rural-urban migration patterns, this low percentage is not surprising. In most parts of the world today, it is these types of people who are abandoning agriculture and swelling the urban centres.[74]

In addition to the number and quality of settlers who remained in the colonatos, the success or failure of rural planned settlement must also be viewed in terms of the government's stated goal to integrate the settlements. (For the location and ethnic composition of the major planned

[74] For a useful bibliography which encompasses a number of studies on rural migration patterns in Africa, see Silberfein, 1969, pp. 311–18.

settlements, refer to Map 1.) In Table 14 we see that just over a third of the settlers admitted by the JPP were located in multiracial colonatos, while the remainder were placed in homogeneous colonatos (comprised of settlers of the same ethnic group).[75] In other words, during the seven-year period under study, the JPP attempted to settle only 1,116 Europeans, Africans and Cape Verdians in multiracial settlements.

TABLE 14

Number and Per Cent of European, Cape Verdian and African Colonos Admitted and Remaining by Racial Type of Settlement

TYPE OF SETTLE-MENT	Europeans			Cape Verdians			Africans			Total		
	Adm.	Rem.	% Rem.	Adm.	Rem.	% Rem.	Adm.	Rem.	% Rem.	Adm.	Rem.	% Rem.
Multiracial	663	210	32	244	162	66	209	123	59	1116	495	44
Homogeneous	1161	630	54	350	266	76	484	405	84	1995	1301	65
Total	1824	840	46	594	428	72	693	528	76	3111	1796	58

Significant at the 0·001 level in the chi-square test.

The percentage of Europeans who remained in the multiracial colonatos (32 per cent) was considerably less than in the homogeneous colonatos (54 per cent).[76] However, before concluding that the multiracial composition caused the higher rate of exodus, it is necessary to control for the variables (age, education, and dependants) which influenced the difference between colonos and ex-colonos in general. A multivariate analysis of these three variables revealed that, if anything, one would have expected a larger number of settlers to have remained in the multiracial colonatos—which did not occur![77] Thus, we are left to conclude that the racial composition must explain the difference observed. In fact, interviews confirmed that the ethnic groups in the multiracial colonatos did not feel comfortable with each other and, in a number of cases, these feelings bordered on outright hostility.

[75] Three colonatos classified as 'homogeneous' were not literally homogeneous in that they did have small minorities. However, as can be seen below, their minorities were too small in number for the colonato to be meaningfully classified as multiracial.
  1. 4 Europeans and 218 Africans
  2. 2 Europeans and 44 Africans
  3. 36 Europeans and 3 Africans
[76] For a figure illustrating the number and per cent of Europeans, Africans, and Cape Verdians in homogeneous and multiracial settlements, see Bender in Heimer (ed.), 1973c, p. 253.
[77] A detailed discussion of this multivariate analysis is found in ibid., pp. 254–5.

MAP I

Angola: Major Planned Settlements as of 31 December 1968

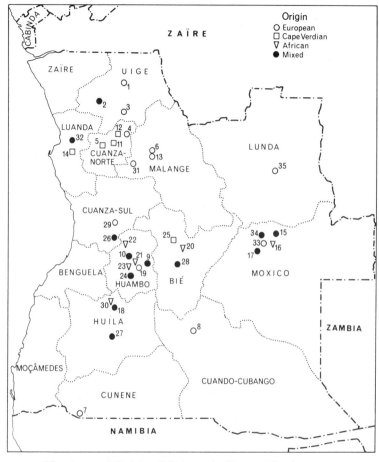

Number and Origin of Colonos in Planned Settlements

10 to 30 Colonos	31 to 60 Colonos	
1. 31 de Janeiro	11. Banga	21. Chinguri
2. Vale do Loge	12. Bolongongo	22. Luvemba
3. Negage	13. Cole	23. Cachaca
4. Luinga	14. Mabuia	
5. Quilombo dos	15. Luxia	**61 to 100 Colonos**
Dembos	16. Caminina	24. Benfica
6. Lutau	17. Sacassange	25. Sande
7. Chitado	18. Lossol	26. Pambangala
8. Missombo	19. São Jorge do	
9. Bela Vista	Cubango	**101 to 300 Colonos**
10. Atuco	20. Missene	27. Matala
		28. Chicava

301 to 600 Colonos
29. Cela
30. Caconda

Abandoned
31. Cacuso
32. São Nicolau
33. Moxico
34. Luangrico
35. Henrique de Carvalho

The most striking feature of the nine multiracial colonatos established by the JPP is the high correlation (r = 0·66) between the number of African colonos admitted and the number of Europeans who left. In Table 15 we see that practically all of the Africans (92 per cent) were located in only four of the nine multiracial colonatos—Chicava, Luxia, Atuco and Sacassange.[78] Yet it is precisely in these four colonatos where the Europeans manifested the least tendency to remain (an average of less than 17 per cent). In the other five multiracial colonatos, where Europeans showed a much higher commitment to remain (61 per cent), only one—Pambangala—admitted more than two African colonos.

TABLE 15

Number and Per Cent of European, Cape Verdian and African Colonos Admitted and Remaining in Multiracial Settlements

SETTLE-MENT	EUROPEANS			CAPE VERDIANS			AFRICANS			TOTAL		
	Adm.	Rem.	%Rem.	Adm.	Rem.	%Rem.	Adm.	Rem.	%Rem.	Adm.	Rem.	%Rem.
Pambangala	92	70	76	—	—	—	12	11	92	104	81	73
Bela Vista	24	15	63	3	3	100	1	0	0	28	18	64
Benfica	22	17	77	104	62	60	1	1	100	127	80	63
Lossol	23	11	48	69	41	59	2	0	0	94	52	55
Vale do Loge	67	25	37	6	5	83	1	0	0	74	30	41
Chicava	186	41	22	8	5	63	97	66	68	291	112	38
Luxia	97	11	11	20	17	85	57	32	56	174	60	34
Atuco	63	18	29	—	—	—	11	3	27	74	21	28
Sacassange	89	2	2	34	29	85	27	10	37	150	41	27
Total	663	210	32	244	162	66	209	123	59	1,116	495	44

Given the JPP's original intention to utilize Cape Verdians to facilitate the integration of Africans and Europeans, it is surprising that only 41 per cent of the Cape Verdians were actually settled in seven of the nine multiracial colonatos. Furthermore, of these seven, only three admitted more than two African colonos—Chicava, Luxia, and Sacassange; the very colonatos from which, as noted above, most of the Europeans left. Thus, the placement of the Cape Verdians in the planned settlements was so limited that practically no opportunity existed for them to fulfill the expected role of racial intermediaries, even had they been capable of such.

[78] Angolan Defence Minister, Iko Carreira, explained to the noted British author Basil Davidson in 1970 why the MPLA decided to spare two of these colonatos (Luxia and Sacassange) from attack:

We've let them be, we haven't touched their cattle. They don't bother us. Even our population doesn't really have anything against them. After all, they're poor folk. They go barefoot, they've no wealth to spare, and actually their lands belong to no one else. Besides, they grow useful things. (Quoted in Davidson, 1972, p. 45.)

From the very beginning the plan to bring in Cape Verdian colonos was fraught with problems. When the programme was initiated in early 1962, there was no preliminary co-ordination or co-operation between the Angolan and Cape Verdian officials. The Governor General of Cape Verde, who had not been consulted previously, viewed the programme as a usurpation of his authority. Apparently the Cape Verdian officials manifested their objections by selecting as colonos the least qualified people on the islands.

For many years well over 90 per cent of all Cape Verdians had received at least primary education; yet more than three-quarters (77 per cent) of those sent to Angola as colonos had never attended school! The 1962 law authorizing the inclusion of Cape Verdian colonos prohibited the selection of any Cape Verdian over the age of forty-five; yet the average age of the Cape Verdian colono was forty and 19 per cent of them were older than forty-five (including six in their sixties and one man in his seventies). In fact, fourteen of the initial ninety-three Cape Verdians settled in one colonato (Benfica) had to be repatriated within the first month because they were either too old or too sick to work as farmers. Finally, the Cape Verdian colonos brought a large number of dependants with them to Angola (an average of five per colono).

These factors help to explain why so few of the Cape Verdian colonos voluntarily left either the multiracial or homogeneous settlements.[79] Their lack of education, older age and large number of dependants severely limited their mobility, increasing the difficulty of returning to Cape Verde or moving to another part of Angola. Even had they desired to return to their homeland, none possessed sufficient property in Cape Verde to sustain their families.

Despite the fact that a significantly higher percentage of Cape Verdians than Europeans chose to remain in both types of colonatos, their presence generally had a negative influence on race relations in rural Angola.[80] The records of the JPP were replete with cases of the anti-social behaviour of a large part of the Cape Verdian colonos towards non-colono neighbouring Africans as well as towards their fellow colonos.

One example of this problem occurred in the colonato of Benfica, located in Huambo District, which was occupied largely by Cape Verdians and some Azorians. Relations between Cape Verdian colonos and neighbouring Africans became so strained that in 1968 the Governor of Huambo District and the Chief of the Military Cabinet confidentially reported their concerns that the nationalist movements could take

[79] In fact, of the 166 Cape Verdian ex-colonos, only 97 voluntarily chose to leave, while 44 were repatriated because of health or age, 19 were expelled, and 6 died.

[80] Sociologically it is not surprising that the Cape Verdian colonos in Angola, the majority of whom were unskilled, illiterate mestiços, would manifest antipathy towards Africans in their attempt to identify with the ruling white sector.

advantage of the situation by infiltrating agents to politicize the Africans in the area of Benfica.[81]

Field reports from colonatos containing Cape Verdians frequently characterized these colonos as individuals with little or no inclination to work the farms or ranches given them. Instead, many of them were often found gambling, drinking or brawling. One official of the JPP complained that the sale and consumption of alcohol in the large Cape Verdian colonato of Sande had become very widespread and that not only fist fights but knife fights were a common occurrence.[82] In Moxico District, the JPP regional head nearly died from knife wounds inflicted by a Cape Verdian colono.

The fact that Cape Verdian colonos did not seem inclined to work the farms given them may not have been completely their fault, especially since, according to the JPP President, the majority of these colonos had been fishermen in Cape Verde.[83] Furthermore, they were not always given lands in Angola conducive to agricultural activities, nor did they receive adequate technical advice concerning the utilization of the soils on their farms.[84]

From nearly every perspective, the Cape Verdian experiment was disastrous for the rural planned settlement programme. From their selection and their abilities as farmers to their role as racial intermediaries and their social behaviour, Cape Verdian colonos were generally failures. Regardless of where the blame for their failure can or should be placed, the JPP did recognize the futility of its innovation and in 1968 ceased all recruitment of new Cape Verdian colonos.[85]

It was suggested in the introduction to this chapter that for planned rural settlement to be considered successful, significant advances would have to be verified in terms of: the establishment of a meaningful Portuguese presence by means of European colonos, economic development in the areas of the planned settlements, racial integration and understanding

[81] Letter from Colonel Aires Martins to Provincial Secretary for Rural Development, Luanda, 19 May 1968 and letter from Governor José Pedro Queimado Pinto to Chefe da Repartição do Gabinete do Governador-Geral, Luanda, 29 August 1968.

[82] The details of this situation are contained in a letter to the JPP headquarters in Luanda from Horácio M. Nunes Quaresma, Chefe da Brigada do Planalto Central, 21 June 1966.

[83] Interview with Fernando Borges Mouzinho, President, JPP, 3 March 1969.

[84] In August 1965 twenty-six Cape Verdian colonos from the colonato of Lossol sent a letter to the Governor General of Angola in which they complained about conditions in Lossol. Among their complaints were: they didn't know how to farm the land they were given nor had they received adequate technical advice from the JPP; their lands were full of trees but only one tractor was available to help them clear the lands; they were 45 kilometres from the nearest health station and had no means of transportation; there was no water in the colonato; and, finally, that one JPP adviser in the colonato treated them 'worse than Africans'.

[85] In answer to a request from a Cape Verdian colono in Moxico District, Borges Mouzinho indicated in a letter (2 October 1968) that the JPP was no longer recruiting Cape Verdian colonos.

both within the planned settlements as well as between the colonos and neighbouring Africans. In fact, these were the JPP's major objectives. We find once again, however, that the government was unable to fulfil its grandiose plans.

For example, by 1968 the JPP could only claim 840 European colonos within its planned settlement programme in rural Angola. In a country twice the size of France or fourteen times larger than metropolitan Portugal, with a population of more than 6 million, the addition of 840 colonos might have been a perceptible increase in the number of European farmers but certainly did not represent a meaningful increase in the overall Portuguese presence in rural Angola. This becomes even more apparent if we separate the colonos actually present in the colonatos in 1968 into two groups—Cela and non-Cela. In Table 16 we see that almost three-fifths (494 of 840) of all European colonos were located within the area of Cela. Therefore the JPP was responsible for settling only 346 European colonos in colonatos other than Cela.

TABLE 16

European Colonos in Cela and Other Planned Settlements (1962–68)

Settlements	Admitted	Remained	% Remained
Cela	685	494	72
Others	1139	346	30
Total	1824	840	46

The breakdown between Cela and non-Cela colonos provides another perspective on the presence of European colonos. Less than one of every three colonos admitted to settlements outside Cela chose to remain. One strongly motivating factor behind the creation of the JPP was to reduce the cost of European planned settlement below that which Cela had incurred during the 1950s. The JPP may have succeeded in lessening the expenditures for planned settlement but the fact that only 30 per cent of the European non-Cela colonos remained indicates a major failure to establish inexpensive planned settlements, especially when compared to the 72 per cent who remained in Cela.

On the other hand, Angolan and Portuguese officials argued that since many of the ex-colonos remained in Angola through the JPP's efforts, the overall white population had been increased.[86] While this does not

[86] This was the position expressed by the following officials during interviews with the author: J. M. da Silva Cunha, former Minister of the Overseas Territories and Defence; Lt. Col. Rebocho Vaz, Governor General of Angola (until October 1972); Fernando Borges Mouzinho, former President of the JPP; Fernando Couto e Silva, former Vice President of the JPP.

address itself to the apparent inability of the government to create a meaningful Portuguese presence in the rural areas of Angola through planned settlement, it does raise an important point. There are no figures indicating the number of European ex-colonos who remained in Angola, but it was almost certainly a majority. Immediately after abandoning the colonatos, a number of them petitioned the government for larger land concessions outside the structures and demands of the JPP.

Since the government of Norton de Matos, more than half a century ago, the land laws presumably guaranteed Africans five times the amount of land they actually cultivated in a given year (in order to take into account their shifting cultivation practices). In reality, however, interpretations of the designation 'cultivated lands' were often in dispute and the law was rarely respected. This led to the concession of many 'legally protected' African lands to Europeans and consequently contributed further to the decline of African agriculture. Ex-colonos, along with other Europeans desirous of these African-held lands, were the main beneficiaries of flagrant misinterpretations of the land laws. Another segment of ex-colonos who remained in the rural areas set up trading posts which, in some cases, they had actually established while still colonos.

Most of the ex-colonos who did not leave Angola migrated to the major cities, especially Luanda. While a few found the skilled jobs (e.g. mechanics or shoemakers) they had once held in the metropole, the majority swelled the ranks of the urban unemployed or underemployed, competing with Africans for the unskilled positions which the latter historically occupied. As a result of this direct competition between European ex-colonos and Africans in both urban and rural settings, the building of a multiracial society in Angola was clearly inhibited, although it is undeniable that the number of ex-colonos contributed to an increase in the overall European presence. Most officials generally viewed the increase as intrinsically good but some officials and business leaders in Angola began to question this position a few years before the April 1974 change of government.[87]

The economic productivity of the rural planned settlements is another important dimension of the general success or failure of the JPP's

---

[87] A conference on settlement held in Luanda in October 1970 was attended by most of the major government and business leaders. While most of the speeches still paid homage to the overriding importance of increasing white settlement, some of the more enlightened did suggest that white settlement should be conditioned by the employment opportunities available. See: 'Congresso de Povoamento', *Actualidade económica*, no. 266 (15 October 1970), pp. 24–9; *Revista de Angola*, no. 225 (15 October 1970) and no. 226 (30 October 1970), *passim*. This position was stated even more forcefully by the former Deputy to the National Assembly and present editor of the influential newspaper, *Expresso*, Pinto Balsemão, who argued that it was not in Portugal's interest to send more unskilled workers to Africa since there were already too many there, and they merely occupied positions which Africans could have filled. 'O tom do futuro', *Notícia*, 57 (9 October 1971), p. 57.

programme. In viewing the colonatos' overall production, it is once again useful to distinguish the settlements within Cela from all others. A study of the annual JPP reports from 1964–67 reveals that the average annual gross income of each colono family outside Cela was less than $300 per year! Within Cela, the gross annual average was $2,800, or almost ten times greater than that in non-Cela colonatos. The JPP did not provide the net income nor sufficient information to determine this figure. It can be said, however, that while the JPP colonatos received a large share of the overall investments made in the rural development sector, they contributed an infinitesimally small percentage to overall agricultural production. For example, in 1967 colonatos contributed the following percentages of production: coffee (0·4 per cent), cotton (1 per cent) and wheat (2 per cent).[88] Only in the case of milk and its by-products (i.e. cream, butter, yogurt), most of which came from Cela, did the colonatos make a substantial contribution to overall agricultural production and processing in Angola.

The multifarious economic ramifications of rural planned settlements in Angola can be illustrated and analysed through a detailed examination of a sample of individual settlements. Two of the eight regional departments (*brigadas*) of the JPP were located in districts which were the most intensive battle zones during the war: Uige District in the north and Moxico District in the east. In Uige, the three colonatos (Vale do Loge, Negage and 31 de Janeiro) and fifteen or so isolated farms under the JPP's jurisdiction were located on lands utilized by Africans before the war (31 de Janeiro was actually founded on the site of the former large African settlement of Damba which had been established by the Agricultural Department in the early 1950s in order to 'modernize' African agriculture). As occurred throughout most of Uige District, these lands were abandoned by Africans in the early days of the war. Shortly thereafter the government embarked on a programme to attract and resettle Africans who had fled. It was decided, however, to settle former European soldiers and some Cape Verdians in the areas of the three colonatos, rather than the original African landholders. Some Africans were allowed to return to these areas, but as workers for the new occupants rather than as landholders.

More than 350 square miles were set aside for the colonatos in Uige, but only a small portion was actually cultivated by the colonos and their African labourers. By 1969 the JPP had spent close to $1 million on developing the infrastructure and annual operating expenses for the Uige colonatos

[88] These percentages were derived by contrasting the figures supplied by the Bank of Angola and the JPP. See Banco de Angola, 1967, pp. 6–24; Junta Provincial de Povoamento, 1967, charts 21 and 22.

—a large expenditure which did not yield promising results.[89] Out of a total of 193 European and Cape Verdian colonos (including 19 Cape Verdians originally settled in the colonato 31 de Janeiro but who were moved to other colonatos for 'security' reasons), only 75 remained by the end of 1968. In Vale do Loge only 30 of the 100 houses originally built for colonos were occupied. Economically, the colonatos did not live up to expectations. In fact, the production of 31 de Janeiro was so disappointing that most of the 33 colonos were transferred in early 1966 to other colonatos outside Uige District.[90] In the remaining two colonatos the average gross income did not exceed $900 per colono family.

The economic results of the colonatos in Moxico District (Luxia, Caminina and Sacassange) were considerably worse than in Uige. Gross income per colono family averaged about $200 per year through 1968, which undoubtedly helps explain why 70 per cent of the colonos in this district left the colonatos. As noted earlier, the JPP extended monthly subsidies to European and Cape Verdian colonos. Theoretically, these subsidies were provided for the first two years while the individual established himself. The colono was then obliged to pay this money back, but in Moxico the subsidies were continued beyond the two-year period because there was no year in which the *gross income* was greater than the annual subsidy.

Because no data were available for African agricultural production in the areas of the colonatos in Uige and Moxico before the colonatos were established, it was not possible to determine if the production of those areas was greater or less as a result of the colonatos. It is clear, however, that the large investments to develop an infrastructure for the colonatos yielded practically no positive economic results.

The same conclusion can be drawn for the colonato of Chitado along the Namibian border in southwestern Angola, but in this case the economic productivity of the area actually decreased. Chitado was built as a series of three-square-mile cattle ranches, extending approximately ninety miles along the Cunene river and incorporating a large amount of the traditional winter-grazing lands of the local (Vahimba) pastoralists.

---

[89] It is not possible to give a precise figure for the money spent on the colonatos in Uige (or any other region) because many expenditures are not broken down in the published reports. The estimate of $1 million was derived by adding all of the investments and operating expenses found in the JPP annual reports (to 1968) on: on preparation of land, water projects, construction of houses and other buildings, cost of livestock, seeds, plants, fertilizers and insecticides distributed, vehicles and the gasoline and oil used to run them, farm machinery and equipment and the difference between the monthly subsidies paid to each colono and the amount which had been repaid from former subsidies. In some cases I had to estimate the cost of construction and cattle purchased as well as the salaries of the personnel hired by the JPP to work in these three colonatos. One million dollars represents the minimal estimate for the total amount expended on the colonatos of Uige during this period.

[90] JPP, 1967, p. 29. Nine of the 33 colonos chose to remain in the colonato.

Some government officials estimated that African family groups with more than 20,000 cattle moved into Namibia after the colonato was created. All of the colonos hired African herdsmen since a large majority had never tended cattle.

Between 1963 and 1967 the government invested just under $1 million in Chitado, of which approximately $300,000 was spent on the 9,462 head of cattle distributed to the colonos.[91] It was estimated that these investments would yield an annual income of about $1,400 per ranch, but this proved illusory given the actual production.[92] While the colonato had as many as 43 colonos at one time, only 19 remained by the end of 1968. The combined gross income for all Chitado colonos by 1968 was less than $10,000, which did not even cover the cost of the barbed-wire fences. Clearly the large expenditures in Chitado were not only wasted but counterproductive to the economic development of the area, given the departure of the African pastoralists.

Thus far it has been suggested that total investments in the colonatos were both expensive and unjustified in light of the resultant small gross agricultural production. It could be argued, however, that Europeans could not be settled in rural Angola for less money and attain even this level of production. Utilizing data collected by the Angolan Board of Agricultural Surveys (Missão de Inquéritos Agrícolas de Angola— M.I.A.A.), this assertion can be answered in relation to the colonatos' agricultural equipment in Malange District. The average investment in equipment for each colonato farm in Malange was $4,150 compared with only $1,750 for comparable non-colonato farms.[93] Despite the fact that the latter investments were less than half the former, the annual gross production of those farms was almost two-thirds higher than the colonato farms ($1,650 compared to $1,075). From these comparisons it can be seen that the non-colonato European farms produced approximately three times as much for each dollar invested in equipment as the colonato farms.

The pattern of large investments and low economic yields found in the four regional departments discussed above was repeated in the remaining planned settlements in Angola, with the possible exception of Cela. Cela is a special case, however, where the astronomically high costs

[91] The estimate of expenditures is based on the same categories of investments and operating expenses noted in note 89. The expenditure on cattle is found in JPP, 1967, p. 96.

[92] JPP, 1963, p. 169.

[93] M.I.A.A. surveyed six of the seven farms in Malange District in 1963–64 which were the same size as those in the colonatos and which produced the same crops. The survey also included the total investment in equipment on each farm. It is, therefore, possible to compare investments for each farm with those farms within the planned settlements in Malange. In the latter case the number of colonos and gross production were averaged over the period 1964–67. For the M.I.A.A. data see Ministério do Ultramar, 1964a, passim.

of investments began to pay off only in the final years of colonialism in terms of providing European colonos with reasonable incomes.

For the most part, the settlements discussed thus far contained Europeans and Cape Verdians, but it is also necessary to examine the exclusively African colonatos maintained by the JPP. Government planners hoped that the changes introduced into the all-African colonatos would be so dramatic that they would serve as catalysts for change among the general rural African population in Angola. Given this goal it is curious to note that, with minor exceptions, the JPP's African colonatos had been founded years before the actual creation of the JPP. Caconda, which encompassed more than 60 per cent of the African colonos claimed by the JPP, had been established in the late 1940s by the Angolan Department of Agriculture while most of the remaining African settlements—located in the Central Highlands—had been organized by the Angolan Cereal Board in the mid-1950s. In most cases the JPP merely assumed jurisdiction of previously established African settlements and called them all colonatos.

The importance of the JPP's role in claiming responsibility for these settlements can best be understood in light of the situation which motivated the initial African settlement schemes in the 1940s and 1950s. Before the 1961 war African agriculture had been suffering serious set-backs which caused considerable concern among the more enlightened members of the government. The combination of low prices paid for agricultural yields, soils depleted by excessive cultivation of cash crops, and increased European confiscation of choice lands reduced the Africans' annual income and obliged many of the men to look for salaried work in order to sustain their families. A large number of African men in the populous Central Highlands were forced either by these economic circumstances or under the 'contract labour' laws to work on coffee plantations in northern Angola. Many of these African families were thus caught in a vicious circle: as their agricultural production annually decreased, more men left the land to seek employment as rural wage earners; and the more men who abandoned their fields, the more African production declined. While this 'proletarianization' of the African countryside proved beneficial to European planters by providing them with an increased number of cheap labourers, it had a devastating impact on African production.

The African settlement schemes of the Department of Agriculture and the Cereal Board were intended to check this trend and provide Africans with enough aid that they would not be forced to leave their lands. Unfortunately, however, the schemes had only limited success. In the first place, they were opposed by practically all European settlers, as well as many high officials in the government, who feared that noticeable improvements in African agriculture would lead to a reduction in the number of Africans available to work as labourers on European plantations and farms. In the second place, little was known about African socio-economic structures and agricultural systems, let alone how to improve them. As a result, much of the available money during the 1950s was spent on long-overdue studies of the Central Highlands rather than to effect major improvements.

The fact that the JPP was unwilling and/or unable to expand the number of African settlements implies that similar pressures and lack of knowledge were as operative after the war began as before. In addition, the JPP was exceedingly (naïvely?) optimistic about the improvements it intended to introduce into the existing African settlements. Plans called for the expansion of the size of African farms and an increase in technical aid and social services which, it was estimated, would greatly increase African earnings to approximately $600 per year.[94]

Once again, however, the beautiful plans and projections on paper were never transformed into reality, for the JPP was unable to make any noticeably positive impact on African agriculture. In 1967 average gross earnings per African farm in exclusively African colonatos in the Central Highlands were $98. The M.I.A.A. sample survey of African agriculture in the Central Highlands in 1964–65 revealed the same annual average gross earnings for farms which were approximately the same size as those in the JPP colonatos.[95] In other words, Africans who were presumably benefiting from JPP material and technical aid were earning no more than the average of the large mass of African farmers in the Central Highlands, most of whom received no government aid. Furthermore, JPP field reports in 1968–69 indicated that none of the African colonatos received adequate social or educational assistance.

Perhaps an important key to the JPP's inability to raise African earnings above those of the general population was the ethnocentric view of the potential for African development which dominated the thinking of most JPP and other government officials. Essentially they believed that the social and technological levels of Africans found in the African colonatos (as well as of some in the integrated colonatos) were very low and therefore not comparable to the more 'technically equipped' European colonos. Furthermore, it was stated that since the general pattern of African colono farmers was oriented to subsistence agriculture, they sold only part of their production.[96] Consequently, two separate development programmes were established within the JPP: one for Europeans, Cape Verdians, and 'civilized' Africans and another for 'uncivilized' Africans—defined as all inhabitants of the African colonatos as well as a portion of

[94] JPP, 1963, p. 140.
[95] M.I.A.A. survey cited in Carriço and Morais, 1971, pp. 23–4; JPP, 1967, pp. 70–3, 79–80.
[96] JPP, 1963, p. 133.

the Africans in the integrated colonatos.[97] 'Civilized' colonos received the bulk of the available resources under the assumption that they could best absorb the financial and technical aid and would produce the most positive economic results.[98] This priority in the allocations of technical and social aid left nearly all the African colonatos badly neglected so that in many ways the occupants had been better off before they came under the JPP's jurisdiction.

The final criterion for measuring the success or failure of Angolan planned settlement centres on the results of the government's attempt to establish racial integration and understanding, both within the planned settlements as well as between the colonos and neighbouring Africans. It is useful to recall the importance which the government accorded this goal in 1961. During the first months of the war Adriano Moreira, Minister of Overseas Territories, addressed himself to the problem of increasing white settlement:

in clearly affirming the high priority given to the settlement of metropolitans we want to emphasize before the community of nations our national decision to continue the policy of multiracial integration, without which there can be no peace nor civilization in Black Africa.[99]

By 1968, however, the JPP could point to only 123 African colonos in integrated colonatos and these colonos, along with their dependants (553), represented less than 0·0004 per cent of Angola's entire rural African population.

Furthermore, the Europeans whom the JPP selected for these multi-racial settlements had the least desirable characteristics for a successful settlement programme: 40 per cent were at least fifty years old in 1968 and only 37 per cent had received any schooling. More than a quarter (28 per cent) were not from Metropolitan Portugal but from the impoverished islands of the Azores and Madeira. Of those from the metropole itself, 53 per cent came from the district of Bragança, one of the poorest in Portugal.

[97] Ibid., pp. 133–6. Interviews with most top officials of the JPP (including the president and vice-president) revealed curious notions concerning the capabilities of Africans to develop. The essence of their views was that Africans must be slowly brought through various stages starting with hand hoes and then gradually moving to animal traction and finally to tractors and other mechanical equipment. Estimates for the length of this transaction ranged from ten to fifty years. Ironically, the European colonos in Cela did not appear to share this anachronistic view, since most of the tractors in Cela were operated by Africans.

[98] The disparity in expenditures can be seen clearly by comparing the expenditures of the two largest colonatos in the JPP, Cela and Caconda. Each was founded more than two decades ago and comprised areas of approximately 300,000 hectares. Furthermore, each contained about 60 per cent of the European and African colonos in the JPP, although Caconda has several hundred more colonos than Cela. While precise expenditures were not available for total preparation of lands, technical advisors, housing, schools, teachers, health facilities and personnel, it appeared that the government spent at least ten times more on each colono in Cela than it spent in Caconda.

[99] Moreira, 1961b, p. 10.

Similar demographic characteristics were also found among Cape Verdians and Africans settled in the multiracial colonatos. In each group more than half the colonos were over the age of forty and less than 20 per cent had ever attended school. Strangely then, the JPP selected what appears to have been the least likely individuals of all three ethnic groups to adapt to a multiracial situation and, as we have already seen, only 32 per cent of the Europeans and 59 per cent of the Africans chose to remain. Furthermore, these colonatos were among the least economically productive of those maintained by the JPP.

Finally, it must be noted that most of the multiracial colonatos were built on lands formerly occupied by Africans. For example, Pambangala, the only multiracial colonato which could be considered successful in terms of a stable population and reasonable economic productivity, was consciously located on the rich soils of an area which had previously supported hundreds of African families who annually had high agricultural yields. Only a dozen African families were incorporated as colonos; most of the remainder were removed to make room for almost a hundred European colonos. Such shifts of African populations not only affected the families forced to move, but also the families in the areas in which they were relocated as a result of the significant increase in population density. This pattern was generally repeated in the areas of nearly every multiracial colonato, seriously disrupting the lives of thousands of African families in rural Angola. Thus, Portugal's attempt to prove to the 'community of nations' that through its planned settlement programme it could successfully pursue a policy of rural multiracial integration was a colossal failure.

Conclusions

The Portuguese government's attempts to establish planned settlements in rural Angola during the twentieth century were based on a number of premises which, for the most part, were strongly influenced by acutely ethnocentric orientations. First, and foremost, was the conviction that transplanting Portuguese rural peasants and their way of life to rural Angola was both feasible and necessary in order to establish meaningful agricultural development. However, not only did very few Portuguese peasants answer their government's call to settle in Angola's rural planned settlements, but a majority of those who did so abandoned the settlements within a short time after their arrival. In addition, those who remained in the settlements did not reproduce their former life style; even in Cela most of the manual work was performed by African labourers, not the colonos themselves.

The government maintained that its large expenditures on rural white settlement were justified in order to raise the level of agricultural production as well as the cultural and economic level of rural Africans. Neither goal was accomplished through the rural settlement programmes, however, nor was there any basis for expecting that those goals could have been attained were the same policies and programmes continued. In fact, an important study of the most densely populated district in Angola (Huambo) suggests that just the opposite occurred. The study by Carriço and Morais demonstrates that on a *per hectare basis* in Huambo District, traditional African farmers in 1970 earned on the average approximately 20 per cent more than European farmers, $18·00 to $14·50 respectively.[100]

Despite this economic reality, the amount of land conceded to Europeans increased each year while the amount of land held by Africans decreased. Between the years 1968–70 the amount of European-held land in Huambo District more than doubled (from 249,039 to 526,270 hectares), while the area cultivated by Africans was reduced by more than a third (36·5 per cent)![101] This reduction in cultivated land, along with a host of other complicating factors, had a catastrophic impact on Africans in the district. For example, gross income per African farm declined from $98·00 in 1964–65 to less than $35·00 in 1970.[102] Because this drop in earnings had to be supplemented in some way, many African men sought salaried work outside their area, engendering new social and psychological as well as economic problems.

Cruz de Carvalho demonstrated that African cattle herders in southwestern Angola were more productive than their European counterparts who maintained large cattle ranches.[103] Once again, however, Africans were under severe pressures to move off their grazing lands to make room for new European ranches. It is within this context that Portuguese rural planned settlements must be viewed and judged. Every European colonato which was located in rural Angola only exacerbated these harmful effects.

The studies cited as well as mere common sense suggest that the more than $100 million expended on planned rural settlements during the last two decades of colonialism could have engendered infinitely more positive economic results, as well as a general development of the African masses, had the money been spent differently. For example, this sum exceeds the total amount expended on all public education in Angola during most of the twentieth century.[104]

[100] Carriço and Morais, 1971, p. 25.

[101] Ibid., p. 24.

[102] Ibid., pp. 23–4.

[103] Cruz de Carvalho, 1974, pp. 199–225.

[104] The estimate utilized for the amount which the Portuguese government spent on all public education in Angola from the turn of the century to 1968 is less than $95 million. Once again, the exact figure for the money spent is difficult to determine because of a lack of adequate statistics before 1950. The most helpful sources were the following: Samuels, 1967, p. 64; 1970, *passim*; Instituto Nacional de Estatística, 1960, p. 313; Sharman, 1954, p. 4. The $100 million spent on settlement during this period is also approximately equal to the total amount spent on all items in the Angolan budgets during the three-year period, 1950–2, including expenditures on the armed forces. See Sharman, 1954, pp. 4–5.

We have seen that after spending this enormous sum of money Portugal, by 1969, was able to successfully settle only 840 European colonos who, along with their dependants, represented approximately one per cent of the entire European population in Angola. It has also been demonstrated that the small portion of this money spent on African colonos made absolutely no difference in their economic productivity in comparison to Africans outside the colonatos. Finally, we have seen that the plan to include Cape Verdian colonos as racial intermediaries backfired both in terms of racial integration as well as economic productivity.

During the past five centuries and especially since the end of the transatlantic slave trade, Portugal attempted to secure its hegemony and 'develop' the rural sectors of Angola through government-sponsored settlement schemes utilizing Portuguese peasants and unskilled workers. Throughout most of this period the overwhelming majority of the settlers were drawn from among the most undesirable inmates of Portuguese prisons. After the overthrow of the First Republic in 1926 they were replaced by free Portuguese whose level of education and skills barely exceeded those of the degredados. With rare exceptions the settlement schemes were costly economic failures and in many cases the removal of Africans from a settlement area resulted in an actual drop in rural productivity.[105] A combination of paternalism, ethnocentricism, and strategic considerations blinded all but a small handful of officials to the pernicious consequences of these white settlement schemes. After the expenditure of more than $100 million to settle a few thousand Portuguese in rural Angola, the most notable legacy of planned settlement was the introduction of racial competition and conflict over land and production. Not surprisingly, all but a few of the colonos and their families fled Angola during the battles prior to and following independence.

[105] It is of interest to note that the failure of large-scale settlement schemes in Africa is not limited to the Portuguese in Angola, for it appears that similar schemes involving Africans in independent countries have also shown poor results. See, for example, Wilde, 1967, p. 221.

PART III

Racial Domination

Introduction

Until the middle of the nineteenth century, Angola did not have a permanent white population other than degredados who had been condemned to perpetual exile in the colony. The soldiers, civil servants, and traders were all principally concerned with staying alive, making a quick fortune by any available means (usually the slave trade), and returning to the metropole as soon as possible. These circumstances were naturally antithetical to the establishment of a sense of community or the development of a spirit of egalitarianism between the Portuguese and African populations in the colony. In fact, Africans were rarely considered as anything other than chattel to be shipped to plantations on the nearby island of São Tomé or as far away as the New World.

With the cessation of the transatlantic slave trade, the initiation of white settlement in 1849, and the scheduled end of domestic slavery in 1878, Portuguese idealists were encouraged to hope that the sins and errors of the past could be rectified and a new basis found for improving relations between the races. Their hopes were crushed, however, by the avarice of the local Portuguese in Angola, who developed new patterns and mechanisms to perpetuate white minority domination. The major patterns and mechanisms, from the end of slavery until the Lisbon military coup on 25 April 1974, constitute the emphasis of Part III.

The *de jure* abolition of slavery near the end of the nineteenth century was followed by a 'forced' or 'contract' labour system which guaranteed that Portuguese settlers could rely on the Government to provide them with cheap or unpaid African labourers. That labour system was only reformed after 1961, in the wake of the war of independence.

Rum had been the principal item used by the Portuguese as barter for slaves, and the end of slavery did not alter the importance of alcohol in Angolan commerce. In fact, Portuguese wine and spirits constituted the backbone of Portugal's trade with Angola—a commercial activity which benefited both the industrialists of Portugal and the Portuguese in Angola but had seriously negative economic and physical consequences for many Africans in the colony.

With the end of the so-called 'wars of pacification', the Portuguese finally penetrated the Angolan interior, ushering in an era of intensive cultural contact which bred new systems of racial differentiation and exploitation. For example, the introduction of the *indigenato* system, whereby all Africans were considered 'uncivilized'—and therefore legally second-class citizens—if they were not judged to have totally adopted the (ideal) Portuguese style of life, merely codified a pattern which had been routinized over the centuries. The movement of Portuguese into the Angolan hinterlands also set off sustained competition between whites and blacks over land, since it has been axiomatic in Angola that the most fertile lands and salubrious zones are always occupied. European expropriation of African lands and large labour migrations provoked by the forced labour system caused acute socioeconomic problems for a significant portion of the African population. These major aspects of minority domination from the end of slavery until the war of independence form the substance of Chapter 5.[1]

The war of independence initially prompted a number of long-overdue reforms designed to establish social equality before the law. But even the abolition of the *indigenato* did not spell the end of white minority rule. The war itself engendered new mechanisms of racial domination. For example, as part of the Portuguese counterinsurgency efforts, over one million Africans were forced off their land and moved into large, 'protected' settlements, further exacerbating the disruption and destruction of traditional African socioeconomic patterns. This policy was widely debated throughout the war within the armed forces and the colonial Government, as military and civilian officials sought to balance the often irreconcilable goals of developing and controlling rural areas. These debates, the actual programmes adopted, their impact on the rural peasantry and the Angolan economy in general, and the implications of large-scale resettlement as a counterinsurgency or development strategy, are analysed in Chapter 6.

[1] The discussion of the major patterns and mechanisms of white domination from the end of slavery to the war of independence in Chapter 5 is necessarily brief because: (1) they are discussed elsewhere throughout this study—especially in the concluding chapter and (2) the aspects of forced labour, land expropriation, the *indigenato*, and *assimilado* status are already extensively documented in numerous books and articles in English and Portuguese. The chapter is therefore intended to provide continuity with the rest of this study by giving a general outline of the period while introducing some new evidence and insights.

CHAPTER 5

Realities of the 'Civilizing Mission': From the End of Slavery to the War of Independence

Western peoples are only capable of giving the African races cloth to dress themselves, spirits to inebriate themselves, and powder to exterminate themselves.

Oliveira Martins (1880)[1]

Introduction

Thus far this discussion of the Portuguese presence in Angola has principally emphasized the European component: Portuguese colonial theories, miscegenation practices, reliance on convict settlers, and the costly—and generally futile—attempts to attract free settlers into planned agricultural settlements. It has been demonstrated that, with rare exceptions, the Portuguese who arrived in Angola lacked the background, preparation, and motivation to fulfil the lofty expectations of Lisbon's colonial theorists. The analysis in the present chapter stresses the contradictions between the infamous 'civilizing mission' and actual colonial practices from the end of slavery until the war of independence.

As early as 1575, when Paulo Dias de Novais arrived in Luanda, Portugal's proclaimed ideal of converting and civilizing Africans with love was all but forgotten. In that same year Padre Garcia Simões sent a letter from Luanda to the Jesuit Provincial in which he argued that arms were necessary to conquer the Africans since 'almost all have verified that the conversion of these barbarians will not be attained by love'.[2] From Dias' first campaigns in 1579, until the 1920s, Padre Simões' attitude

---

[1] Oliveira Martins, 1887, p. 287.
[2] The letter of Padre Garcia Simões was sent 20 October 1575 and can be found in Brásio, 1953, pp. 129–42. The quote can be found on p. 142.

prevailed and hardly a year passed when Portuguese troops did not conduct at least one campaign against Africans in Angola.[3]

Prior to the second half of the nineteenth century, most of the battles between Portuguese and Africans revolved around the slave trade, but following the Berlin Conference in 1885 Portuguese attacks were principally motivated by desires for territorial conquest and the subjugation of the African peoples. Portuguese attacks and African counterattacks in the late nineteenth and early twentieth centuries—euphemistically called the 'wars of pacification'—began in the south against the proud Ovambo, who battled for more than a quarter of a century.[4] The wars spread to the Bie Plateau in 1902, when the normally pacific Ovimbundu revolted against labour conditions, the rum trade, and Portuguese interruption of the rubber trade.[5] Finally the Portuguese engaged the Dembos in the north in their most difficult campaign, which endured until 1920, at which time Portugal could finally claim to have conquered or gained the acquiescence of most Africans in Angola.[6] One of the most important ramifications of 'pacification' for the Africans was that it subjected them to recruitment as forced labourers under the Portuguese labour system which replaced slavery.

From Slave to Forced Labour

The campaign to end all forms of slavery in Angola, initiated in 1836 with the legal cessation of the transatlantic slave trade, persisted for almost half a century. Pressure by those, like the humanitarian statesman Sá da Bandeira, who argued that total abolition of slavery was indispensable for the development of Africa, led to the adoption of a series of anti-slave laws between 1854 and 1858. While these laws did not immediately end all legalized forms of slavery in Angola, they did free some slaves and established 1878 as the final date for abolition.[7] It was thought that the twenty-year period of gradual abolition should suffice for an orderly

[3] Wheeler and Pelissier, 1971, p. 41. Also see: Wheeler, 1969, p. 428. The most detailed account of wars between the Portuguese and Africans in Angola over the past century and a half can be found in Pelissier, 1975, 3 vols.

[4] For accounts of the battles in the south, see Almeida, 1936, passim; Eduardo da Costa, 1906, passim.

[5] Childs, 1949, p. 211; Rodney, 1968, pp. 64–5. The most complete study of this revolt can be found in Christensen and Wheeler, 1973, pp. 53–92.

[6] The most detailed accounts of the Dembos campaigns have been written by David Magno, a Portuguese major who fought in the wars against the Dembos. He originally published a nine-part series in Revista militar, nos. 8–12 (1916) and nos. 1–4 (1917) as well as a book, Guerras angolanas (Porto: Companhia Portuguesa Editora, 1934), pp. 37–106. For further information on these wars of 'pacification', see Silva Rego, 1970, pp. 261–71; Duffy, 1962a, pp. 118–19.

[7] Oliveira Martins, 1887, pp. 187–8, note 2; Duffy, 1967, pp. 7–21; and Junior, A. D., n.d., pp. 76–82. The latter book was published some time after 1965.

transition from slave to free labour on European farms and in the cities.[8]

Sá da Bandeira hoped his legislation would end the practice of 'whites continuing to exploit the service of the Negroes, as they have done for centuries', but whites in Angola were not interested in utopian theories or legislation that presumed Africans to be anything more than beasts of burden.[9] Their incomes depended on cheap labour and if they were to be prohibited from enslaving Africans legally, new methods would have to be found. Their pressure on the Angolan administration to ignore the new anti-slavery legislation was so strong and effective that the administration capitulated and chose not to enforce the laws.[10] In fact, by 1873— only five years before the scheduled end of slavery—the Governor General of Angola advised the King to abandon forever any illusions that the whites would cease exploiting the Africans.[11]

New guises were found under which to continue the old labour practices. For example, the 1875 legislation, supposedly designed to further refine categories of freed slaves, introduced a vagrancy clause which considered all 'non-productive' Africans as 'vagrants' and therefore subject to non-paying labour 'contracts'.[12] The determination of 'productivity' was usually left to local administrators, who had no difficulty finding enough 'vagrants' to meet the settlers' demands for free labour. Legislation abolishing forced labour in 1878 was largely ignored. Finally, a new labour code, promulgated in the closing days of the nineteenth century, established a legal and moral obligation for all Africans to work.[13] Africans found in violation of the ambiguously worded law could be forced to work for the State or private individuals. Such workers were seldom paid and, according to one British diplomat in Angola at the turn of the twentieth century, nobody regarded the contract labourers as anything other than slaves.[14]

[8] In 1850 almost half (6,020 of 12,565) of Luanda's population consisted of slaves. This is roughly the same percentage of slaves as reported by Meneses in the early part of the century when the slave trade was in full force. See Oliveira, M. A. F. de, 1964, p. 9 (of reprint).

[9] Sá da Bandeira, 1873, p. 84.

[10] Duffy, 1967, p. 115; Davidson, 1972, pp. 106–8.

[11] The Governor General's confidential letter to the King, sent 4 June 1873, is quoted in Sá da Bandeira, 1873, p. 68.

[12] Silva Cunha, 1955, pp. 141–2. Some Portuguese officials considered all Africans not contracted as vagrants.

[13] Silva Cunha, 1955, pp. 147–8; Duffy, 1959, p. 153.

[14] The dispatch, sent in April 1902 by the British Consul of the Congo Independent State after he had visited a number of farms in Angola, is quoted in Duffy, 1967, p. 169. Another Englishman, Henry Nevinson, who travelled in Angola a year later, notes the rationalization of one Portuguese official who argued that this form of slavery was beneficial to the slave because it allowed him to come into contact with a higher civilization and afforded him 'a comfort and well-being which would have been forever beyond his reach if he had not become a slave' (1906, p. 54). Nevinson estimated that at the time of his visit about half of the Angolan population lived under some form of slavery. Ibid., pp. 48–9. Also see Davidson, 1972, pp. 125–6.

The blatant exploitation of Africans which the new labour system represented was partially veiled by the pseudo-pragmatism and moral rationalizations offered by the new generation of hard-headed 'colonialistas'—led by António Enes—who came to dominate Portuguese colonial thinking and policies by the end of the nineteenth century. Following Oliveira Martins and others, they believed that Africans were so inferior to the Portuguese that it was futile to attempt to civilize them through education.[15] Enes, and later Mousinho de Albuquerque, argued that the only efficacious means of imparting Portuguese civilization to Africans was through manual labour which, they held, was necessary in order for Africans to appreciate the dignity of work.[16] In addition to the 'benefits' forced labour could bring to Africans, Enes was not oblivious to the benefits which Portugal would accrue: 'If we do not learn how, or if we refuse to make the Negro work and cannot take advantage of his work, within a short while we will be obliged to abandon Africa.'[17]

A few courageous whites in Angola tried to carry on Sá da Bandeira's tradition by speaking out against the new labour policies. For example, Gomes dos Santos condemned his countrymen for cheating Africans out of their labour, and worse, for considering Africans as nothing more than beasts of burden without rights or privileges.[18] The editor of one outspoken weekly, *Defeza de Angola*, continually attacked forced labour even after he and one of his reporters were assaulted by a gang of thugs in Luanda, which resulted in his reporter's expulsion from Angola.[19] A number of assimilado newspapers also joined the attack, condemning not only the forced labour practices but Portuguese 'civilization' itself, which connoted for them little more than the 'sacking, devastating, selling, torturing, killing' of the African populations.[20]

---

[15] While Oliveira Martins did try to defend Africans against Portuguese mistreatment, he also tried to prove that blacks are 'an inferior anthropological type, close to the ape, and barely deserve the name of man'. Employing his 'scientific evidence' he attacked the missionary effort in Africa and rhetorically asked:

why not teach the bible to the gorilla and the ourangoutang, who have ears even though they can't speak, and must understand almost as much as the black, of the metaphysics of the incarnation of the Word and the dogma of the Trinity (1887, p. 285).

[16] Duffy, 1959, pp. 236–42, 365, notes 17–18 and Samuels, 1972, pp. 58–9.

[17] Quoted in Duffy, 1959, p. 239.

[18] Gomes dos Santos, 1903, p. 148. Five years later he wrote: 'Our anti-social policy does not know how to civilize the black, it only knows how to punish him, and punishes as treason that which is merely ignorance.' G. S., 'A situação em Angola', 1908. I assume that 'G. S.' is Gomes dos Santos as the article is written in his style in addition to the fact that he did write for the Holy Ghost Mission's journal *Portugal em Africa* during this period.

[19] Macedo, 1910, pp. 163–5. Macedo, the editor referred to, gives in these pages a fascinating account of how he arrived in Angola and the difficulties he encountered while fighting to end the abuses against Africans.

[20] Wheeler and Pelissier, 1971, pp. 106–8. For an insightful examination of African and mestiço radical journalism at the end of the nineteenth century, see the following studies by Wheeler: 1970, pp. 854–76; 1968, pp. 40–59; and 1972a, 67–87.

The critics' pleas were drowned out by settler demands for more black labourers, and most critics turned their energies and attention to aiding the Republican forces attempting to assume power in Portugal. However, the revolution of October 1910, which established the Republic, did not lead to the anticipated reforms in 'native policies'. The Republican constitution of 1911 maintained the obligation of Africans to work but limited the contracts to two years and prohibited employers from using corporal punishment.[21] The first Republican Governor sent to Angola, Colonel Manuel Maria Coelho, had previously spent many years there, including five as a degredado for earlier political activities. He briefly rekindled the reformers' hopes by expelling eleven Portuguese colonos for violating the new laws regulating contract workers; but after a year of futile attempts to change the well-entrenched system, he resigned in frustration.[22] When the enlightened Governor Norton de Matos first took charge of the government in Angola in 1912, he found 'a system of native labour which, with only rare exceptions, could not be called *free labour*'.[23] While Norton de Matos was able to effectuate some changes, settler reactions after his departure in 1915 led to the re-establishment of nearly all forced labour practices.[24]

The end of the Republic and the rise of Salazar's *Estado Novo* (New State) brought new modifications and refinements to the contract labour laws. Decrees of 1926 and 1928 established new 'native laws' which theoretically abolished the vagrancy clause, but added the stipulation that Africans must work for paid wages during a given period of each year and if they refused to volunteer to work they could be 'contracted' by the State.[25] A 'protection clause' in the 1928 labour code stated that Africans could only be forced to work on services of pressing public interest, but the 'public interest' legally included private white farms, thereby guaranteeing the colonos' supply of cheap labour.[26]

The fifteenth-century Portuguese view that Africans benefited from white subjugation because of the opportunity it gave them for contact with a higher civilization prevailed during the first three decades of Salazar's

[21] Wilensky, 1968, pp. 37–44 and Silva Cunha, 1955, pp. 197–99. For an interesting and more recent account of the still widely debated 'Revolution of 1910,' see Wheeler, 1972c, pp. 172–94.

[22] Norton de Matos, 1944, pp. 26–7.

[23] Norton de Matos, 1926, p. 126.

[24] In a speech before the Angolan Legislative Council on 1 December 1922, Norton de Matos said that the return to forced labour after his departure in 1915 'constituted the greatest error which has been practised in matters of colonial administration in this province' (ibid., p. 128).

[25] Silva Cunha, 1955, pp. 42, 221, 257; Duffy, 1959, p. 319.

[26] Silva Cunha, 1955, pp. 41–2, 201–3; Santa Rita, 1940, pp. 42–3.

In 1921 Norton de Matos passed a decree which forbade the furnishing of forced labourers to private employers, but this was largely ignored and he was bitterly attacked for his insensitivity to the needs of Portugese farmers. See Davidson, 1972, pp. 113–14.

Estado Novo.[27] Africans continued to be regarded generally as subhuman, 'still the savage man of the iron age ... full of simple virtues like any animal'.[28] The role of the white man remained, according to the Minister of Colonies in the mid-1930s, to direct and teach the Africans to work, rather than work alongside them in the fields.[29]

It was difficult to see how Africans would benefit from participation in the Portuguese labour system when as late as 1942 that system guaranteed them payment of less than $1·50 per *month*.[30] For many Africans the only escape from this modern form of slavery was to flee the colony; by 1954 the United Nations estimated that about 500,000 Angolans were living outside the country.[31] This exodus naturally exacerbated the labour scarcity which, in turn, moved the Portuguese to increase their reliance on 'contract' labourers, thereby further worsening economic and social conditions for Africans and thus engendering an even greater exodus. Some officials perceived the vicious circle in which Portugal was caught in Angola but their warnings went unheeded. For example, Marcello Caetano, deposed as Prime Minister in April 1974, looked into African labour conditions in the mid-1940s as Salazar's Minister of Colonies. He stated that the large labour migration was caused by the blind selfishness of Portuguese employers and the system of forced labour which used Africans 'like pieces of equipment without any concern for their yearning, interests, or desires'.[32]

[27] For an example of this fifteenth-century view see the writings of Gomes Eannes de Azurara concerning the arrival of the first African slaves which were brought to Portugal in 1443. Azurara was the private chronicler of the famous navigator Prince Henry, who inspired most of the Portuguese discoveries during the fifteenth century. Azurara, 1896–9, vol. 1, pp. 51,.81–2 and vol. 2, p. 321, note 81.

[28] Maria Archer, 1935, p. 7.

[29] Monteiro, A., 1935, pp. 43–4.

[30] Freitas Morna, 1944, p. 241. More than a decade later the salaries of contract workers 'rose' to U.S. $3·00–$4·00/month. Gaspar, M. da C., 1966, p. 59.
One of the main beneficiaries of the 'contract labour' system was the large private diamond mining company, Diamang. In 1947, for example, approximately 5,500 of Diamang's 17,500 African workers were provided 'by intervention of the authorities' and they received an average of $25·00 per year in combined wages, rations and 'various goods'. By 1954 these wages, etc. 'rose' to $29·50 and after some unrest among the workers the government urged the company to double the salaries of African employees. This increase would have cost the company $410,000 in additional wages but the directors declared the company could not afford it. What they could afford, however, was to pay their stockholders dividends of $4,100,000—ten times greater than the proposed salary increases! See Davidson, 1972, p. 128.

[31] United Nations, 1962, p. 38.

[32] Caetano, 1946, p. 72. Gladwyn Murray Childs, an American missionary who worked for more than forty years among the Ovimbundu, Angola's largest ethnic group, reported in 1949 that 'the constant demand for labour and the means used to supply it have come to constitute the most severe trial which has yet come to the Ovimbundu'. He further noted that their location in the centre of Angola made it more difficult for them to emigrate. Nevertheless, he found thousands of Ovimbundu outside Angola in places as far away as Natal in South Africa and the former French colonies in West Africa (pp. 214–15).

During Caetano's four-month study mission in Angola and Mozambique, he consulted with top officials including the Colonial High Inspector, Henrique Galvão, who was in the process of preparing a full report on labour conditions in Angola and Mozambique. Caetano was sufficiently impressed by Galvão to encourage him to run for the position of Angolan Deputy to the National Assembly.[33] Galvão was elected in 1946 and the following year he delivered the famous 'Report on Native Problems in the Portuguese Colonies' to a closed session of parliament, which led to his downfall and eventual arrest in 1952.[34] In his confidential report to the Assembly, Galvão noted that the scarcity of labour, which concerned Caetano, had reached such catastrophic proportions that

> to cover the deficit the most shameful outrages are committed, including forced labour of independent self-employed workers, of women, of children, of the sick, of decrepit old men, etc. *Only the dead are really exempt from forced labour.*[35]

He argued that the worst aspect of the labour situation was the government's willingness to openly recruit and supply free African labour to the settlers to such a degree that the settlers assumed the government was 'obligated' to provide them with that labour.[36] This echoes Caetano's complaint after his trip the previous year: ' "I need to be given Blacks" is a phrase which I frequently heard from colonos: as if the Blacks were something to be given!'[37]

Despite critical reports by Caetano, Galvão and others, Africans continued to be 'given' to the colonos, who often treated them worse

---

[33] Galvão, 1949, p. 8.

[34] A complete English version of this report can be found in Galvão, 1961, pp. 57–71. Also see Kay, H., 1970, p. 215. Galvão served seven years in prison until he finally escaped. In 1961 he hijacked the Portuguese luxury liner, the Santa Maria, to publicize his various causes against the Salazar regime. Many argue that Galvão's seizing the Santa Maria precipitated the outbreak of the 1961 Angolan war and Duffy described it as 'the symbolic beginning of the end for Portugal in Africa'. Duffy, 1962a, p. 214. Another comprehensive version of the hijacking can be found in Zeiger, 1961, pp. 9–125.

[35] Galvão, 1961, p. 63. Emphasis in original. One reason why Galvão found little support was that almost all Portuguese, including those critics who cited the inhumanity of forced labour, maintained that forced labour was necessary for the development of Angola. As late as 1959 F. B. Pacheco de Amorim, the outspoken critic of Portugal's African policies, argued that forced labour was 'offensive to the dignity and freedom of human beings'. He went on to state, however, that the 'shocking increase' in its usage was understandable since 'the system can not be developed without recourse to it' (1958, pp. 110–11). His defence of forced labour is reminiscent of the nineteenth-century critics of the inhumanity of slavery, such as Oliveira Martins, who maintained that it was, nevertheless, necessary for the development of Brazil.

[36] Galvão, 1961, p. 64. For a moving condemnation of forced labour in Mozambique, see portions of the diary of D. Sebastião Soares de Resende, the first Catholic Bishop in Beira, covering the years 1944–62, cited in Martins, 1974, pp. 12–21.

[37] Caetano, 1946, p. 73.

than their forefathers had treated their animals or slaves.[38] In the case of slaves and work animals, the owner had an interest in keeping his 'property' healthy and strong; otherwise he would have to pay money to replace them. Under the forced labour system, however, the employer cared little if his worker became incapacitated or died, for he could always ask that another labourer be furnished. Galvão reported that the death rate for Africans supplied by the government to certain employers reached as high as 35 per cent during the two-year contract period.[39] As late as 1954 an observer in Angola estimated that almost 10 per cent of the entire African population were 'contract workers'.[40] The forced labour system was only abolished in 1961 after African nationalists attacked the coffee plantations in the north, where the greatest concentration of 'contract workers' in Angola was found.

The Degradation of Alcohol

While slavery and the forced labour system in Angola have been well documented in studies of Portuguese imperialism and colonial exploitation, practically no detailed studies exist on the importance of the alcohol trade between Portugal and her colonies.[41] This trade extended back to the earliest stages of Portuguese contact with Africa and continued until the final days of colonialism. It was a classical example of imperial exploitation by which metropolitan industries reaped enormous profits from selling to the colonies inferior products for inflated prices. The devastating human consequences of the alcohol trade merit further study; the following merely represents the tip of the iceberg.

From the middle of the seventeenth century until the abolition of

[38] For an excellent and strong critique of the forced labour system just prior to its abolition by one of Portugal's leading geographers, see Ribeiro, 1961, pp. 13–14.

[39] Galvão, 1961, pp. 64–5. Concerning the brutality towards the *contractados* (forced labourers), one southern Angolan said that 'it is better go to Mahonda [Namibia] to work because the white man [South Africans] does not beat one there as he does [in Angola] with those on contract'. Quoted in Mendes, 1958, pp. 96–7.

[40] Basil Davidson calculated that there were no fewer than 379,000 contract workers in 1954 (1955, p. 196; and 1972, p. 127). The Portuguese government sent another Englishman to Angola to retrace Davidson's path and interview the same people whom Davidson had spoken to. The result, not surprisingly, was the publication of a pamphlet denying Davidson's charges. F. Clement Edgerton argued that there were only 142,674 Africans on contract in 1953 and 99,771 in 1954. Much of the confusion over precise figures arises from the fact that generally the 'contracts' for both *contractados* and *voluntários* were oral, not written, thereby making it almost impossible to distinguish between the two kinds of workers, as Galvão confirms in his 'Report' cited above. See Edgerton, 1955, pp. 12, 20.

[41] A notable exception is the valuable set of documents compiled by José Soares Martins (published under the pseudonym José Capela), which he prefaces with an excellent introduction. While most of the book is devoted to the alcohol trade's impact on Mozambique, there is a good discussion of the general problem of wine exports to the colonies and a helpful review of legislation which governed that trade in the final years of colonialism (1973, *passim*).

slavery, most Portuguese in Angola who were not involved in the slave trade engaged in the trade of some form of alcohol. For over a century and a half (1660–1830) Brazilian rum was the most important commodity imported into Angola.[42] When the end of the slave trade with Brazil also stopped the importation of Brazilian rum, the Portuguese in Angola turned their attention to the expanding Angolan rum industry. While many officials complained of the ruin and even death which the alcohol trade brought to the African population, as in the case of slavery and forced labour, there was little they could do to curb this invidious commercial activity.

The alcohol trade was not only injurious to the health of the Africans but detrimental to the Angolan economy as well. High profits in alcohol encouraged farmers to grow sugar cane. For nearly a century (1830–1930) sugar cane was the most important European crop in Angola while almost all other European agricultural activities declined.[43] In addition, the Portuguese sought to monopolize the alcohol trade through laws which prohibited Africans from distilling their own fermented fruit drinks.

Alcohol dominated the commercial activities of a large portion of Portuguese, prominent among whom were the degredados.[44] The official yearbook for 1898 reveals that 30 per cent of all Portuguese engaged in Angolan commerce were *exclusively* involved in the wholesale or retail sale of alcohol. This figure does not include the even greater percentage of Portuguese traders in the interior who relied on rum and wine as almost their only item of barter with Africans.[45]

In order to fulfil international treaty obligations as well as to stimulate exports of metropolitan wines, Portugal promulgated a law in 1902 which prohibited the manufacture and sale of rum by Europeans in Angola. While the law did curtail the production of rum by European-owned distilleries, it had little effect on alcohol consumption, since the Europeans merely sold their sugar cane directly to the Africans.[46]

---

[42] See Wheeler and Pelissier, 1971, p. 48 and Duffy, 1959, pp. 256–7. Between 1848 and 1851, a period when few slaves were exported, liquor represented 25 per cent of all Angolan imports. *Almanak statístico da Provincia d'Angola e suas dependências para o anno de 1852*, 1851, calculated from chart, p. 28. This was the first almanac published in Angola.

[43] See Nascimento and Mattos, 1912, p. 17 and Cruz, 1928, pp. 13–14.

[44] In his comprehensive study of Angolan degredados at the turn of the twentieth century, Silva Telles notes that whereas degredados were once 'considered the best traffickers in *black* ivory' during slave times, they shifted their commercial 'talents' to the alcohol trade—selling most of their liquor to Africans (1903, pp. 86–7). The eminent Governor Paiva Couceiro (1907–9) lamented a few years later that while practically no public services were provided to the large African quarter in Luanda, called Ingombotas, there were 21 taverns which sold *aguardente* (firewater), of which 11 were owned by former degredados. Couceiro, 1948, pp. 163–4.

[45] Governo Geral da Província de Angola, 1900, p. 105, chart 1.

[46] Duffy, 1959, p. 256.

Furthermore, many settlers made their own rum on a small scale and used it to 'pay' their African workers, a practice which lamentably survived until the end of colonialism. By the 1920s many observers were convinced that alcohol had brought total ruin to the African population and the economy of Angola.[47] Once again Norton de Matos was among the most outspoken critics, arguing in 1926 that 'the supplying of alcoholic drinks to the natives is the most vile exploitation which has been invented. It is a thousand times more repugnant than slavery of old.'[48]

Norton de Matos and other crusaders against the pernicious effects of alcohol in Angola had to fight not only the interests of Angolan whites but also the metropolitan industries which greatly profited from the export of alcoholic beverages to the colonies. In the same year, 1926, in which Norton de Matos deplored the exploitation which alcohol visited upon Angola, 8,010,000 litres of alcoholic beverages were imported into the colony.[49] The enormity of this trade can be seen more clearly when compared with that of other colonizing powers. For example, during the five-year period 1919–23, 8,972,211 litres of alcoholic beverages were imported into all of the French West African colonies and 16,644,421 litres into all of the former British West African colonies. Since the former French and British West African colonies had approximately five and ten times more inhabitants, respectively, than Angola in the early 1920s, this means that Angola annually imported between *22 and 25 times more* alcohol, on a per capita basis, than was imported into the former French and British West African colonies.[50]

By the mid-1930s the Salazar regime had succeeded in sharply curtailing the production of alcoholic beverages in Angola. Rather than spelling an end to the inebriation of the African population, this action merely passed the profits from Angolan to metropolitan hands. For centuries wine had been a leading export of Portugal, but faced with growing European tariffs during the depression, Portugal had to find new outlets for its precious product and the protected markets of Angola and Mozambique were logical choices. Almost immediately Portuguese wine became Angola's number one import item, a position it maintained until the early 1960s.[51] The importance of this market for the Portuguese wine industry can be seen in the fact that between 1934 and 1969 more than

---

[47] See Cruz, 1928, pp. 13–14 and Barns, 1928, p. 104.

[48] Norton de Matos, 1926, p. 141.

[49] Bullock, 1932, Appendix 8, p. 41.

[50] *Renseignements coloniaux et documents publiés par le Comité du Maroc. Supplement de l'Afrique Français et le Comité du Maroc. Supplement de l'Afrique Française de Mars 1925*, p. 97. I would like to thank Dr. Jennifer Ward for calling this source to my attention.

[51] Between 1959 and 1961, 10 per cent of all Angolan imports were alcoholic beverages (mostly wine), 99·1 per cent of which came from the metropole. Marques, W., 1964–5, vol. 1, p. 131 and vol. 2, p. 734. The only import which occasionally exceeded wines was Portuguese textiles. See, for example, Sharman, 1954, Appendix 5, p. 41. The total cost of importing Portuguese wine from 1958 to 1962 was $62·5 million! Diogo, 1963, p. 133.

two-thirds of all Portuguese wine exports went to Angola and Mozambique.[52]

Shifting from Brazilian to Angolan rum and finally to Portuguese wine as the primary form of alcohol consumed in Angola did not change the devastating effect which the alcohol trade had on the health, morale, and economic activities of the African population.[53] The Portuguese bush trader who monopolized African trade in the interior always preferred to barter the highly profitable alcoholic beverages. In large parts of Angola, Africans were unable to trade their cattle or agricultural produce for anything other than wine. Wherever this occurred, the Africans had little incentive to expand crop production or increase their herds. Thus, the centuries-old dependence on alcohol as the major item of trade in Angola enriched metropolitan interests and brought large profits to bush traders and a number of Portuguese businessmen in Angola; but economic development suffered in both the African and European sectors and alcoholism became one of Angola's principle social problems.[54]

Questions of Land Rights

Before the twentieth century, Portuguese expropriation of African lands was not widespread, since there were few Portuguese in the colony and almost all of them shared a strong aversion to agriculture. This is not to imply, however, that the problem did not exist. For example, nineteenth-century laws governing land concessions (e.g. 1838 and 1865) were ambiguously worded and rarely heeded.[55] They allowed 'unoccupied'

[52] See the speech by Fonseca, F. P. da, 1969. In 1969 Angola and Mozambique imported 86·6 million and 37 million litres of wine respectively. This compares with approximately 70 million litres which Portugal exported to all foreign markets during the same year. United Nations, 1971a, p. 33.

The pattern of Portuguese wine exports dramatically shifted in 1972, when wine exports abroad exceeded those to the African colonies for the first time in decades. This shift in trade patterns resulted from a decree in November 1970 which limited metropolitan exports to the colonies of certain products, the prominent one being wine. See Overseas Companies of Portugal, *Intelligence Report* (June 1973). For more on the background and effect of the legislation curbing metropolitan exports to Angola, see Bender, 1974, pp. 126–8.

[53] J. Bacelar Bebiano points out in 1938 that Portuguese wines completely replaced African-produced alcoholic beverages in parts of Angola and added that 'almost all of the cheap [metropolitan] wines shipped to Africa are consumed by the Africans' (1938, p. 10).

[54] It was not uncommon to find, especially in the south, entire villages drunk on Portuguese wine. In 1969, metropolitan restrictions on the production of alcoholic beverages in Angola were loosened to allow the fabricating of fruit wines. At the same time restrictions were put on the amount of wine which could be exported from the metropole, which effectively transferred a significant portion of the alcohol commerce back into the hands of Angolan whites.

For a classic defence of the policy of increasing wine exports to Angola and Mozambique in order to augment profits for metropolitan industries, and an attack on proposals to allow local fruit wine industries to develop in Angola the year before they were officially approved, see Banco Nacional Ultramarino, *Boletim Trimestral*, 1968,.pp. 44–6.

[55] Santa Rita, 1940, p. 47.

land to be given as concessions to Europeans; but 'occupied' land was interpreted as that land being farmed at the moment in question and did not include those lands lying fallow as part of the Africans' shifting agricultural patterns. Since the definition of 'occupied' land had not been resolved satisfactorily by the time more Portuguese began settling in rural Angola, it was natural that conflict over land rights would increase.

The first major attempt to legally dispossess Africans of their land came in 1907 with a decree which allowed fixed zones to be set aside for the exclusive use of Africans.[56] The practical result of this decree was to provide Europeans with a legal vehicle for taking over the choice plateau areas in rural Angola. The renowned High Commissioner Vicente Ferreira was only one of many who argued that Africans should be moved from the plateau areas to the hot and humid zones where 'whites showed little desire or capacity to settle'.[57] Between 1912 and 1932, 98 square miles of land were set aside for 'native reserves' and four square miles were given (with titles) to individual Africans.[58] During the same period over twice as much land (242 square miles) was given to 198 foreigners and fifteen times as much (1,563 square miles) was given as land concessions to Portuguese settlers.

The grandiose schemes of Ferreira and others for creating large-scale native reserves were never implemented, largely because Europeans could obtain land almost anywhere they desired. If Africans resisted, they were simply forced off their lands. Childs cites numerous instances of the forced removal of Africans from the Central Highlands between 1941 and 1944.[59] Ironically, a few years later many European land concessions in the Central Highlands reverted to the State as a result of the owners' failure to meet certain requirements, especially that of cultivating a specified percentage of the land.[60] The intensification of European settlement in the Central Highlands during the 1950s, however, renewed European land hunger and the expropriation of African lands reached crisis proportions by the end of the 1960s.[61]

---

[56] Ibid., pp. 47–8.

[57] Ferreira, 1954a, pp. 48–50. Ferreira also argues here that such reserves did not impose segregation on Angola because separation between Africans and Europeans was already in practice in Angola 'as a result of the repugnance felt by certain native tribes for the proximity of whites'. Also see: Ferreira, 1933, p. 116; Barreiros, 1929, pp. 27, 34; Dias, M. da C., 1913, pp. 9–10, 22–9.

[58] *Angola: relatório da repartição dos serviços de cadastro e colonização*, 1935, pp. 12–13. The legislation covering these native reserves can be found on pp. 14–15. I have converted the areas of land from hectares to square miles.

[59] Childs, 1944, pp. 2–4.

[60] Childs, 1949, pp. 216–17.

[61] For a discussion of the economic consequences of expanded white settlement in the Central Highlands, see Carriço and Morais, 1971, pp. 23–5 and *passim*, and Possinger, 1973, pp. 32–52.

Farther south on the Huila plateau most of the best African agricultural land had been appropriated much earlier by Portuguese settlers, since it was an area of early and intensive colonization. Thus, by the 1950s African agriculture on the Huila plateau was in serious decline, a problem which was only exacerbated by the widespread contracting of Africans to work on Portuguese farms, industries, road construction and other public work projects.[62]

Few land problems had occurred in the eastern districts by the 1950s because of the negligible size of the white population, but serious problems did exist in the northern districts (Uige and Zaïre), principally in the coffee and palm areas where there were already 7,000 Portuguese settlers, many of whom were occupying lands traditionally held by Africans.[63] Only three years before the outbreak of the 1961 war in northern Angola, one Portuguese observer reported that many Africans in this area were convinced their lands had been stolen and he warned that trouble could result unless the practice were altered.[64] But even after the war had begun, the expropriation of fertile African lands continued. In fact, in the early 1970s there were more European requests for land than at any other time in Angolan history.[65]

Restoration of the 'Civilizing Mission' Under the New State

The alleged justification for Portuguese colonization in Africa was to bring civilization to Africans. Yet during the first four and a half centuries of Angolan colonization, the Portuguese treated the Africans as little more than a resource of unpaid labour. The overthrow of the Republic and the rise of Salazar's New State rekindled interest in carrying out Portugal's 'historic mission'—the transformation of Africans into Portuguese.[66] The blueprint for this mission was contained in the *indigenato* system incorporated into the New State's colonial policy. Ostensibly intended to protect the interests of Africans, the *indigenato* explicitly set up a regime of social and political inequality by dividing the population into two separate juridical categories: *indigena* (also referred to as uncivilized, unassimilated, or native), which included all Africans and

[62] Urquhart, 1963, p. 137.

[63] Província de Angola, 1953, pp. 68–70.

[64] Santos, O., 1957–8, p. 80.

[65] It is of interest in this regard to note that land distribution was one of the first major questions addressed by the governing Angola Junta after the April 1974 coup. The Junta set up a land commission in mid-October 1974 to survey all land occupation in each district, regardless of the legality of such occupation. *BBC Summary of World Broadcasts* ME/4733/B/4 (19 October 1974).

[66] The first Colonial Minister of the New State, Armindo Monteiro, was among the strongest believers and most vociferous propagandists for the civilizing mission in Africa. See, for example, n.d., p. 108. A more complete discussion of the contradictions in the Portuguese 'civilizing mission' can be found in the concluding chapter of this book. Also see Chapter 1.

mestiços not adjudged to be civilized; and *não-indígena* (or civilized), which included all whites and *assimilados* (mestiços and Africans considered civilized).[67]

Officially it was possible for any African or mestiço to be classified as an *assimilado* (*não-indígena*) and thus achieve the same legal status as a European. To qualify for the classification, however, the individual had to be eighteen years old, demonstrate the ability to read, write, and speak Portuguese fluently, earn wages from a trade, eat, dress, and worship as the Portuguese, maintain a standard of living and customs similar to the European way of life, and have no record with the police.[68] The leaders of the New State ubiquitously believed that the assimilation process would take centuries. Armindo Monteiro, speaking as Colonial Minister in June 1933, warned the First Colonial Governors Conference:

> We don't believe that a rapid passage from their African superstitions to our civilization is possible. For us to have arrived where we are presently, hundreds of generations before us fought, suffered and learned, minute by minute, the most intimate secrets in the fountain of life. It is impossible for them to traverse this distance of centuries in a single jump.[69]

Since the implantation of 'modern civilization' in Portugal was not complete after centuries of contact with the western world, it is not surprising that Salazar, Monteiro, and others could believe that the same process would take at least as long in Africa, if not longer.

For those persuaded that it would take centuries to civilize Africans, the small number of *assimilados* in Angola was natural and expected; for others, concerned with the rapid integration of Africans into the modern sector, the dearth of African *assimilados* was shocking. The actual number of *assimilados* in Angola at the time of the 1940 and 1950 censuses (the only two censuses which divided the population into 'civilized' and 'uncivilized' categories) is open to serious question. Normally, the decision as to whether an individual qualified as an *assimilado* was arbitrarily determined by local administrators (*chefes dos postos*)—the same individuals who were often responsible for providing 'contract labourers'. Since *assimilados* were not subject to be 'contracted', there was a clear incentive to attain this status, but it was not uncommon for local administrators to deny 'qualified' Africans the *assimilado* status in order to maintain a large repository of potential contract workers. Furthermore, *assimilados* were subject to higher taxes and military conscription, which

[67] Wilensky, 1968, pp. 129–50; Duffy, 1962b, pp. 160–5; Marques, 1964, vol. 2, pp. 86, 227–9; and Wheeler and Pelissier, 1971, pp. 130–6.

[68] For descriptions of the qualifications required for the classification of 'civilized' or *assimilado* see: Lemos, 1941, pp. 49–52; Moreira, 1956, p. 465; and 1955, pp. 22–3.

[69] Monteiro A., 1935, pp. 108–9. Also see Salazar, A. de O., 1968, p. 272.

Portuguese officials and scholars indefatigably offered as the explanation for the low number. It is unlikely, however, that more than a few thousand Africans chose not to accept the status because of these obligations.[70] Nevertheless, even if the number of Africans who could have qualified were double or even triple the official number of Africans legally considered to be 'civilized', the total would still have represented an infinitesimal fraction of the overall African population, as can be seen in Table 17.

TABLE 17
Angolan Population by Race and 'Civilization Status', 1940 and 1950[71]

Race	Total Population	Total 'Civilized'	Per Cent 'Civilized'
1940			
a) African	3,665,829	24,221	0·7
b) Mestiço	28,035	23,244	82·9
c) White	44,083	44,083	100·0
1950			
a) African	4,036,689	30,089	0·7
b) Mestiço	29,648	26,335	88·8
c) White	78,826	78,826	100·0

The principal reason for the small number of *assimilados* in Angola by the middle of the twentieth century is that few Africans had access to the institutions which could impart Portuguese civilization.[72] In fact, Angola had scarcely any institutions which could contribute to the 'civilization' of either Africans, mestiços, or Europeans. Less than 5 per cent of all children between the ages of five and fourteen were enrolled in school in 1950, while 97 per cent of all Africans fifteen years and older were classified as illiterate. Two years later, there were only 37 high school graduates in the entire colony, most of whom were white.[73] The low priority which education was accorded is blatantly

[70] Moreira, 1956, pp. 464–5; 1961c, pp. 140–1; and Coissoro, 1961, p. 79.
Gwendolen Carter, among others, has argued on the contrary that the number of *assimilados* was inflated by the inclusion of wives and children of *assimilado* men who would not have qualified on their own. She therefore estimates that there were no more than 8,000 to 10,000 Africans who were 'true assimilados' in Angola in 1950 (1960, p. 99).

[71] The data used in compiling this table are found in: Colónia de Angola, 1941, pp. 78–9, 99, 118 and Provincia de Angola, 1953, pp. 68–9, 89, 109.

[72] Domingos António de Mascarenhas Arouca cogently observed in a strong attack on the *indigenato* that assimilation demanded that Africans possess habits, skills, etc. which could only be acquired after one was already considered an *assimilado* (1961, p. 13).

[73] For a comprehensive analysis of Portuguese educational policies and practices in the former colonies, see Sousa Ferreira, 1974b. pp. 74–108. Also see United Nations, 1962, p. 33; Wohlgemuth, 1963, p. 40; Amaral, 1960, p. 59.

obvious when the number of students in Angola is contrasted with other former European colonies: in 1952, for example, Angola had 14,898 primary school students (more than two-thirds of whom were white) compared with African enrolments the same year of 418,898 in Ghana and 943,494 in Zaïre (formerly the Belgian Congo).[74] Portugal did not attempt to emulate the Belgian, French, and British colonial policies of inculcating their cultures through formal education. The Portuguese agent of civilization was not the formal school teacher but the 'informal' (and often less educated) Portuguese employer.

While the *indigenato* was juridically based on cultural and not racial criteria, its application was strictly racial. Legally, any mestiço who did not live like an African in the bush and *all* whites were automatically considered civilized; thus, their 'cultural level' was deduced *ipso facto* from their colour. Some Africans and mestiços argued that the criteria for determining whether one was civilized or not should be applied to whites as well—especially those who were *cafrealizados* ('had gone native'). A Mozambican *assimilado* lawyer asked rhetorically in 1961 if it wasn't an 'insult to put the *assimilado* on par with Europeans living by primitive standards', but his logic escaped colonial officials and he was eventually imprisoned for almost a decade in a case which became an international *cause célèbre*.[75] In contrast, Africans who could read and write Portuguese, were Christian wage-earners, and dressed in a European manner were not classified as *assimilados* if an official believed they manifested 'a few traces of their ethnic identity'.[76]

Few Portuguese officials or citizens viewed these legal and social dis-

---

[74] It should be noted that the population of Ghana was approximately twice as large as Angola at the time, while Zaïre was almost three times more populous. See Hailey, 1956, p. 1258; and Silva Cunha, 1963, pp. 17–18.

[75] Arouca, 1961, pp. 14–15. Domingos Arouca was working as a male nurse in Lourenço Marques when he won about $750 in a lottery, which he used to go to Lisbon to study law. He returned to Mozambique in 1960, as the colony's first black lawyer. Shortly after his arrival he was refused admission into a Lourenço Marques movie theatre on racial grounds, which he vociferously protested. In 1961 he published his study attacking the *indigenato*. In 1965 he was elected President of the Association of Mozambican Negroes and was arrested the following month when the Association was closed by the government. He was held in prison for thirteen months before his trial and was finally sentenced to four years in prison for subversion and an additional three years as a security measure. Once he had served his sentence, he was still not released for more than a year. Arouca was finally released less than a year before the military overthrow of the Caetano regime. Following the coup he assumed a leadership role in FRELIMO and was active diplomatically in the Provisional Government of Mozambique, headed by Joaquim Chissano. See: *New Statesman* (London), 5 January 1973, *Guardian* (London), 25 June 1973 and *The Daily News* (Dar es Salaam), 28 June 1973. Following independence Arouca had a falling out with FRELIMO and moved to Lisbon where he became the leader of an anti-FRELIMO exile group called FUMO.

For a classical and convoluted defence for considering all whites as civilized, the position which Arouca so bitterly attacked, see Monteiro, J. A. P., 1961, pp. 34–5.

[76] Lemos, 1941, p. 50.

tinctions as indications of racial prejudice, exploitation, or discrimination. On the contrary, the creation of special institutions and laws for Africans was interpreted as magnanimity—proof of the Portuguese altruistic recognition of the need to provide special protection for those judged to be inferior.[77] Fervently believing in the superiority of their own civilization, the Portuguese held that it was in the Africans' best interests to change completely every aspect of their lives, including their social, economic, and political organizations, religious beliefs, clothes, food, cosmology, habitat as well as agricultural techniques. From these premises, it followed that anything which broke down traditional African institutions, beliefs and practices—including forced labour—was positive since it took Africans further away from their own cultures and closer to the Portuguese way of life.[78]

The attainment of the *assimilado* status may have exempted Africans from contract labour and facilitated their access to European economic and educational institutions but in actual practice it did not guarantee them first-class citizenship. In fact, both the private and public sectors paid *assimilados* lower wages under the premise that the wages reflected the differential productivity of the races. For example, Afonso Mendes argued in 1958 that these wage differences could not be considered an example of racial discrimination because the lower wages merely represented the value of the output.[79] It is apparent that both one's

[77] Adriano Moreira averred in 1956 that 'Portuguese culture, in its contact with native culture, adjudges it inferior in many respects' (1956, p. 460). The following year António Salazar maintained that 'we believe that there are races, decadent or backward, as you will, whom we have taken upon ourselves the duty of leading towards civilization'. Speech broadcast on Portuguese radio, 1 November 1957 and cited by Ehnmark and Wastberg, 1963, p. 41.

[78] Manuel da Silveira Ramos argued in 1952 that 'there cannot be any noticeable progress in any Negro society on the African continent by allowing it to exist according to its traditional patterns. Civilization implies profound political evolution, as happened with European societies, forced to accept new institutions and new social practices' (1952, p. 63). For an excellent critique of this ethnocentric notion of change, see Whitaker, 1967, pp. 190–217.

[79] Mendes, 1957–8, pp. 87–8. In this same article he also argues strongly against allowing Africans to join any kind of labour unions by cautioning that:

we should never forget that unionism would be an optimum medium for the Africans to make constant social demands and, with such a means, it would be a miracle if they did not let themselves become absorbed by the success of the concessions, outside propaganda, and the invalid but always attractive principles of liberty and equality; the certain result would be social agitation, followed by a mutual lack of understanding, repression and violence. The country cannot now run the risk of seeing its territories transformed into battlefields as, unfortunately, is happening in other African territories' (p. 93).

Afonso Mendes served as Director of the Angolan Labour Institute from 1962 to 1970, when he was transferred to Mozambique, where he held the same job until his return to Angola following the April 1974 coup. He was appointed to the cabinet of the first provisional government, in charge of labour relations, but strong protests and demonstrations cultural level and economic productivity were prejudged on a racial, not cultural or even individual, basis. In sum, Portuguese laws and practices guaranteed that any white person in Angola—even if judged by compatriots to be parasitic, indolent, or morally degenerate—was accorded higher social consideration and earned better wages than all but a handful of non-whites.

While the Portuguese and their foreign supporters comforted themselves with the belief that social and political inequalities in Angola reflected cultural realities rather than racial discrimination, there were few *assimilados* or mestiços who did not experience daily manifestations of racial (not cultural) discrimination. The history of protest against Portuguese discriminatory practices extends back to the nineteenth century, but it was only after the Second World War that this protest took on a decidedly political tone. A number of *assimilados* and mestiços studied and travelled outside Angola and were exposed to individuals and ideas which encouraged them to seek more than the reform of a colonial system which offered little promise of ever ceasing the exploitation of Angola's blacks. In Leopoldville (Kinshasa), Brazzaville, Accra, Conakry, Paris, and Lisbon, they were caught up in the forces which brought an end to the English, French, and Belgian empires in Africa. Many who studied in the metropole were surprised to discover that the majority of the Portuguese whom they encountered were (in the terms they had been taught to use) considerably less 'civilized' than themselves, which further intensified their desire to be rid of Portuguese colonialism altogether. When their poems, petitions, manifestos, and peaceful protests proved to be ineffective in achieving even minuscule reforms, they turned their talents and energies towards the goal of total national independence. Thus, *assimilados* and mestiços organized the Popular Movement for the Liberation of Angola (MPLA) and the Union of Angolan Peoples (UPA), which launched the first attacks of the Angolan war for independence in February and March of 1961.[80]

by Africans forced his removal within weeks. Despite the reactionary stance he adopted in the quotations cited here and again in his 1966 book on salaried labour in Angola, the negative role he played in the Portuguese whitewash of the 1971 ILO investigation of labour conditions in Angola, and the general failure of the Angolan Labour Institute to adequately protect African workers during his tenure as Director, he gained a reputation abroad as a strong liberal, which helps explain his appointment by the provisional government. His liberal reputation is undoubtedly attributable to the leak of a secret report he prepared in early 1969 on the realities of the labour situation in Angola. The report, which he prepared for the Angolan Council on Counter-Subversion, was published by the Angolan Comité in Amsterdam in 1972. For further information see: Mendes, 1966, *passim*; International Labour Organization, 1971, pp. 3–54; Angola Comité, 1972, pp. 1–27; Luanda newspapers carried reports of the protests against Afonso Mendes. See, for example, *O Comércio*, 21 June 1974.

[80] There were no mestiços among the organizers of UPA but most of the leaders were either *assimilados* or *évolués* (a more or less equivalent status which Belgians used in the

Within a matter of months, these armed attacks provoked more reforms in Portuguese colonialism than the combined protests of an entire century: the *indigenato* was repealed, thereby abolishing the distinction between 'civilized' and 'non-civilized' citizens; local African administrative bodies were organized; Portuguese and African customary laws were co-ordinated; the regulation of land concessions and occupation was tightened; and the system of unpaid forced labour was abolished.[81] While many of these reforms later proved to be merely a change in form rather than substance, the war did finally awaken Portugal to the recognition of some of the anachronisms in its colonial system. At the very time when other European colonizing powers were divesting themselves of their African territories, Portugal committed itself to resist the forces of nationalism and to seriously attempt to develop the land, resources, and people of its colony—in short, to colonize Angola. But it was too little and too late, as even General António de Spínola was to observe almost a decade and a half later in his book *Portugal e o Futuro*.[82] The legacy of five hundred years of abuses against Africans was too great to overcome with a few overdue reforms. That legacy has seldom been captured more graphically than in the uncharacteristically candid secret report by Afonso Mendes, presented in January 1969 to the Angolan Council on Counter-Subversion, in which he outlined the 'errors and abuses committed in the very recent past by our political and administrative structure':

Slavery, the wars of pacification, the abuses of power, physical violence carried out by administrative authorities, forced labour with all the accompanying consequences which are not pleasant to relate, the lack of protection during the 'indigenato' regime, administrative measures, the confiscation of lands which belonged to the community by customary law and were not meant for individual ownership, the dislocation of the population, the compulsory cultivation, numerous offences against traditional laws and the African system of values, etc., etc. ... Among Africans the white man will always be presented as a bad and greedy human being, as the sole cause of all the misery of the past, and perhaps as the traditional enemy of the black. And if this is the way the white man was in the past, it is quite probable that he will be considered this way in the present and future.[83]

Congo). For further information on the role of *assimilados* and mestiços in the formation of the liberation movements, see: Marcum, 1969, pp. 18–100; Davidson, 1972, pp. 146–54; and Wheeler and Pelissier, 1971, pp. 97–8, 126–36.

[81] For further information on these 1961 reforms, see *supra*, pp. 108–9.

[82] Spínola, 1974, p. 237.

[83] Mendes, 1969, p. 4. English versions can be found in the report published by the Angola Comité (see note 79) which was later reprinted in *Rural Africana*, no. 24 (Spring 1974), pp. 75–88.

CHAPTER 6

Wartime Response Towards African Civilians: The Dilemma of Development Versus Control

Introduction

Angola was the archetype of a colonial society at the time of the African nationalist uprising in February–March 1961.[1] A white minority exercised almost total control over the economy, civil service, politics, and the destinies of approximately five million Africans. The thrust of the colonial system had all but guaranteed that Africans could not break out of the cycle of poverty which engulfed their lives. A good number of the civilian and military officials in Angola recognized that Africans had sufficient reasons to be hostile towards a system which had oppressed them for centuries and to be receptive either to joining or at least to assisting one or another of the nationalist movements. It was apparent to most of these officials that the system had to be radically restructured in order to prevent the occurrence of either possibility; but the question was how?

Some civilian and military officials argued that the Portuguese should prove to Africans that they could benefit by remaining loyal to the colonial regime. This group proposed that all forms of racial discrimination be abolished and that the Government implement economic and educational programmes which would provide Africans with meaningful opportunities to improve their social and economic positions. In other words, they argued, give the Africans a true stake in the system and they will ignore the nationalists' appeals.

This approach was opposed by those who believed that Portugal had neither the time nor resources to make such radical changes in the system

---

[1] Some of the major accounts in English of the Angolan independence war and nationalist movements before the Portuguese coup of April 1974 can be found in: Marcum, 1967, pp. 9–17; *idem*, 1969; *idem*, 'Liberation Movements of Portuguese Africa', paper written for the United Nations Association of the United States of America, Inc., 1 June 1970; Davidson, 1972; Chilcote, 1967; 1969; 1972a; Wheeler and Pelissier, 1971; Bell, 1971, pp. 112–58; and Grundy, 1973.

before the nationalists could extend their influence in Angola. They maintained that the first priority would have to be to 'control' the African populations; i.e. to make it physically impossible for the nationalists to reach them. They proposed concentrating rural Africans into large hamlets or villages, supervised and/or guarded by the army with the aid of the secret police, thereby inhibiting civilian African co-operation with the nationalists. Once the rural Africans were 'secured' in the villages, they argued, developmental programmes could be implemented.

The policies which were actually carried out represented a series of attempts to reach a compromise between the opposing philosophies of development and control. Unfortunately, the overall impact of the massive resettlement programmes was merely to perpetuate the colonial system which placed the interests and security of whites above those of Africans. For the most part, Portuguese policy-makers viewed the situation in terms of a zero-sum game whereby benefits to one racial group would accrue at the expense of the other; and there was seldom doubt among whites that their interests should always be paramount.

Important objections were raised against the resettlement programmes by top officials in the army, civil service and police—especially between 1967 and 1969 when there was a massive expansion of the programmes. The Angolan General Council on Counter-Subversion held two series of meetings at this time during which confidential papers were presented on the actual status of all counterinsurgency efforts. Many of these papers are cited throughout this discussion in order to illustrate the full scope of the official debates about policies relating to rural Africans during the war.[2]

The widespread disruption which resettlement visited upon rural Angola suggests the need for a careful examination of its history, nature, and rationale. While resettlement failed to stop or even attenuate the insurgency, the radical changes it provoked in traditional societies

[2] The General Council on Counter-Subversion, formed in the late 1960s, studied, discussed and made recommendations on the theoretical and practical aspects of counterinsurgency measures. The Commander and Chief of the Armed Forces in Angola supervised the Council but the majority of members were high civilian officials (directors and assistant directors) in the colonial government. In 1968 the Council held two important symposia: one on the 'Settlement Problem' (*O Problema do Povoamento*) initiated 7 February 1968; the other 'Symposium on Counter-Subversion' (*Simpósio de Contra-Subversão*) initiated 10 July 1968.

The papers on the 'Settlement Problem' were broken down by sector: rural, commercial, industrial, civil service, liberal professions, and military. In addition to these papers there was a final report containing the conclusions and recommendations of each sectorial group: General Council on Counter-Subversion, 1968.

Participants in the Symposium on Counter-Subversion were also divided into six sections: (I) 'General Plan of Counter-Subversion', (II) 'Organization of Counter-Subversion'; (III) 'Regroupment and Control of Populations'; (IV) 'Civil Defence—Self-Defence and Militias'; (V) 'Psychological Action—Public Information'; and (VI) 'Social Advancement—Rural Settlement'. The authors and titles of twenty-five papers can be found in IDOC, 1974, pp. 14–18.

were so profound that rural Angola will never again be the same. Thus, resettlement is not only analysed as a counterinsurgency strategy but it is also discussed in terms of its implications for the period of reconstruction and development in independent Angola.

An Overview of Portuguese Responses to the War

The Portuguese response to the unexpected armed attacks by Angolan nationalists in early 1961 was a mixture of violence and reform. The element of surprise, which gave the nationalist forces a significant initial advantage, caught the small and inexperienced Portuguese army unprepared and unable to maintain control over a territory fourteen times larger than the metropole.[3] Thus, while the army was being greatly augmented from Lisbon, Angolan whites organized into vigilante groups that indiscriminately killed Africans in all parts of Angola, sometimes hundreds of miles from the areas of fighting.[4] The civilian violence, numerous political arrests, and widespread napalm bombing succeeded in driving most of the nationalist forces out of the colony within months. By the end of the summer of 1961, Portugal had regained control of nearly the entire territory, but the official death toll had reached more than 2,000 Europeans and 50,000 Africans. In addition, almost one-tenth of the African population had fled across the northern border into Zaïre.

Once the guerrilla forces had been repulsed, suspected nationalist leaders had been murdered or imprisoned, and the colonial whites had finished their catharsis of violence, Lisbon turned its attention to reforms. The decrees of September 1961, intended to abolish forced labour, illegal land expropriation, and other practices which had contributed to the degradation of Africans and to the deterioration of the rural African economy, were part of an overall effort to win the hearts and minds of Africans.[5] Officials in Lisbon hoped to show Africans that they had

[3] The size of the Portuguese army in Angola in early 1961 was approximately 8,000 men, consisting of 2,000 to 3,000 Europeans and 5,000 Africans (none of whom held officer's rank). Herrick *et al.*, 1967, p. 377, and Wheeler, 1969, p. 431.

By the end of the first year of the war, the army had been expanded to 50,000 and, while the number of soldiers fluctuated annually, the average was approximately 60,000 which, on a per capita basis, was three times more than the maximum United States commitment in Vietnam. See Wheeler, 1975, Table, p. 15.

At the time of the initial attacks, the Governor of the District of Luanda, Brigadier General Martin Soares, noted that there had been warnings from the Portuguese embassy in Leopoldville six to eight months before the first attacks, but added that nobody had believed the reports. Quoted in Venter, 1969, p. 13.

[4] The nature of these groups varied with respect to official government support. Some acted completely on their own with no government aid or endorsement, while others received weapons from the Government. All, however, were voluntary. The Government never officially endorsed the terror perpetrated, but it did not always discourage it, since in the beginning it was often the only effective method of stopping the spread of the insurgency. Once the situation began to normalize, however, the army did a great deal to curb the abuses of these vigilante groups.

[5] *Supra*, pp. 108–9.

more to gain by staying with Portugal than by supporting the liberation movements and, relative to its pre-war performance, Portugal expended considerable effort and money in an attempt to improve social and economic opportunities for Africans. During the early years of the war, when guerrilla activity was essentially confined to border attacks launched from sanctuaries in neighbouring countries, it was possible to implement programmes of assistance for Africans. Outside small pockets in the enclave of Cabinda and the northern coffee districts, there was little contact between the guerrillas and the civilian African population, which allowed the Portuguese considerable latitude for effecting their reforms and promulgating their propaganda. These efforts to win the loyalty of Africans ultimately failed, however, partially because there was more emphasis on propaganda than actual reform.

In late 1966, the nationalists changed tactics and shifted the battleground to eastern Angola. Operating out of border sanctuaries in Zambia, they began an intensive mobilization of peasants in the East. Their success demonstrated Portuguese vulnerability in that area to attacks which were based internally with some peasant support. Within a short time, the eastern front constituted an area of over 100,000 square miles (twice the size of metropolitan Portugal) and extended more than 350 miles inside the territory from the Zambian border. The initial effectiveness of the guerrillas' new strategy to politically mobilize peasant support before undertaking military missions convinced many Portuguese officials that it was too late to try reforms since African peasants had already demonstrated their willingness to co-operate with the nationalists. They concluded that civilian or noncombatant Africans must be isolated immediately from the guerrillas; to accomplish this they borrowed some pages from the guerrilla warfare manuals of the British, French and American armies and undertook a massive campaign to regroup Africans into strategic hamlets.

The regrouping of Africans into artificial villages had been employed previously in Angola, Mozambique and Guinea-Bissau but the programme initiated in eastern Angola in late 1967 marked the first time that Portugal had used this strategy as the major focus of its counterinsurgency efforts. It also marked yet another sad chapter in the chronicle of destruction of Angola's traditional African social, economic and political patterns—a chronicle which began with slavery, continued through the 'pacification wars' and contract-labour period, and finally ended with the forced resettlement of over one million Africans during the war.

The Counterinsurgency Programme of Population Resettlement

There were two basic types of population resettlement or regroupment schemes in Angola which were viewed as vital to the general counterinsurgency effort.[6] The first type, *aldeamentos* (hereafter referred to as 'strategic resettlements'), were large villages organized by the military, often surrounded by barbed wire, into which formerly dispersed Africans were grouped together.[7] Ostensibly, the primary functions of these strategic resettlements (generally located in eastern Angola and to a lesser extent in the northwest) were to provide organized local defence against attacks and to prevent insurgent infiltration and mobilization among non-combatant peasants. The other type of resettlement, *reordenamento rural* (referred to hereafter as 'rural resettlement'), occurred in most parts of Angola outside the immediate fighting zones.[8] Generally sponsored by the civilian government, the rural resettlements were often similar in appearance to the strategic resettlements (without barbed wire), but had the ostensible purpose of promoting economic and social development rather than providing military outposts against attacks. In essence, both resettlement schemes grouped previously dispersed Africans into large organized villages alongside roads which were regularly patrolled by the military. Each family had to build its own hut and keep all gardens and animals within a prescribed area, usually about

[6] A variety of terms was used in Angola to describe the resettlement or regroupment plans. A partial list would include: *aldeamentos, regedorias, aldeias estratégicas, agroupamentos, concentraçoes, reagroupamentos, reordenamento rural, colonatos, desenvolvimento comunitário, ndandandas,* and *aldeias fortificadas.* Because of the confusion over the imprecise use of these terms—some words were used to describe more than one type of resettlement while others occasionally referred to phenomena outside 'resettlement'—I will use my own nomenclature. I distinguish these two types primarily on the basis of the purpose they ostensibly, but not necessarily, were designed to serve. While it is true that there were a number of well-intentioned and altruistic supporters and executors of these programmes, the primary function of all resettlement programmes was their contribution to the general counterinsurgency effort.

[7] U.N., 1969, paragraphs 53–8. There is a close similarity between the strategic resettlements in Angola and the Strategic and New Life Hamlet Programs in South Vietnam. See Smith, H. H., *et al.*, 1967, pp. 231–4.

[8] Rural resettlement officially began in May 1962, but was neglected until the late 1960s. While the rationale behind the programme was to provide economic and social development for rural Africans, the timing and location of the new villages were often a result of military and police priorities. Nevertheless, those responsible for the programme were frequently motivated by altruistic intentions and they vigorously attempted to distinguish their programme from strategic resettlement. The best statement on *reordenamento rural* and how the programme was intended to be different from strategic resettlement is found in one of the papers presented to the General Council on Counter-Subversion's Symposium on Counter-Subversion, prepared by six men who were responsible for the *Reordenamento Rural* programme. Afredo Jorge de Passos Guerra, Fernando Diogo da Silva, and Amilcar Santos Martins da Silva, 'Relatório e Conclusões: Comissão de Estudo da Secção VI ("Promoção Social-Reordenamento Rural")', presented 24 January 1969, pp. 7–26. Also assisting in the preparation of this report were Florentino Ramalho da Rocha, Jorge Bonucci Veiga, and José Carmo Maria Brandão. Also see Mouzinho *et al.*, 1969, pp. 45–6. For an excellent critical examination of the problems attendant to resettlement in Angola, see Guerra and Veiga, 1970, pp. 113–29.

thirty square metres. All residents were required to sleep in the new village every night and were responsible, under penalty, for reporting to the authorities any stranger in the area or any person missing from the village.[9]

Small military quarters were established in many of the strategic re-settlements where the males were organized into militia units. The actual number of Africans who were in the militia is probably not known (they were frequently organized *ad hoc* and the accuracy of the figures reported was often questionable) but it can be assumed that there were roughly 30,000 by the end of the war. In public, the Portuguese vociferously defended the militias as necessary for the defence of the resettlements' inhabitants against attacks by the nationalist guerrillas. Yet only about 10 per cent of the Africans in the militia were ever issued weapons—the remainder used wooden models of rifles or sticks to train, and bows and arrows or spears in combat. Furthermore, the nationalists rarely attacked a resettlement unless they were provoked, betrayed, or attacked by the inhabitants and, when such confrontations occurred, the local militia was usually little match for the better-armed and trained guerrilla forces.[10] The papers delivered at the Symposium on Counter-Subversion leave no doubt that the Portuguese had little inten-tion of properly arming the African militia because they feared the Africans might defect to 'the enemy' with the weapons. Instead, the militia's primary function was to compromise its members with the nationalists. For example, the group responsible for the report to the Symposium on 'The General Plan of Counter-Subversion' argued:

It would be beneficial to obtain their [Africans in the resettlements] collaboration and take advantage of every opportunity to provoke a division between them and the enemy through their participation in public acts, such as speeches at civic ceremonies and through their participation in self-defence, organized militias, etc. Once they are

---

[9] The failure to report such knowledge was considered a punishable violation (the punish-ment often being a public beating) and was used at times to punish large numbers of people in a resettlement.

An attempt was also made to control the movement of the inhabitants in the new resettlements as they travelled to and from their fields. Ostensibly this was done for their own protection, but more importantly it allowed the authorities to know where everybody was at a given time, and helped reduce contacts between those outside the resettlement villages and the nationalists. See Prego, 1969, p. 4.

[10] Africans in these village militias should not be confused with the Africans who served in the regular Portuguese army, or the famed 'Grupos Especiais' or 'Flechas'—speci-ally trained auxiliary forces attached to the secret police (PIDE/DGS), who had the reputa-tion of being the best counterinsurgency troops on offensive missions. See U.N., 1972, p. 162; and Dash, 1974. For further information on the 'flechas' see *Diário de Luanda*, 10 October 1973 and *Diário de Notícias* (Lisbon), 13 December 1973.

compromised they will begin to fear reprisals from the enemy and, consequently, will seek our protection.[11]

Population control was further extended in each resettlement through the establishment of a network of spies and informers who were coerced or recruited among the villagers by the secret police (PIDE/DGS). The informers were exempted from paying taxes and were paid either a small monthly retainer or according to the importance of the information they supplied.[12] Individuals considered suspicious or exposed as co-operating with the guerrillas were frequently beaten in public as an object lesson to the others. Captain Magalhaes J. Cruz Azevedo, a district commander in the Angolan police (PSPA), argued that the violence could be advantageous for the counterinsurgency effort if it were well publicized: 'We have to take action against elements who live in our midst and promote subversion. Violence still is a strong argument, especially when applied against blacks whose entire concept of God is imbedded in the idea of violence.'[13] In addition, the fact that Africans were usually employed to administer the punishments meant that more individuals were compromised with the nationalists—a strategy also apparent in the occasional public exposure of informers. In sum, control over the African population—the primary goal of resettlement—was attempted through the interaction of a variety of methods such as restricting and regulating their movements, creating a network of spies and informers, violence, and sowing distrust both among the villagers and between the villagers and the nationalists.

Another goal of resettlement was to win the loyalty of the African population through economic and social development. A third goal, which became apparent as resettlement spread but which was not always endorsed by the government, was to free certain African-held

[11] Comissão de Estudo da Secção I, 'Plano de Contra-Subversão: relatório, conclusões e sugestões', presented to the Symposium on Counter-Subversion, January, 1969, p. 13. A similar argument is made by one of the other commissions when they aver that 'The simple fact of belonging to a militia constitutes a certain form of compromise with our side' for Africans incorporated into the militias. See Grupo de Coordenação e Inspecção da Contra-Subversão, 1968, p. 11.

[12] Morais, C. A. de, n.d., cited in IDOC, 1974, pp. 35–6.

[13] Captain Magalhaes J. Cruz Azevedo, 'Acção psicológica', presented to the Symposium on Counter-Subversion, p. 1, cited in IDOC, 1974, pp. 54–5.

In September 1973 a new Security Council (Conselho Provincial de Segurança) was formed, with the main function of analysing 'repressive measures used in other parts of Portugal and study their adaptation to Angola' and to defend the priorities in the use of repressive measures. The Council was comprised of the Chief of the DGS in Angola, the Chief of the Judiciary Police (*Policia Judiciária*), and the Commander-General of the Public Security Police (PSP) and was presided over by the Secretary-General. *Diário de Notícias* (Lisbon), 13 September 1973.

MAP 2: *Wartime resettlement zones*

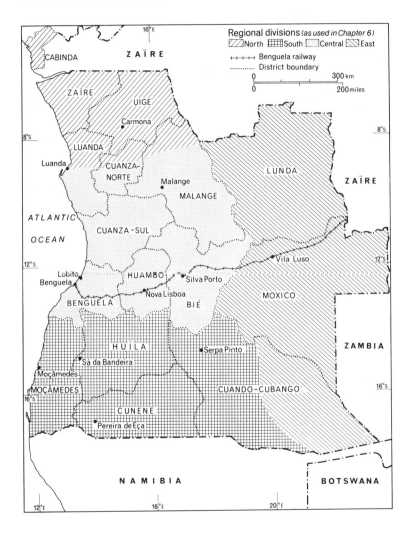

lands for further European settlement.[14] Basically, all resettlement programmes in Angola were intended to satisfy at least one of these three goals of population control, promoting development and increasing the amount of land for European settlement. Obviously, these goals were often mutually exclusive, especially when the exigencies of population control resulted in a loss of land and decrease in economic productivity.

Strategic and rural resettlements were distinguished in Angola on the basis of the former emphasizing population control while the latter were intended principally to promote social and economic development. In reality, however, the strategic and rural resettlement schemes were frequently indistinguishable both in appearance and results. The government services provided, the military interests served and the economic consequences which resulted were so similar that it is not particularly useful to distinguish the two programmes analytically; therefore the overall impact of African resettlement will be analysed here by region, rather than by the specific programme (see Map 2).[15]

Finally, it is important to underscore the fact that there was relatively little opposition to resettlement from either military or civilian officials. As noted above, the military endorsed resettlement as an expedient means of facilitating population control while a large number of civilian officials enthusiastically supported it in the hope that it would provide them with a better opportunity to extend governmental services such as medical care, education, agricultural aid and sanitation. The hopes and plans of both civilian and military supporters, however, often went unrealized or actually boomeranged, largely because no detailed plan for all of Angola was ever promulgated in spite of the fact that the strategic resettlement programme was first incorporated into the counterinsurgency effort as early as 1961. It was never clarified, for example, whether strategic resettlements should have been confined to the war zones or adopted for Angola as a whole or whether the programme was to be restricted to agricultural peoples or extended to cattle herders as well.[16]

[14] A number of papers presented to the Symposium warn of the dangers in the trend of white settlers taking over African lands abandoned when the former occupants were moved into resettlements, but whites' avarice for land continued to supersede military considerations in many parts of Angola up to the change in government in late April 1974. The problem is also discussed in *A Província de Angola* (Luanda), 16 April 1970.

[15] For a discussion on the lack of distinction among the various types of resettlements, see the paper presented by Colonel Fialho Prego, p. 3. Also see 'Relatório e Conclusões: Commissão de Estudo da Secção VI', pp. 17 and 19–20.

[16] A number of interesting and significant differences of opinions over these questions emerge in the papers presented to the Symposium on Counter-Subversion. For example, those who drafted the 'Relatório e Conclusões: Commissão de Estudo da Secção VI' were principally civilians responsible for rural development programmes and they strongly urged that strategic resettlements be confined to combat zones, on a temporary basis, because of the negative social and economic consequences. On the other hand, the military officers who drafted the report, 'Breves Reflexões Sobre Os Problemas da Contra-Subversão na

In other words, neither the social and economic structures nor the location were considered to any great extent by those responsible for the regroupings. In 1967 when the green light was given to emphasize and expand resettlement, many zealous local administrators, often anxious to fulfil what they perceived as a superior's wishes, began to regroup indiscriminately hundreds of thousands of Africans from every type of social and economic system in Angola. In the following pages the resettlement programmes in Angola are described and analysed within the geographical classification: north, east, central and south.[17]

THE NORTH

The mass exodus of Africans from northern Angola immediately after the outbreak of the war (estimated to be between 400,000 and 500,000) not only helped to swell the nationalist forces but also dealt a serious blow to the important coffee industry.[18] Most of those who fled to Zaïre or hid in the forests either had provided the labour on the large European coffee plantations or had been producing coffee on their own small plots. Resettlement became the focus of the military programme undertaken in the North to attract the refugees back to Angola. The army argued that resettlement villages offered the only hope of stemming the exodus, and therefore much time and money were devoted to the construction of 130 to 150 resettlements and a number of new schools, which were staffed at the primary level essentially by non-commissioned officers.[19] Despite the observation of a Portuguese military doctor who served with the Portuguese forces in the North that the programme was carried out 'without

Zona do G. C. I., N.º 3', which covered the four districts where no armed activity occurred throughout the war (Huambo, Huila, Benguela, and Cuanza-Sul), dismissed the objections of the civilians and urged the expansion of resettlements in these districts on the basis of their conviction that the strategic resettlements not only were requisite for population control but were also well accepted by the people and successfully promoted development (pp. 6–9).

[17] This regional division is based on the economic and social structures of the populations, the type of resettlement programme, and geographic location. It should be noted that many of the conditions (such as the general economic situation in Angola, the Government's attitude and available resources) were relevant more or less equally to all four regions, although some of them are discussed here in relation to one region only.
  The northern region included the districts of Zaïre, Uige, and the northern parts of Malange and Cuanza-Norte. The eastern region was composed of the districts of Moxico, Lunda, and Cuando Cubango. The central region comprised the districts of Cuanza-Sul, Huambo, Bie, and the southern half of Malange. The southern region included the districts of Moçamedes, Huila, Cunene, and the western half of Cuando Cubango.

[18] Between 1956 and 1961, coffee accounted for 35–40 per cent of Angola's total exports. In 1967 coffee represented over half (52.5 per cent) the value of all Angolan exports; but in 1971 and 1973 its importance declined to 34.2 per cent and 27 per cent, respectively, principally because of the growing importance of oil and mineral exports. For the latter figures see International Defence and Aid Fund, *Southern African Information Service* (January–June 1973), p. 226 and U.N., 1975, p. 28.

[19] See Maciel, 1963, pp. 279–80; and Laidley, 1964, pp. 80–2.

depth, without interest, or without friendship for the African', approximately 200,000 Africans returned and were located in the resettlement.[20]

Throughout most of the 1960s the Portuguese viewed the resettlement programme in the North as a major success, principally because of the large numbers of Africans who were located in the strategic resettlements and because their relocation opened up a considerable amount of African lands for distribution to white settlers. This perspective, which later encouraged policy makers to spread the programme to other parts of the colony, proved in the end to be myopic and eurocentric. Moreover, it ignored the basic reasons why it was relatively easy for the Portuguese to move hundreds of thousands of Africans into the new resettlements.

With few exceptions, most of the Africans who became inhabitants of the strategic resettlements had no other choice. To have remained hiding in the forests would have made them vulnerable to attack from both sides. In addition, a number of those who had crossed the border into Zaïre were unable to secure urban employment or work on the land. Because they were faced with starvation, attacks from the Portuguese and nationalist troops, and almost no possibility of returning to their lands or finding employment, the strategic resettlements offered them some important advantages—especially protection and the likelihood of obtaining land or jobs on nearby coffee plantations. Furthermore, the resettlements' size and structure were not so disruptive of living patterns among the Bakongo in the North—who traditionally live in relatively large groups and have worked as farm labourers—as later occurred among other ethnic groups in Angola. These and other factors enabled the Portuguese to settle large numbers of Angolans in strategic resettlements in the North with a minimum of resistance and occasionally even co-operation from the inhabitants.

The strategic resettlements were also viewed as successful because they restored the European coffee economy. (The African economy was devastated by the war.) Portuguese plantation owners faced economic ruin without African labourers, and the resettlements were ready repositories of coffee workers. Furthermore, large areas of land formerly held by many of the Africans in the resettlements were seized or 'legally' conceded to whites.[21] Consequently, the 'success' which the Portuguese

[20] Padua, 1963, p. 83. Padua served as a doctor with the Portuguese army in northern Angola in 1961, after which he moved to Brazil.

A Portuguese military commander in the North estimated that about 200,000 of the approximately 500,000 (his estimate) refugees returned to live in resettlements established by the military. Quoted in U.N., 1970, p. 51.

[21] The expropriation of African land in the North was most intensive during the 1950s. See ibid., p. 340. A number of high officials were involved in this robbery of African lands; for example, virtually everybody questioned maintained that the former Governor General Rebocho Vaz (1966–72)—Governor of Uige District at the time the war started—was a partner in an anonymous company which took over some of the largest and richest coffee lands in Uige. This accusation was never proven, due to the difficulty of establishing under Portuguese law the identity of partners in anonymous firms.

perceived in the strategic resettlement programme in northern Angola during the early years of the war stemmed almost exclusively from white interests. The propensity of the Portuguese in Angola to evaluate programmes and policies directed toward Africans by the degree to which they benefited white interests proved to be a fatal error for colonial officials, who considered the resettlement programme in the North so successful that they believed it to be a key to winning the war.

If the resettlements in the North proved to be compatible with white goals, they failed miserably to satisfy even the most minimal African goals or aspirations. A notable lack of planning and insufficient government aid undermined African development possibilities from the start. For the most part, Africans in the resettlements could not maintain, let alone improve, their previous standard of living. Beyond cash crops (e.g. coffee), traditional agriculture in the area was almost moribund, as described in one of the papers presented to the Council on Counter-Subversion:

> The traditional economy of this population [in the District of Zaïre] has become impossible, since its land is reduced to that surrounding the villages [which] live in a continuous state of alarm. In this way the tragedy of an already undernourished population which has to live from the harvest of an unproductive agriculture becomes greater still . . . We must strive for economic progress; this goal will have to be a high priority.
> In the district of Zaïre, increase of agricultural productivity is the main lever for this process. Therefore, the State has to help the population to develop agriculture. We are responsible for the economic backwardness of the population of Zaïre [district], and we should not forget that economic backwardness is a sign of political bankruptcy.[22]

'Political bankruptcy' was also apparent in the educational 'backwardness' of the population. For example, the Governor of Zaïre District noted in the late 1960s that there were 'only four qualified teachers' for the 4,500 primary school pupils in his district.[23]

The economic situation of the other major northern district, Uige, was similar to Zaïre's. In 1969 the Governor of Uige admitted that the Government could not afford to stimulate investment because of the high cost of the war.[24] In addition to the shortage of government financial assistance, there was an acute shortage of government personnel. In Uige, for example, the civil service was 50 per cent understaffed.[25] By

[22] Quoted in IDOC, 1974, pp. 106–7.

[23] The Governor also noted that 'primary education not only is too academic and too abstract, but it is left to "accidental" teachers and school directors'. Quoted in ibid., p. 91.

[24] Cited in Dennis Gordon, 'How Peace Returned to Uige', *The Natal Mercury* (Durban), 27 June 1969.

[25] Nunes and Morào, n.d., p. 1.

the end of 1969, the economic climate of the area had deteriorated to the point where the only newspaper published in the North editorialized that the situation had become a crisis:

> The majority of the people in the Uige District are spending much more money than they earn ... Productivity is not increasing. The subsistence crops are being abandoned, or are handled in the most primitive fashion of using the almost forced labour of women ... Not a single goat or pig is being raised, nor are there any eggs produced for sale in the population centres.... As is obvious, this condition does not exist in a void—it must be based on the economic, political and social structures which practical life demonstrates to be terribly inadequate ... the situation has reached such a point that figures are no longer necessary. Everyone knows and feels this trend. When a dog dies, a veterinarian is not needed to certify the fact. The odour more than suffices.[26]

The economic decline in the North affected all races, but Africans were especially hard hit. The approximately 60,000 independent African coffee growers were paid artificially low prices (about 30 per cent of export value) for their coffee, while some 140,000 who worked on the coffee plantations found the official daily minimal wage (which ranged between US$0·70 and $1·00 during the late 1960s and early 1970s) inadequate to meet their essential needs. Moreover, it was rare to encounter a white farmer who paid his workers *as much* as the legal minimum wage! The plight of Africans was further exacerbated by high taxes and a sharp rise in the cost of living (79 per cent between 1965 and 1973).[27] Predictably, the deterioration of social and economic conditions in the North encouraged Africans to co-operate with nationalists—a matter of grave concern for some Portuguese officials. For example, in one of the most

---

[26] 'Editorial' in *Jornal do Congo* (Carmona), 18 December 1969. The response to this editorial by an Angolan economic periodical was to state that part of the problem of the decline in productivity in Uige (as well as in most of Angola) was caused by the Africans' 'declared desire for idleness, supported by a tribal solidarity which permits them to eat a crust of bread here, to drink a cup of water there ... and to outdo each other in the practice of theft and other violations'. *Actualidade económica*, 1970, p. 2.

[27] For figures concerning the increase in the cost of living in Angola, see *Economia Portuguesa*, 1970, p. 16; *A Província de Angola* (Luanda), 8 February 1973; and *Notícias de Portugal* 27 (1 September 1973, p. 6). In 1973 the cost of living in Luanda increased 13·2 per cent! Banco de Angola, 1973a, p. 31; and 1973b, pp. 231–6.

During the first half of the war direct taxes increased 97 per cent, indirect taxes 114 per cent, and a special consumer tax on items such as beer, sugar, petroleum, and tobacco increased 412 per cent! Furthermore, between 1966 and 1973 the general minimum tax varied from district to district but averaged about 300 escudos (in Uige it was 380 escudos), which for many workers represented approximately one month's work. See *A Província de Angola*, 8 March 1973 and 14 November 1973.

Finally, it is important to note that during nine months in Angola, I did not find one instance of a European who paid his African farm labourers as much as the minimum-wage law required. Consequently, the word 'minimum' is quite misleading since it really represents the 'maximum' paid to African farm labourers.

important papers presented to the Symposium on Counter-Subversion, Ramiro Ladeiro Monteiro warned that the following conditions on the coffee plantations contributed to feeding the subversion in the North: occasional food deficiencies, labour relations which were 'hardly honourable', low wages, and a disproportionate profit for the employers.[28]

Once it was apparent that conditions in the strategic resettlements represented no alteration in the pre-war colonial structure—when Africans either provided cheap labour for European planters or produced coffee which was purchased for considerably less money than the market value or the price paid to Portuguese farmers—the only Africans who 'volunteered' to live in the resettlements did so at the point of a gun. Consequently, instead of reducing the exodus of African labour as occurred in 1961–62, the strategic resettlements actually began to provoke it. In fact, between 1960 and 1970, the population declined in both northern districts. In Zaïre District alone the population dropped sixty per cent over the previous census.[29] Not surprisingly, by 1973 the number of Angolans living in the Republic of Zaïre had grown to over 600,000.[30]

This exodus from the North necessitated greater reliance on labour imported from other parts of Angola (principally Ovimbundu from the Central Highlands), but there were never enough African workers to satisfy the Portuguese planters.[31] While they tended to blame the government for the labour shortage, a leading Angolan newspaper in mid-1973 suggested that the farmers bore equal responsibility, since low wages along with inadequate benefits such as food, housing, health care, etc. 'might be' one reason for the labour exodus.[32] In August of the same year, another Angolan newspaper—despite rigid censorship—acknowledged that the liberation movements had intensified their activities in the North compared with recent years.[33] Herein lies the most

[28] Monteiro, R. L. n.d., p. 5. Monteiro was Chief of Cabinet of the Services for the Centralization and Coordination of Intelligence of Angola (SCCIA) at the time he presented this. SCCIA was responsible for overseeing all intelligence activities in Angola.

[29] The total number of inhabitants in the districts of Zaïre and Uige in 1960 were 103,906 and 399,412 respectively, while in 1970 there were 41,766 and 386,037 inhabitants, respectively. See Província de Angola, 1964, p. 35; and Estado de Angola, 1972, p. 7.

[30] Cited in U.N., 1974, p. 3.

[31] Shortly before the signing of the cease-fire in October 1974, a large number of Ovimbundu workers on the coffee plantations in the North suddenly left and returned to the Central Highlands. It was estimated that as many as a third of the 100,000 migrants fled, which crippled coffee farming in certain areas. One white farmer who employed 2,000 Africans before the exodus reflected on the 11 Africans who remained and said that there was no way he could stay in business unless they returned. The manager of the largest grower conglomerate (10,000 acres of coffee) lamented that it would take three years of hard work to restore his fields if the African workers stayed away six months. See Thomas A. Johnson, 'Labourers Fleeing Farms in Angola', New York Times, 20 October 1974. This flight appears to have been caused by the Ovimbundu fear of attack from the forces of FNLA (principally comprised of Bakongo people), and a desire to return to the central highlands while an important land survey was under way.

[32] A Província de Angola, 26 April 1973.

convincing evidence that the resettlement programme had failed.

Few officials were unaware of the social and economic decay afflicting Africans in the northern resettlements; nevertheless the programme was defended on the grounds that these artificial villages were necessary to extinguish the subversion. Yet, with the exception of the first year of the war, the fighting reached its height in the North in the months just prior to and after the April 1974 coup in Portugal. Whether the strategic resettlements prevented an earlier loss for Portugal is not possible to determine, but it is clear that the resettlement programme in the North failed to contain, let alone defeat, the nationalist guerrillas. Ironically, it is equally clear that this lesson was lost on at least a portion of the Portuguese military, for they continued to capture Africans and put them into resettlements in the months immediately following the Lisbon coup.[34]

THE EAST

The strategy employed by the guerrillas throughout most of the war in the North was to conduct raids from sanctuaries across the border in Zaïre. With the exception of selected pockets (e.g. the Dembos area), the nationalist troops in the North were never permanently based inside the colony; therefore their military operations did not require nor receive intimate collaboration from African peasants. The shortcomings of this strategy were perceived by the leaders of the MPLA and UNITA nationalist movements as they prepared to concentrate their military activities in the East during the mid-1960s. They argued that if the struggle were to progress beyond occasional border raids and ambushes, roots would have to be established among the rural peasantry, who could then help the guerrillas sustain themselves internally. They were aided during this period of mobilization by the Portuguese misperception that the war was caused exclusively by outside forces with no support among the internal population. In short, the Portuguese assumed that if guerrilla warfare moved to the East, it would be carried out in the pattern found in the North. This led Portugal to station her troops along the Zambian border, leaving most of the countryside unprotected. Thus, in late 1966, with some internal peasant support, the nationalists opened the eastern front

---

[33] Cited in U.N., 1974, p. 5.

[34] See Henry Kamm, 'Soldiers in Angola Unsure and Bored', *New York Times*, 5 June 1974. General Leao Correira, commander of the Portuguese forces in the North, told the reporter that any civilians found in the area (Santa Eulalia) who were not living in resettlements were rounded up as collaborators with the nationalists. Kamm confirmed that the strategic resettlements were neglected right up to the end of the war:

Across the airstrip from this base and enclosed with the same barbed wire is a resettlement area containing about 1,000 people. It is considered a transit camp but many of its inhabitants have been there for three or four years.

Also see *New York Times*, 25 August 1974.

and rapidly challenged Portuguese hegemony over more than 100,000 square miles of eastern Angola.[35]

Portugal's initial reprisals, such as the napalming of many villages, did not have the same deterrent effect on an insurgency with internal support as they had in 1961 against the externally-based insurgency in the North. Once again, streams of Africans began to flee Angola, this time into Zambia and Botswana.[36] Desperate to stop both the infiltration—which soon spread hundreds of miles inland—and a potentially massive emigration, the Portuguese embarked on a crash programme of moving Africans into strategic resettlements. The relocation progressed rapidly and by November 1968 military officials claimed that over 70 per cent of the Africans in Lunda and Moxico Districts were living in resettlements. In late 1969 the Governor of Moxico stated that 80 per cent of those (140,000) Africans 'under guerrilla control' in his district had been recovered under the strategic resettlement programme. Even larger numbers of Africans would have been resettled by this time had not the presence of nomadic pastoralists created problems for the administration. The Governor of Cuando Cubango, for example, privately admitted in 1969 that the resettlement of agricultural peoples in his district had been almost impossible but that the task he faced to resettle nomadic pastoral peoples would be considerably more difficult.

The process of resettling Africans in the East was more complex for the Portuguese because of the prior mobilization by the nationalists. Unlike the North, where the civilian population feared reprisals from the nationalists and the Portuguese alike, in the East the principal fear was of the Portuguese. This forced the Portuguese army to resort to violence in moving civilians from their traditional lands to the new resettlements. One woman who escaped from a strategic resettlement in Moxico (Sangezo, near Cuete) described the day her village was forced to move:

> The Portuguese came at dawn and surrounded the village. They broke into the huts and told us to get out. They tied the men's hands behind their backs. There were more than 50 white soldiers with guns, and a few black ones. The soldiers were very brutal, beating us with the butts

[35] For more on the guerrilla strategy employed in the East and the initial results, see Davidson, 1972, pp. 254–61, 264–5, 282–98; and Valentim, 1969, pp. 44–7. For further information on the mistaken strategy Portugal utilized during the early years of fighting in the East, see Vieira, n.d., p. 3; and Marques, S. S., 1969a, pp. 329–30. It is of interest to note that when General Silvino Silvério Marques left his position as Governor General of Angola in 1966, he was strongly criticized by whites for being too sympathetic to African demands. However, as head of the first provisional government in Angola following the April 1974 coup, he was bitterly attacked by Africans for being too sympathetic to white demands, which led to his rapid dismissal.

[36] It was reported in South Africa that by the end of 1968 the number of Angolan refugees who fled across the Caprivi Strip in order to escape Portuguese bombing had quadrupled Botswana's refugee population, causing serious resettlement problems for the Botswana Government. See *The Natal Mercury* (Durban), 24 December 1968. Also see Davidson, pp. 133–4.

of their guns and then kicking us when we fell to the ground. Women and children were beaten too, and not just those who resisted or tried to escape. Nobody escaped.

They said that we had been helping the terrorists ... My uncle was very reluctant to go with the Portuguese to the aldeamento, and was there and then beaten to death. In all, two men and two women were killed in this way. They just left the bodies lying there without burying them.

After a while the lorries came for us. The Portuguese gathered together our personal possessions—blankets, pots, etc.—and burned them. Our huts were burned too. We were allowed to take nothing with us; we were just thrown on the lorries.[37]

By 1970 almost all Africans in the East who were outside the nationalist-controlled areas lived in strategic resettlements and, due to the programme's rapid implementation and insufficient planning, their lives quickly became disordered. Most of them were required to give up a large portion of their traditional social and economic patterns and to accept what one military officer described to me as an 'artificial life'. They were told that the need to abandon many traditional ways would be more than compensated for by new benefits which the Government could now provide. The Government explained that in the past it simply had not been able to extend its services over an area of more than 200,000 square miles, inhabited by fewer than two people per square mile. However, once the resettlements were established, practically none of the promised services was ever implemented. Furthermore, the new living pattern exacerbated previously neglected problems—such as lack of sanitation, communicable diseases, little or no agricultural aid—which required not only the promised services but new ones.

One reason these services were not provided was the expansion of the war; i.e. the extra money and personnel which could have been used for social and economic improvements were consumed by the increased military requirements. But the problem was not totally a result of the war effort. Many positions budgeted for rural Angola were unfilled because of the understandable reluctance of civil servants or professionals to risk their lives for extremely low salaries and harsh, often dangerous, living conditions. Furthermore, there was a decline not only in the number of civil servants in the interior after 1961 but also in the qualifications of individuals hired to replace some of those who left. This dramatic decrease in number and qualification of civil servants in the interior gravely concerned the Director of Civil Administration, Adelino Amaral Lopes, in mid-1968. He further feared that the low salaries paid civil servants portended an even greater exodus. Lopes argued that there were at least three serious consequences of this decline in the civil service: 'the large mass of the African population who live in the bush

[37] Quoted in Rivers, 1974, p. 43.

are not assisted as they should be'; 'sovereignty and the security and defence of people and goods are placed in danger'; and the development of an already underdeveloped interior becomes less and less likely.[38]

Despite the much-heralded expansion of education after the start of the war, there was a severe deficiency of schools and teachers in the rural sector, especially in the strategic resettlements.[39] In 1971, for example, 57 per cent of all villages had no schools and many of the schools which were constructed were not staffed.[40] Between 1964 and 1969 an average of only 100 primary school teachers per year were trained in Angola's four teacher-training schools and only 200 primary school monitors per year. Furthermore, just over two-thirds of all teachers in rural Angola in 1971 received no more than four years of primary education.[41] The situation was most critical in the East, where few teachers chose to locate when there were acute teacher shortages in the safer and more comfortable major cities. The low enrolment figures of the pre-resettlement period in the East—less than 7 per cent of those eligible were enrolled in the final two years of primary school (grades 3 and 4)—were not appreciably improved by the resettlements.[42] Finally, it was not possible for over 99 per cent of the inhabitants of the East to progress beyond primary school, since there was only one public secondary school in the area (Luso), which opened in the mid-1960s and was attended primarily by Europeans.

Inadequate health care has been an endemic problem in Angola in both the urban and rural sectors. The principal factor has been the lack of doctors and nurses, which appeared to worsen during the course of the war, according to a 1973 editorial in a Luanda newspaper: 'Despite the encouraging fact that every year more and more doctors come out of our universities, the shortage of physicians in our State [Angola] seems to be increasing rather than diminishing.'[43] Furthermore, the distribution

---

[38] See Lopes, A. A., 1968, pp. 1–5; and 'Relatório e conclusões: comissão de estudo da Secção VI', pp. 5, 18.

[39] For further information on the expansion of Angolan education during the war see: Samuels, 1967, pp. 63–6; Samuels and Bailey, 1969, pp. 180–9; Heimer, 1973b, pp. 111–43; Silva, E. M. da, 1973, pp. 193–210.

[40] Heimer, 1973a, p. 91. It is of interest to note the observation of Lt. Col. Julio Carvalho Costa on the problem of unstaffed schools:

A widespread and deeply rooted idea is that the problem of education is solved by building schools. We have seen many new school buildings, here and there, both in Africa and in Portugal, which were not in use because of a lack of teachers. ('Promoção socio-económica', paper presented to the Symposium on Counter-Subversion, p. 9.)

[41] Heimer, 1973a p. 93. 'Monitors' were primary-school teachers, usually found in African schools, who received minimal training. See U.N., 1970, pp. 42–3.

[42] Província de Angola, Direcção dos Serviços de Estatística, 1967, pp. 54, 61. It is interesting to note that only 40 per cent of the students enrolled in primary schools in the East passed (p. 53).

[43] Editorial in *A Província de Angola* entitled 'The Price of Health', cited in Overseas Companies of Portugal, *Intelligence Report* (June 1973). Also see Bender, 1975b, p. 479, note 43.

of doctors and nurses grossly favoured the areas of white population; in early 1968, 68 per cent of all private physicians were located in only three districts (Luanda, Huambo and Benguela), while there were merely ten private doctors in the eastern districts, Moxico, Cuando Cubango and Lunda.[44] Moreover, besides doctors in the armed forces, few government doctors were sent to the East.

Numerous reports from Portuguese officials and doctors in the nationalist movements confirmed that health and sanitation conditions in the eastern resettlements were critical in the late 1960s and early 1970s. To a considerable degree these problems were exacerbated by the resettlements themselves, which concentrated large numbers of people under dubious sanitary conditions. For example, one of the reports submitted to the Symposium on Counter-Subversion outlined some of the negative health consequences of the resettlements:

> an increase in the number of contagious diseases as a result of greater pollution of the soil and of drinking water ... (tuberculosis, leprosy, common childhood diseases, intestinal parasites, diarrhoea, etc.); [and] a greater possibility of outbreaks of epidemics, especially measles, whooping-cough, jaundice, intestinal troubles capable of causing an increase in mortality.[45]

In fact the feared epidemic outbreaks did occur and were confirmed by two respected MPLA doctors who worked in the East, Dr. Eduardo dos Santos and the late Dr. Américo Boavida.[46]

The dearth of qualified people to staff schools and medical posts was equally apparent in practically every skilled profession in Angola. Generally, the colony looked to the metropole for professional skilled personnel, but Portugal was suffering from its own crisis of skilled manpower throughout the 1960s and especially during the early 1970s, when more then one hundred thousand Portuguese emigrated annually to Western Europe and the Americas. Traditionally, Angola had attempted to attract skilled Portuguese immigrants by offering higher salaries, but the labour shortage in Portugal raised metropolitan wages above those in Angola which, combined with the dramatic increase in Angola's cost of living, encouraged the emigration, not immigration, of Portuguese skilled

[44] Monteiro, R. L., 1968, table entitled 'Quadro das profissões liberais'. This table (21) can be found *infra*, p. 231. It is of interest to note that if one assumed that all of the 1,205 people practising a liberal profession were white (which was not true), the total represented less than one half of one per cent (0·48 per cent) of all whites in Angola! For a further discussion of this situation, see Bender and Yoder, 1974, pp. 34–5.

[45] See Comissão de Estudo da Secção VI, 'Relatório e conclusões', p. 22 and Nunes, J. P., n.d., pp. 8–9.

[46] Before his tragic death in a Portuguese bombing attack in Moxico in November 1968, Dr. Américo Boavida, along with Dr. Eduardo dos Santos, recorded findings of the widespread incidence in the East of tuberculosis, syphilis, malaria, sleeping sickness, leprosy, hookworm, malnutrition, and hunger. Cited in Davidson, 1972, pp. 302–3.

manpower.[47] In early 1968, a confidential report revealed that only 1,205 people of all races in Angola were considered to be practising a 'liberal profession' (the professions ranged from doctors, lawyers and engineers to bookkeepers, nurses, private teachers, masseurs and insurance agents). Furthermore, almost half were located in Luanda, the capital.[48] Thus during the final years of the war, at the very time when more money and personnel were needed to cushion the disruptive shock of resettlement life, the Government found itself with less money and available personnel. The result was disastrous for Portuguese counterinsurgency efforts, to say nothing of the Africans who were relocated.

The nature of the social and economic problems engendered by the resettlements in the East can perhaps best be illustrated with three examples.[49] The first concerns Paulo, a fisherman in Moxico District. In 1968 he was moved into a strategic resettlement over fifty miles from the waters which had sustained him and his family and ancestors for centuries. Never having farmed before, he seldom tilled the land given him to grow crops which were totally unfamiliar to him. In addition, the soil on his new land was bad—perhaps an explanation for its being unoccupied when the resettlement site was chosen. Thus when Paulo saw that even the good farmers were having poor results, he ceased working his land altogether. Part of his time was occupied by militia training so that he could defend the resettlement and his new way of life against the insurgents, who promised the people in Paulo's area that they would restore the traditional ways and lands.

The second example is that of Manecas, whose hut was next to Paulo's. He was from a different ethnic group and was only moved eight miles, so he still lived in a familiar area and was even within walking distance of his rice fields. He soon found it impossible, however, to walk to his fields each day, do his necessary work and return by sundown as was required. He was often tempted to stay overnight in his old hut next to his fields, but he knew that if one night his absence were noticed he could be arrested or even shot mistakenly as a 'terrorist', or at least accused of collaborating with the nationalists. Because Manecas could devote so little time to his fields, his production was less than one-tenth of the year before he entered the resettlement. After the first year he rarely went to his fields, as he decided that the results of his first attempt were hardly worth his efforts. The children of both Manecas and Paulo were accustomed to helping their families in the fields or at the river. However, in the resettlement they had nothing to do but await the arrival of the promised teacher—who never appeared, even though

[47] See Mouzinho et al., 1969, pp. 52–3 and Bender and Yoder, 1974, pp. 35–6.

[48] Cf. infra, Table 21, p. 231.

[49] The examples of Paulo and Manecas are based on information I collected in Angola in 1968–9; the example of Chiyana is drawn from information gathered by two journalists, Leon Dash and Bernard Rivers, who travelled 800 miles in eastern Angola during the summer of 1973.

the resettlement residents complied with the authorities' order to build themselves a school.

The third example concerns Chiyana, who was moved with her husband and six children into a strategic resettlement in Mexico. Because of the proximity of the resettlement to the battle zone, none of the inhabitants was allowed to have fields outside the village. Instead, Chiyana and her husband had to work for their food. They would work two twelve-hour days gathering stones for road building and line up on the third day to receive their payment—one mug of maize flour. Thus their family of eight had to share two mugs of flour every three days. This was the only food they had. Chiyana and her husband saw no difference between life in the resettlement and the forced labour of 'the past', and eventually they managed to escape to the refuge of a nationalist camp.

The experiences of Paulo, Manecas and Chiyana were so ubiquitous in the East that it was considered an economic disaster area within two years of the resettlement programme's initiation. A 1969 report by the Benguela Railroad Company, for example, noted that the eastern half of Angola was almost completely lost as a productive agricultural area.[50] In 1969 manioc production dropped 90 per cent in Mexico District and the rice crop was down to practically nothing, paralysing the rice shelling factories. The amount of fish caught and honey and wax gathered also decreased seriously.[54] Agricultural production was so low in the East that one Catholic charity in Angola, CARITAS, asked the United States (in vain) to provide aid (P.L. 480) to supplement the food shortage. Despite this grave food shortage, the military greatly intensified its use of defoliants and herbicides in 1970, further exacerbating the food crisis.[52] One government administrator admonished those responsible for counter-insurgency efforts because of their neglect of the food shortage problems:

[50] 'Relatório de Companhia do Caminho de Ferro de Benguela, 1969', cited in *A Província de Angola* (Luanda), 18 June 1970. Further manifestations of concern over the economic crisis in the east were reflected in the debates in the Legislative Council of Angola in April 1970. Accounts of these debates can be found in *A Província de Angola* (Luanda), 25 April 1970, pp. 4, 7.

[51] One African who was asked why he no longer fished in the Cuando river replied that it was too dangerous since the 'white men always bring their helicopters down by the river to catch any people to try and force them to tell where the guerrilla camps are'. Quoted in the *Times of Zambia*, 6 January 1970.

[52] While Portugal denied throughout the war that it used herbicides, the U.S. Government confirmed that they were used extensively by 1970; see *New York Times*, 9 December 1970. In 1972 and 1973 the nationalist movements presented considerable evidence of the use of herbicides and defoliants. For example, the MPLA estimated that about 4,000 persons died in the East from eating poisoned crops during an eighteen-month period, while FNLA reported more than 2,500 cases of diarrhoea, of which more than 200 were fatal during the period from November 1972 to July 1973. See 'Herbicides—Another Form of Massacre in Angola', *Southern Africa* 6 (October 1973), p. 22. The commander of the Portuguese armed forces in Angola after the coup, General Joaquim António Franco Pinheiro, indicated that Portugal halted all defoliation in May 1974 as an act of goodwill towards the nationalists. Cited in the *New York Times*, 2 June 1974.

The food problem is being given too little attention within the framework of counter-subversion. On the contrary, it is almost systematically ignored ... The population eats food that is disgusting to most people—for example, worms, insects, and birds. The native population normally eats three times a day. Due to the lack of food this is frequently reduced to twice or once. It occasionally occurs that they do not eat at all, or only eat leaves and wild fruits, because of the lack of food.[53]

The food crisis finally received recognition when it reached the white urban centres. In 1972–73, Luanda's newspapers were filled with articles on the acute shortage of rice, potatoes, onions and maize—products which once were exported and now had to be imported. Resettlement was a major contributor to the crisis, both directly (e.g. by causing the reduction of African land cultivated) and indirectly (e.g. by causing the flight of many African farmers either to neighbouring countries or to nationalist-held areas in the colony). During the 1960s the latter problem of population loss was particularly severe in the East, where the population was 42 per cent less by 1970 than expected from the 1960 census.[54]

The Government's response to the crisis did not reassure many Africans. Desperately in need of food, medical care, and education, they received paved roads instead, parts of which they were forced to help build. Between 1965 and 1967 expenditures on improving transportation and communication facilities were almost six times greater than expenditures on health and education, the former consuming half of all expenditures under the Third Development Plan (1968–70).[55] The economic im-

---

[53] Sigurd von Willer Salazar, 'A alimentação nos agregados africanos do Districto de Malange', paper presented to the Symposium on Counter-Subversion, p. 1. Salazar was an administrator in Malange District, not the East; therefore the peoples whom he describes are outside the districts under discussion. This quote was included here, however, since the food crisis was always considered to be worse in the East than the Malange area.

[54] For a study of the impact of the war on population growth and estimates of the number of Africans who were outside Portuguese-controlled areas in all three Portuguese African colonies, see Pelissier, 1974, pp. 34–73. Also see Bender, 1975b, p. 482, note 55.

[55] The importance which the military accorded to road construction cannot be over-emphasized. In 1953 Angola had only 53 miles of asphalted roads, which increased to 250 miles by 1960, the year before the war. By the end of 1972, however, the number of miles of asphalted roads increased eighteen-fold to 4,400! A large portion of these paved roads was built in zones which suffered the most intensive guerrilla challenge—areas which frequently were also the least populated. This leaves an independent Angola with a well-developed road system reaching many remote areas—a situation which is unique in Africa. While asphalt roads consumed most of the money spent by the Government on road construction, a considerably greater amount of non-paved roads were also built. Thus by mid-1973 it was reported that Angola had a total of 45,000 miles of roads. See: Brandenburg, 1969, p. 326; Niddrie, 1969, p. 5; U.N. 1974, p. 25; Diário de Notícias (Lisbon), 10 July 1973; A Província de Angola (Luanda), 13 and 14 January 1973; and Diário de Luanda, 7 April 1973.

portance of the roads built was negligible but they were considered logistically vital to the counterinsurgency programme, as one of the papers delivered at the Symposium on Counter-Subversion clearly indicates: 'It can be said that revolt starts where the roads end. Beyond any doubt, counter-subversion depends far more on connecting roads than on direct confrontation with subversives.'[56] However, although the 'connecting roads' were built, they did not stop the 'revolt' or African resentment.

The Government could not count on the private sector for assistance in the development of the East—practically no company showed interest in locating there. Between 1967 and 1971 the total capital investment in the East was 4·6 million escudos, or an average of about $40,000 per year.[57] Even the Government was reticent to invest in the area. For example, the 'Development Plan for the East, 1972–74' allocated only $700,000— most of which was to be spent on resettlement of Africans.[58] After experiencing more than five disastrous years with the strategic resettlement programme in the East—voluminously documented in confidential and public government reports—the military still remained steadfast in its conviction that population control was the key to winning the war.

While the resettlement programme undoubtedly improved Portugal's control over the population in the East, it did not cut off frequent contacts between the nationalist guerrillas and the civilian population. Intensification of guerrilla activity and eye-witness accounts from noted foreigners verified that the nationalists had 'intimate daily contact with the civilian population'.[59] In fact, it appears that there was a definite correlation between the number of Africans forced into resettlements and the intensity of the war. In 1970, for example, when the Government had already resettled the overwhelming majority of people under its control, according to U.S. intelligence sources the nationalists initiated over 60 per cent more combat actions than the previous year, which resulted in an increase of about 25 per cent in Portuguese casualties. Furthermore, in the same year, the number of nationalist attacks against resettlement militias nearly doubled, which dramatically demonstrated that Portugal lacked the means to guarantee the safety of Africans whom it promised to protect in the resettlements.[60] Thus, the resettlement

[56] Cited in IDOC, 1974, p. 89.

[57] See U.N., 1974, p. 29.

[58] Ibid., p. 8.

[59] See Davidson, 1972, pp. 207–22, 229 note; 1970, p. 16; Rivers, 1974, pp. 41–5; and the excellent series by the *Washington Post* reporter Leon Dash (who won the Overseas Press Award for these articles) in the *Washington Post*, 23–25 December 1973. Dash also reported that nationalist leaders maintained that the poor conditions in the strategic resettlements provided them with fertile recruiting grounds. *Washington Post*, 24 March 1974.

[60] After an extensive trip through Moxico in the spring of 1970, a reporter from Luanda wrote about the 'climate of insecurity' and the 'need for greater protection', and finally suggested that the urban centres appeared to offer the only protective shelter. *A Província de Angola*, 11 April 1970. For an excellent account of the situation just prior to the end of the war, see U.N., 1974, p. 6.

programme failed in its major objective of stopping the internal support extended to the nationalists, who continued to expand their areas of control until the coup of April 1974. At best the resettlements helped to maintain a stalemate in the war—which ultimately proved to be Portugal's Achilles' heel. The stalemate was also costly for the resettled Africans, who not only lost their lands but their health and often their lives as well.

CENTRAL ANGOLA

In the North and East the principal purpose of the resettlements, which were generally constructed in or near areas directly affected by the war, was population control. In central and southern Angola (excluding small pockets in Bie District), armed conflict did not occur throughout the war nor was any seriously expected before the resettlement programme was initiated there. However, there had long been direct competition between Europeans and Africans for land and markets in both central and southern Angola, whereas in the East and most of the North, the small amount of European settlement precluded that type of direct competition. It is not surprising, therefore, that in the former areas there was far more interest in freeing African-held lands than in population control.

The central plains, the most densely populated area of Angola, are largely inhabited by the Ovimbundu peoples, who constitute approximately one-third of the country's population.[61] Both the willingness of the Ovimbundu to fight on the side of the Portuguese Government in the North at the outset of the war, and the fact that most Ovimbundu lived over five hundred miles from either the Zambian or Zaïrean borders, indicated to most officials that there was little danger of widespread Ovimbundu collaboration with the nationalists. For these and other reasons, the Government promised in 1966–67 that no resettlements would be constructed in central Angola. It was feared that the introduction of resettlement could result in the alienation of Africans considered friendly to the Portuguese. This promise was broken, however, 'in 1968 by a governmental order which required all landholders to settle in huge, hastily [sic] constructed villages comprising about 100 to 500 family dwellings'.[62]

The order was partially a product of the panic produced among the Portuguese military by the nationalists' totally unexpected success in the East in 1967. The study group (No. 3) concerned with the central and southern (non-combat) areas reported to the Symposium on Counter-Subversion that since it was an accepted 'fact' that the more dispersed

[61] Rella, 1974, pp. 5–8; Silva Rego and Santos, 1974, pp. 55–7; Redinha, 1967, pp. 15–17 and map; and Silva, F. D., n.d., pp. 83–143. The latter was originally presented as a Master's thesis (ISCSPU) in December 1968, then published as a book in the early 1970s.

[62] Possinger, 1973, p. 46.

the people were the more easily they would be taken in by 'the enemy', the most viable way to prevent this occurrence would be to regroup the population during the period of 'subversion incubation' (pre-insurrection). They further maintained that this policy would not only serve military exigencies but would stimulate social and economic development.[63] Thus this group of officers and administrators felt that the resettlements in central and southern Angola would benefit everybody.

Another officer revealed unmitigated admiration for the Ovimbundu's unmatched adaptation to 'our pattern of life', hard work as agricultural labourers, success as independent farmers and their support of the Portuguese war effort 'by denouncing traitors and even by taking arms against the enemies of Portugal'; he decided, nevertheless, that the Ovimbundu should be concentrated into resettlements. His recommendation was based on his belief that heavy demographic pressure was caused by the Africans' poor exploitation of their natural resources. He concluded that 'on the principle that the best possible use has to be made of the land, it is necessary to intensify the campaign for settling [white] people on it'. Essentially, Lieutenant Gonçalves Coelho saw no contradiction between expanding white settlement and social and economic progress for the Ovimbundu; on the contrary, he averred that 'this regrouping could serve as a model for economic development'.[64]

The gross misunderstanding of the Ovimbundu, shared by so many officials who equated resettlement with economic development, in fact led the Portuguese to stifle an important process of development which had been occurring for decades. The introduction of cash crops (e.g. coffee, corn, beans and wheat) to the Central Highlands, soil depletion, overpopulation, and other external factors had stimulated the Ovimbundu to expand their holdings outside the village structure. In other words, social and economic organization had become more individualized—more Portuguese as it were—with the breakdown of clan or village-bound society. The disintegration of village communities was still progressing when the resettlement programme was implemented in 1968. A German agronomist, who had studied and worked in the area for a number of years, observed:

> The general and highly emotional opposition of the peasants against the government measure [to force Ovimbundu into resettlements] was indeed far more than a protest against the actual economic damage; it nearly led to a complete breakdown of cash-crop production. The attitude of the peasants illustrated that the demand for clearly marked individual family landholdings, not bound to clan and community, was not only conditioned by a specific technical and economic situation

[63] Grupo de Coordenação e Inspecção da Contra-Subversão, 1968, pp. 6 and 10.

[64] Coelho, n.d.(b), paper presented to the Council on Counter-Subversion, quoted in IDOC, 1974, pp. 110–11.

which made subsistence in large villages next to impossible. Their refusal of resettlement must moreover be interpreted as an indication that large villages symbolized a way of life the Mbundu peasants no longer accept.[65]

Ovimbundu resentment was further exacerbated by the fact that most lived hundreds of miles from the war zones and therefore they could not understand the 'strategic' necessities for their resettlement. It seemed to be a form of punishment, an idea which was encouraged, in part, by the methods used to move the people. One elderly man who lived over two hundred miles from any fighting told a Canadian missionary in 1969:

It's really tough. Those who didn't build their new huts immediately after being told had their old ones, including all of their belongings, burned by the troops. N ... came up last week and told me how the troops burned the house and granary of a friend who had been given permission to stay by the administrator. [He concluded] even the Ovimbundu won't stand for this kind of treatment.[66]

Between 1968 and 1970 many local administrators pushed the expansion of the resettlements with such zeal that large numbers of people were either removed immediately after they had planted their fields—often they were then unable to tend them—and/or they arrived in the new villages after the planting season. A further irritation resulted from the fact that the new fields were often smaller than their former lands and with inferior soils. One resettlement in Huambo District was located on land with so much shale that it was impossible for the inhabitants to grow their maize.

To most Africans in the Central Highlands, the resettlement programme appeared to be just another ruse to cheat them out of their lands, especially since there had been intensive competition with the Portuguese for the best lands for decades. The climate and soils attracted Europeans to the already highly populated area, resulting in the loss of thousands of African holdings. After the reforms of September 1961, African lands were theoretically protected under the decree (43 894) which established three classes of land in Angola: (a) first-class—land in the urban areas and immediate suburbs; (b) second-class—communally-held African lands; and (c) third-class—any land residually considered as neither first- nor second-class and which could therefore be conceded to Europeans. The law further stipulated that second-class land must encompass an area five times that occupied by a village (in order to take into account patterns of shifting cultivation) and, recognizing the Africans' 'inalienable' rights

[65] Possinger in Heimer, 1973c, p. 46. For an excellent summary of developments in Ovimbundu agriculture during the period preceding resettlement, see pp. 43–6.

[66] I would like to acknowledge the assistance of and information from the late Betty Gilchrist (including the sharing of this quote) on resettlements in the Cuima area of Huambo District.

to this land, the law prohibited their expulsion.[67] White farmers strongly objected to the second-class land delimitation, for they knew that if the law were scrupulously applied there would be no third-class lands available for concessions in the Highlands. Thus, although legally third-class lands could not only be determined after the first- and second-class lands had been, in practice the second-class lands were never delimited, often causing them to be defined as those tracts which did not fall under the categories of first- or third-class lands. In short, neither the white settlers nor many government officials—especially those responsible for land demarcation (Direcção dos Serviços Geográficos e Cadastrais)— understood, accepted, or respected African land rights.[68]

Despite this generalized attitude towards African land rights, it was not always easy to physically displace Africans from their land in the crowded Highlands. It is in this context that resettlement should be seen, for it immediately 'opened up' hundreds of thousands of acres. This presented military and civilian officials with a major problem when they realized that the land which the Africans were forced to abandon would 'arouse the greed of Europeans' who would covet it.[69] Almost all the papers presented to the Symposium on Counter-Subversion which touched on this problem strongly recommended government protection of such lands and that under no condition should they be given as concessions to European farmers.[70]

---

[67] Further information on the system of land laws in Angola after September 1961 can be found in: Guimaraes, F. De V., 1969, pp. 1–8; Moreira, 1961a, pp. 204–21; U.N., 1965, pp. 7–35; and Raposo, 1972, pp. 35–43.

[68] Discussions of violations of African land rights can be found in: Guimaraes, F. de V., 1969, pp. 3–5; Polanah, 1972, pp. 12–13; Mendes, 1969, p. 6; IDOC, 1974, pp. 71–4; and three Commissions of Study for the Symposium on Counter-Subversion (previously cited); Section, I, pp. 8–9, 14; Section III, p. 3; Section VI, p. 4.

[69] See Study Commission of Section I, p. 8.

[70] See especially those papers cited in *supra*, note 68.

From the day the new land law was promulgated (6 September 1961), the provision protecting African communal lands (second-class lands) was strongly attacked by white settlers and a number of public officials. Pressure was directed towards the Council on Counter-Subversion in 1968–9 to abolish second-class lands, but there appears to have been a strong conviction in the Council that the law should be preserved. For example, the minutes of one of the debates in the Council on this question reveal:

There are great doubts on whether the abolition of second-class land is opportune, since it is certain that such a distinction, with all the defects it may have, constitutes in a manner of speaking an arm—perhaps the only arm—for the defence of the strata of the population to which it is relevant. (*Minutes of the Meeting of the Council on Counter-Subversion* (Luanda) taken by Joaquim Nogueira Jordão, 15 July 1968, p. 4. Also see minutes of 19 July 1968, pp. 1–3.)

After failing in their attempt to overturn the second-class land category, the settlers turned to Lisbon and, in December 1972, the Corporative Chamber considered a bill which would have revised the 1961 land concession legislation. Significantly, the introduction

The importance of this issue can be appreciated better by considering land pressures in Huambo District, Angola's breadbasket, whose population is approximately 88 per cent Ovimbundu. At the time of the resettlement campaign it was estimated that 'by present technological standards of land occupation, there is already an excess of about 150,000 people (or 23 per cent of the rural population) on the land left to the Ovimbundu in the Huambo District', which forced approximately 60,000 Ovimbundu to migrate annually to other parts of the colony in search of work.[71] Despite this dismal situation and the military's awareness of the delicacy of the land problem and its attendant economic and military consequences, the avarice of the whites prevailed. Between 1968 and 1970 the amount of land held by Europeans in Huambo District *more than doubled* (from 249,039 to 526,270 hectares); during the same period the amount of land cultivated by Africans was reduced by more than a third (36·5 per cent)![72] Once again, as it had done for five centuries, white greed undermined and ridiculed official policy and, also once again, Africans were expected to accept the bitter consequences stoically and peacefully.

One important reason why more efforts were not made to stop the white land grab in the Central Highlands was that most officials were convinced that the expansion of white settlement represented an expansion of Portuguese security. In fact, this was precisely the position advanced in the meetings of the Council on Counter-Subversion by the Director of SCCIA, Angola's former top intelligence organization.[73] For the most part, those responsible for the strategic resettlements were ignorant of traditional social and economic systems extant in the colony, which contributed to their myopic perception of the impact of expanded white settlement. A few lonely individuals, however, indefatigably fought to prevent further white settlement in densely populated areas of the colony —especially the Central Highlands—but they framed their criticisms within the perspective of counterinsurgency exigencies. One of the most penetrating expositions of this perspective is found in a paper presented by an agronomist, Francisco Sá Pereira, to the Council on Counter-Subversion within months of the mid-1968 initiation of the resettlement

---

to the bill affirmed the Government's continuing concern about protecting the white settler population in the colonies and developing the natural resources; but there was no mention of protecting the interests of the indigenous populations. The thrust of the bill was to change the three categories of land to two—urban and rural—which would have made it easier for Portuguese individuals and enterprises to acquire the large areas of land. See U.N., 1973, pp. 18–19.

[71] Vierra da Silva and Morais, 1973, p. 98.

[72] Carriço and Morais, 1971, p. 24.

[73] Recorded in the Minutes of the meeting of the Council on Counter-Subversion in Luanda, 29 July 1968, p. 2.

programme in the Central Highlands. The following is a paraphrase of his argument to the Council:[74]

While we cannot doubt the role which European occupation of agricultural land plays in security considerations, we also cannot forget that this frequently comes at the cost of yet another security factor whose importance is rarely recognized: the development of traditional agriculture. Innumerable examples can be presented which show that European agrarian occupation enters into competition with African agrarian development, often in the form of serious shocks, such as occurred with agrarian settlement in Cela, tobacco of Quilengues, cellulose and sisal of Ganda and Cubal, the pasture lands in Mucope, etc., etc. In every case, the best lands and marketing channels were taken from the Africans.

The general opinion in Angola is that there are vast areas of uninhabited land which should leave room for Europeans and Africans to farm side by side, but this view ignores the fact that traditional agricultural methods require large areas of land which can only be reduced in size (thus freeing areas for white settlement) through significant government assistance. In other words, the first step toward expansion of white agriculture settlement should be the development of traditional agriculture. As it is, the amount of African lands is being reduced without any technical compensations, which can only contribute to the deterioration of conditions for African farmers and herders. At the present time further white agricultural settlement can only be realized to the detriment of traditional agriculture. Thus, the political alternative is clear: one must decide which security factor is more important—European agrarian occupation or the development of traditional agriculture—because they are at present mutually exclusive.

The resettlement of Africans away from their lands and the concession of those lands to whites is not only a tough blow to the Africans' ideas of individual freedom but a severe impediment to the progress of their culture, which in many areas of Angola (e.g. central plateau) was clearly developing before the advent of this programme. The Africans view these changes as a regression and with each regression we create a new potential stratum of subversion in the traditional milieu.

[74] Sá Pereira, 1968. Sá Pereira was Assistant Director of the Missão de Inquéritos Agrícolas de Angola (Angolan Board of Agricultural Census and Surveys). He presented this paper in the place of the Director of MIAA, Eduardo Cruz de Carvalho, who was away from the colony at the time. The position expressed by Sá Pereira epitomized the general orientation of the entire MIAA staff, whose decade-long, difficult and, at times, dangerous daily battles against white settler interests evoke considerable admiration. Without the guidance and teachings of MIAA personnel— such as Eduardo Cruz de Carvalho, Francisco Sá Pereira, Julio Morais, Ze and Jaime Almeida, Elias and Duarte Candeías, Manuel Dias, Manuel de Oliveira, and many others—on a 3,000-mile trip through the interior of Angola, it would never have been possible for me to have gained a fraction of my present understanding of rural Angola.

Within months the opposition to resettlement advanced by Sá Pereira, Eduardo Cruz de Carvalho (the Deputy Director and the Director of the Missão de Inquéritos Agricolas de Angola, respectively), and others drew harsh criticism from their fellow participants in the Council on Counter-Subversion. The two heads of the Department of Economic Services, for example, argued that:

> it has been mentioned that as a means of arresting subversion it is important to rapidly improve the technical processes of the native populations, in such a way as to provide them with a substantial increase in wealth. We believe that this is of enormous interest to the province's economy, but it is not the safest road to avoid subversion at this time. Only the settlement of [white] men in the interior can be [effective].[75]

The group responsible for the central and southern districts went even further and argued that resettlement in these areas was so popular and successful that Africans were actually asking to be moved. In a strong attack against government officials who opposed resettlement, they remonstrated that there was no evidence for 'the so-called ancestral habits' impeding the success of resettlement, and further contended that those who opposed resettlement on these (and other) grounds were 'covering up their incapacity and damned aloofness from their responsibilities and obligations by continuing to speak only of the difficulties'.[76]

Both critics and defenders of resettlement had an opportunity to translate their beliefs into policy in Bie, the easternmost district of central Angola, which both nationalists and Portuguese considered as the military key to the Central Highlands. By way of background it should be noted that African farmers began having considerable success after the mid-1960s—especially those who grew coffee on small plots in northern Bie. A few government officials and agricultural experts described the increased coffee production as the most promising agricultural development in all Angola, further noting that these Africans had probably developed a stake in the *status quo*.

Some minor nationalist infiltration (although no fighting) was noticed in Bie in 1967 and early the following year a small group of Africans claimed to have been 'vaccinated' against 'white men's bullets'. With strong urging from nervous white settlers in the area, local administrators

[75] Pedriras and Pinto, 1968, pp. 1–2.
[76] Grupo de Coordenação e Inspecção da Contra-Subversào, 1968, pp. 8–9.

and the army killed several hundred Africans as an 'object lesson'. The incident persuaded Angolan officials, particularly the military, that population control measures—notably resettlement villages—were necessary. They were convinced that if the nationalists gained a foothold in this gateway to the populous Central Highlands, the course of the war could be changed; i.e. they feared that they did not have enough manpower to contain the insurgency if it incorporated appreciably more Africans.

The plans for the resettlements, which had been on the drawing boards for over a year, were immediately implemented, and over wide areas of Bie Africans were moved into large resettlement villages. At the same time, many of the younger men who had not been drafted into the Portuguese military were recruited to work as labourers on the coffee plantations in the North. This left an unusually high percentage of elderly men, women and children to work the fields. Often far from their original plots, the remaining population was unable to match the record crops of the past years and coffee production dropped dramatically. The resettlement programme may have reduced the infiltration, but the critics began to warn of future trouble because of the agricultural setbacks.

In 1970 their worst fears were realized. According to a U.S. intelligence report, all three major nationalist groups were active in Bie District (in the northeast where Bie, Moxico and Lunda Districts meet; in the southeast at the tripoint of Bie, Moxico, and Cuando Cubango Districts; and in central Bie, east of the Cuanza river). Portugal immediately began moving inactive troops from other areas into Bie in an attempt to stop the guerrillas at the Cuanza river. It is impossible to speculate if and when the insurgency would have arrived in Bie had the Portuguese not undertaken the resettlement of the African population, but it is clear that the guerrillas were able to capitalize greatly on the dissatisfaction engendered by the programme.

The outbreak of fighting in Bie forced a major reassessment of counterinsurgency policy for the district. Critics of resettlement, who had failed to convert government officials from the lowest *chefe de posto* to Governor General Rebocho Vaz, now directed their lobbying to the new Commander in Chief of the Armed Forces, General Costa Gomes—who would later become Chief of Staff of the Portuguese Armed Forces until being fired in March 1974 and who, on 30 September 1974, would be named President of Portugal following General Spínola's resignation. After months of discussion, the critics finally convinced Costa Gomes and he ordered a rollback in the resettlement programme. The General approved a plan which disbanded the resettlements in the Andulo area and established a rural extension pilot project in the locality headed by a German agronomist, Hermann Possinger, perhaps the most vociferous critic of the resettlement programme.[77]

The goal of the pilot project was to show that social and economic development within traditional patterns was not only possible but inevitable if the Government invested its money and energies in improving, rather than destroying, those 'so-called ancestral habits'. It was argued that this was the only hope for containing an insurgency in the area. In fact, however, those responsible for the extension programme were not seriously interested in contributing to the counter-insurgency effort, but in launching another form of revolution whose goals were essentially consistent with those of the nationalists. Both aimed at eradicating the oppressive colonial mechanisms which not only impeded but reversed African social and economic development.[78] The extension pilot project involved a comprehensive attack on well-entrenched exploitive systems of credit, marketing and transportation networks, and provided substantial relevant technical assistance (training, seeds, fertilizers, etc.), built new storage facilities, and started agricultural clubs for the purpose of taking advantage of better prices through co-operative buying and selling.[79] The results were so impressive that even the most intransigent critic of rural extension had to admit to the conspicuous success of the programme. On 16 October 1971, the rural extension programme was made permanent and greatly expanded in Bie and Huambo. By the end of 1973 there were fifty-six teams of extension workers in the two districts assisting over half a million people.[80] Not all African farmers in the extension programme experienced the dramatic increases of the maize farmers, who in some zones improved their per hectare yield more than ten times. Generally, however, there were vast improvements in all sectors.[81]

It is not possible to credit or blame (depending on one's perspective)

[77] Hermann Possinger, after working in Brazil for a decade (1952–62), turned his attention to problems of rural development in Africa as a senior researcher in tropical agriculture and economy at the IFO–Institut in Munich. He has conducted research in Tanzania, Kenya, Uganda, Madagascar, South Africa, Ethiopia, Sudan, Mozambique, and Angola. He first visited Angola in 1963 and over the following decade he stayed in Angola for a total of more than four years. His influence in convincing important members of the Government and military in Angola to substitute positive rural assistance for resettlement cannot be overestimated. An excellent statement of the general views which he expounded in Angola at this time can be found in a speech, 'Congresso de Povoamento e Promoção Social', delivered 9 October 1970 in Andulo, Angola (mimeo).

[78] Despite the fact that the Portuguese Government eventually gave prominence to the rural extension programme in the over-all counterinsurgency effort, Possinger never viewed the programme as counterrevolutionary. On the contrary, he strongly believed that societies undergoing rapid development were potentially more revolutionary than those which exist in abject poverty. Conversations with Hermann Possinger in Munich, Germany, May 1969.

[79] Missão de Extensão Rural de Angola, *Relatório de Actividades, 1972* (Nova Lisboa: MERA, 1973), pp. 1–61 and *Diário de Luanda*, 13 May 1973.

[80] Estado de Angola, 1973a, pp. 11–12 and *A Província de Angola* (Luanda), 15 August 1973.

[81] Missão de Extensão Rural de Angola, *Relatório de Actividades, 1972*, p. 29.

the rural extension programme for the fact that the insurgency in the central plateau did not appreciably expand before the end of the war the zones established in 1970. Undoubtedly many factors account for this lack of expansion, such as logistical problems of supplying an insurgency four to five hundred miles from a friendly border, ethnic considerations, the relative weakness of the nationalist military forces near the end of the war (caused in part by internal factional divisions), demographic and topographic differences from the East, etc. Nevertheless, it is a fact that the insurgency did not spread into areas incorporated into the extension programme—a statement which cannot be made about resettlement. Because the extension programme was not moved into areas of actual fighting, it is not known whether the government could have successfully employed it as a counterinsurgency strategy. It is clear, however, that Africans incorporated into the rural extension programme were *infinitely better off* economically, socially, politically and educationally at the end of the war than Africans who had been resettled!

THE SOUTH

Nowhere in the colony was the programme of resettlement more superfluous to the exigencies of counterinsurgency or antithetical to traditional African social and economic patterns than in southern Angola (i.e. the districts of Cunene, Huila, Moçamedes and the western half of Cuando Cubango). While the area contained sedentary African and Portuguese farmers, most of the inhabitants were pastoral or agropastoral populations who tended approximately two million head of cattle in a nomadic and semi-nomadic existence.[82] Similar to most African cattle-keepers, the Angolan pastoralists have assimilated relatively few western traits and have always manifested a fierce sense of independence and a strong commitment to preserving their traditional way of life against any encroachments from either Europeans or other Africans. These cultural and historical realities, combined with the fact that the open, arid and semiarid zones in the South would have made it extremely difficult to camouflage armed guerrillas, suggested to some enlightened military and government officials that there was little likelihood of the pastoralists participating in the armed struggle—*if they were essentially left alone.*

However, in 1968, zealous local officials, anxious to make a 'contribution' to the war effort and generally ignorant of African traditions, ordered some of the semi-nomadic pastoralists (e.g. Ovambos, Handas and Herreros) to construct and occupy huts in fixed resettlement villages. The resettlements represented cultural genocide and economic ruin for the

[82] The most comprehensive analyses of the area's human and physical ecology can be found in: Cruz de Carvalho, 1974, pp. 199–225, and Cruz de Carvalho and Vieira da Silva, 1973, pp. 145–92. Also see Urquhart, 1963, *passim*; Estermann, 1960a, pp. 21–262; 1960b, pp. 13–278; and Murdock, 1959, pp. 369–74.

pastoralists, whose social and economic way of life is dependent upon the careful ecological balance they have evolved within their annual transhumances.[83] The order to settle permanently in fixed villages was especially resented because the war had not even remotely touched (nor did it ever touch) this area. Within months major problems arose in the South for the Portuguese. An important Ovambo chief refused to move his people into a resettlement they had been forced to construct, and told a government official that the only way they could get him into the resettlement would be to kill him and carry his body in. This and similar incidents brought a number of PIDE agents and SCCIA personnel into the area, not only because of resistance to resettlement, but to investigate reports of incipient contacts between nationalist guerrillas and the pastoralists.

Military considerations were not the only factors involved in the initial decision to resettle African pastoralists. For decades Portuguese ranchers had been moving into the area and they, along with many others, were anxious to expand the size and number of European holdings. White expansion in the South had been hindered, however, by the law which included African pastoral areas under the protection of second-class lands. Consequently, support for the white settlers' demands to abolish the second-class lands began to appear in newspapers, magazines and Legislative Council debates. It was argued that African cattle-raising practices were hopelessly primitive, unproductive, and not responsive to marketing needs, and therefore a portion of their land should be given to white ranchers who, it was alleged, would vastly increase productivity. While this argument had no basis in fact (i.e. African herds were often equally or more productive than cattle raised on European ranches in the same zone), the spurious 'technological' appeals won considerable support within the Government—although not sufficient to overturn the land law.[84]

[83] For a remarkable map showing the paths of the transhumances in the area, see Missão de Inquéritos Agrícolas de Angola, *Recenseamento Agrícola de Angola*, vol. 20 (1968), map 2.

[84] It is hoped that the widely held myth (and belief) that the so-called modern or western methods of cattle raising are more efficient and productive than traditional methods will be laid to rest after Cruz de Carvalho's unparalleled comparative study of the two systems (see note 82). This myth was sustained in Angola in part because of the marketing system, which tended to obscure the origin of cattle marketed. Frequently, African cattle were purchased by Portuguese ranchers and integrated into their own herds before being sold, which gave the impression that a significantly greater proportion of the cattle marketed in Angola were raised by Europeans than was actually the case. Cattle merchants, however, finally admitted in 1970 that 90–95 per cent of Angola's meat export came from traditional herds. Actas das Sessões do Conselho Legislativo de Angola, Acta no. 191 (Luanda 1970), cited in Cruz de Carvalho and Vieira da Silva, 1973, pp. 162–3.

The Portuguese received encouragement in their efforts to transform nomadic pastoralists into sedentary cattle ranchers by some reputedly 'high-power' American consultants from the Hudson Institute, led by Herman Kahn. The 1969 Hudson study of Angola (sponsored by the infamous Portuguese conglomerate, Companhia União Fabril-CUF)

Some lands in the South were simply seized by Portuguese ranchers (who either expelled the occupants or hired them to tend cattle) and, in the case of the colonato Chitado on the Namibian border, the land was taken over by the Government itself.[85] More frequently, however, whites obtained their land through pseudo-legal methods. All petitions for land concessions required certification that the plot was not inhabited or utilized by Africans. Local, district, and provincial authorities would often sign these certificates without prior investigation, or even if they knew that the land was occupied by Africans. While bribery played a role in the false certifications, it was not always necessary since most of the officials believed that the expansion of European farms and ranches was economically and politically desirable. At times the clamour for African land took on such decidedly anti-African tones that the Governor General (Rebocho Vas) was forced on several occasions to remind white settlers in Huila District that Africans were also people with their own civilizations which deserved respect, and he warned that a failure to recognize this fact could undermine Portugal's goal to remain in Angola.[86]

Whereas white farmers and ranchers enthusiastically endorsed resettlement in the South because of the land they hoped it would bring them, another powerful white interest group—*comerciantes* or bush traders—was less than supportive and frequently opposed the programme because

---

underscores the limitations and, at times, folly of believing that American (or other Western) 'think tanks' or 'brain trusts' are capable of providing useful analysis and/or advice on every issue in every part of the world. Edmond Stillman, an American political scientist and member of the Hudson 'team' which studied Angola, argued, for example, that:

There is no reason why cattle ranches of relatively modern dimensions might not be run by the cattle tribes of the south ... The ability of blacks in the Carmana [*sic*] area to adapt to European-style coffee farming would suggest that this could be done.

Stillman, not unlike most of the Portuguese officials who supported the resettlement programme in the South, manifests a profound ignorance of African cultural and economic patterns in his inability to distinguish between sedentary agriculturalists and nomadic cattle herders. The substitution of a cash crop (e.g. coffee in the Carmona region) for a subsistence crop is by no means analogous to a nomadic pastoralist denying all of his cultural, religious, and economic practices to become a stationary cattle rancher. See Stillman, 1969, p. 171.

[85] The area of Chitado was seized in order to locate a number of Portuguese ex-soldiers on expensive European-style ranches which the Government built on African lands. The experiment of trying to increase 'security' and 'economic productivity' by using ex-soldiers was such a social and economic disaster that it was never attempted again. Further information on Chitado can be found in *supra*, pp. 109–10, especially note 68.

Despite the overwhelmingly negative results which occurred in trying to settle ex-servicemen on rural farms in Angola, a number of Portuguese continued to praise the programme. See for example: Araujo, 1964; pp. 52–4 and the articles by Maurício R. Soares in *A Província de Angola* (Luanda), 19 October 1968 and 22 February 1969.

[86] Interview with Lieutenant-Colonel Rebocho Vaz, in the Governor's Luanda office, 11 March 1969. The Governor General made similar remarks in public the following year. See U.N., 1970, p. 79.

of the resultant loss of African trade. During most of the present century the Portuguese bush trader offered Africans the only means for commercializing their cattle and agricultural production. During the war, attempts in the South to break their exploitive monopoly through the introduction of government-run markets failed, principally because of opposition by the traders.[87] As a general rule the trading system operated in the following manner.[88] Transactions were based on the barter of goods, the value of which was set by the bush trader. Because Africans had practically no access to sources of credit, they were forced to rely on the bush trader for credit to purchase goods between harvests. The refusal of most traders to allow Africans to pay off their debts in cash prevented them from selling their products in the government-run rural markets (which usually paid higher prices but did not extend credit). Furthermore, without access to the middlemen from whom the bush trader bought and sold goods, Africans were tied into a system in which they had to sell their products to the local bush trader or not sell at all. European farmers and ranchers, on the other hand, sold directly to the middlemen and only rarely went through the bush traders. Many traders complained that resettlement was ruining their business because of the resultant drop in African production. For example, one trader, who was located along the former path of a group of nomadic cattle people who had been moved into a permanent resettlement, indicated that the number of cattle he bought from Africans in late 1968 dropped from about thirty to one or two per month.

The bush traders' opposition to resettlement had only minimal impact on government or military officials, principally because of their well-deserved reputation as racists, thieves, and supreme exploiters of Africans. These men—who evoked such admiration among the lusotropicalists because they 'lived in the bush among the people and spoke their language'—used every imaginable means to cheat Africans (e.g. regularly fixing the balances on their scales to underweigh cattle and produce, adding items which were never purchased to the credit accounts, paying extremely low prices for African products, and charging exorbitant prices for their goods—especially wine).[89] In Angola there were absolutely no illusions about the exploitive nature of this system of trade,

[87] See Bender, 1972b, p. 35; and Comissão de Estudo da Secção I of the Symposium on Counter-Subversion, pp. 10–11.

[88] More extensive descriptions of the exploitive nature of the bush trading system of barter can be found in: Missão de Extensão Rural de Angola, *Relatório, 1972*, pp. 35–7; Polanah, 1972, pp. 10 and 15; Comissão de Estudo da Secção VI of the Symposium on Counter-Subversion, p. 3; and Ribeiro, 1975, p. 56.

[89] It should be noted that the overwhelming majority of bush traders were themselves blatantly exploited by wholesalers in the major cities who supplied the traders with credit and goods. In fact, it can probably be said that the bush traders were forced to operate on such a small margin of profit that it would not have been possible for them to have survived economically unless they cheated the Africans.

as can be seen in the following observations by an excellent govern-ment anthropologist and a contributor to the Symposium on Counter-Subversion:

> the man in the rural area recognizes that his situation is unjust, that he should live better. There are many who have had years of good harvest, earning money as never before: 'But we continue like this' (pointing to their clothes, huts, children, their ailments). 'The one who earns', they add, 'is the bush trader'. Their vision does not ex-tend beyond the bush trader where, for ages, all of their production has been channelled. Also the money they have earned.[90]

> We know that the [African] farmer continues to be robbed, although to a lesser extent. He is aware of this, but refrains from saying anything because for the basic necessities of life he needs credit, which he has to pay back at harvest time with usurious interest charges.[91]

Before the war the interplay of two such powerful interest groups as the settlers and traders would have been resolved by the appropriate government bureaucracies towards which these groups focused most of their lobbying on the question of African resettlement. During the war, however—especially during the last half—the military dominated the decision-making processes in most sectors and became the major arbiter of conflicts among white interest groups. Neither the traders nor settlers in the South evoked much sympathy among the military (i.e. their anti-African attitude and behaviour were condemned as detrimental to the war effort) and they were essentially ignored during the 1969 military debates about whether to expand or cut back the resettlement of Africans in the South.[92]

A special report to the Symposium on Counter-Subversion by the study group responsible for regroupment and control of Africans presented the dilemma of attempting to regroup the pastoral peoples. On the one hand, they agreed that the dispersion and migratory patterns of the pastoralists leave them considerably more vulnerable (i.e. accessible) to nationalist 'subversion', since they generally live beyond the scope of government surveillance. They also knew, however, that if the Government attempted to remedy this problem by forcing the pastoralists into fixed villages, it would remove the very means by which the people have always 'resolved their anxieties and problems', and thus there would be little hope of ever winning their support. The study group concluded (and was supported by other contributors to the Symposium) that surveillance merited a higher priority than the economic productivity and social cohesion of the people, and therefore

---

[90] Polanah, 1972, pp. 14–15.

[91] Quoted in IDOC, 1974, p. 76.

[92] For further discussion on the reactions of white interest groups to the resettlement programme, see Bender, 1972a, pp. 352–3.

recommended that they be regrouped.[93] A minority of the participants in the Symposium rejected this solution categorically, arguing that it was technically impossible for the pastoralists to maintain any semblance of economic activity in fixed villages. Others tried to forge a compromise, calling for militia units to accompany all pastoralists on their trans-humances, but this was rejected as impractical.[94] Ultimately, those responsible for resettlement in the South were persuaded to curtail the programme on the basis of reports from military officers and PIDE agents indicating that there was considerably more nationalist activity and propaganda among pastoralists who had already been resettled than among those unaffected by the programme.

The military's decision to slow down their resettlement programme in the South did not, however, end the forced settlement of pastoralists in the region. The pastoralists' way of life was further jeopardized by the accord signed between Portugal and South Africa in 1969, known as the Cunene River Basin Scheme. The plan to build a series of dams along the six hundred-mile Cunene river interested South Africa because of the cheap electricity which could be derived from the Calueque Dam along the Namibian border. The Portuguese were princi-pally interested in irrigating large areas of land which could support the expansion of white ranches and farms.[95] The plan envisioned the irrigation of 320,000 acres of agricultural land and an additional 865,000 acres for cattle grazing, but the first phase was reduced to approximately 230,000 acres for agriculture and 250,000 acres of pasture land.[96]

[93] Grupo de Coordenação e Inspecção de Contra-Subversão, 1968, pp. 2–3. José Gonçalves Coelho, (n.d.(a), p. 4) in his paper to the Symposium on the regrouping of pastoral populations of Huila District, demonstrates considerable knowledge and understanding of the traditional social and economic systems of the pastoralists, but nevertheless concludes that 'the pastoral populations can and should be regrouped'.

[94] Morais, C. A. de, n.d., cited in IDOC, 1974, pp. 36–7 and Prego, 1969, p. 3.

[95] It should be noted that the political interests of Portugal and South Africa outweighed the economic considerations behind the joint accord to carry out the Cunene River Basin Scheme. South Africa correctly worried that Portugal's resolve and ability to maintain its control over Angola and Mozambique were waning and they hoped that the Cunene Scheme would give the Portuguese a greater stake in staying. The Portuguese, moreover, were anxious to attract significant amounts of foreign capital both to help develop economic sectors which were beyond her means and to give her allies a greater stake in her sur-vival in Africa.

The complete text of the Portuguese-South African agreement on the first phase of the Cunene River Basin Scheme can be found (in Portuguese and English) in *Diário do Governo* (Lisbon), first series, number 250 (28 October 1970), pp. 1589–96. Further infor-mation on the rationale behind the agreement and the initial plans can be found in: Sousa Ferreira, 1974a, pp. 159–69; Niddrie, 1970, pp. 1–17, 57–8; U.N., 1971, pp. 62–4; and Overseas Companies of Portugal, n.d., pp. 1–12.

[96] 'Cunene Scheme May Attract More Guerrillas Than Settlers', *African Development* (July 1972), pp. 14–16; U.N., 1973b, p. 11; Castelinho, 1972, pp. 23–5; 'Plano Cunene', *Notícias de Portugal* 27 (5 September 1973), p. 11; and *Jornal do Comércio* (Lisbon), 20 July 1971, p. 21.

Initial reports in the international media that the Cunene River Basin Scheme would result in the settlement of 500,000 new Portuguese settlers were illusory and immediately denied by the Portuguese Government. However, by the end of 1974, 6,233 Portuguese families were reported to have settled on the newly irrigated land.[97] In order to make room for these and other families and to clear an area of seventy square miles for an artificial lake behind the dam, tens of thousands of African farmers and pastoralists were moved into permanent resettlements. In Cunene District the plan would have resulted in the reduction of communal grazing lands by half and would have lowered the herd size in the region from 207,800 to 60,000–70,000 animal units. Ironically, agronomists estimated that the white ranches would not have enough carrying capacity to supplement the anticipated loss of African cattle![98]

Thus, at the very time the military decided to de-emphasize the strategic importance of resettlement in the South, the Government began its own campaign to resettle Africans under the Cunene River Basin Scheme. While the latter resettlement was rationalized on the basis of the purported economic and social development it would bring to the area, 'development' implied the expansion of the white or Portuguese economic sector at the expense of the African sector. This naturally represented an anathema to Africans because of both the land loss and the forced adoption of an entirely new way of life.

Most Portuguese familiar with resettlement in the South entertained few illusions about the repercussions for Africans. It was understood that resettlement engendered strong resentments against the regime and carried little hope of contributing to winning the 'hearts and minds' of the people. Yet resettlement continued because the expansion of white settlement and Portuguese economic patterns were considered to be of greater importance. It is not possible to maintain (as some Portuguese spuriously did) that resettlement was responsible for the absence of armed conflict in the South, because there was never a serious threat of armed action before the programme began, nor did the topography favour guerrilla warfare. It is possible to assert, however, that the expansion of resettlement encouraged Africans in the South to more actively enter into contact with the nationalists for reasons which undoubtedly had more to do with the preservation of the basic way of life than with the achievement of political independence.

Conclusion

During more than thirteen years of armed warfare in Angola, the Portuguese colonial government and military sought to cut all contact between

[97] Committee for Freedom in Mozambique, Angola and Guiné, n.d., p. 5; and *Comércio do Funchal* (Madeira), 19 December 1974, p. 11.
[98] Cruz de Carvalho and Vieira da Silva, 1973, p. 164.

the nationalist forces and the civilian African population and, at the same time, to win Africans over to the Portuguese side through programmes of social and economic development. The resettlement of African peasants into large circumscribed villages was the vehicle chosen to fulfil these two goals in the countryside. By the end of the independence war over one million peasants had been moved into resettlements and the results of this relocation show that, with rare exceptions, the two goals were incompatible. That is to say, the maximization of population control led to serious breakdowns in the social and psychological security of the peasantry and to a marked decline in economic productivity and food supplies.[99] Military theorists will undoubtedly debate and speculate for years whether Portugal's resettlement programme provided sufficient population control to avert an actual military defeat, or if the programme boomeranged and guaranteed the nationalists an inexhaustible supply of soldiers and supporters among the inhabitants of the resettlements. Whatever strategic advantages the resettlements may have provided, one inescapable truth is that they were not enough to break the military deadlock which ultimately drained Portugal's resources and her will to continue the armed struggle.

There is considerable evidence to suggest that while the Portuguese generals in Angola, Mozambique and Guinea-Bissau were indefatigably defending the thesis that resettlement held the key to victory, the negative effects of the massive dislocation of Africans alienated rather than attracted the peasantry and ultimately fed the very insurgency it was intended to extinguish. As early as January 1969, it was obvious to at least one of the six study commissions of the Symposium on Counter-Subversion that the strategic resettlements had provoked a number of serious problems which were capitalized on by the nationalists. The commission's synthesis—which follows—of the economic, health and social problems engendered by the strategic resettlements merits attention not only because it proved prophetic, but also because it provides (inadvertently) an excellent summary of the overall negative impact which all resettlements produced in rural Angola:[100]

A. *From an economic standpoint*:

1. the abandonment, by resettled populations, of an economic organization which provided a stable basis for their subsistence;
2. the need to reorganize economic life in a new locale with a corresponding drop in output;

[99] For an extensive analysis comparing the resettlement of peasants under wartime conditions (into strategic hamlets) in Angola, Mozambique, Guinea-Bissau, Malaya, Algeria, Vietnam, and Rhodesia, as well as resettlement under peacetime conditions (into *ujamaa* villages) in Tanzania, see Bender, 1975b, pp. 448–63, 491–97; and 1972a, pp. 353–60.

[100] This synthesis is found in the paper prepared for the Symposium on Counter-Subversion by the Study Commission of section VI (Social Advancement—Rural Resettlement), 'Relatório e Conclusões', presented 24 January 1969, pp. 21–3.

3. the need for the State, in an emergency situation, to support these populations until the subsistence balance is restored;
4. the loss of income—for an indefinite period of time and not easily recuperated—from perennial crops;
5. the difficulty or impossibility of maintaining the herds of cattle because of the loss of the natural equilibrium between the number of cattle and available pasture land, which will also result in a greater risk of spreading contagious cattle diseases;
6. the acceleration of the depletion of the soils in areas intensively occupied.

B. *From a health standpoint:*

1. the worsening of the population's nutritional condition;
2. the higher frequency of contagious diseases (tuberculosis, leprosy, childhood diseases, intestinal parasites, diarrhoea, etc.) as a result of greater pollution of the soil and drinking water in the surrounding area and as a result of the increased human contact;
3. the greater possibility of epidemic outbreaks—specifically measles, whooping cough, hepatitis, gastroenteritis—capable of causing an increase in mortality.

C. *From a social standpoint:*

1. a forced change in behaviour patterns involving various aspects of individual and collective life;
2. a change in hierarchical relationships, friendships, and intimate relationships and an adjustment of social, economic and other interests;
3. the possibility that populations not included in resettlement will use the lands abandoned by their neighbours for agriculture and animal husbandry in a less careful way;
4. the greater possibility of social conflict and the deterioration of customs because of the irreconcilability between traditional norms and the new living conditions;
5. the discontent and deprivation will increase migration which will then intensify the urbanization process and decrease the production of the resettled populations because of the flight of the more able-bodied people.

From all the above it can be concluded that because 'resettlement' aggravates the cycle of underdevelopment, it favours subversion.

These problems, and others, can result from any programme which involves the massive resettlement of peasants—whether it occurs under wartime conditions or conditions of peace. When traditional social, and economic structures are destroyed, social unrest and economic decline will inevitably result unless the regime can effectively provide new structures to mediate the peasants' transition and integration into the larger society.

PART IV

Conclusion

CHAPTER 7

The Reality of Race in Angola[1]

General Perspectives

For centuries Portuguese and foreign writers have published opposing views of race relations in Angola. During the war of liberation Portugal justified her continued presence in Africa on the ground that this was necessary to preserve the allegedly harmonious multiracial societies that had been created under the Portuguese flag. The well-documented arguments advanced by those who condemned Portuguese colonialism were so diametrically opposed to the equally well-documented Portuguese viewpoint that their reference to the same situation is indeed remarkable. How is it that so many writers sincerely believed that the Portuguese in Angola were devoid of racism, while many others found them to be at least as racist as any other European colonizer? An answer to that question, which has been posed at various points in this study, may now be suggested.

Most discussions of race (e.g. discrimination, prejudice, conflict, harmony, etc.) are beclouded by misunderstandings which result from the different experiences, assumptions, values and cognitions of the observers. For example, were a white South African and black American to arrive together in colonial Luanda and not encounter separate facilities for blacks and whites or discriminatory legislation, but occasionally see interracial couples on the streets, the South African would most likely conclude that black-white relationships in the Angolan capital were harmonious. On the other hand, the absence of 'whites only' signs and the presence of integrated couples would hardly impress a black American as being evidence of racial harmony; he or she would certainly demand verification of equal economic, social, educational and political opportuni-

[1] In this chapter I have allowed considerably more latitude for my personal views of the matters and works at issue than heretofore. Most of the writers, studies, and 'schools' to which I shall refer in this chapter have already been cited and reviewed in previous chapters. In addition, Allen Isaacman and I have recently published a comprehensive review and analysis of changes in the scholarly literature on Angola and Mozambique from *Estado Novo* to independence, which includes a major section on race relations. (Over 350 major books and articles are reviewed in that essay.) See Bender and Isaacman, 1976, pp. 220–48.

ties and rewards. If there are no laws which segregate blacks and whites, are they in fact integrated? Do they live in the same neighbourhoods, frequent the same schools, restaurants, clubs and stores? Do they respect each other's cultures? Unless these questions could be answered affirmatively with respect to Angola, the black American would not be likely to share the white South African's assumption of 'racial harmony'.

When the criteria for our judgments are spelled out, as in this example, misunderstandings are not likely to occur. However, we rarely know the background, values, or racial attitudes of those who have commented on the importance of race in Angola. Furthermore, since few writers are explicit about the standards they employ to form their judgments, it is difficult to know whether their support or rejection of lusotropical claims of racial harmony have been based on criteria similar to those of the hypothetical white South African or black American.

Given this caveat, we can assume that most of the Portuguese and foreigners who accepted the lusotropical myth of racial bliss in the African colonies employed the superficial criteria of the hypothetical South African, avoiding the implications of the questions posed by the black American. It would not be difficult to find 'examples' of racial harmony at a shallow level of perception.

There have always been token 'representative Africans' who would express their gratitude about 'being' Portuguese and whom many commentators mistakenly assumed to be 'representative' of the Africans rather than the Portuguese. Moreover, after 1961 there were no laws or organized white groups which prevented Africans from living in middle- and upper-class neighbourhoods, eating in the finest restaurants, studying in the university, holding high positions in the government or the military, or owning their own businesses. For many commentators, this was sufficient proof of Angolan racial harmony. Yet further investigation into the actual number of Africans who could take advantage of these celebrated 'freedoms' would have uncovered no more than a few dozen—hardly confirmation of a racially integrated society.

The absence of racist laws or separate racial facilities is clearly not indicative of the absence of racial segregation. Americans in the northern part of the United States used to feel as smug about their 'non-racism' *vis-à-vis* their compatriots in the south as the Portuguese felt with respect to South Africa. Both deluded themselves into believing that the absence of overt forms of racial discrimination *ipso facto* connoted the presence of racial integration. Many writers on Angolan race relations adopted this spurious logic and in doing so proclaimed the reality of racial integration where its achievement was, at best, minimal.

Certainly the formal sanction of law is not requisite to the existence of a segregated society; an infinite number of informal mechanisms can sustain such a society. For instance, rigid educational standards and Draconian class barriers effectively precluded Africans in Angola from seriously threatening the white bastions of exclusivity (e.g. jobs, neighbour-hoods, private schools, social clubs). These conventional and technically non-racial mechanisms were, in fact, so effective that they obviated the necessity (after 1961) to adopt explicitly racial legislation or to develop segregated institutions in order to guarantee the preservation of white superiority and domination.

Significantly, the Portuguese never felt sufficiently secure (or threat-ened) to train and employ even a token number of Africans in responsible positions. Thus, in early 1971 when a *Washington Post* reporter asked to meet prominent Africans in government or business, he was told by the director of Angolan Information and Tourism that 'unfortunately, he left last week'.[2] 'He', in this instance, referred to the former Provincial Secre-tary of Education, Pinheiro de Silva—a mestiço who had assimilated more Portuguese culture than 99 per cent of the Portuguese in the colony, and who was the last 'black' to occupy a top-level position in the colonial administration.

What racial integration did occur in colonial Angola normally reflected the downward mobility of the Portuguese rather than the upward mobility of blacks. When I commented to the then Governor General Rebocho Vaz that after travelling over five thousand miles during nearly a year in Angola I frankly had been unable to find the vaunted integrated multiracial society, he asked me if I had toured the capital's slums (*musseques*) where I *would* find blacks and whites living together. He was alluding to the few thousand Portuguese who inhabited the sprawling African slums because they owned shops there or were too indolent and poor to live in the Portuguese part of the city.[3] Ironically, this singular testimony for Portuguese integration vanished within months of the over-throw of the Caetano regime, when riots provoked by whites and blacks led to the departure of the Portuguese (and Cape Verdians) from the slums.

The absence of discriminatory legislation, separate racial facilities, and overt racism, combined with the presence of Portuguese living side by side with Africans in the slums, clearly convinced most Portuguese and many foreigners that whites in Angola did not harbour racial prejudice. In fact a number of observers needed no more evidence than the alleged

---

[2] See Hoagland, 1971; and 1972, p. 273. Hoagland directed the same request to govern-ment officials in Mozambique. Like their counterparts in Angola, they were unable to come up with names of any prominent Africans.

[3] Interview with Lieutenant-Colonel Rebocho Vaz, Governor General of Angola, Luanda, 11 March 1969. Before the war almost all of the Portuguese who lived in the *musseques* (slums) were traders. An increase in the number of impoverished Portuguese immigrants, the spiralling cost of living, and the scarcity of economical housing in Luanda during the 1960s and early 1970s resulted in an influx of the Portuguese to the slums. In 1970/71 the Public Security Police (PSP) estimated that 3·7 per cent of the 160,985 inhabitants of fourteen *musseques* were European. Ramiro Ladeiro Monteiro noted a tendency among the Europeans to settle near urbanized zones or at least along the main roads leading through the *musseques*; 1973a, p. 83; and 1973b, pp. 212–14.

openness of interracial sex and, occasionally, marriage. It would appear that this factor, more than any other, convinced many in the western world—and especially the Portuguese themselves—that Angolan race relations were harmonious.

To assume, however, that individuals of different races who engage in sexual relations must also respect each other's race or culture is not only contrary to the Portuguese experience throughout the world, but to the experience of all European colonizers in the New World and Africa. The assumption mistakes passion for respect and confuses eroticism with egalitarianism. Most importantly, it ignores the significance of demographic pressures. As we have seen in Chapter 2, the frequency of miscegenation and the attitudes of whites towards mestiços are primarily a function of two demographic factors: the ratio of European men to European women and the proportion of whites in relation to non-whites. Accordingly, the continuance of Portuguese miscegenation in Africa decades after miscegenation between Africans and Europeans in non-Portuguese territories had become insignificant was attributable to the absence of Portuguese women in the colonies, rather than to something *sui generis* in the Portuguese national character.[4]

The personal testimonies of individual Portuguese settlers and administrators about their own purported freedom from racial prejudice have provided another familiar source of misleading information and superficial evidence concerning Angolan race relations. As though trained by a combination of Pavlov and Gilberto Freyre, almost every Portuguese in colonial Angola automatically professed his or her abhorrence of all forms of cultural and racial discrimination. In fact, most Portuguese arrived in Angola already convinced that they were not racists. Their luso-tropical ideology was reinforced by the knowledge that they had not previously engaged in acts of racial discrimination in Portugal. Generally this was true not because of their freedom from racial prejudice but because of the tiny number of blacks in the metropole.

It is revealing that a good historical study of the centuries-old presence of black slaves in Portugal remains to be written.[5] However, since the middle of the nineteenth century there were practically no blacks in the country other than occasional transient students from the colonies, a dozen or so soccer players, and a few Africans employed in the Banco de Angola, Banco Nacional Ultramarino and the Overseas Ministry. In fact, until the first waves of Cape Verdian workers arrived in the early 1970s (to

---

[4] The late Amílcar Cabral strongly attacked the lusotropical assertion that miscegenation was concomitant with racial harmony, noting ironically:

Perhaps unconsciously confusing realities that are biological or necessary with realities that are socioeconomic and historical, Gilberto Freyre transformed all of us who live in the colony-provinces of Portugal into the fortunate inhabitants of a Luso-Tropical paradise (Cabral, 1969a, p. 9)

[5] For a brief discussion about the African slaves in Metropolitan Portugal, see Chapter 2, note 33, pp. 30-1.

replace the Portuguese labourers who had emigrated), it was possible to live for years in the country without seeing a black—let alone have personal contact.[6] This created a propitious basis for convincing most metropolitan Portuguese that they harboured no racial prejudice.

The pronouncements of non-racism by most Portuguese were stated with such sincerity that a large number of writers assumed this reflected reality. Sincerity, however, is not always consonant with reality. Most Portuguese attitudes towards Africans were steeped in paternalism; and even sincere, well-meaning paternalism should not be confused with genuine respect for African cultures and peoples. On the contrary, Portuguese paternalism was based on cultural arrogance and connoted a profound disrespect for African cultures and peoples. In fact, these attitudes of arrogance and disrespect were the very core of the 'civilizing mission' and the *indigenato* system which sought to 'raise' Africans from an assumed backward and inferior existence to the allegedly superior level of Portuguese civilization.

Guided by their ethnocentric perspective, the Portuguese were able to rationalize even the most outrageous acts against humanity for over

[6] The Portuguese did not react differently from other Europeans or Americans who live in multiracial communities—where most of the blacks occupy the lowest rungs of society—when about one hundred thousand Cape Verdians (most of whom are dark mestiços from the Island of Sal) arrived in Portugal in the early 1970s. Before the arrival of the Cape Verdians, visitors were frequently warned to avoid certain poor sections of Lisbon, especially at night, because most of the inhabitants of these barrios were said to be infected with venereal disease, were prone to robbery and assault, smelled etc. By early 1975 some of these same barrios had become virtually Cape Verdian ghettos, but this time the warnings did not elaborate on the reasons for avoidance. It sufficed to say that the inhabitants were black because, for a large number of Portuguese, that colour was synonymous with all their negative views about the barrios' previous inhabitants. In addition clashes between Cape Verdians and the police were attributed by blacks to racial antagonism. (See, for example, *Comércio do Funchal* [Madeira], 6 September 1973.)

In late 1976 racial tension between Portuguese and Cape Verdian miners erupted into violence in central Portugal. Two Cape Verdians were killed and almost two dozen Cape Verdians and Portuguese were hospitalized as a result of what Portuguese termed their 'country's first major race riot'. *Expresso* (Lisbon) 8 October 1976 and the *New York Times* 8 October 1976.

There has been strong racial antagonism between white Portuguese and Cape Verdians in the United States. George N. Leighton, an Illinois appellate court judge and second-generation Cape Verdian who grew up in the area of New Bedford, Massachusetts, maintains that the white Portuguese he knew in Massachusetts were 'every bit as prejudiced as Southern white rednecks'. Ironically, a large number of the Cape Verdians in the U.S. (200,000 to 300,000) have alienated American blacks by their refusal to acknowledge that they are black and by their aloofness. In fact, anti-black phrases have been common among Cape Verdians in the U.S., who have generally considered themselves 'just Portuguese'. For an excellent discussion of Cape Verdians in the U.S. (and Judge Leighton's quote), see Francis Ward, 'Cape Verdian Mixed Race Seeks Identity', *Los Angeles Times*, 23 June 1975. For further insight into the problem of racial identity among Cape Verdians in the U.S., see Leon Dash, 'Black Roots in Angola', *Washington Post*, 26 December 1973.

Almost all of the approximately 40,000 Cape Verdians who were in Angola before the April 1974 coup resembled Cape Verdians in the U.S. in that they identified with the Portuguese in the colony, not with the Africans.

five centuries, since the time of Prince Henry, when it was believed that the first African slaves brought to Portugal were fortunate. Through their enslavement, it was argued, they would be able to receive the light of the holy faith and live in civilized surroundings rather than in 'bestial sloth'.[7] The same perspective was later used to justify the forced labour system, which replaced slavery at the end of the nineteenth century, and the massive resettlement programme (*aldeamentos*) during the war of independence. In short, any policy or activity which destroyed traditional African institutions, settlement patterns, or beliefs was perceived by most Portuguese as inherently good and, at times, even magnanimous! Moreover, those who shared the Portuguese presupposition of the cultural or racial inferiority of Africans and belief in the efficacy of paternalism also generally accepted lusitanian pretensions to a special aptitude for establishing harmonious multiracial societies in the tropics.

Finally, distortions in studies of Angolan race relations which resulted from an exaggerated emphasis on the absence of explicitly racial laws and institutions, the presence of racially integrated slums, the ethnocentric or paternalistic self-appraisals by settlers and officials, and the evidence of miscegenation have been compounded by the relative dearth of serious works which view Angolan race relations through African eyes. This ignorance of an African perspective is symptomatic of the pervasive eurocentric bias which dominates the historiography of Angola.[8] Just as most historians have generally assumed that events within the European communities constituted the only significant history of Angola, Portuguese perceptions have been used to epitomize the only meaningful perspective of race relations. Yet infinitesimally few Africans have ever shared this perspective. In fact, most Africans were certainly not aware that Portugal even subscribed to principles of cultural and racial egalitarianism, let alone that the Portuguese actually believed they practised such principles in Angola.

These contradictory perceptions of the fundamental nature of relations between Africans and Portuguese dominate the history (and historiography) of colonial Angola—especially the final decades. African perceptions of white domination fomented and fed the armed revolt against Portuguese colonialism. On the other hand, Portuguese perceptions of their divinely inspired mission sustained their conviction that the defeat of the nationalist forces was both inevitable and necessary for the maintenance of progress and racial harmony. It has been difficult for many non-Portuguese to understand how the overwhelming majority of the Portuguese people could sincerely believe that their perspective was realistic. Hence it is important to understand the historical and philosophical foundations of the Portuguese point of view.

[7] See Chapter 1, pp. 12–13.

[8] For an extensive critique of the eurocentric bias in the historiography of Angola and Mozambique, see Bender and Isaacman, 1976.

The Development and Maintenance of Portuguese Attitudes Towards Africans

Portugal had been enslaving Africans for almost half a century by the time Diogo Cão reached the shores of Angola in 1483, and it was not long before Angola had become Africa's major source of slaves for the New World. Sixty thousand of the three to four million slaves exported from Angola were captured during the first two decades of the Portuguese presence. Lusotropical historians advanced sophistic arguments that the Portuguese who engaged in the slave trade were somehow more tolerant and humane than other European slavers. Yet all evidence indicates that during those long centuries of transatlantic slave trading, none of the nations engaged in the trade could be described as humane or tolerant. The Portuguese people, like other European colonizers, firmly believed Africans to be congenitally inferior to Europeans, and therefore were convinced that Africans should serve Europeans. By the end of the slave trade in the mid-nineteenth century, such attitudes were deeply rooted in Portugal. Since the Portuguese universally manifested attitudes of racial superiority during their first four centuries in Angola, it is important to determine if and when these attitudes attenuated during the last one hundred years —from abolition to independence.

In any consideration of possible changes in Portuguese racial attitudes following the abolition of slavery, it is critical to recall that until the early decades of the twentieth century most Portuguese in Angola were degredados whose misanthropy towards Africans is richly documented (see Chapter 3). The degredados were in direct competition with Africans for the lowest position in the social structure. In the eyes of many military officers, civil servants and foreign visitors, the superior comportment of Africans within the Portuguese sphere —especially those in the army — gave them an edge over the exiled convicts. Thus the degredados were forced increasingly to differentiate themselves from Africans, usually resulting in an exaggeration of the relevance of the one trait they possessed which was esteemed in the colony—their colour!

The post-abolition rigidity of racist attitudes was not confined to the lowly degredado; it was endemic to all levels of society, including the petty traders, the civil service, the army, cabinet and even the Crown. Oliveira Martins, Mousinho de Albuquerque, Antonio Enes, Serpa Pinto, and most of the other prominent personalities in Portuguese colonial affairs during the latter half of the nineteenth century continued to propagate the notion that Africans were inherently inferior.[9] In fact, throughout the great colonial debates over 'native policies' in government circles and the Lisbon Geographical Society, this notion was rarely questioned. Instead, the debates focused principally on the extent to which Portugal

---

[9] For further information on the racist views of these and other important Portuguese of this period, see Hammond, 1967, pp. 205–16.

was justified in continuing the exploitation of those who were 'inferior'. From the Africans' perspective these debates over nuances were irrelevant; no matter which appellation was used, e.g. slaves, libertos, forced labourers or contract labourers, there were almost no perceptible differences in the treatment of Africans by Portuguese overlords.

The ingrained racist attitudes and behaviour changed little if at all during the twentieth century, whether colonial policies were fashioned by liberals in the First Republic (1910–26) or fascists in the *Estado Novo* (1930–74). António de Oliveira Salazar was patently explicit about his belief in white superiority.[10] Even the most caustic critics of the abuses against Africans, such as Norton de Matos (twice Governor of Angola), considered Africans to be inferior to whites and vigorously opposed miscegenation. Many have equated the attempts to protect Africans by Sá da Bandeira, Norton de Matos and others as manifestations of Portuguese egalitarianism. However, empathy for the suffering of others does not presuppose a belief in equality. For example, as Salazar's Colonial Minister in the mid-1940s, Marcello Caetano castigated the 'blind selfishness' of Portuguese employers in Angola and Mozambique who used Africans 'like pieces of equipment'. Nevertheless he could still argue that:

> The blacks in Africa must be directed and moulded by Europeans but they are indispensable as assistants to the latter. I do not affirm this out of prejudice—I merely formulate an observation. In one or other case the European family can do without African workers but, as a whole, the African economy cannot do without the European. The Africans by themselves did not know how to develop the territories they have inhabited for millennia, they did not account for a single useful invention nor any usable technical discovery, no conquest that counts in the evolution of Humanity, nothing that can compare to the accomplishments in the areas of culture and technology by Europeans or even by Asians.[11]

Caetano, Salazar, and most of the other prominent officials during the *Estado Novo* were profoundly influenced by nineteenth-century, pseudo-scientific, American and European schools of racist thought. They shared

[10] See Chapter 1, p. 7. Salazar never wavered from this view. In one of the last interviews he gave before his stroke in 1968, he told a reporter for the Argentinian magazine *Extra* who asked him how long it would take before African countries were capable of governing themselves: 'It is a problem for centuries; within 300 to 500 years. And in the meantime, they will have to go on participating in the process of development.' Large excerpts of this interview appeared in *A Província de Angola* (Luanda), 3 July 1968. Also see Moura, 1968, p. 272 and *passim*.

[11] Caetano, 1954, p. 16. For Caetano's criticism of the treatment of Africans by Portuguese employers, see 1946, p. 72.

Some Portuguese thought that the 'moulding' of Africans should be carried out with an iron hand. Carlos Eduardo de Soveral (1952, p. 136) for example, argued in his sociological study of Angola that an African 'likes to be strongly commanded [by Europeans] and, as all primitive beings, is so close in this aspect to the animal, he wants and loves the vigorous hand rather than the gentle hand'.

the polygenists' assumption that physical differences (e.g. skin colour, skull shape, nose contour) proved the existence of cultural and intellectual differences. They also accepted the Social Darwinists' premise that all civilizations must traverse similar processes of historical development. Since the evolution of the species resulted in higher and lower forms of natural life, they concluded that the same laws must operate among human races and civilizations. Thus, race was viewed as the fundamental cause of cultural differentiation. Within this perspective Africans were viewed as a separate or 'incipient species', while Europeans were considered to have attained the highest stage of human development. The same pseudo-scientific racist theories also had a great impact on virtually every Brazilian social thinker before World War I: however, the Brazilians later discarded these theories, whereas most Portuguese tenaciously clung to them.[12]

The writings of the Brazilian Modernists in the 1920s and 1930s, especially those of Gilberto Freyre, provided strong refutations of the polygenist and Social Darwinian racial theories. Contrary to the racial determinists, Freyre asserted the importance of societal factors in the Brazilian socialization process, among them the master-slave relationships, the importance of the patriarchal society, education and the effects of diet. He further argued that the significant impact of African civilizations on the Brazilian national character proved these civilizations to be advanced. This in turn provided the rationale for a multiracial society in which the component races could be considered equally valuable and important.[13] Yet many Brazilians, frequently including Freyre himself, ignored the full ramifications of their conclusions on the importance of race in society.

Portuguese academics and politicians also did not perceive or understand the full implications of Freyre's works on their own racial theories. Instead, they combined his concept of a harmonious and egalitarian multiracial society with their Social Darwinism and produced a bastardized version of lusotropicalism. This theoretical cross-fertilization did not yield a new hybrid society in Africa but a typical colonial society, characterized by the same omnipresent white domination which had marked all other European colonization in Africa. In fact, Portuguese lusotropicalism did not work in theory *or* practice. There can be no racial harmony in a

[12] For a penetrating discussion of the racism in pre-World War I schools of thought in Brazil, see Skidmore, 1974, pp. 48–53 and *passim*. For a general summary of the views of blacks among French intellectuals from the eighteenth to the twentieth century, see Cohen, 1975, pp. 1–11.

For a discussion of the influence of genetic theories on historical explanations, see Gallie, 1959, pp. 386–402.

[13] Skidmore, 1974, pp. 190–2. Skidmore's analysis of the role and importance of Gilberto Freyre and other major writers in Brazilian social thought between 1870 and 1930 is essential for a comprehensive understanding of the importance of race in Brazil. Also see: Bastide, 1972, pp. 225–40; 1974, p. 19, and *passim*; and António de Figueiredo, 1965, p. 207.

multiracial society where individuals of one race consider themselves superior, because they will inevitably try to dominate those they view as inferior. This occurred in every Portuguese colony throughout the world. However, Portuguese scholars and politicians rarely perceived the contradiction between white domination and racial harmony.

Portuguese educators provided much of the reasoning that gave legitimacy to the maintenance of attitudes of cultural and racial superiority. The basic tenets of pseudo-scientific racist theories were so widely accepted and espoused in Portuguese academia that generations of students were unable to examine critically the contradictions in lusotropicalism. For example, before the outbreak of the Angolan war most Portuguese anthropological studies were unabashedly eurocentric and racist. Physical anthropologists, following the polygenists, compiled prodigious tables of cranial, skeletal and other anatomical measurements to prove not only that physical differences actually existed among the races but, more importantly, that Europeans were superior to Africans and mestiços. Cultural anthropologists emphasized the esoteric aspects of African religions and ceremonies, concentrating most of their efforts on describing rites, dress, hair styles and scarification.[14] By stressing the esoteric rather than the functional interactions of Africans with each other and their environment, they reinforced *a priori* beliefs that African cultures were stagnant and backward. Such studies furnished the 'scientific' documentation for the Social Darwinian view that Africans were indeed lower than the Portuguese on the (unilineal) scale of cultural development.

Even Portugal's best anthropologists manifested this ethnocentricism — frequently accompanied by strong doses of paternalism. For example, Jorge Dias, one of the few Portuguese anthropologists whose work has received international recognition and whom many consider to have been Portugal's leading anthropological specialist on the colonies, wrote as late as 1960:

> all men are in principle equal and we, as older brothers, have the duty of protecting and guiding our younger brothers ... Although we may be convinced that our civilization is superior to many indigenous societies of our Overseas Provinces, we never try to impose it.[15]

While Dias acknowledged that Africans, under the *indigenato*, were only treated as equal citizens when they 'acquired a European mentality and

---

[14] For further discussion of Portuguese anthropologists and especially the impact on the Portuguese of their ahistorical assumptions about the unchanging nature of 'primitive' societies, see Bender and Isaacman, 1976. For an example of an Overseas Minister's manifestation of this view, see Silva Cunha, 1963, p. 19.

[15] Jorge Dias, 1960, pp. 25–6.
Dias' five-volume study on the Macondes of Mozambique was largely responsible for his being named a fellow at the Institute of Advanced Behavioral Studies in Palo Alto, California, in the late 1960s.

customs', he did not perceive this as constituting an imposition of Portuguese culture.

A. A. Mendes Correia, Jorge Dias' mentor and usually considered to be the father of 'modern' anthropology in Portugal, wrote and taught that both Africans *and* mestiços were intrinsically inferior to Europeans. He argued that no matter how brilliant, mestiços were incapable of making a complete identification with the Portuguese in terms of temperament, will, feelings, or ideas. From this he concluded that mestiços 'must never hold high posts in the general politics of the country'.[16] Despite these pronouncements, he frequently explained that Portugal's 'success' in Africa was due to 'the absence of intolerant attitudes or racial prejudices' among the Portuguese.[17]

Mendes Correia was the first director of the Higher Institute of Colonial Studies (1946–58). (Its name was later changed to the Higher Institute of Social Sciences and Overseas Studies—Instituto Superior de Ciências Sociais e Política Ultramarina, ISCSPU.) The Institute was entrusted with the education and training of the (intended) elite of the colonial service. In addition to Mendes Correia and Jorge Dias, the faculty included most of Portugal's leading African specialists, e.g. António da Silva Rego, António de Almeida, Silva Cunha and Adriano Moreira, who succeeded Mendes Correia as Director and was Portugal's best-known political theorist on colonialism.[18] These and other professors in the Institute were

---

[16] Corrêa, A. A. Mendes, 1940, p. 132.

[17] See, for example, Corrêa, 1953, pp. 33–50; also see 1943.

Mendes Correia's failure to perceive the contradictions in his views of Africans and mestiços juxtaposed to his professed belief in non-racism is a commonplace blind spot in Portuguese scholarship. Another interesting example can be seen in the following excerpt from an essay which argued in favour of miscegenation in the African colonies:

> It is rare in Portugal for someone to be attacked for being a mestiço. Mixed blood or the colour of the face never prevented a man from reaching any position in Portuguese life. Everyone respected, for example, Sousa Martins, the great man of science, or Gonçalves Crespo, the great and perfect poet. *No one ever threw in the faces of these men the portion of negro blood which ran in their veins.* But when mulattoes are politicians, those who oppose their ideas use, at times, their racial mixture as an arm of personal attack. (Oliveira, O. de, 1934, p. 367. Emphasis added.)

[18] Adriano Moreira exerted an enormous influence over colonial affairs in Portugal from the late 1950s, when he became Director of ISCSPU, until the early 1970s, when he was fired by Marcello Caetano over matters which were probably more personal than political. Politically mercurial, Moreira attempted to use his academic position to advance his personal political career. Initially, he attempted to build upon his ill-deserved reputation as a 'liberal', gained during his brief stint as Overseas Minister in 1961–62. That reputation was principally nurtured by his much-publicized reforms of 6 September 1961 (e.g. abolition of the *indigenato, et al.*). The 'reforms', however, did not lead to any fundamental change in white domination, partially because Moreira himself prevented it. During the long years of war in Africa, Moreira adopted more conservative political views until by the time of Caetano's overthrow he was reputedly the choice of the ultrarightists, led by Américo Tomás, to replace Caetano. Moreira was never more than a rumour away from being Prime Minister but, after the April 1974 coup, he chose exile in Brazil over further waiting in the wings to be called.

responsible for most of the scholarship and propaganda on the colonies published in Portugal during the last quarter-century of colonialism. With rare exceptions their works were unmitigatedly eurocentric and dominated by lusotropical themes. Only a few of the thousands of student master's theses and published works of the faculty presented analyses or evidence contrary to the idyllic image of harmonious race relations in the colonies.

The lack of analytical rigour in colonial scholarship was characteristic of the general Portuguese educational system which, under Salazar and Caetano, discouraged independent thinking, especially when it trod on sacred dogmas such as lusotropicalism. There were a small number of creative scholars at the ISCSPU and other Portuguese universities but, like all teachers and researchers in the country before April 1974, they risked professional, economic and political sanctions if they were too vigorous in challenging official orthodoxies. Consequently, most were forced either to pursue politically safe subjects or to carry out their work in exile (e.g. A. H. de Oliveira Marques and Jose Cutileiro). Moreover, Portuguese scholars also suffered from most of the handicaps which plagued foreign researchers, including restricted access to archival materials, limited opportunities for fieldwork, concern over potential problems for one's informants as well as the omnipresent preoccupation with the political repercussions of any study.

The Universities of Coimbra, Porto and Lisbon (including the ISCSPU) were not the only Portuguese institutions of higher learning which indoctrinated colonial administrators with ethnocentric and racist teachings. Thousands of officers who became colonial administrators were equally influenced by such doctrines in the Military Academy. For example, prior to his becoming the Military Commander-in-Chief in Mozambique (1969–73), General Kaúlza de Arriaga argued in the *Lessons of Strategy in the Course of High Command, 1966/67* that 'blacks are not highly intelligent, on the contrary, of all peoples in the world they are the least intelligent'. He concluded that since 'one needs to have superior intelligence to carry on subversion', African nationalists were doomed to failure. He further noted:

> We shall only be able to maintain white control in Angola and Mozambique, which is a national objective, if the (white) population grows at a rate which at least accompanies and slightly surpasses the production of assimilated blacks ...
>
> Clearly this brings up another problem: which is that we should also not be too efficient in the advancement of the blacks; of course we should advance them, but let us not exaggerate.[19]

---

[19] These and other quotations from General Kaúlza de Arriaga's *Lições de estratégia de curso de altos comandos—1966/67*, vol. 12 can be found in: Amílcar Cabral, 'A Brief Report on the Situation of the Struggle', September 1971, pp. 6–7 (mimeographed); and *República* (Lisbon), 14 May 1974.

Just how ethnocentric the Portuguese military elites were before April 1974 can be seen in a sociological survey the army administered in 1968 under the direction of the former Chief of Staff, General Luís Maria da Câmara Pina. The purpose of the survey was to determine 'the influence of the army in the diffusion of Portuguese culture', but the questions were so blatantly ethnocentric that the responses were useless. The survey asked, for example, whether or not Portuguese soldiers (as the carriers of Portuguese culture in Africa) were breaking down such 'traditional customs' as community violence, inter-tribal warfare, and ethnic segregation. The survey also tried to elicit whether or not the Africans:

participated, without reluctance, on work projects in the public interest. Do they understand the necessity of contributing to the collective good (paying taxes and submitting to legal and administrative authority)?[20]

The strong influence of Social Darwinism on General Pina is apparent in his view of cultures:

All cultures are equally respectable but some are more prominent than others, more historical, because 'historical is everything that exercises or exercised influence'. There are also isolated cultures which die.

This perspective led General Pina to believe, for example, that African languages in the colonies would inevitably atrophy and Portuguese would become the only common language.[21] Yet there was little in the past to support the General's blind faith in the superiority of the Portuguese language. After almost five hundred years of a Portuguese presence in Angola, only 1 per cent of the African adults and 2 per cent of the children in rural Angola used the Portuguese language regularly in 1970–71.[22]

[20] The questions in the survey which were asked in Angola, Mozambique, and Guinea-Bissau can be found in Pina, 1968, pp. 645–51.

[21] Ibid., part 1 (August–September 1968), pp. 540–1 (quote on cultures) and p. 544 (future of Portugese language in Africa).

[22] These and other valuable data on the use of Portuguese by Africans in rural Angola can be found in Franz-Wilhelm Heimer's superb survey and analysis (1974, preliminary draft). The data cited are found on p. 76.

The belief in the superiority of the Portuguese language was ubiquitously shared by the Portuguese in the colonies. It was even incorporated into the curriculum of the teacher-training programme. For example, the first dozen pages of a basic textbook for all primary school teachers in Angola are dominated by a long footnote which reproduces a 1944 report of the jury of high school admissions in Benguela. The report begins:

A good part of its [African] population unconsciously cultivates bad habits, acquired in infancy, in pronunciation and other things of equal or greater gravity such as the grammar; these bad habits are the result not of the crossing of races directly but the crossing of languages with completely different constitutions and vocabulary; Bantu, with reduced inherited vocabulary, poor in grammatical forms, fit for serving a civilization in its infancy; and Portuguese, with a tableau of morphemes and a vocabulary rich in gradations to the point of serving peoples who are in the vanguard of civilization, capable of being adapted effortlessly to each special intent of the numerous writers who, over almost a millennium, made it their interpreter.

The report, written by Dr. J. Brilhante de Paiva, is quoted in Rosa, 1961, pp. 12–13, note 1. The entire note can be found on pp. 12–21.

This familiar gap between ideology and reality in the African colonies helped to bolster and sustain the Portuguese political, military, economic and intellectual elites' support of the war effort. Seldom could the facts modify their lusotropical illusions. Prime Ministers Salazar and Caetano, Generals Pina and Kaúlza de Arriaga, Professors and Overseas Ministers Adriano Moreira and Silva Cunha, Governor General Rebocho Vaz, Foreign Minister Franco Nogueira, and Professors Mendes Correia and Jorge Dias disagreed on many matters but they shared a common delusion—the natural laws of history guaranteed that Portugal would ultimately triumph in the African 'provinces'. Thus, for this elite to accept the principle of decolonization or to admit that military victory was not possible was tantamount not only to abandoning the divinely inspired 'civilizing mission', but to abandoning the very cornerstone of Portuguese historical thought.

Despite the ubiquity of lusitanian attitudes of cultural and racial superiority, Portuguese scholars, officials and many foreign observers have strongly objected to the application of the term racism in analyses of discrimination against Africans in Angola. They argue instead that any discrimination which occurred was based on cultural or class, not racial, criteria. I have argued against the utility of distinguishing between these congruent categories in the Brazilian context; in Angola these distinctions are even less helpful.[23]

A society, such as colonial Angola, structured on racial inequality and excluding blacks from equal participation, can be considered a racist society, irrespective of any direct invocation of the physical criterion of colour. Attitudes of racial superiority and a system of racial privilege may be rationalized on cultural grounds, but the fact remains that the objective exclusion of blacks is the same.[24]

Few Portuguese in Angola bothered (or were able) to discern distinctions between race and culture; white was viewed conterminously with Portuguese culture while blacks were residually perceived as being part of an undifferentiated 'culture', labelled African. Under the *indigenato* and within lusotropical theory, one could be considered racially black and culturally Portuguese (i.e. assimilado), but less than 1 per cent of Africans ever officially attained this status.

More importantly, when Africans did qualify as assimilados, the attitudes of most whites towards them reflected not the ideals of Gilberto Freyre but the invidious views of the former Angolan High Commissioner, Vicente Ferreira, who argued that 'so-called civilized Africans ... are generally no more than grotesque imitations of white men ... [with] a

---

[23] See Chapter 2, pp. 42–5.

[24] For a stimulating essay on how race and culture have been ideologically linked in systems of racial domination, see Leo Kuper, 'Ideologies of Cultural Differences in Race Relations', in his valuable collection of writings, 1974, pp. 11–39, and *passim*. I also want to express my appreciation to Professor Kuper for his assistance in helping me clarify this and other points in this section.

primitive mentality, poorly concealed by the speech, gestures and dress copied from Europeans'.[25] Thus, while 'culture' was portrayed in Portuguese theory and law as a product of one's environment, not race, in practice almost all Portuguese accepted Vicente Ferreira's assumption that culture and race were inseparable. Within their perspective, black was not a colour but a condition.

Whites in Angola rarely needed to resort to explicit or legalistic forms of racial discrimination because the virulent system of cultural and class discrimination effectively precluded Africans from participating as equals in Portuguese social, economic, or political institutions. Prior to the repeal of the *indigenato* in 1961, the laws of Angola all but guaranteed the impossibility of Africans advancing beyond the lower class. If an African were able to overcome the almost insurmountable cultural barriers and qualify for the status of assimilado, he or she immediately faced additional economic barriers, since being an assimilado did not accord one the right to earn equal wages for performing the same job as a white.[26] Furthermore, even 'white wages' were low and often did not suffice for parents to pay for their children's education beyond the fourth grade. Consequently the cost of educating children was prohibitive for all but a very small number of Africans, and without education there was little hope of ever breaking out of the vicious circle of poverty which engulfed their lives.

Neither the heralded reforms of September 1961 (which abolished the *indigenato* and other repressive legislation) nor the fourfold expansion of primary education during the decade of the 1960s appreciably mitigated the harsh conditions which afflicted the lives of Africans in the colony. The recognition of all Africans as equal Portuguese citizens was as beneficial to their advancement as manumission or even emancipation was for poor, illiterate, and unskilled slaves in almost any nineteenth-century slavocracy. Equality in legal and political status is worth little unless accompanied by increased opportunities for upward economic and social mobility. The 1961 and subsequent reforms extended to Africans the freedom but not the means to compete as equals with whites. Thus, the rigid class divisions in colonial Angola served as effective racial divisions. Just how effective these divisions ultimately were is manifested by the minute number of Africans who graduated from a Portuguese university or who earned salaries commensurate with even a middle-class income before independence.[27] When I questioned the former Overseas Minister

[25] Ferreira, 1954a, vol. 3, p. 40.

[26] See Chapter 5, pp. 152–5.

[27] In a confidential report on aspects relevant to counter-subversion presented to the Angolan Council on Counter-Subversion (17 January 1969), Afonso Mendes (who was then the Director of the Angolan Labour Institute) argued:

The estrangement of blacks from commercial and industrial activities constitutes one more aspect of the lack of economic roots and fixed material interests [of Africans]. This results in the absence of a black middle class. (Mendes, 1969, p. 10).

Silva Cunha why Portugal did not attempt to rectify this situation with compensatory assistance, he replied that 'this would constitute reverse discrimination and we are adamantly opposed to all forms of discrimination'.[28]

This same point is made in another paper presented to the Council on Counter-Subversion; see Comissão de Estudo da Secção I, 1969, p. 16.

Also see Oliveira, W. F., 1965, pp. 33–9. Oliveira was the Director of Afro-Asian Studies at the University of Bahia (Brazil) at the time he wrote this article following a trip through Angola. He was shocked by the white domination he saw: 'There are no rich black Angolans, neither do they occupy important positions in the administration or in local commerce' (p. 34).

While considerable data have been presented to substantiate this point, the rarity of middle- or upper-class Africans in Angola was vividly expressed by an anecdote which was circulating during my stay:

One afternoon '*um preto com pasta*' ('a black with a briefcase') was seen entering a large government office building along the Bay of Luanda. So unusual was the sight of a 'preto com pasta' that his appearance created quite a stir. Naturally his movements were closely observed and when, after a few moments, he 'disappeared', a hasty search was made of all the building's bathrooms, stairways, and corridors. Failing to locate him, the building's occupants fled into the street in panic, certain that their building would explode at any moment. They only returned to their offices when it was verified that the 'preto com pasta' was quietly attending to his business in one of the offices.

The absence of urban terrorism in Angola during the war underscores the significance of such an anecdote.

[28] Interview with J. M. da Silva Cunha, Minister of the Overseas Territories, Lisbon, 19 June 1969.

Silva Cunha cited General Silvino Silverio Marques—former Governor General of Angola, 1962–66—as a perfect example of the folly of trying to implement 'reverse discrimination'. His view of the General in the context of events surrounding Silvino's brief return to Angola as High Commissioner following the military coup provides a fascinating illustration of how ignorant major Portuguese officials were of the views of Africans and mestiços in Angola.

Silvino Silverio Marques already had a reputation as a 'liberal' in the Portuguese army when he was appointed Governor General in Angola a year after the outbreak of the war of independence. His governorship coincided with a period in which Portugal was forced to implement major reforms in the colonies, which reinforced his 'liberal' reputation. Among conservatives and reactionaries in the Salazar and Caetano regimes (e.g. Silva Cunha, Franco Nogueira, and Américo Tomás), Silvino was considered a radical and probably subversive. One indication of the latter view emerged during the interview when Silva Cunha questioned Silvino's motives for publishing a broad attack on Portuguese civilian and military strategies in the colonies, which included the suggestion that Portugal was abandoning its traditional policy of non-racism. (See Marques, S. S., 1969a, pp. 329–32; and 1969b, pp. 385–9.)

It is therefore not surprising that General Spínola and the first transitional government following Caetano's overthrow selected Silvino Silverio Marques to be High Commissioner in Angola. They were convinced that Africans would rejoice at the return of 'the enlightened Africanista Governor'. What they failed to perceive was that the man whom they viewed as liberal to radical and 'pro-African' in the metropolitan political context was widely condemned in Angola. For while it is true that Silvino implemented a number of reforms, Africans, mestiços, and a few whites argued that these reforms never altered the basic structure of white domination and exploitation. Moreover, they recalled the harsh

It took almost a century after the abolition of slavery for white Americans to recognize and admit that without special efforts to eradicate the handicaps which white racism had inflicted on blacks in America, the latter would have only limited opportunities to compete successfully in the economic and social structure. The maintenance of inflexible 'standards' with a *laissez-faire* approach to the advancement of blacks (i.e. 'no reverse discrimination') proved to be inherently more discriminatory against blacks in Angola than in the United States because the former lacked even the most minimal skills and 'qualifications' necessary for equitable competition.

While many Portuguese acknowledged the strong correlation between race and socioeconomic status in Angola, few recognized—let alone acknowledged—that white racism was the primary cause. On the contrary, secure in their conviction that miscegenation connoted racial harmony and that neither they nor their laws manifested a scintilla of racial prejudice, most Portuguese were absolutely certain that the preeminence of whites could not have resulted from racism. They concluded, therefore, that since they did not discriminate against Africans on a racial basis, the fact that Africans were not rising above their low condition in Angola must be a result of their own inabilities. For example, in the early 1970s the general manager of the Benguela Railroad said he had only one African among his 130 senior staff members because: 'They don't seem to be interested in this work. There is nothing against a coloured man getting one of these jobs. But they don't do anything for themselves.'[29]

This was precisely the position taken by Rebocho Vaz when I asked him why so few Africans were found outside the lower class. He responded by reminding me that there were no laws preventing Africans from bettering their position in Angola and therefore if they had not done so it was really their own fault. 'Africans', the Governor General explained, 'lack ambition and are not geared to the same kind of thinking as the white

repression of Africans during his four years as Governor General. In fact, A. Bobela-Motta, in an 'Open Letter' to Silvino published in *A Província de Angola* (8 June 1974), suggested that the key to success of his second government would be to do everything contrary to his first government: 'You need only say yes to that which, twelve years ago, you said no; to call black those whom you called white; to applaud those whom you then condemned; to reverse your scale of values.'

Silvino Silverio Marques was replaced as High Commissioner (by Admiral Rosa Coutinho) after serving little more than a month. He and his traditional government were bitterly attacked in Angola and Lisbon for being soft on white extremists and hard on African nationalists. He was clearly bewildered by the strong reaction against him as High Commissioner and, by ensconcing himself in the Governor's Palace, he appeared almost frightened of venturing out among the people. From the content of the numerous letters he published after his final departure from Angola (19 July 1974), it would seem that Silvino may still be bewildered. For examples of these letters, see *Vida Mundial*, no. 1845 (23 January 1975), pp. 51–2; *Expresso* (Lisbon), 28 June 1975 and 12 July 1975.

[29] Quoted in Hoagland, 1971.

man in terms of initiative and getting ahead'. He added that he believed it would take generations for Africans to develop the ambition and initiative necessary to improve themselves. While he recognized that the government had a responsibility to assist Africans, like his superior Silva Cunha, he was concerned that his government would not be liable to any charge of racial discrimination—including 'reverse discrimination'.[30]

This Governor General personifies the racial myopia which has blinded so many Portuguese and other whites throughout the world to the self-fulfilling prophecy underlying their views of black inferiority. First they posit the inherent inferiority of blacks, then proceed to institutionalize that inferiority by denying blacks the opportunity to acquire the skills and means to participate effectively as equals. Angolan Africans were expected to prove themselves worthy before a beneficent Portuguese civilization would bestow the largesse of 'citizenship', yet access to the institutions which could impart 'worthy' comportment was generally limited to citizens. This systematic exclusion resulted in patterns of behaviour which, upon superficial examination, appeared to provide credence and validity to the contention that Africans were intrinsically and inherently inferior to Portuguese.[31]

While this self-fulfilling prophecy helped to sustain white attitudes of superiority, it conditioned very few Africans to accept a definition of themselves as inferior. The etiology and basic manifestations of racial inferiority complexes in Angola were almost identical to those described by Fanon, Memmi and Mannoni, yet they were infinitely less prevalent there than these authors would lead one to believe.[32] In fact, such in-

---

[30] Interview with Lieutenant-Colonel Rebocho Vaz, Governor General of Angola, Luanda, 11 March 1969. The Governor General's view that Africans were reluctant to better themselves through study and hard work was shared by most whites and many mestiços. Even Afonso Mendes, the Director of the Angolan Labour Institute from 1962 to 1970, argued shortly before assuming this post that 'the Angolan native is, in a general way, highly reluctant to work … he doesn't find within his society the guiding example which would lead him to acquire regular and continuous work habits' ('A não discriminação e o direito de associação nos territórios não metropolitanos e os trabalhadores indígenas em Angola', *Estudos Ultramarinos* 7 [1957–58], p. 85). For further background on Afonso Mendes and other contradictory positions he maintained concerning African labour problems, see *supra*, Chapter 5, note 79, pp. 153–4.

[31] For a brilliant analysis of the development and sustenance of (white) superiority and (black) inferiority complexes which derived from the exclusion of blacks by whites in the United States and the world in general, see Tillman, 1963, pp. 2–5. I am deeply indebted to the cogency of his words and thoughts on this and many other issues discussed in this chapter. Also see: Merton, 1962, p. 430; and the authors cited in note 32 (below).

[32] Memmi, 1965, pp. 79–111 and *passim*; Mannoni, 1964, Chapter 1 ('Dependence and Inferiority'), pp. 39–60 and *passim*; and Fanon, 1963, 1967. For an excellent discussion of the general problem of subordinated races accepting denigrating definitions of themselves, see Kuper, 1974, pp. 16–20.

feriority complexes were confined principally to assimilados in the major urban centres.[33]

Studies (e.g. Fanon) which attribute to all Africans the inferiority complexes of the numerically insignificant assimilated blacks are flawed by their acceptance of the colonialist's ethnocentric beliefs in the omnipotence of western civilization and the fragility of African cultures. In fact, as Amilcar Cabral and others have argued, the penetration of Portuguese culture was extremely limited and ineffective against the cultural resistance of the masses.[34]

[33] Most mestiços closely identified with Portuguese culture, including believing in the inherent inferiority of Africans. Yet, the majority of Portuguese also considered mestiços to be racially inferior—an attitude which some mestiços actually accepted.

The depth of these self-deprecating attitudes among mestiços was dramatically demonstrated to me one Sunday during lunch with six middle-class mestiço couples (50–65 years old). Following an animated discussion of the 'laziness' and 'stupidity' of Africans, I asked them to explain the cause. They unanimously responded that it stemmed from the racial and cultural inferiority of Africans. When I suggested that the logic of their response indicated that, as racially mixed individuals, they would also have to be considered inferior to whites, they did not hesitate to assure me that this was true. They hastened to explain, however, that while they, personally, happened to constitute exceptions, mestiços as a general rule were inferior to whites.

A common Portuguese perspective on mestiços is epitomized in the following ISCSPU Master's thesis on 'Aspects of Multiracialism in Angola':

In Angola the mestiços have always tried to identify themselves with the Europeans and western culture. If they were lucky enough to be recognized by their white fathers, their lives came to be like that of the Europeans and, if they grew up with complexes, it wasn't the fault of the society which received them'. Gaspar, M. da C., 1966, p. 109.

[34] Amílcar Cabral cogently elaborated this point in an address ('Identity and Dignity in the National Liberation Struggle', 1972, pp. 39–47) given at Lincoln University, 15 October 1972, upon receipt of an honorary doctoral degree:

With certain exceptions the period of colonization was not long enough, at least in Africa, for there to be a significant degree of damage to the most important facets of the culture and traditions of the subject people ... Outside the capital and other urban centres this [Portuguese cultural] influence is almost nil. It only leaves its mark at the very top of the colonial social pyramid which created colonialism itself, influencing the indigenous petite bourgeoisie, and a very small number of urban workers. The masses in the rural areas and the larger section of the urban population, over 99 per cent of the indigenous population, are untouched, or almost untouched, by the culture of the colonial power. This is partially the result of the ... effectiveness of the cultural resistance of the people, who, subjected to political domination and colonial exploitation, find their own culture acts as a bulwark in preserving their identity. Where the indigenous society has a vertical structure this defence of their cultural heritage is further strengthened by the colonial powers' interest in protecting the influence of the ruling class, their allies.

The quote is found on p. 41. Cabral expands on this theme in two other major speeches: 'National Liberation and Culture', 1970; and 'The Role of Culture in the Struggle for Independence', delivered to UNESCO, Paris, 3–7 July 1972.

In contrast, Fanon argued in *The Wretched of the Earth*:

Colonialism is not satisfied merely with holding a people in its grip and emptying the native's brain of all form and content. By a kind of perverted logic, it turns to the past of the oppressed people, and distorts, disfigures and destroys it (p. 170).

It should not be assumed that simply because the Portuguese lauded their own supposed cultural and material 'superiority' and demeaned the cultures of Africans that Africans necessarily believed them. The opposite may have appeared as the case from the works of Portuguese scholars and in the themes of assimilado writers, but for at least 80 per cent of the Angolan population neither of these perspectives represented the reality of cultural contacts. Most Africans remained psychologically, if not physically, outside the pale of Portuguese culture. At times, even Africans who married Portuguese appeared to be as impervious to Portuguese cultural influences as the latter were to African influences. This fact was vividly illustrated to me by an elderly, redoubtable Ovambo woman whom I met in southern Angola.

Senhora Almeida had lived with a former Portuguese army officer for over twenty years, during most of which time she was his legal wife. When they were married by a priest her husband was forced to abandon his military career. She had already been considered an outcast by most Ovambo because of her relationship with the army officer. All six of the Almeida children graduated from high school (a rarity even for Portuguese families) and were well integrated in the Portuguese system: among her five sons two became government agricultural experts, one was a bush trader, and of the two youngest, one was a soldier and the other a student at the time I knew them. A number of Portuguese settlers in the area confirmed the sons' memories that their parents had an extremely happy marriage until their father's death in the early 1960s.

Because of this background (and perhaps because of my own ethnocentrism) I was surprised by Senhora Almeida's demeanour when I met her at the campsite where her children had gathered for the Christmas and New Year's holidays. Her dress and behaviour seemed to be indistinguishable from any other African woman in the area. She refused to eat at the makeshift table or to use a knife and fork, preferring the ground and her hands instead. Whenever she spoke to me or one of her Portuguese daughters-in-law, it was necessary for one of her sons to act as an interpreter.

Finding myself alone with her one afternoon, I tried to engage her in a simple conversation, assuming that she must have learned some Portuguese from her husband and because her children had obviously grown up speaking the language. Yet, from the look on her face and her stony silence, it appeared that she did not understand a word of Portuguese. As I left her I wondered out loud if her husband (and children) had spoken to her only in Ovambo. Suddenly she spoke to me, saying in impeccable Portuguese, 'Oh no, my husband *never* spoke it. He knew my language as well as I, but he *never* spoke it.' When I asked why, she replied in a strong voice: 'he said that he would never speak the language of dogs'. I further inquired why she had refused earlier to speak Portuguese since she was obviously fluent. Her answer was to return to the same empty, silent look I had received during my first attempts to speak with her.[35]

Senhora Almeida exemplifies the fact that the Portuguese in the colony had no monopoly on ethnic pride. She also illustrates the reality that not all Africans who were intensively exposed to Portuguese culture chose to assimilate it. Equally important, however, her relationship with her husband provides an important key to the understanding of race relations in Angola. Neither respected the other's culture or race but, as she personally verified, they loved and respected each other. Thus, each compartmentalized their racial feelings and by doing so were able to interact as equals at some, though not all, levels. In this way it was possible for the Portuguese to isolate their genuine affection or respect for an African wife, mistress, or servant without acknowledging the full equality of the culture or race of that individual.

Finally, Senhora Almeida's uniqueness among Africans in Angola stemmed not from the personal confidence and cultural pride, which led her to reject most aspects of Portuguese culture, but from the fact that she was actually in a position to accept or discard salient features of Portuguese culture intimately familiar to her. By contrast, the overwhelming majority of Africans had so little knowledge of Portuguese culture that the decision to assimilate it never arose.

Assimilation Revisited

The Portuguese viewed the assimilation process as occurring in three stages: the destruction of traditional societies, followed by the inculcation of Portuguese culture and finally the integration of 'detribalized' and 'Portuguesized' Africans into Portuguese society.[36] This was precisely the

[35] The Portuguese frequently referred to Kimbundu, the language spoken by most Africans in the area surrounding the capital, as 'a language of dogs or of monkeys and claimed that to study it was an aberration of the spirit'. Matta, 1970, p. 35. Also see *supra*, note 22.

A few nights after my conversation with Sra. Almeida, her older sons (who had strong nationalist sympathies) began to tease their younger brother who had just been drafted into the Portuguese army. They warned him to keep his head down at all times because his uncles 'on the other side' were far better marksmen than he ever would be. Suddenly Sra. Almeida announced that she did not appreciate the humour and if anybody mentioned her son entering the army again she would leave the campsite immediately. The subject was not brought up again.

[36] Amadeu Castilho Soares (1960, p. 101) epitomized the view of most Portuguese scholars and politicians when he argued that the more the colonizing process breaks down 'tribal societies', the more 'integration will be accomplished, resulting in the pluricultural harmony of our political doctrine'.

While Mannoni agreed that for assimilation to succeed traditional social structures had to be destroyed first, he added that 'assimilation is only practicable where an individual has been isolated from his group, wrenched from his environment and transplanted elsewhere' (1964, p. 27).

course followed in Brazil and everyone 'knew' how successfully the Portuguese had assimilated blacks in Brazil. Yet, as we have seen (see Chapter 2), Brazil's economy, ecology, racial demography and long history of slavery were distant from Angolan realities. The uprooted Africans brought to Brazil were unable to draw upon their traditional institutions, social patterns, or values to sustain their cultural identities under the exigencies of adopting the language, cosmology, dress, food and gods of the ruling culture. Thus, by the end of the nineteenth century it was possible to identify a 'Brazilian society' which included all racial groups. While blacks were not incorporated into every level of Brazilian society they were, nevertheless, almost totally assimilated and therefore culturally Brazilian rather than Kimbundu, KiKongo, or Yoruba.

In Angola the Portuguese were unable to effectuate even the first stage of the assimilation process. The physical subjugation of Africans was not completed until the early decades of the twentieth century and, like all European colonizers in Africa, the Portuguese were incapable of eradicating the foundations of African societies. Moreover, they lacked the capacity *and* the volition to implement the second stage—the inculcation of Portuguese culture—despite the fact that it was the very heart of the civilizing mission. For example, only 1,012 Africans in 1940 could read and write Portuguese, which represented less than 0·03 per cent of all Africans in the colony.[37]

While the number of Africans enrolled in school increased over tenfold during the final quarter century of colonialism, the poor quality and rigidity of the educational system precluded all but 5 per cent of the Africans enrolled from completing the four years of primary school. Thus, the one instrument which Portugal possessed for effectively assimilating Africans in Angola was accorded such a low priority and was so poorly utilized that only a minute proportion of Africans were ever meaningfully exposed to Portuguese culture, let alone desirous of assimilating it.[38]

---

[37] Colónia de Angola, 1943, p. 25. The total number of Africans counted in this census was 3,665,829.

One indication of the differential levels of assimilation between blacks (*not* including mestiços) in Angola and Brazil is seen in the proportion who are literate in Portuguese. In the same year (1940) when there were only 1,012 literate blacks in Angola, 34 per cent of the (524,441) blacks in the Brazilian state of São Paulo were classified as literate. Furthermore, all blacks in Brazil who were not literate nevertheless spoke Portuguese as their native (and usually only) language. See: Fernandes, 1969, p. 455, note 6; and Pierson, 1953, pp. 101–8.

For further information on the assimilation process and assimilados in Angola, see *supra*, Chapter 5, pp. 149–55.

[38] The inadequacy of education in Angola was recognized by the Portuguese educational and economic planners themselves. For example, in the studies preparatory to the Fourth Development Plan (1974–79), they argue that:

Most of the population (and nearly all the rural population) attend only the first two, or at most three, grades, leaving school with only the sketchiest knowledge, so rudimentary that within a short while they fall back into illiteracy.

Trabalhos Preparatórios do IV Plano de Fomento (1974–1979), Educação, Serviços de Planeamento

The small number of Africans who absorbed Portuguese culture is dramatically illustrated in Heimer's studies on education in rural Angola. Using sophisticated survey research techniques and a large sample (2,976) covering approximately 80 per cent of Angolan Africans, he found that few Africans had knowledge of the Portuguese language, history, leaders, or geography.[39] For example, only 6·5 per cent of the rural heads of families in 1970–71 named Salazar, Caetano, or Américo Tomás as the 'Chief of the Portuguese Government' and less than 1 per cent identified Lisbon as the capital of Portugal. Furthermore, 85 per cent did not know 'What is Mozambique' while only 0·6 per cent identified it as a Portuguese territory.[40] Obviously, most rural Africans continued to orient

---

e Integração Económica (Luanda, 1972), p. 20 quoted in Sousa Ferreira, 1974b, p. 90. Sousa Ferreira notes that only 4·4 per cent of all students enrolled in Angolan primary schools between 1967 and 1970 completed primary education, i.e. passed the final examination of the fourth grade.

For comprehensive critical discussions of the role of education in the assimilation process in Angola, see: Sousa Ferreira, 1974b, pp. 74–126; Heimer, 1974, vol. 2, pp. 82–98 and *passim*; and Melo, Capela, Moita and Pereira, eds., 1974, pp. 51–67 and *passim*.

The low priority which education was accorded in Angola is underscored by the fact that 1967 was the first year in more than a quarter-century when more money was spent on education than on white settlement. Nevertheless, the approximately $11 million spent on education that year represented only half of what England spent on education in Ghana in 1950. See Chapter 5, pp. 151–2.

[39] For detailed information on the sampling strategy, methodology, and questionnaire used in this study, see Heimer, 1972, Anexos 1–8, pp. 400–516 and 19/4, p. ii and Anexos 1–3. The survey and analysis were carried out with the close collaboration of Eduardo Cruz de Carvalho, Julio Artur de Morais, and more than ninety other employees of the Missão de Inquéritos Agrícolas de Angola.

Concerning the level of 'domination of the Portuguese language', the following breakdown was obtained for rural Africans:

(a) Perfectly fluent   01 %
(b) Relatively fluent   04 %
(c) Reasonably fluent   16 %
(d) Few rudimentary ideas   24 %
(e) No knowledge   53 %

Heimer, vol. 2 (1974), p. 75.

Another measure of the degree of African acculturation is the frequency of the use of Portuguese by Africans in the rural areas:

(a) Regularly   01 %
(b) Some frequently   08 %
(c) Very rarely   31 %
(d) Never   59 %

ibid., p. 76.

[40] For these and other tables covering the ability of rural Africans to identify facts and places as a measure of acculturation, see Heimer, vol. 1 (1972), Tables 89–99, pp. 347–58. One of the most important conclusions emerging from Heimer's study is that mere school attendance is not as important a determinant of the level of acculturation as has been generally thought. As previously noted, this is partially accounted for by the inadequacy and inefficiency of rural education in colonial Angola. See Heimer, 1974, pp. 88–9. For further reading on problems associated with using education to determine acculturation, see Clignet, 1970, pp. 425–44.

themselves within their own historical and geographic context and remained relatively unaffected by Portuguese culture.

Knowledge about the Portuguese which most rural Africans gained from contact was not the type which would even remotely promote assimilation. Local administrators, bush traders, soldiers and colono farmers and ranchers had little interest in the assimilation of Africans. Instead they were principally concerned with collecting taxes, recruiting cheap labour, imposing the cultivation of cash crops, cheating peasant farmers and herders in commercial transactions, expropriating communal lands, and containing any protest which these and other similar activities engendered. To assist Africans to absorb Portuguese culture (i.e. 'progress') was contrary to their personal 'missions' of exploitation and domination. Each viewed African progress as a threat to their livelihood and duties—in other words, *their* own future progress. Any attempt to inculcate Portuguese culture and values or to treat rural Africans as equals was perceived by most whites as jeopardizing the well-entrenched patterns of exploitation which had enriched so many of them.

The same rationale influenced most Portuguese attitudes and policies towards the assimilation of Africans living in the urban centres. The approximately 600,000 Africans in Angolan cities and towns were naturally exposed to considerable Portuguese influence and were under strong pressures to adapt to Portuguese patterns.[41] In fact, a certain degree of assimilation was almost requisite for finding employment since all but a handful of employers were Portuguese. Yet full assimilation connoted equality and equality for Africans spelled the end of white exploitation and domination. Thus little effort was expended on imparting Portuguese civilization to urban Africans beyond that which was necessary for them to function as useful, but cheap employees. Consequently, urban Africans may have been more acculturated than their rural counterparts, but they were never fully assimilated or integrated as equals into the Portuguese sector.

Portuguese domination of urban life was so complete prior to independence that Angolan cities—unlike most other African cities—afforded Africans few opportunities for significant upward mobility. By the middle of the twentieth century the number of Portuguese living in the urban centres had grown to the point where they (and mestiços) occupied all responsible and remunerative positions as well as a large portion of the

---

[41] According to the preliminary results of the 1970 Angolan census, there were 568,503 Africans living in cities or towns containing 2,500 or more inhabitants. Fifty-five per cent (312,290) of these urban-dwelling Africans lived in the capital. Estado de Angola, 1972, p. 8. (The final results of the 1970 census were never published.)

Monteiro maintains that 100 per cent of all men and 85 per cent of the women who inhabit Luanda's slums (*musseques*) were able to speak Portuguese. Unfortunately, however, he does not distinguish the various levels of competency, which prevents comparisons with Heimer's data on rural Angola, 1973a, p. 332. For a general discussion of the education of Luanda's slum dwellers, see pp. 331–55.

unskilled jobs such as waiters, taxi-drivers and even lottery ticket salesmen. Moreover, thousands of Portuguese women worked as maids and market women; the latter actually displacing all of the African women from Luanda's central market-place.[42] Even the possibility to advance within the confines of the massive urban slums was denied to Africans by the fact that wherever there was an opportunity for profit or prestige there was also a Portuguese (or mestiço) ready to take advantage. With the death of an African herbalist (Snr. Sambo) in the early 1970s, there were no African businessmen left in Luanda.

The development of poor black ghettos in Angolan cities has paralleled the pattern of urbanization found in the United States, South Africa and most other multiracial societies in the world. However, the growth of ghettos in the U.S.—and to a much lesser extent in South Africa—was accompanied by the growth of a black middle and upper class whose wealth and prestige were direct products of the ghetto. Black professionals, businessmen, landlords, etc., were forced to endure the humiliation of segregation and prejudice but were nevertheless able to enjoy some of the amenities of wealth which could be obtained within the ghetto. Thus, urbanization may not have changed the *caste* of blacks in the United States but it did enable many to change their *class*. Neither changed for blacks in Angolan cities.

The Portuguese colonial system dominated Africans in both the rural and urban sectors without absorbing them; it drained the Africans economically without ever fully integrating them into the system. Whereas this reality was diametrically opposed to the goals of the 'civilizing mission' and 'lusotropicalism', it was a direct consequence of the goals and interests of most of the Portuguese settlers in the colony. Under these circumstances it is not surprising that so few Africans in Angola were considered (*de jure* or *de facto*) assimilados before independence.

Finally, lusotropical theory envisaged the assimilation process in terms of reciprocal borrowing and adaptation of the cultures in contact. In Brazil this involved the Portuguese and other Europeans both influencing

[42] Africans were displaced not only from market-places and jobs but residential areas as well. As the number of whites in the major urban centres grew, the 'white city' began to expand its borders into the African slums. In Luanda, for example, so many whites constructed clandestine houses and businesses in areas inhabited by Africans that at least four *musseques* (slums) disappeared completely (i.e. Bairro Operáio, Viuva Leal, Caldeira, and Burity). Clandestine houses—or houses constructed on land not owned by the constructor, without building permits, etc.—numbered in the thousands. They were almost invariably linked into municipal water and sanitation networks after completion and were frequently 'legalized'—if for no other reason than to collect for the services provided and to make them eligible to be taxed. For further information on the displacement of urban Africans from their residences see: Monteiro, 1973a, pp. 78–80 and *passim*; Bailey, 1968, pp. 405–7. For an in-depth study (despite heavy censorship) of the impact of clandestine housing among the Axiluando fishermen who lived along the coast just south of Luanda, see Morais, J. D. de, 1972, pp. 40–5.

and being influenced by African and Indian cultures. The Portuguese in Africa, however, viewed assimilation in a unilinear fashion; that is, assimilation connoted the Europeanization of Africans but never the reverse. In fact, Africanization ('cafrealization') of the Portuguese was viewed as retrogressive and was strongly disparaged. The result is that Portuguese culture in colonial Angola was hardly modified at all. Even superficial African influences on food, dress, music, and language—which the Portuguese in Brazil easily assimilated—scarcely permeated the Portuguese community in Angola. African music was not even played on Angolan radio stations until 1968 when the military decided it might be an effective way to capture an African audience for their propaganda. In short, there was infinitely less African influence on the Portuguese community in Angola (who never constituted more than 5 per cent of the population) than American black influence on American culture (where, for more than a century, whites have never constituted less than 80 per cent of the population).

Despite verbose lusotropical proclamations to the contrary, the Africans and Portuguese in Angola assimilated little from one another. In fact, they barely knew each other. In the words of General Galvão do Melo, one of the original seven members of the Portuguese Junta of National Salvation following the overthrow of the Caetano regime:

Pouco aproveitamos da África, e a África pouco aproveitou de nós. O Povo Português e o Povo Africano permaneceram desconhecidos um do outro: estrangeiros.

We benefited little from África and África benefited little from us. The Portuguese people and the African people remained unknown to each other: foreigners.[43]

Whites in Colonial Angola: A Last Look

Lusotropicologists and many foreign writers have extolled the virtues of the poor, uneducated Portuguese peasant, praising him as the bulwark of white settlement in Angola. Their argument, in short, was that the closer Europeans and Africans were to each other's cultural level (usually interpreted by class), the more amicable would be relations between the races. This belief not only appeared in the fantasies of Gilberto Freyre, Salazar and Caetano, but in the works of respected scholars such as

---

[43] Galvão de Melo, 1975, p. 60. It is interesting to read this quote in light of the fact that one of the (accurate) charges against General Galvão de Melo when he was purged (along with General Spínola and others) from the Junta in late September 1974 was that he was a serious obstacle to decolonization.

Jorge Dias and Ralph Delgado—who considered these rustic peasants the *fina flor* of Portuguese colonization.[44]

The conviction that poor, unskilled and uneducated peasants represented Portugal's best racial 'integrators' stemmed from the same fallacious reasoning which held that Cape Verdian and Angolan mestiços were the best racial 'intermediaries' in the colony. Both tenets were rooted in the Social Darwinian view that everyone can be classified on a unilineal scale of cultural or racial development *and* that the greatest cordiality exists among those groups which are most proximate on these scales. This mechanistic logic dominated Portuguese theories of race relations despite the fact that it was contradicted daily in actual relations between the races. Just as mestiços proved to be the worst racial intermediaries—given their strong identification with Portuguese society—the *fina flor* proved to be the most recalcitrant to establishing egalitarian relations with Africans.

The Portuguese in colonial Angola were no different in this respect from whites in any other multiracial society in the world. The poor white is directly threatened in any multiracial society which strives for equal racial opportunities and meaningful racial integration. As blacks ascend the social and economic ladders, the improved jobs and neighbourhoods they normally seek are occupied by unskilled and semiskilled whites —the 'hard hats', not the aristocrats. Angola afforded most of the Portuguese settlers their first opportunity for social mobility. Almost overnight *saloios* (hicks) became *senhores* and they were not prepared to jeopardize this newly found status through open and fair competition with blacks who, after all, represented 95 per cent of the colony's population.

The attitudes of whites in Angola towards human labour never developed beyond the reactions which had evolved during slavery, characterized by the popular saying: 'trabalho é para o cachorro e o preto' ('manual labour is for the dog and the black'). For most colonists—who frequently had been farmers and manual labourers in Portugal—the idea of working with one's hands in Angola was considered degrading, a mark of inferior social status and therefore to be avoided if possible. Many of them employed at least one servant in their homes and, if they owned a farm or business, a number of African labourers (seldom paid more

[44] Variations of this argument can be found in the following: Freyre, 1953, pp. 181–2; Delgado, 1960, p. 48; Bettencourt, 1961, p. 80; Dias, J., 1960, p. 27; Abecasis, 1965, pp. 20–1; and Neto, 1971, pp. 6–7.

A classical lusotropical position assumed by a foreigner on the importance of poor Portuguese peasants can be found in the work of Mugur Valahu, who argues:

Portuguese paternalism, in relation to the natives, permits a real assimilation. Integration became possible not only thanks to official policy, tending to the creation of a pluriracial society, but also because this material distance diminished constantly. It doubtlessly becomes easier for the non-evolved Negro to rise to a higher social level when the very white has an extremely modest standard of living (1968, p. 116). (This book was originally published in French in 1966.)

For a more recent (and more guarded) development of this position, see Adelman, 1975, p. 564.

than U.S.$.75 a day before the Portuguese coup).[45] The colonies provided the first opportunity for most settlers to employ others to do their work, and they were not adverse to abusing and deprecating their employees, since a large majority had themselves suffered as employees/servants in the metropole. The prerogatives of being an 'employer' in pre-coup Portugal—including the (unchallenged) 'right' to denigrate and exploit employees judged inferior—were exported *in toto* to Angola and expanded to include the use of corporal punishment. Thus, everyday metropolitan social and labour problems became acute racial problems as well in the colonies.

Furthermore, the average white employer earned between ten and one hundred times more than his African employees, which established an almost insurmountable barrier in life-style between them—even if the cultural gap was not always great. This difference in life-style enabled many Portuguese to rationalize their attitudes of superiority and, consequently, their harsh treatment of their African employees. Since little contact between the races in colonial Angola transcended that of employer-employee/master-servant, most racial interaction reinforced the dichotomous view that whites were superior and blacks inferior.

A brief profile of the Portuguese in Angola at the end of the colonial era reveals not only how dependent their 'superior' status was on colour (not achievement) but also how few skills they possessed which could have contributed to the economic or social development of an independent

---

[45] The reactionary journalist and novelist, Reis Ventura, argued in 1955 that each 'civilized family' in Angola utilized an average of three African workers: a maid, a cook, and a laundress. Three years later Afonso Mendes maintained that there were few colonos who did not 'have one, two, or more native servants. There were few colonos who did not unload the least physical effort on the native's shoulders.' See: Ventura, 1955; and Mendes, 1957–8, p. 85.

For a discussion of similar Portuguese attitudes against manual labour in Brazil, see Smith, T. L., 1972, pp. 231–2.

Ninety-five per cent of the (105,925) salaried rural workers in Angola earned less than 250 escudos per month in 1965 (an escudo equalled approximately U.S.$.03 at this time). If one were to translate this monthly salary to an hourly wage based on the number of hours worked per month, the average hourly wage for salaried rural workers was approximately $0.03. The minimum wage was raised in 1970 (for all those over 18 years of age) to 30 escudos per day in Luanda and Cabinda, 25 escudos/day in Carmona and São Salvador, and 20 escudos/day in all other areas. The employer, however, was allowed to deduct up to 50 per cent of these wages to cover his cost of food, clothing, housing, etc.—which frequently were never provided. One example of the blatant exploitation of African workers can be seen in the fishing industry at Mossamedes. In 1974 the more than 10,000 Africans who worked over 16 hours a day on the fishing boats under extremely precarious conditions earned an average of less than 650 escudos a month. In contrast, the owners of the boats earned approximately 2,200 escudos an hour! See: *Expresso* (Lisbon), 11 May 1974; U.N., 1973, pp. 42–5; and Grupo de Trabalho Sectorial, n.d., p. 120, chart 11.

Angola.[46] The massive white exodus which occurred during the months prior to independence was undoubtedly provoked by the open warfare among the three nationalist movements; but a look into the background of the whites leaves little doubt that most would have left eventually even if the transition to independence had been peaceful. Either they would have been sent back to Portugal in the interest of curbing forms of economic exploitation, or they would have left on their own out of the realization that they could not (or would not) adapt to an egalitarian multiracial society.

It has been evident throughout this study that the image of the Portuguese population in Angola, portrayed in pre-coup Portuguese scholarship and propaganda as a settled and stable population with five centuries of roots in the colony, does not match the reality of Portuguese immigration and settlement patterns. In fact, Table 18 clearly illustrates that *over half* of the whites in the colony by the end of 1974 had immigrated or were born *after the outbreak of the war of independence*! Moreover, only about 28 per cent of the whites present in 1970 were actually born in the colony; in the capital of Luanda (where almost 45 per cent of all whites resided) the proportion of 'native-born' Portuguese dropped to less than 20 per cent.[47]

---

[46] Governor General Robocho Vaz had no illusions about the low level of skills and education possessed by most Portuguese immigrants. He even acknowledged during my interview with him (11 March 1969) that most did not contribute to the development of the colony. When I asked him how, then, he could justify the continuation of this type of immigration, he responded that he hoped the poor and uneducated peasants would some day attract relatives who had more education and skills.

Another important factor behind the massive exodus of whites before independence was the fear of retribution by Africans whom they had mistreated. In part, these fears resulted from projections, since whites had rarely been punished for crimes committed against Africans. Nowhere was this more evident than in the trial of five white taxi drivers who, because of a false rumour, indiscriminately attacked the *musseque* Cazenga on the night of 16 September 1972, killing four Africans and burning down at least six houses. All five were found 'not guilty' for lack of evidence, even though there were a number of (African) eyewitnesses and considerable evidence. For example, one of the accused taxi drivers (António Grilo) was seen by witnesses killing Bernardo Gouveia with a 22 calibre pistol. The police later found a 22 Long Baretta pistol in his cab (identified as being at the scene of the crime) which ballistics reports indicated was the probable (50–70 per cent) murder weapon. While Grilo's fingerprints were presumed to be on the gun, it was determined that since neither the science of ballistics nor fingerprinting is exact, there was a 'reasonable doubt' that Grilo committed the crime and he was released accordingly. A moving account of the crimes, evidence, and trial is contained in the eloquent appeal for justice by the public defender, Albertino dos Santos Fonseca Almeida, a mimeographed copy of which I have in my possession.

When white taxi drivers again attacked Africans in Cazenga shortly after the Lisbon coup, the Africans fought back and some of the taxi drivers were arrested.

[47] The data for native-born whites in 1960 can be found in the census: Província de Angola, 1967, p. 13. The figures for 1970 are based on my projections from the 1960 census, since the 1970 census was not published.

TABLE 18

Number of Whites Living in Angola: 1845–1974[48]

1845	1,832
1900	9,198
1920	20,200
1940	44,083
1950	78,826
1960	172,529
1961	162,387
1970	290,000[a]
1974	335,000[a]

[a]estimates

It is not possible to present a precise evaluation of the educational background of Angolan whites, since the most recent data which included a racial breakdown of school attendance were published in 1950 (see Table 19). It is significant to note, however, that in 1950 almost half

TABLE 19

Number of Years of Education of Whites in Angola,
Five Years Old And More, 1950[49]

Years of Education	Number	Percentage
None	30,506	44·2
1–4	27,042	39·2
5–11	10,058	14·6
12 +	1,389	2·0
Total	68,995	100·0

[48] The sources used in compiling this table can be found above in Table 1, p. 20 and in Bender and Yoder, 1974, pp. 26–31. The latter article was written as an attempt to correct a number of misconceptions concerning the size of the Angolan white population, generally assumed (in the media) as approximately 500,000 at the time of the Portuguese coup—a gross exaggeration. This exaggeration was possible because the statistics concerning the white population obtained in the 1970 census were never published. The total number of Angolans counted in the 1970 census was known by early 1972, including a racial breakdown of all those living in cities or towns containing 2,500 or more inhabitants. Yet, by independence time it was still not known how many whites had been counted in the census, making it necessary for one to rely on estimates for all references to the size of the white population after 1960.

[49] This table was adapted from Provincia de Angola, 1955, p. 5.

of all whites in the colony who were five years old and over never attended school, and *less than 17 per cent* had obtained more than four years of education. Official data published after 1950 which bear on this subject not only lack racial designations but are incomplete and frequently unreliable. Nevertheless, a meaningful expansion of the educational system occurred so late (late 1960s) and the number of students reportedly enrolled in secondary schools (or their equivalents) or higher educational institutions was still so small that the Angolan educational system could not have substantially raised the educational level of whites in the colony.[50]

Since most of the fourfold increase in the white population during the last quarter-century of colonialism resulted from the influx of Portuguese immigrants, an analysis of their educational background broadens our perspective of the Angolan whites just prior to independence. Less than *six per cent* of the approximately 100,000 Portuguese immigrants between 1950 and 1964 who were seven years and older attended school beyond the fourth grade![51] While Table 20 indicates that the proportion

[50] In 1970, 27,916 students of *all races* were enrolled in secondary schools of all types, including trade and commercial schools, ecclesiastical and art schools, and the University of Luanda. While the total rose to 34,237 in 1972, it still represented only a small portion of eligible school-age whites and only about 3 per cent of all children in the colony between the ages of 10 and 19 years. Instituto Nacional de Estatística, 1972, p. 60; and Estado de Angola, 1972, p. 10.

In an article in *Expresso* (Lisbon), it was argued that only 15 per cent of the Europeans in Angola were skilled (31 May 1975).

[51] The only method employed by Portuguese statisticians and demographers for calculating the number of 'white' immigrants who arrived in Angola each year was to subtract the total number of people who annually left the colony (by land, sea, and air) from the number of those who entered. The balance was considered to be the number of white immigrants, despite the fact that not all of these 'immigrants' were white or necessarily people intent on immigrating. For example, almost all of the approximately 40,000 Cape Verdians who emigrated to Angola in recent decades were mestiços. Nevertheless, since no racial breakdown of the passengers is provided, I am considering all immigrants as white (with the knowledge that it skews the white population upward).

My figure of 6 per cent as the proportion of immigrants to Angola with more than four years of education is an extremely conservative estimate. The actual proportion could be less than 2 per cent! The official data did not discriminate the education of Portuguese by colony before 1965 and therefore all data published before this time refer to those who emigrated to all of the Portuguese overseas colonies. Nevertheless, approximately two-thirds of all emigrants during this period emigrated to Angola *and*, as a general rule, Angola attracted those with the lowest education. My own survey of the government's statistical annuals covering 1953 to 1964 revealed that there was actually a net loss of 128 settlers with five to eleven years of education (i.e. 128 more people with five to eleven years education left the colonies than arrived). During the same period there was a positive balance of 1,994 immigrants with twelve or more years education, representing only 1·8 per cent of all immigrants. Barata presents data on the education of those who went to the colonies (i.e. he did not subtract those who left during the same period). The percentages of those with some high school (five to eleven years) or university (twelve or more) education were, respectively: 1950–54, 6·0 per cent and 2·7 per cent; 1955–59, 1·9 per cent and 2·3 per cent; and 1960–62, 5·2 per cent and 2·0 per cent. Barata, 1965, p. 136, Table 51. Also see Bender and Yoder, 1974, p. 33.

of immigrants with post-primary school education rose during the 1965–72 period, it still did not exceed the 1950 level of less than 17 per cent. Moreover, the percentage of immigrants who arrived without any schooling at all during the last decade of colonialism rose to more than 55 per cent. Clearly, after a century of successive government campaigns to raise the cultural and educational level of Portuguese immigrants in Angola, the *fina flor* continued to predominate until the very end of colonialism.

PART IV CONCLUSION

TABLE 20

Number of Years of Education of Portuguese Emigrants to Angola, Seven Years and Older, 1965–72 [52]

Years of Education	Number	Percentage
None	33,063	55·7
1–4	16,412	27·6
5–11	8,649	14·6
12 +	1,256	2·1
Total	59,380	100·0

[52] The data used in compiling this table were found in: *Boletim Mensal de Estatística de Angola,* Luanda (January 1966), pp. 20–3; the *Anuários Estatísticos* of Angola from 1966 to 1971; and *Anuário Estatístico,* 1972, vol. 2 (Lisbon: Instituto Nacional de Estatística, 1972), pp. 22–3. The totals and percentages do not include those immigrants whose educational background was unknown.

[53] Monteiro, Ramiro Ladeiro 1968. SCCIA's estimate of the total white population (excluding soldiers) as of December 1967 was 270,000.

It is important to note that this table of those in the 'liberal professions' *does not include all* professionals extant in Angola. For example, all 'professionals' who worked in the civil service or army were excluded *unless* they maintained a private practice or business on the side. The possibility of government employees having a private practice naturally varied among the professions. For example, practically every government or military doctor in Angola had a private practice on the side. Therefore while the table approximates the total number of doctors in Angola in 1968, this would not be true for engineers, land surveyors, etc.

Finally, it should be noted that those professions assumed under the rubric of 'liberal professions' correspond to the tax code (i.e. those who had to pay a 'professional tax'). Clearly those who designed the tax code made little effort to adhere to common sociological interpretations of the 'liberal professions'.

TABLE 21

Number and Location of those Practising a Liberal Profession in Angola, 1968[53]

	LUANDA	BENGUELA	HUAMBO	HUILA	CUANZA SUL	MALANGE	BIE	MOÇAMEDES	CUANZA NORTE	UIGE	MOXICO	CABINDA	CUANDO CUBANGO	LUNDA	ZAÏRE	TOTALS
Lawyers	43	12	7	4	3	4	2	2	4	3	1	2	—	—	—	87
Land Surveyors	9	3	1	2	1	—	—	—	1	—	—	—	—	—	—	17
Canvassers (collectors)	—	5	7	4	—	5	9	3	—	—	3	—	—	—	—	36
Architects	20	2	—	1	—	1	—	—	—	—	—	—	—	—	—	24
Engineering Technicians	22	1	1	—	1	—	—	2	—	—	1	—	—	—	—	28
Analysts	—	—	1	—	—	—	—	—	—	—	—	—	—	—	—	1
Insurance Agents	4	—	3	—	1	—	—	—	—	—	—	—	—	—	—	8
Accountants	9	4	1	—	—	—	—	1	—	6	—	1	—	—	—	22
Builders	10	7	—	—	—	—	—	—	—	2	3	1	1	—	—	24
Customhouse Brokers	45	38	2	2	3	—	—	8	—	—	1	5	—	—	—	104
Draftsmen	11	3	—	—	1	—	—	—	1	—	—	—	—	1	—	17
Nurses	39	15	16	8	11	6	11	4	4	6	3	—	—	—	—	123
Electricians	20	8	4	2	2	2	1	3	3	1	4	1	—	—	1	52
Engineers	51	3	5	4	—	3	1	1	—	—	—	1	—	—	—	69
Bookkeepers	14	6	6	3	9	4	5	2	5	—	3	—	—	—	—	57
Physicians	146	46	38	22	20	13	10	6	14	11	7	3	2	1	1	340
Foremen	20	6	12	8	3	5	3	6	1	—	—	—	—	—	—	64
Masseurs	9	1	1	—	—	—	—	—	—	—	—	—	—	—	—	11
Musicians	8	—	—	—	—	—	—	—	—	—	—	—	—	—	—	8
Extrajudicial Attorneys	13	6	4	2	3	1	2	2	3	3	1	2	—	—	—	42
Private Teachers	10	6	3	—	1	8	—	—	—	3	—	—	—	—	—	31
Agrarian Regents	—	—	—	—	1	—	—	—	—	—	—	—	—	—	—	1
Solicitors	9	—	—	5	—	1	—	1	—	—	1	—	—	—	—	17
Topographers	—	1	—	—	1	—	—	—	—	—	—	—	—	—	—	2
Veterinarians	6	4	2	6	1	—	—	1	—	—	—	—	—	—	—	20
TOTALS	518	177	114	73	62	53	44	42	36	35	28	16	3	2	2	1205

The extremely low educational level of whites in colonial Angola and, by extension, the minimal degree of skills they possessed are confirmed in a confidential report on the liberal professions presented to the Angolan Council on Counter-Subversion in June, 1968. As can be seen in Table 21, the term 'liberal profession' incorporates a number of diverse professions ranging from doctors to insurance agents. Moreover, some of those included were mestiços and a few were black Africans. But even if we consider all of them to be white, the 1,205 professionals in Angola in early 1968 represented less than a half of one per cent (0·48 per cent) of the total white population.

The geographic distribution of individuals practising a liberal profession indicates that the bulk of Angola's population did not benefit from whatever skills they possessed. Two-thirds of the professionals in Angola in 1968 lived in only three of Angola's sixteen districts, 42 per cent in the capital alone. Not unexpectedly, these three districts (Luanda, Benguela and Huambo) contained over 60 per cent of the whites in the colony. No data exist for the number and location of professionals in Angola after 1968; but, given that social and working conditions (including salaries) were admittedly better in the metropole than in Angola, it is unlikely that the number of professionals rose appreciably between 1968 and 1975—when the massive white exodus occurred.

The limited capacity of the educational system to train meaningful numbers of Angolans beyond the equivalent of (an American) junior high-school education, the extremely small number of trained professionals, the difficulty of recruiting highly skilled metropolitans, and the arduous working conditions and low wages found in the public sector severely compromised the size and quality of the colonial civil service. The former Director of the Civil Administration not only pointed out an overall drop in the quality of civil service by the late 1960s but added that large numbers of civil servants had abandoned the rural areas for the cities with the result that: 'the mission of the Portuguese presence in Angola is betrayed because the large masses of the African population are not assisted as they should be'.[54]

If only a few per cent of the Portuguese in Angola worked in the civil service or exercised a liberal profession, and if only 10 per cent were

[54] Lopes, A. A., 1968, p. 2.

I do not know how many Portuguese worked in the civil service prior to independence, but in 1965 an unpublished document prepared by the Angolan Department of Civil Administration listed the following categories according to the occupants' place of birth: (a) employees of metropolitan government in line and auxiliary positions, 1,038 (born in Portugal) and 715 (born in colonies); (b) high administrative officers, 148 (Portugal) and 34 (colonies); (c) political figures (e.g. deputies to the National Assembly, members of the economic and social councils, legislative councils, etc.), 27 (Portugal) and 25 (colonies). Cited in Norman A. Bailey in Abshire and Samuels, 1969, pp. 149–50. A significant proportion of those listed as born in the colonies were actually Cape Verdians, most of whom left during the 1975 pre-independence exodus.

farmers or fishermen, how did the remainder—nearly all of whom had less than five years of education—earn a living? The answer is that most were engaged in commerce. By the end of 1967 whites (and a few mestiços) owned 21,297 licensed commercial establishments; if all illegal/clandestine establishments were included, the actual number would be at least double (according to official estimates).[55] When other Portuguese who worked for the owners of these businesses are added, along with the families of those who worked in the commercial sector, it would appear that over two-thirds of all whites in the colony were dependent on commerce. The reason for this large concentration of Portuguese in the Angolan commercial sector and the background of those who engaged in commerce were described by the former heads of the Department of Economic Services in the following:

> It is an accepted truth that each Portuguese who makes his way to Angola harbours the desire to enter into the commercial sector, going into business for himself, if possible. Coming almost always from the agricultural sector, where they were simple workers with little education and little knowledge of the country (many totally illiterate), they do not hesitate to enter into business, despite their lack of training ... the principal reason which propels the Portuguese into commerce originates in their lack of technical knowledge and secondly from the fact that they had previously lived a difficult life in agriculture which frustrated all enthusiasm to continue as farmers ... They adopt this new activity, for which they are not prepared, because it gives them new hope for earning easy money ... [and] because it is actually a far easier means of earning a living than agriculture.[56]

These data on the educational and occupational background of the Portuguese settlers in Angola clearly show that after five centuries Portugal was still dependent on its lowest class for the impetus to the colonization of Angola: the same *petit blanc* who traditionally had manifested the most virulent white racism in multiracial societies throughout the world. The only difference was that the *petit blanc* in Angola made up a significantly larger proportion of the overall white population than did his counterparts elsewhere in Africa.[57]

[55] A complete breakdown of the number of commercial establishments, the number of specialized employees, and the amount of capital investment by region can be found in Pedriras and Pinto, 1968, table following p. 14. Their estimate that the inclusion of clandestine commercial establishments would double the number of legal establishments is found on pp. 2–3.

[56] Ibid., pp. 1–3.

[57] The educational and occupational background of the whites in Angola compared unfavourably not only with the English gentry who settled in the Kenyan Highlands and with the French colons in Senegal but even with the Portuguese who emigrated to Mozambique and Brazil.

Final Thoughts

In this chapter I have tried to emphasize the cognitions, modes of rationalization, myths, biases and ideologies which blinded most Portuguese and many foreigners to the realities of white racism and domination in Angola. Fortunately for Africans in the former colonies (and for the citizens of Portugal), not all colonial administrators or military officers shared the conviction that the *petit blanc* represented the *fina flor* of colonization, or that an 'intrinsic superiority' of Portuguese civilization guaranteed victory in the colonial wars. Through their contacts with the settlers, some junior officers and enlightened administrators realized that a large portion of whites manifested attitudes and behaviour totally antithetical to all of the basic tenets of lusotropicalism.[58] They concluded that the widespread presence of white racism had produced a vast number of alienated Africans which, in turn, guaranteed an unending supply of nationalist recruits—in other words, the prospect of a perpetual military stalemate. For many Portuguese officers the ramifications of white racism precluded the thought, let alone the possibility, of a military victory. When

---

[58] Most of the papers presented to the Angolan General Council on Counter-Subversion reveal that, while metropolitan politicians and academicians publicly exalted the virtuous *fina flor* as being non-racist, a number of military officers and civil servants in Angola privately condemned them for causing and sustaining the war:

[The] European population is still not conscious of the gravity of the situation in which they live. They remain tied to old concepts which have served as the basis for their relations with Africans; in most cases, this has merely led to a commingling because contacts are limited to working relations which do not always proceed according to plans. [The European population] does not want to abdicate the prerogatives they have been permitted to enjoy ... They turn their back on and ignore the problems of the war with which we struggle. Most of them think that it is a problem exclusively for the armed forces who, together with the police, have to defend the peace and their farms because of the simple fact that they pay taxes.

[The] relationship between Europeans and Africans is one of the fundamental aspects to be considered in the context of counter-subversion. There is a tendency among Europeans, especially those less educated, to adopt a feeling of superiority because of the colour of their skin in their relations with Africans. These Europeans do not even know how to distinguish between evolved and less-evolved Africans and frequently fall into generalizations. Besides this, at times, Europeans adopt these attitudes in their contacts with Africans purposefully to be spiteful and to taunt them.

These quotes can be found in, respectively: Grupo de Coordenação e Inspecção da Contra-Subversão, 1968, p. 2; and Comissão de Estudo da Secção I, 1969, pp. 13–14.

For further background on the participants and purpose of the Angolan General Council on Counter-Subversion's symposia in the late 1960s see above, Chapter 6, note 2, p. 157. It should be noted that not all of the authors of papers critical of the racial attitudes of whites in Angola were 'enlightened' or necessarily favoured independence under majority rule. Some, for example, merely saw white racism as a serious problem and error which had to be combated in order to win the war. What makes these studies unique is that they present a side of 'official opinion' which never found its way into the government's propaganda or the treatises of Portuguese scholars.

it became obvious to them that their superior officers and the political leaders in Lisbon were incapable of transcending anachronistic racial, colonial and ideological beliefs, the junior officers, frustrated both by the unending and apparently fruitless fighting and by the lack of response to their suggestions and criticisms, seized the reins of the Portuguese Government on 25 April 1974.[59]

The overthrow of the Caetano regime by the Armed Forces Movement portended not only the end of Portuguese colonization in Angola but also the demise of the Portuguese colonial community described in this study. Few genuine or meaningful steps towards decolonization were taken during General Spinola's five months in office, which encouraged many settlers to believe that white domination was still possible. In fact, during the summer of 1974 some whites in Luanda resorted to previous patterns of asserting their dominance during times of crisis by attacking Africans living in the *musseques* (slums).[60] Instead of being intimidated as in the past, however, the Africans were provoked into counter-attacks which led to an immediate departure from the *musseques* of Portuguese and Cape Verdian merchants. For a time it appeared that Luanda would prove to be the racial keg of dynamite so many had feared.

Undoubtedly the racial violence would have continued and grown had the Armed Forces Movement not succeeded in removing General Spinola from office in late September 1974. The departure of Spinola placed Angola firmly on course towards independence and made it possible for the nationalist parties to surface and assume an active role in the de colonization process. Initially, the nationalists' campaign for support throughout the colony mollified racial antagonisms as Africans, mestiços and whites joined the three recognized nationalist parties (MPLA, UNITA, and FNLA). By the time the Transitional Government assumed power on 31 January 1975, relatively few Portuguese had fled the colony.

---

[59] The background, causes, and wider implications of the Portuguese coup of April, 1974 are beyond the scope of this study. I have discussed these matters elsewhere: 1974, pp. 121–62; and 1975a. Also see Kenneth Maxwell's two-part analysis of the coup and the Armed Forces Movement 1975a, pp. 29–35 and 1975b, pp. 20–30.

[60] Detailed accounts of the Luanda race riots during the summer of 1974 can be found in *Noticia* (Luanda), no. 763 (July 1974), pp. 26–41; *Comércio do Funchal* (Madeira), 1 August 1974, pp. 8–16; *Expresso* (Lisbon), 27 July 1974; *BBC Summary of World Broadcasts*, 2nd series: ME/4677/B/5 (14 August 1974); and *Newsweek* (26 August 1974), p. 41. For an analysis of the reactionary behaviour of whites who provoked most of the rioting, see the interview with General Silva Cardoso, the Portuguese High Commissioner in Angola during the Transitional Government, in *Expresso* (Lisbon), 17 May 1975.

Many whites in Angola believed that they would be safe in Luanda (where they were outnumbered by Africans almost four to one) if they could terrorize the *musseques*. This belief stems in part from their experience during the early months of the war in 1961 when they slaughtered over a thousand Africans in the slums. Many whites told me in the late 1960s that they had guns loaded and hand grenades ready to attack the slums at the first sign of trouble. For a description of one of these attacks in 1972, see above, note 46.

The first nine months following the Lisbon coup proved to be the most peaceful phase of decolonization in Angola. The Transitional Government was barely in place, however, before the internecine conflicts which had dominated relations among Angolan nationalists during the past two decades were resumed. In previous years their attacks on each other had been generally verbal, carried out in foreign languages in the pages of international newspapers and periodicals; occasionally they had fought physically on the battlefield in remote parts of the colony. Once they were able to campaign openly for support, however, the insecurities, distrust, fears and hatred which had been nurtured during the long years of underground and exile politics threatened to engulf millions of Angolans of all races.

The impotency of the Transitional Government to restore peace after the FNLA's violent attacks on the MPLA in late March 1975 marked the beginning of the collapse of law and order throughout the country. In subsequent months it became evident that neither the Transitional Government nor the Portuguese Armed Forces could protect the lives or property of anyone living in the country. Most Angolans had nowhere to flee, but whites increasingly began to look to Portugal as a place of refuge.

Approximately 60,000 Portuguese had fled Angola by the time the international airlift began on 1 May. In the wake of the uncontrolled violence which spread through Angola, a reported 235,315 refugees of all races left during the airlift (which ended 31 October 1975).[61] Additional thousands of Portuguese left in early 1976, during a second airlift, leaving an estimated 30,000 to 40,000 Portuguese remaining in the Peoples Republic of Angola at the end of the war.[62]

This massive white exodus was a mixed blessing for the Peoples Republic of Angola. It removed as many as a quarter of a million Portuguese from the country, the majority of whom had deeply ingrained racist predispositions and whose livelihood had directly or indirectly depended upon the exploitation of Africans. With their departure went a potentially explosive source of racial friction. On the other hand, their exodus also disrupted the economy, reduced the scope and effectiveness of government services and diminished the material quality of urban life. While these short-run problems are severe and problematical, they are surmountable. Moreover, it may ultimately be fortunate for the Peoples

---

[61] The figure of 60,000 Portuguese fleeing before June 1975 was given by Correia Jesuino, then Portuguese Minister of Information. See *Diário de Notícias* (Lisbon), 13 June 1975. The Ministry of Co-operation announced in early 1976 that between 1 May and 31 October 1975, 235,315 refugees were airlifted out of Angola. Cited in the *New York Times*, 18 January 1976.

[62] The estimate of 30,000 to 40,000 Portuguese still in Angola by March 1976 was given by José Gomes Mota, who served as State Secretary of the Ministry of Co-operation in the VI Provisional Government in Portugal. *Expresso* (Lisbon), 20 March 1976, interview on p. 13.

Republic of Angola that they occurred sooner rather than later.

The thrust of the activities of all but a small minority of whites in colonial Angola—whether they had lived in urban or rural areas or had worked in the private or public sector—was to develop and enrich a very narrow stratum of Angola's population. In the long run, therefore, it may be beneficial to start almost from scratch, to reorient the economy and government services to better serve the more than 90 per cent of the population who had either been exploited or neglected by the colonial system.

Bibliography

Bibliography

Sources cited in this study

Books, Articles, Reports and Documents

Abecasis, Carlos Krus, 1965, 'Fundamentos de uma política de povoamento', *Boletim da Sociedade de Geografia de Lisboa* 83, pp. 9–23 (January–June).

Abshire, David M. and Bailey, Norman A., 1969, 'Current Race Character', in *Portuguese Africa: A Handbook*, pp. 202–16, eds. David M. Abshire and Michael A. Samuels. New York: Praeger.

Abshire, David M. and Samuels, Michael A., eds., 1969, *Portuguese Africa: A Handbook*. New York: Praeger.

Acheson, Dean, 1967, Foreword to *The Third World*, by Franco Nogueira. London: Johnson.

Actualidade economica, 1970 (Luanda) 1 (January).

Adams, Richard N. *et al.*, 1960, *Social Change in Latin America Today*. New York: Vintage Books.

Adelman, Kenneth L., 1975, 'Report from Angola', *Foreign Affairs* 53 (April), pp. 558–76.

Afonso, A. Martins, 1961, 'O colonato europeu de Cela, em Angola', *Boletim Geral do Ultramar* 37 (February), pp. 261–88.

Agência Geral do Ultramar, 1961, *Províncias ultramarinas portuguesas: dados informativos*, no. 1. Lisbon: Agência Geral do Ultramar.

——, 1968, *Províncias ultramarinas portuguesas: dados informativos*, no. 4. Lisbon: Agência Geral do Ultramar.

Alden, Dauril, ed., 1973, *Colonial Roots of Modern Brazil*. Berkeley: University of California Press.

Almanak statístico da Província d'Angola e suas dependências para o anno de 1852, Luanda: Imprensa do Governo.

Almeida, João de, 1936, *Sul d'Angola: relatório de um governo de distrito*, 2nd ed. Lisbon: Agência Geral das Colónias.

Alves, Carlos, 1960, *O povoamento de Angola*. Lisbon: Bertrand.

Amaral, Ilídio do, 1960, *Aspectos do povoamento branco de Angola*, Estudos, Ensaios e Documentos, no. 74. Lisbon: Junta de Investigações do Ultramar.

——, 1962, *Ensaio de um Estudo Geográfico da Rede Urbana de Angola*. Lisbon: Junta de Investigações do Ultramar.

——, 1964, *Santiago de Cabo Verde—a terra e os homens*. Lisbon: Junta de Investigações do Ultramar.

——, 1967, 'Santiago de Cabo Verde, Guiné e São Tomé', in *Curso de Extensão*

Universitária—Cabo Verde, Guiné, São Tomé e Principe. Lisbon: Instituto Superior de Ciêncías Sociais e Política Ultramarina.

——, 1968, *Luanda: Estudo de Geografia Urbana*. Lisbon: Junta de Investigações do Ultramar.

Amorim, Fernando Bayolo Pacheco de, 1958–9, 'A concentração urbana em Angola: contribuição para o estudo da demografia de Angola', *Revista do Centro de Estudos Demográficos* 11, pp. 89–111.

Andrade, Mario Pinto de [Buanga Fele], 1955, 'Qu'est-ce que le "luso tropicalism"?', *Présence africaine* 4 (October–November), pp. 24–35.

Andrade, Mario Pinto de, 1958, *Antologia da poesia negra de expressão portuguesa*. Paris: Pierre Jean Oswald.

Angola Comité, 1972, *Petition by the Angola Comité Concerning the Report by Mr. Pierre Juvigny*. Amsterdam: Angola Comité.

——, 1973, *Facts and Reports*, vol. 23, no. 24, p. 9. Amsterdam: Angola Comité.

Angola: relatório da repartição dos serviços de cadastro e colonização, 1935, no. 16. Lisbon: Agência Geral das Colónias.

Araujo, A. Correira de, 1964, *Aspectos de desenvolvimento económico e social de Angola*. Lisbon: Junta de Investigações do Ultramar.

Archer, Maria, 1935, 'A carta', *O mundo português* (January), pp. 7–12.

——, 1936, *Sertanejos*, Cadernos Coloniais, no. 9. Lisbon: Editorial Cosmos.

Arouca, Domingos António de Mascarenhas, 1961, *Análise social de regime do indigenato*. Lisbon: by the Author.

Associação Industrial Portuguesa, 1952, 'Situação da Industria Nacional', *Grande Congresso Nacional de Lisboa*, Lisbon, 1910, cited by José Gonçalo Santa-Rita, 'Oliveira Martins e política colonial', *Estudos Ultramarinos* 2 (January–June).

Atkinson, William C., 1960, *A History of Spain and Portugal*. Harmondsworth: Penguin Books.

Azevedo, Lucio d', 1913, 'Estudos para a história dos Cristãos-Novos em Portugal', *Revista de História* 3, pp. 76–93.

Azevedo, Thales de, 1959, *Ensaios de antropologia social*. Salvador-Bahia: Publicações da Universidade da Bahia.

Azurara, Gomes Eannes de, 1896, 1899, *The Chronical of the Discovery and Conquest of Guinea*, 2 vols., trans. Charles Raymond Beazley and Edgar Prestage. London: Hakluyt Society.

Bacelar, João, 1924, 'O problema da transportação penal', paper presented to the 2.º Congresso Colonial Nacional. Lisbon.

Baião, Antonio, 1972–3, *Episódios dramáticos da Inquisição portuguesa*. 3 vols. 3rd ed. Lisbon: Seara Nova.

Baião, Rodrigo José, 1966, 'Angola, espaço aberto', in *Migrações e povoamento*. Luanda: Instituto de Angola.

Bailey, Norman A., 1968, 'Local and Community Power in Angola', *Western Political Quarterly* 21 (September), pp. 400–8.

——, 1969, 'The Political Process and Interest Groups', in *Portuguese Africa: A Handbook*, pp. 146–64, eds. David M. Abshire and Michael A. Samuels. New York: Praeger.

Ball, George W., 1968, *The Discipline of Power*. Boston: Little, Brown and Company.

Balsemão, Francisco Pinto, 1971, 'O tom do futuro', *Notícia*, no. 616 (9 October).

Banco de Angola, 1967, *Annual Report and Economic and Financial Survey of Angola, 1967*. Lisbon: Banco de Angola.

——, 1973a, *Boletim Trimestral*, no. 64 (October–December).

Banco de Angola, 1973b, *Relatório e Contas, 1973*. Lisbon: Banco de Angola.

Banco Nacional Ultramarino, 1968, *Boletim Trimestral*, no. 68.

Barata, José Fernando Nunes, 1963, *Estudos sobre a economia do ultramar*. Lisbon: Centro de Estudos Político-Sociais.

——, 1966, 'Êxodo rural, emigração e povoamento do ultramar', *Ultramar* 7, pp. 71–99.

——, 1970, 'O aproveitamento do Cunene e o desenvolvimento do sul de Angola', *Ultramar* 10, pp. 51–73.

Barata, Oscar Soares, 1965, *Migrações e povoamento*. Lisbon: Sociedade de Geografia de Lisboa.

——, 1966, 'O povoamento de Cabo Verde, Guiné e São Tomé', reprint from *Curso de Extensão Universitária—Cabo Verde, Guiné e São Tomé*. Lisbon: Instituto Superior de Ciências Sociais e Política Ultramarina.

Barbosa, Ilidío, 1948, *Possibilidades de colonização branca em Angola*. Lisbon: Edições da J.A.C. de Portugal.

——, 1968, 'Inquéritos às missões rurais de colonizaçao', Luanda, 1947. Quoted in Fernando L. de Couto e Silva, 'A tentativa de colonização oficial de 1928', Master's thesis, Instituto Superior de Ciências Sociais e Política Ultramarina, Lisbon.

Barnes, T. Alexander, 1928, *Angolan Sketches*. London: Methuen and Co.

Barreiros, José Baptista, 1929, *Missão histórica de Portugal: colonisação branca da África portuguesa*. Ponta Delgada: Editor Gremio Açoreano.

Bastide, Roger, 1967, 'Color, Racism and Christianity', *Daedalus* 96 (Spring), pp. 312–27.

——, 1972, 'Lusotropicology, Race, and Nationalism, and Class Protest and Development', in *Protest and Resistance in Angola and Brazil*, pp. 225–40, ed. Ronald H. Chilcote. Berkeley: University of California Press.

——, 1974, 'The Present Status of Afro-American Research in Latin America', *Daedalus* 103 (Spring), pp. 111–23.

Beazley, C. Raymond, 1894, 'The Colonial Empire of the Portuguese to the Death of Albuquerque', *Transactions of the Royal Historical Society*, vol. 8. London: Longman, Green.

Bebiano, J. Bacelar, 1938, *Angola: alguns problemas*. Lisbon: Imprensa Nacional.

Bell, J. Bowyer, 1971, *The Myth of the Guerrilla*. New York: Alfred A. Knopf.

Bell, Wendell, 1964, *Jamaican Leaders: Political Attitudes in a New Nation*. Berkeley: University of California Press.

Beltran, Gonzalo Aguirre, 1970, 'The Integration of the Negro into the National Society of Mexico', in *Race and Class in Latin America*, pp. 11–27, ed. Magnus Morner. New York: Columbia University Press.

Bender, Gerald J., 1967, 'Political Socialization and Political Change', *Western Political Quarterly* 20 (July), pp. 390–407.

——, 1972a, 'The Limits of Counterinsurgency: an African Case', *Comparative Politics* 4 (April), pp. 331–60.

——, 1972b, 'Angola: History, Insurgency and Social Change', *Afirca Today* 19 (Winter), pp. 30–6.

——, 1974, 'Portugal and her Colonies Join the Twentieth Century: Causes and Initial Implications of the Military Coup', *Ufahamu* 4 (Winter), pp. 121–62.

——, 1975a, 'Portugal, Angola and Mozambique: A Year Later'. Unpublished paper presented to Yale University's Seven Springs Center's Symposium on Change in Contemporary Southern Africa, 9 May.

Bender, Gerald J., 1975b, 'The Myth and Reality of Portuguese Rule in Angola: A Study of Racial Domination', Ph.D dissertation, University of California, Los Angeles.

Bender, Gerald J. and Isaacman, Allen, 1976, 'The Changing Historiography of Angola and Mozambique', in *African Studies Since 1945: A Tribute to Basil Davidson*, pp. 220–48, ed. Christopher Fyfe. London: Longman.

Bender, Gerald J. and Yoder, P. Stanley, 1974, 'Whites in Angola on the Eve of Independence: The Politics of Numbers', *Africa Today* 21 (Fall), pp. 23–37.

Bender, Tamara L., 1973, 'The Fortress of São Miguel', *Jornal Português* (Oakland, California) (9 August).

Benguela, Depósito de Degredados Registo dos Ofícios, 1883–1895 (972/132). Arquivo Histórico de Angola, Códice No. 2–3–21.

Benguela, Depósito Subalterna de Degredados; Copiador de Ofícios, 1903–1904. Arquivo Histórico de Angola, Códice No. 3–6–3.

Benguela Quartel, Colónia Penal Militar, Registo da Correspondência Expedida (1506/317). Códice 3–6–1.

Benguela Quartel, Colónia Penal Militar Agrícola, Registo da Correspondência Expedida (1411/222). Códice 3–4–45.

Benguela Quartel, Depósito Subalterno de Degredados, Registo da Correspondência Oficial Expedida, 1905–1907 (1494/305). Arquivo Histórico de Angola. Códice No. 3–5–64.

Bettencourt, José de Sousa, 1961, *O fenómeno da emigração portuguesa.* Luanda: Instituto de Investigação Científica de Angola.

——, 1965, 'Subsidio para o estudo sociologico da população de Luanda', *Boletim do Instituto de Investigação Científica de Angola* 2 (Luanda), pp. 83–130.

Biggs-Davison, John, 1971, 'The Current Situation in Portuguese Guinea', *African Affairs* 70 (October), pp. 385–94.

Birmingham, David, 1965, *The Portuguese Conquest of Angola.* London: Oxford University Press.

Boavida, Américo, 1967, *Angola: cinco séculos de exploração portuguesa.* Rio de Janeiro: Editora Civilização Brasileira.

Bobela-Motta, A., 1974, 'Carta Aberta ao General Silvino Silverio Marques', *A Província de Angola* (Luanda), 8 June.

Boletim da Junta da Emigração, 1965, 1967. Porto: Ministério do Ultramar.

Boletim Geral do Ultramar, 1970, 46 (January–June).

Boletim Official do Governo Geral da Província D'Angola, 1851, no. 298 (14 June).

Bosman, William, 1963, *A New and Accurate Description of the Coast of Guinea,* quoted in C. R. Boxer, *Race Relations in the Portuguese Colonial Empire: 1415–1825.* Oxford: Clarendon Press.

Boxer, C. R., 1962, *Golden Age of Brazil.* Berkeley: University of California Press.

——, 1963, *Race Relations in the Portuguese Colonial Empire: 1415–1825.* Oxford: Clarendon Press.

——, 1965, *Portuguese Society in the Tropics: The Municipal Councils of Goa, Macao, Bahia, and Luanda, 1510–1800.* Madison: University of Wisconsin Press.

——, 1969, *Four Centuries of Portuguese Expansion: 1415–1825.* Berkeley: University of California Press.

Branco, João Bentes Castelo, 1894, 'Colónias militares', *Portugal in Africa* (Lisbon) 1.

Brandenburg, Frank, 1969, 'Transport Systems and Their External Ramifications', in *Portuguese Africa: A Handbook,* pp. 320–44, eds. David M. Abshire and Michael A. Samuels. New York: Praeger.

Brásio, António, 1944, *Os pretos em Portugal*. Lisbon: Agência Geral das Colónias.
———, 1953, *Monumenta missionária africana*, vols. 2 and 3. Lisbon: Agência Geral do Ultramar.
Brathwaite, Edward, 1971, *The Development of Creole Society in Jamaica, 1770–1820*. Oxford: Clarendon Press.
Brito, Raquel Soeiro de, 1967, 'A Ilha do Principe', *Geográphica* 3, (April), pp. 2–19.
Bullock, G. H., 1932, *Economic Conditions in Angola (Portuguese West Africa)*. London: Department of Overseas Trade.
Burns, E. Bradford, 1970, *A History of Brazil*. New York: Columbia University Press.
Cabral, Amílcar, 1969a, Foreword to *The Liberation of Guiné*, by Basil Davidson. Baltimore: Penguin Books.
———, 1969b, *Revolution in Guinea*. London: Stage I.
———, 1970, 'National Liberation and Culture', speech delivered at Syracuse University, 20 February and published by the Syracuse Program of Eastern African Studies. Occasional Paper No. 57.
———, 1972, 'Identity and Dignity in the National Liberation Struggle', *Africa Today* 19 (Fall), pp. 39–47.
———, 1974, *Guiné-Bissau: nação africana forjada na luta*. Lisbon: Nova Aurora.
Cadornega, António de Oliveira de, 1942, *História geral das guerras angolanas*, 3 vols., rev. ed. Lisbon: Agência Geral das Colónias.
Caetano, Marcello, 1946, *Relações das colónias de Angola e Moçambique com os territórios estrangeiros vizinhos*. Lisbon: Imprensa Nacional.
———, 1951a, 'Os antecedentes legislativos do Acto Colonial', *Estudos Ultramarinos* 1 (October–December), pp. 1–9.
———, 1951b, *Colonizing Traditions, Principles and Methods of the Portuguese*. Lisbon: Agência Geral do Ultramar.
———, 1954, *Os nativos na economia africana*. Coimbra: Coimbra Editora.
———, 1970, 'È na linha das reformas profundas que temos de prosseguir', *Notícias de Portugal*, no. 23 (October).
———, 1973a, 'Grito de Alarme', speech delivered to the Acção Nacional Popular, 9 April.
———, 1973b, interview with German newspaper *Die Welt* and reprinted in *Notícias de Portugal*, no. 27 (8 September).
———, 1973c, *Razões da presença de Portugal no Ultramar*. Lisbon: n.p.
———, 1974a, 'Linha de rumo para o Ultramar', speech presented to the National Assembly, Lisbon, 5 March 1974. Reprinted in *Notícias de Portugal*, no. 1401 (9 March).
———, 1974b, 'Conversa em família', speech over Portuguese radio and television, 28 March 1974. Reprinted in *Notícias de Portugal*, no. 1405 (6 April).
———, 1974c, interview with French magazine *Le Point* and reprinted in *Notícias de Portugal*, no. 1407 (20 April).
Camacho, Brito, 1930, *Gente Boer*. Lisbon: Editora Guimaraes.
Capela, José, see Martins, José Soares.
Capello, Guilherme Augusto de Brito, 1889a, *Aspects of Angolan History*. Lisbon: Imprensa Nacional.
———, 1889b, 'Relatório do Governador Geral da Província de Angola—1887', *Relatórios dos Governadores das Províncias Ultramarinas*. Lisbon: Imprensa Nacional.
Cardoso, Carlos Alberto Lopes, 1968, 'A traição de D. Nicolau de Agua Rosada e Sardonia', *Tribuna dos Musseques* (Luanda), no. 63 (8 August).
Carriço, Jacinto dos Santos and Morais, Julio Artur, 1971, *Perspectivas do desen-*

volvimento regional do Huambo. Nova Lisboa: Instituto de Investigação Agronómica de Angola.

Carter, Gwendolen, 1960, *Independence for Africa*. New York: Praeger.

Carvalho, Sebastião José de, 1940, 'Estudo histórico de problema da colonização em Angola e Moçambique, principalmente no período contemporâneo', *Congresso do Mundo Português*, vol. 15, book 2, part 2, pp. 71–114. Lisbon: Comissão Executiva dos Centenários.

Cascais, Fernando, 1975, 'Angola: accordo de transição para independência complexa', *Vida Mundial*, no. 1845:53–6 (23 January).

Castelinho, I., 1972, 'Cunene', *Portugal: An Informative Review*, no. 25 (July), pp. 22–5.

Chaliand, Gérard, 1969, *Armed Struggle in Africa: With the Guerrillas in Portuguese Guinea*, trans. David Rattray and Robert Leonhardt, Introduction by Basil Davidson. New York: Monthly Review Press.

Chilcote, Ronald, 1967, *Portuguese Africa*. Englewood Cliffs: Prentice-Hall.

——, 1969, *Emerging Nationalism in Portuguese Africa*. Stanford: Hoover Institution Press.

——, 1972a, *Emerging Nationalism in Portuguese Africa: Documents*. Stanford: Hoover Institution Press.

——, ed., 1972b, *Protest and Resistance in Angola and Brazil*. Berkeley: University of California Press.

Childs, Gladwyn Murray, 1944, 'Notes on Civil Administration in Angola: Civilizing Words', unpublished paper written 11 September.

——, 1949, *Umbundu Kinship and Character*. London: Oxford University Press.

Christensen, C. Diane and Wheeler, Douglas L., 1973, 'To Rise with One Mind: The Bailundu War of 1902, an Introductory Analysis', in *Social Change in Angola*, pp. 53–92, ed. Franz-Wilhelm Heimer. Munich: Weltforum.

Cidade, Hernani and Santos, Carlos Afonso [Carlos Selvagem], 1967, *Cultura Portuguesa*. Lisbon: Empresa Nacional de Publicidade.

Clignet, Remi, 1970, 'Inadequacies of the Notion of Assimilation in African Education', *Journal of Modern African Studies* 8 (October), pp. 425–44.

Coelho, José Gonçalves, n.d.(a), 'Condicionalismo de reagrupamento das populações pastoris da Huíla', paper presented to the Angolan Council on Counter-Subversion.

——, n.d.(b), 'Uma política de reordenamento da população de Angola, com base na expansão Vimbundos', paper presented to the Angolan Council on Counter-Subversion.

Cohen, William B., 1975, 'French Racism and Its African Impact', paper presented at UCLA African Studies Center Coloquium on 'New Perspectives on French Imperialism in Africa', 1 May.

Coissoro, Narana Sinai, 1961, 'Política de assimilação na África portuguesa', *Estudos Ultramarinos* 3, pp. 69–85.

——, 1966, *The Customary Laws of Succession in Central Africa*. Lisbon: Junta de Investigações do Ultramar.

Colecção oficial de legislação portuguesa: publicada no ano de 1932, 1940, first and second half. Lisbon: Imprensa Nacional.

Collins, Robert O., 1971, *Europeans in Africa*. New York: Alfred A. Knopf.

Colónia de Angola, 1941, *Censo geral da população, 1940*, vol. I. Luanda: Imprensa Nacional.

——, 1943, *Censo geral da população, 1940*, vol. VII. Luanda: Imprensa Nacional.

Comissão de Estudo da Secção I, 1969, 'Plano de Contra-Subversão: relatório, conclusões e sugestões', paper presented to the Symposium on Counter-Subversion, Luanda, January.

Comissão de Estudos, 1968, *O problema do povoamento visto e analisado em Angola*, presented to the General Council on Counter-Subversion, Luanda, September.

Committee for Freedom in Mozambique, Angola and Guiné, n.d., *White Power: The Cunene River Scheme*. London.

Congresso do Mundo Português, 1940, vol. 15, book 2, part 2. Lisbon: Comissão Executiva dos Centenários.

Conselho do Governo, 1886, *Acta da Reunião do Conselho do Governo de Angola*, 10 June.

Conselho Legislativo, 1926, *Representação do 1.º Conselho Legislativo aos poderes centrais*. Luanda: Empreza de Propaganda Colonial.

Cordeiro, Luciano, 1934a, *Obras de Luciano Cordeiro*. Coimbra: Imprensa da Universidade.

——, 1934b, 'Relatório da Comissão dos Negócios Externos da Câmara dos Senhors Deputados', presented 20 May 1885 and reprinted in *Obras de Luciano Cordeiro: questões coloniais*, pp. 590–632. Coimbra: Imprensa da Universidade.

Corrêa, A. A. Mendes, 1940, 'O mestiçamento nas colonias Portuguesas', in *Congresso do Mundo Português*, vol. XIV, Tomo 1, Lisbon: Comissão Executiva dos Centenários, Secção de Congressos.

——, 1943, *Raças do império*. Porto: Portucalense Editora.

——, 1953, 'A cultura portuguesa na África e no Oriente', in *Atas do colóquio internacional de estudos luso-brasileiros*. Nashville, Tenn.: Vanderbilt University Press.

Correia, António Simões, 1955, *Código penal português* Lisbon: Livraria Ferin.

Costa, Eduardo da, 1906, *A questão do Cuanhama*. Lisbon.

Costa, Julio Carvalho, n.d., 'Promoção socio-económica', paper presented to the Symposium on Counter-Subversion.

Couceira, Henrique de Paiva, 1948, *Angola (dois anos de governo junho 1970–junho 1909): história e comentários*. Lisbon: Edições Gama, Comemorative Edition.

Couto e Silva, Fernando L., 1968, 'A tentativa da colonização oficial de 1928', Master's thesis, Instituto Superior de Ciências Sociais e Política Ultramarina, Lisbon.

Crawford, William Rex, 1961, *A Century of Latin American Thought*, rev. ed. Cambridge, Mass.: Harvard University Press.

Crowder, Michael, 1962, *The Story of Nigeria*. London: Faber and Faber.

Cruz, Domingos da, 1928, *A crise de Angola*. Lisbon: Imprensa Lucas.

Cruz de Carvalho, Eduardo, 1974, ' "Traditional" and "Modern" Patterns of Cattle Raising in Southwestern Angola: A Critical Evaluation of Change from Pastoralism to Ranching', *Journal of Developing Areas* 8 (January), pp. 199–226.

Cruz de Carvalho, Eduardo and Guimarães, Francisco de Vasconcelos, 1968, 'A evoluço do crédito agrícola em Angola', paper presented at the Symposium of the Southern African Regional Commission for Conservation and Utilization of the Soil, Salisbury, Rhodesia, 23–30 May.

Cruz de Carvalho, Eduardo and Vieira da Silva, Jorge, 1973, 'The Cunene Region Ecological Analysis of an African Agropastoral System', in *Social Change in Angola*, pp. 145–92, ed. Franz-Wilhelm Heimer. Munich: Weltforum Verlag.

'Cunene Scheme May Attract More Guerrillas Than Settlers', 1972, *African Development*, July, pp. 14–16.

Dash, Leon, 1973, 'Black Roots in Angola', *Washington Post* (26 December).
———, 1974, 'After 13 Years, Angola War Remains a Stalemate', *Washington Post* (5 August).
Davidson, Basil, 1955, *The African Awakening*. London: Macmillan.
———, 1961, *The African Slave Trade: Precolonial History, 1450–1850*. Boston: Little, Brown; Atlantic Monthly Press Book.
———, 1969, *The Liberation of Guinea: Aspects of an African Revolution*, Foreword by Amílcar Cabral. Baltimore: Penguin Books.
———, 1970, 'An Inside Look at Angola's Fight for Freedom', *African Report* 15 (December), pp. 16–18.
———, 1972, *In the Eye of the Storm: Angola's People*. Garden City: Doubleday.
Degler, Carl N., 1971, *Neither Black nor White*. New York: Macmillan.
'Os degredados e a ordem pública', 1908, *Portugal em África* 15 (no. 178), 22 May.
Delgado, Ralph, n.d., *História de Angola*, 4 vols. Lisbon: Edição do Banco de Angola.
———, 1944, *Ao sul do Cuanza: ocupação e aproveitamento do antigo Reino de Benguela*. Lisbon.
———, 1960, 'A ocupação de Angola durante os séculos XVII e XVIII e os tipos e os rumos do respectivos colonatos europeus', *Actas: Congresso Internacional de História dos Descobrimentos*, vol. 5, part 2. Lisbon.
Diário do Governo (Lisbon), 1961, first series, no. 207, 6 September.
Diário do Governo (Lisbon), 1970, first series, no. 250, 28 October.
Dias, Gastão Sousa, 1947, *A mulher portuguesa na colonização de Angola*. Luanda: Cadernos Coloniais de Propaganda e Informação, no. 10.
———, 1959, *Os portugueses em Angola*. Lisbon: Agência Geral do Ultramar.
———, 1971, *Pioneiros de Angola*, 2nd ed. Lisbon: Agência Geral do Ultramar.
Dias, Jorge, 1960, 'Convívio entre pretos e brancos nas províncias ultramarinas portuguesas', *Estudos Ultramarinos* 3, pp. 21–32.
Dias, Manuel da Costa, 1913, *Colonização dos Planaltos de Angola*. Lisbon: by the Author.
Diogo, Alberto, 1963, *Rumo à industrialização de Angola*. Luanda: Junta de Desenvolvimento Industrial.
Direcção dos Serviços de Economia, 1953, *Angola, Província de Portugal em Africa*. Luanda: Realização Gráfica de Publicações Unidade.
'Dispatches from U.S. Consuls in Saint Paul de Loanda, 1854–93', roll 5, vol. 5, no. 17.
Dollard, John, 1937, *Caste and Class in a Southern Town*. New Haven, Conn.: Yale University Press.
Donald, Cleveland, Jr., 1972, 'Equality in Brazil: Confronting Reality', *Black World* 22 (November), pp. 23–34.
DuBois, W. E. B., 1925, 'Worlds of Color', *Foreign Affairs* 3 (April), pp. 23–34.
Duffy, James, 1959, *Portuguese Africa*. Cambridge, Mass.: Harvard University Press.
———, 1962a, *Portugal in Africa*. Cambridge, Mass.: Harvard University Press.
———, 1962b, *Portugal's African Territories: Present Realities*, Occasional Paper no. 1. New York: Carnegie Endowment for International Peace.
———, 1967, *A Question of Slavery*. Cambridge, Mass.: Harvard University Press.
Dzidzienyo, Anani, 1971, *The Position of Blacks in Brazilian Society*. London: Minority Rights Group.
Economia Portuguesa (Lisbon), 1970, no. 2 (November).

Edgerton, F. Clement C., 1955, *Angola Without Prejudice*. Lisbon: Agência Geral do Ultramar.

———, 1957, *Angola in Perspective: Endeavour and Achievement in Portuguese West Africa*. London: Routledge and Kegan Paul.

Ehnmark, Anders and Wastberg, Per, 1963, *Angola and Mozambique: The Case Against Portugal*. London: Pall Mall Press.

Enes, António, 1946, *Moçambique: relatório apresentado ao governo*, 3rd ed. Lisbon: Agência Geral das Colónias.

Estado de Angola, 1972, *Informações estatísticas*. Luanda: Direcção Provincial dos Serviços de Estatística.

———, 1973a, *Alguns elementos acerca da Missão de Extensão Rural de Angola*. Nova Lisboa: MERA.

———, 1973b, Missão de Extensão Rural de Angola, *Relatório de actividades, 1972*. Nova Lisboa: MERA.

Estermann, Carlos, 1960a, *Etnografia do sudoeste de Angola: os povos não Bantos e o grupo étnico dos Ambos*, 2nd ed., vol. 1. Lisbon: Junta de Investigações do Ultramar.

———, 1960b, *Etnografia do sudoeste de Angola: grupo étnico Nhaneca-Humbe*, 2nd ed., vol. 2. Lisbon: Junta de Investigações do Ultramar.

Fanon, Franz, 1963, *The Wretched of the Earth*. New York: Grove Press.

———, 1967, *Black Skin, White Masks*. New York: Grove Press.

Faria e Maia, Carlos Roma Machado, 1924, 'Zonas colonisaveis, estudo de adaptação de europeus', reprint from *2.º Congresso Colonial Nacional*.

———, 1930, 'Colonisação da raça branca portuguesa em Angola', reprint from *3.º Congresso Colonial Nacional*.

Farinha, António Lourenço, 1969, *D. Afonso I, rei do Congo*, 2nd ed. Lisbon: Agência Geral do Ultramar.

Felner, Alfredo de Albuquerque, 1933, *Angola: apontamentos sobre a ocupação e início de estabelecimento dos portugueses no Congo, Angola e Benguela*. Coimbra: Imprensa do Universidade.

Fernandes, Florestan, 1969, *The Negro in Brazilian Society*, trans. Jacqueline D. Skiles, A. Brunel and Arthur Rothwell. New York: Columbia University Press.

———, 1967, 'The Weight of the Past', *Daedalus* 96 (Spring), 560–79.

———, 1970, 'Immigration and Race Relations in São Paulo', in *Race and Class in Latin America*, pp. 122–42, ed. Magnus Morner. New York: Columbia University Press.

Ferrão, F. da Silva, 1856–7, *Theoria do direito penal aplicada ao Código Penal Português*, vol. 2. Lisbon.

Ferreira, Vicente, 1933, 'A capital de Angola', *Boletim geral das colonias* 19 (October), pp. 100–19.

———, 1936, 'A ciência e o empirismo na colonização moderna', *Anais do Instituto Superior de Ciências Económicas e Financeiras* 4.

———, 1954a, 'Alguns aspectos da política indígena de Angola', originally published in 1934 and reprinted in Vicente Ferreira, *Estudos Ultramarinos*. Lisbon: Agência Geral do Ultramar, vol. 3, pp. 35–50.

———, 1954b, *Estudos Ultramarinos*, 4 vols. Lisbon: Agência Geral do Ultramar.

———, 1954c, 'Regiões de povoamento europeu nos planaltos de Angola', *Estudos Ultramarinos*, vol. 3, part 2, *Angola e os seus problemas*, pp. 87–128. Lisbon: Agência Geral do Ultramar.

Figueiredo, Alphonse de, 1966, *Le Portugal: considérations sur l'état de l'administration, des finances, de l'industrie et du ce royaume*, Lisbon, 1866, in R. J. Hammond, *Portugal and Africa: 1815–1910*. Stanford: Stanford University Press.

Figueiredo, António de, 1965, 'The Children of Rape', *The New African* 4 (November), pp. 203–7.

First, Ruth, 1963, *South West Africa*. Baltimore: Penguin Books.

Fonseca, Armando Xavier da, 1940, 'Caudais emigratórios da metrópole e sua arrumação no império colonial português', *Congresso do Mundo Portugues* 15, pp. 563–78.

Fonseca, Francisco Pereira da, 1969, 'A evolução e perspectivas das exportações de vinhos para as províncias ultramarinas', *Diário de Notícias* (Lisbon), 13 June.

Freitas Morna, Álvaro de, 1944, *Angola, un ano no Governo Geral (1942–1943)*, vol. 1. Lisbon: Livraria Popular de F. Franco.

Freyre, Gilberto, 1940, *O mundo que o português criou*. Rio de Janeiro: Livraria José Olympio Editora.

——, 1953, *Um brasileiro em terras portuguesas*. Rio de Janeiro: Livraria José Olympio Editora.

——, 1957, *Casa grande e senzala*, 9th ed. Lisbon: Edição Livros do Brasil.

——, 1958, *Integração portuguesa nos trópicos*. Lisbon: Junta de Investigações do Ultramar.

——, 1961, *The Portuguese and the Tropics*. Lisbon: Executive Committee for the Commemoration of the Vth Centenary of the Death of Prince Henry the Navigator.

——, 1963, *Mansions and Shanties: The Making of Modern Brazil*, trans. Harriet de Onis. New York: Alfred A. Knopf.

——, 1964, *The Masters and the Slaves: A Study in the Development of Brazilian Civilization*, 2nd ed., abridged, trans. Samuel Putnam. New York: Alfred A. Knopf.

Fyfe, Christopher, ed., 1976, *African Studies Since 1945: A Tribute to Basil Davidson*. London: Longman.

Gabriel, D. Manuel Nunes, 1958, 'De aquem e alem-mar', speech presented to the Legislative Council of Angola and reprinted in *Portugal em África* 15 (May–June), pp. 184–90.

Gallie, W. B., 1959, 'Explanations in History and the Genetic Sciences', in *Theories of History*, pp. 386–402, ed. Patrick Gardiner. Glencoe: The Free Press.

Galvão, Henrique, 1932, 'Um critério do povoamento europeu nas colónias portuguesas', *Boletim Geral das Colónias* 8 (May), pp. 3–26.

——, 1937, *Angola: para uma nova política*, vol. 1: *Fisionomia do passado, aspectos do presente*. Lisbon: Livraria Popular de Francisco Franco.

——, 1949, *Por Angola: quatro anos de actividade parlamentar, 1945–49*. Lisbon: by the Author.

——, 1961, *Santa Maria: My Crusade for Portugal*, trans. William Longfellow. Cleveland: World Publishing Co.

Galvão, Henrique and Selvagem, Carlos [Carlos Alfonso dos Santos], 1952, *Império ultramarino portugues*. Lisbon: Empresa Nacional de Publicadade.

Galvao de Melo, 1975, *MFA: Movimento Revolucionario*. Lisbon: Portugalia Editora.

Gann, L. H. and Duignan, Peter, 1962, *White Settlers in Tropical Africa*. Baltimore: Penguin Books.

——, 1969, 'Reflections on Imperialism and the Scramble for Africa', in

Colonialism in Africa, vol. 1: *The History and Politics of Colonialism 1870–1914*, pp. 100–32. Cambridge: Cambridge University Press.

Gaspar, José Maria, 1958, 'A colonização branca em Angola e Moçambique', *Estudos de ciências políticas e sociais* 7, pp. 31–54.

——, 1960, 'Sistemas de povoamento', *Colóquios sobre problemas de povoamento*, Estudos de ciências políticas e sociais, no. 33. Lisbon: Junta de Investigações do Ultramar.

——, 1961,'Angola e Moçambique e o problema do seu povoamento nos séculos XIX e actual', *Estudos Ultramarinos* 3, pp. 19–26.

Gaspar, Manuel da Cruz, 1966, 'Aspectos do multiracialismo em Angola', Master's thesis, Instituto Superior de Ciências Sociais e Política Ultramarina, Lisbon.

General Council on Counter-Subversion, 1968, *O problema do povoamento visto e analisado em Angola: relatório*. Luanda.

Gomes dos Santos, José A, 1903, *As nossas colónias*. Lisbon: Empreza do 'Portugal em África' Editora.

——, 1908, 'A situação em Angola', *Portugal em África: Supplemento Colonial* 15 (7 September).

Gourou, Pierre, 1965, 'Étude comparée de l'Amazonie et du Congo Central', *Actas do III colóquio internacional de estudos luso-brasileiros*, Lisbon, 1959, cited by José Honório, *Brazil and Africa*, p. 17. Berkeley: University of California Press.

Governo do Brasil, 1956, *VI Recenseamento Geral do Brasil (1950)*, vol. 1. Rio de Janeiro.

Governo Geral da Província de Angola, 1900, *Annuário estatística da província de Angola, 1898*. Luanda: Imprensa Nacional.

Governo Geral de Angola, 1968, *Secretaria Provincial de Educação: Sintese das actividades dos serviços, 1966–1967*. Luanda: Edição do Centro de Informação e Turismo de Angola.

Graham, Richard, 1970, 'Action and Ideas in the Abolitionist Movement in Brazil', in *Race and Class in Latin America*, pp. 51–69, ed. Magnus Morner. New York: Columbia University Press.

Grande enciclopedia portuguesa e brasileira, n.d., vol. 4. Lisbon and Rio de Janeiro: Editorial Enciclopedia.

Grundy, Kenneth, 1973, *Confrontation and Accommodation in Southern Africa*. Berkeley: University of California Press.

Grupo de Coordenação e Inspecção de Contra-Subversão, 1968, no. 3, 'Relatório especial; breves reflexões sobre os problemas da contra-subversão na zona do G. C. I', paper presented to the Symposium on Counter-Subversion, 20 October.

Grupo de Trabalho Sectorial, n.d., no. 19, 'Relatorio: mão de obra e politica de emprego, promoção e ordenamento das populações nacionais', unpublished government report. Luanda.

Guerra, A. J. de Passos and Veiga, Jorge Bonucci, 1970, *Revisão do III Plano de Fomento: promoção social*. Luanda: Junta Provincial de Povoamento.

Guerreiro, Manual Viegas, 1958, 'Boers de Angola', *Garcia de Orta* 6, pp. 11–31.

Guimarães, Francisco de Vasconcelos, 1969, 'Aspectos do "regulamento de ocupação e concessão de terrenos nas provincias ultramarinas" com interesse para a contra-subversão', paper presented to the Council on Counter-Subversion, 7 January.

Guimarães Sobrinho, Venancio, 1964, Acta da Sessão no. 121 of the Conselho Legislativo de Angola, 14 May 1964, p. 2416, quoted in João Pereira Neto,

Angola, meio século de integração, p. 214. Lisbon: Instituto Superior de Ciências Sociais e Política Ultramarina.

Hailey, Lord, 1956, *An African Survey*, rev. ed. London: Oxford University Press.

Hammond, R. J., 1966, *Portugal and Africa, 1815–1910: A Study in Economic Imperialism*. Stanford: Stanford University Press.

——, 1967, 'Race Attitudes and Policies in Portuguese Africa in the Nineteenth and Twentieth Centuries', *Race* 9, pp. 205–16.

Hargreaves, John, D., 1967, *West Africa: The Former French States*. Englewood Cliffs: Prentice-Hall.

Haring, C. H., 1958, *Empire in Brazil*. Cambridge, Mass.: Harvard University Press.

Harris, Marvin, 1952, 'Race Relations in Minhas Velhas, A Community in the Mountain Region of Central Brazil', in *Race and Class in Rural Brazil*, ed. Charles Wagley. Paris: UNESCO.

——, 1970, 'Referential Ambiguity in the Calculus of Brazilian Racial Identity', in *Afro-American Anthropology*, pp. 75–86, ed. Norman E. Whitten, Jr. and J. F. Szwed. New York: The Free Press.

Heath, Dwight B. and Adams, Richard N., eds., 1965, *Contemporary Cultures and Societies of Latin America*. New York: Random House.

Heilbroner, Robert L., 1963, *The Great Ascent*. New York: Harper and Row.

Heimer, Franz-Wilhelm, 1972, *Educação e sociedade nas áreas rurais de Angola: resultados de um inquérito*, vol. 1, preliminary draft (Luanda).

——, 1973a. *Educação e sociedade nas áreas rurais de Angola: resultados de um inquerito*, vol. 2, preliminary draft (Luanda).

——, 1973b, 'Education, Economics and Social Change in Rural Angola: The Case of the Cuima Region', in *Social Change in Angola*, pp. 111–44, ed. Franz-Wilhelm Heimer. Munich: Weltforum Verlag.

——, ed., 1973c, *Social Change in Angola*. Munich: Weltforum Verlag.

——, 1974, *Educação e sociedade nas áreas rurais de Angola: resultados de um inquérito, análise do universo agrícola*, vol. 2, preliminary draft (Luanda).

'Herbicides—Another Form of Massacre in Angola', 1973, *Southern Africa* 6 (October), p. 22.

Herrick, Allison Butler *et al.*, 1967, *Area Handbook for Angola*. Washington, D.C.: Government Printing Office.

Herring, Hubert, 1961, *A History of Latin America from the Beginnings to the Present*, 2nd ed. New York: Alfred A. Knopf.

Herskovits, M. J., 1930, *The Anthropometry of the American Negro*. New York: Columbia University Press.

Hill, M. F., 1960, 'The White Settler's Role in Kenya', *Foreign Affairs* 38 (July), pp. 638–45.

Hoagland, Jim, 1971, 'White Elite Rules Portuguese Africa', *Washington Post*, 18 April.

——, 1972, *South Africa: Civilizations in Conflict*. Boston: Houghton Mifflin.

Hoetink, Harry, 1970, 'The Dominican Republic in the Nineteenth Century: Some Notes on Stratification, Immigration, and Race', in *Race and Class in Latin America*, pp. 96–121, ed. Magnus Morner. New York: Columbia University Press.

Hoppe, Fritz, 1970, *A África Oriental portuguesa no tempo do Marques de Pombal: 1750–1777*. Lisbon: Agência Geral do Ultramar.

Horrell, Muriel, 1967, *South-West Africa*. Johannesburg: South African Institute of Race Relations.

Horrell, Muriel, 1968, *Introduction to South Africa, Basic Facts and Figures*. Johannesburg: South African Institute of Race Relations.

——, 1971, *A Survey of Race Relations in South Africa, 1970*. Johannesburg: South African Institute of Race Relations.

IDOC, 1974, *Angola: Secret Government Documents on Counter-Subversion*, trans. and ed. Caroline Reuver-Cohen and William Jerman. Rome: IDOC.

Institute for Strategic Studies, 1970, *The Military Balance 1970–1971*. London: Institute for Strategic Studies.

Instituto Nacional de Estatística, 1955, *I.º Congresso dos Economistas Portugueses (Problemas das economias ultramarinas); IV Secção—colonização étnica (Comunicações e debates)*. Lisbon.

——, 1960, *Anuário estatístico do ultramar, 1959*. Lisbon.

——, 1972, *Anuário Estatístico, 1970: Províncias Ultramarinas*, vol. 2. Lisbon: Imprensa Nacional.

International Labour Organization, 1971, *Report by Pierre Juvigny, Representative of the Director-General of the International Labour Office, On Direct Contact with the Government of Portugal Regarding the Implementation of the Abolition of Forced Labour Convention, 1957* (no. 105). Geneva: International Labour Organization.

Isaacman, Allen F., 1972, *Mozambique: The Africanization of a European Institution*. Madison: University of Wisconsin Press.

——, 1976, *The Tradition of Resistance in Mozambique: Anti-Colonial Activity in the Zambesi Valley, 1850–1921*. Berkeley: University of California Press.

Isaacman, Allen and Isaacman, Barbara, 1975, 'The Prazeros as Transfrontiersmen: A Study in Social and Culture Change', *The International Journal of African Historical Studies* 8, pp. 1–39.

Jaspert, Willem, 1929, *Through Unknown Africa*, trans. Agnes Platt. London: Jarrolds Publishers.

Jesus, Quirino Avelino de, 1885, 'A colonização luso-africana', *Portugal em Africa* 22.

——, 1894, 'Uma proposta de lei de colonisação', *Portugal em Africa* 1.

Jordan, Winthrop D., 1968, *White Over Black: American Attitudes Toward the Negro 1550–1812*. Baltimore: Penguin.

Jordão, Joaquim Pedro M. Vasconcelos No., 1969, *Povoamento em Angola: 1962–1967*. Luanda: Junta Provincial de Povoamento de Angola.

Jorge, Ricardo, 1940, *Origem e desenvolvimento da população do Porto: notas históricas e estatísticas*, Porto, 1897, cited by J. A. Pires da Lima, *Mouros, judeus e negros na história de Portugal*. Porto: Livraria Civilização-Editora.

July, Robert W., 1970, *A History of the African People*. New York: Charles Scribner's Sons.

Jundanian, Brendan F., 1974, 'Resettlement Programs: Counterinsurgency in Mozambique', *Comparative Politics* 6 (July), pp. 519–40.

Junior, Alfredo Diago, n.d., *Angola perante a escravatura*. Luanda: Editorial Quissange.

Junior, Faria Blanc, 1916, *O depósito de degredados*. Luanda: Imprensa Nacional de Angola.

Junior, M. M. de Brito, 1974, 'Multiracialidade portuguesa—um mita', *Província de Angola* (Luanda) (6 June).

Junta Provincial de Povoamento de Angola, 1963, *Relatório anual das actividades, 1963*. Luanda: Junta Provincial de Povoamento de Angola.

——, 1967, *Relatório anual das actividades, 1966*. Luanda: Junta Provincial de Povoamento de Angola.

Junta Provincial de Povoamento de Angola, 1968, *Relatório anual das actividades, 1967*. Luanda: Junta Provincial de Povoamento de Angola.

Kalili, Narciso and Mattos, Odacir de, 1967, 'Existe preconceito de côr no Brasil', *Realidade* (Rio de Janeiro) 2 (October), pp. 35–60.

Kaplan, Irving *et al.*, 1969, *Area Handbook for Zambia*. Washington, D.C.: U.S. Government Printing Office.

Katzen, M. F., 1969, 'White Settlers and the Origin of a New Society, 1652–1778', in *The Oxford History of South Africa, vol. I—South Africa to 1870*, pp. 183–232, ed. Monica Wilson and Leonard Thompson. New York: Oxford University Press.

Kaúlza de Arriaga, 1971, *Lições de estratégia do curso altos comandos—1966/67*, vol. 12, cited by Amílcar Cabral, 'A Brief Report on the Situation of the Struggle' (mimeographed) September.

Kay, George, 1970, *Rhodesia: A Human Geography*. New York: Africana Publishing Corp.

Kay, Hugh, 1970, *Salazar and Modern Portugal*. New York: Hawthorn Books.

Kennan, George F., 1971, 'Hazardous Courses in Southern Africa', *Foreign Affairs* 49 (January), pp. 218–36.

Klineberg, O., ed., 1944, *Characteristics of the American Negro*. New York: Harper.

Knapic, Dragomir, 1964, *Geografia económica de Portugal*, vol. 2, part 2. Lisbon: Instituto Comercial de Lisboa.

Kroeber, A. L., 1937, 'Diffusionism', in *The Encyclopedia of the Social Sciences*, vol. 3, eds. Edwin R. A. Seligman and Alvin Johnson. New York: Macmillan.

Kuper, Leo, 1965, *An African Bourgeoisie: Race, Class and Politics in South Africa*. New Haven, Conn.: Yale University Press.

——, 1974, *Race, Class and Power*. Chicago: Aldine Publishing Company.

Laidley, Fernando, 1964, *Missões de Guerra e da paz no norte de Angola*. Lisbon: Tapete Mágico.

Lasswell, Harold D. and Kaplan, Abraham, 1950, *Power and Society: A Framework for Political Inquiry*. New Haven, Conn.: Yale University Press.

Lavrádio, Marques do, 1936, *Portugal em África depois de 1851*. Lisbon: Agência Geral das Colónias.

Lebre, António, 1934, *Africa desconhecida*, Cadernos Coloniais, no. 2. Lisbon: Editorial Cosmos.

Leitão, Fernando Rodrigues, 1963, 'Contribuição para o estudo do sistema prisional no ultramar', Master's thesis, Instituto Superior de Ciências Sociais e Política Ultramarina, Lisbon.

Lemos, Alberto de, 1936, *Bases para a solução dos problemas da colonização de Angola*. Lisbon: by the Author.

——, 1941, 'Introdução ao primeiro censo geral da população de Angola', Colónia de Angola, *Censo geral da população, 1940*, vol. 1. Luanda: Imprensa Nacional.

——, 1957, 'Colonização étnica', *Brotheria* 64 (April), pp. 445–60.

Lenz, Oscar, 1886, 'La cote occidentale de l'Afrique', *Bulletin de la Union Géographique du Nord de la France* 8.

Leonard, Olen D. and Loomis, Charles P., eds., 1953, *Readings in Latin American Social Organization and Institutions*. East Lansing: Michigan State College.

Lewis, M. G., 1971, *Journal of a West India Proprietor, Kept During a Residence in the Island of Jamaica*, cited by Edward Brathwaite, *The Development of Creole Society in Jamaica, 1770–1820*, p. 175. Oxford: Clarendon Press.

Lima, J. A. Pires da, 1940, *Mouros, judeus e negros na história de Portugal*. Porto: Livraria Civilização-Editora.

Linton, Ralph, 1936, *The Study of Man*. New York: Appleton-Century.

Livermore, H. V., 1966, *A New History of Portugal*. Cambridge: Cambridge University Press.

Long, Edward, 1968, *The History of Jamaica*, vol. 2. London, 1774, quoted in Winthrop D. Jordan, *White Over Black: American Attitudes Toward the Negro, 1550–1812*. Baltimore: Penguin Books.

Lopes, Adelino Amaral, 1968, 'O funcionalismo público no conjunto do "problema do povoamento"', paper presented to the Council on Counter-Subversion (June).

Lopes, Vicente, 1936, 'Angola, 1906–1910', *O mundo português* 2 (August–September), pp. 347–55.

Lopez de Lima, José Joaquim, 1846, *Ensaios sobre a statística das possessões portuguezas no ultramar*, vol. 3. Lisbon: Imprensa Nacional.

Lopo, Julio de Castro, 1964a, *Jornalismo de Angola: subsídios para a sua história*. Luanda: C.I.T.A.

———, compiler, 1964b, *Governadores-gerais e outras entidades de função governativa da província de Angola: 1575–1964*. Luanda: C.I.T.A.

Lowenthal, David, 1969, 'Race and Color in the West Indies', *Daedalus* 96 (Spring 1967), reprinted in *Comparative Perspectives on Race Relations*, pp. 293–312, ed. Melvin M. Tumin. Boston: Little, Brown and Co.

Luanda: Copiador dos Ofícios Expedidos pela Secretaria do Depósito dos Degredados, 1883–1885 (1381/192). Arquivo Histórico de Angola. Códice No. 3-4-15.

Macedo, José de, 1910, *Autonomia de Angola*. Lisbon: by the Author.

Machado, Álvaro, 1935, 'Colonização', *Boletim da Sociedade de Geografia de Lisboa* 53 (May–June), pp. 228–37.

Machado, José Vieira, 1940, *Colonização—projectos de decretos*. Lisbon: Agência Geral das Colónias.

Maciel, Artur, 1963, *Angola Heróica: 120 dias com os nossos soldados*. Lisbon: Livraria Bertrand.

Madeiros, Carlos Alberto, 1976, *A colonização das Terras Altas da Huíla*. Lisbon: Centro de Estudos Geograficos.

Magalhães, António Miranda de, 1934, 'Colonização branca no Ultramar: erros do passado', in *Conclusões das teses apresentadas ao Primeiro Congresso de Colonização*, pp. 13–14. Porto: Imprensa Moderna.

Magno, David, 1916–17, *Revista militar*, nos. 8–12 (1916) and nos. 1–4 (1917); a nine-part series.

———, 1934, *Guerras angolanas*. Porto: Companhia Portuguesa Editora.

Mannoni, O., 1964, *Prospero and Caliban: The Psychology of Colonization*, 2nd ed. New York: Praeger.

Mantero, Francisco, 1969, *Manual Labour in S. Thome and Principe*. New York: Negro Universities Press.

Marcelino, Anibal Artur, 1930, *Colonização de Angola por brancos*. Funchal: Livraria Popular.

Marcum, John, 1967, 'Three Revolutions', *Africa Report* 12 (November), pp. 8–22.

———, 1969, *The Angolan Revolution: The Anatomy of an Explosion*, vol. 1. Cambridge, Mass. M.I.T. Press.

Marques, A. H. de Oliveira, 1964, *A sociedade medieval portuguesa*. Lisbon: Sá da Costa Editora.

Marques, A. H. de Oliveira, 1972, *History of Portugal*, 2 vols. New York: Columbia University Press.

Marques, Silvino Silvério, 1969a, 'Estrategia estrutural portuguesa', *Defesa Nacional* 35 (January), pp. 329–32.

——, 1969b, 'Estrategia estrutural portuguesa', *Defesa Nacional* 35 (part 2), (February), pp. 385–9.

Marques, Walter, 1964, *Problemas do desenvolvimento económico de Angola*, 2 vols. Luanda: Junta de Desenvolvimento Industrial.

Martins, José Soares (José Capela), 1973, *O Vinho Para o Preto*. Porto: Afrontamento.

——, 1974, *Escravatura: a empresa de Saque, o abolicionisma (1810–1875)*. Porto: Afrontamento.

Matta, J. D. Cordeiro da, 1970, *Cartilha racional para se aprender a ler Kimbundu (ou lingua Angolense)*, Lisbon, 1892, cited by Michael A. Samuels, *Education in Angola, 1878–1914*. New York: Teachers College Press.

Maurício, Fernando Gomes, 1966, speech given during 'Overseas Week', 1965, reprinted in *Migrações e povoamento, conferências e palestras proferidas em Angola, na 'Semana do Ultramar, 1965'*. Luanda: Instituto de Angola.

Maxwell, Kenneth, 1975a, 'The Hidden Revolution in Portugal', *The New York Review of Books* 22 (17 April), pp. 29–35.

——, 1975b, 'Portugal Under Pressure', *The New York Review of Books* 22 (29 May), pp. 20–30.

Melo, Antonio, Capela, Jose, Moita, Luis and Pereira, Nuno, eds., *Colonialismo e lutas de libertação (7 cadernos sobre a guerra colonial)*. Porto: Afrontamento.

Melo, Vasco Marinho Homem de, 1940, 'O degrêdado', *Boletim dos institutos de criminologia*, no. 6, pp. 133–97.

Memmi, Albert, 1975, *The Colonizer and the Colonized*. Boston: Beacon Press.

Mendes, Afonso, 1957–58, 'A não discriminação e o direito da associação nos territórios não metropolitanos e os trabalhadores indígenas em Angola', *Estudos ultramarinos* 7, pp. 83–95.

——, 1958, *A Huila e Moçâmedes: considerações sobre o trabalho indigena*. Lisbon: Junta de Investigaçoes do Ultramar.

——, 1966, *O trabalho assalariado em Angola*. Lisbon: Instituto Superior de Ciências Sociais e Política Ultramarina.

——, 1969, 'Aspectos relevantes da contra-subversão', paper presented to the Council on Counter-Subversion, 17 January.

Mendonça, R. Zuzarte de, 1965, 'O desenvolvimento social das populações rurais', *Actividade económica de Angola* 71 (January–April).

Menezes, Sebastião Lopes de Calheiro, 1867, *Relatórios dos governadores das províncias ultramarinas*. Lisbon: Imprensa Nacional.

Merton, Robert K., 1962, *Social Theory and Social Structure*. Glencoe: The Free Press.

Miller, Joseph, 1973, 'Requiem for the "Jaga"', *Cahiers d'études africaines* 13, pp. 121–49.

Ministério do Interior, 1965, *Boletim da Junta da Emigração*. Lisbon: Ministério do Interior.

——, 1967, *Boletim da Junta da Emigração, 1965*. Porto: Ministerio do Interior.

Ministério do Ultramar, Missão de Inquéritos Agrícolas de Angola, 1964a, *Recenseamento agrícola de Angola, IV: Planalto de Malange: Agricultura empresarial*. Luanda: M.I.A.A.

Ministério do Ultramar, *et al.*, 1964b, *Recenseamento agrícola de Angola: Bacia Leiteira Cela-Catofe (First Part)*, *1962–63*. Luanda: M.I.A.A.

——, 1968, *Recenseamento agrícola de Angola*. vol. 20. Luanda: M.I.A.A.

Minter, William, 1972, *Imperial Network and External Dependency: The Case of Angola*. Beverly Hills: Sage Publications.

Mintz, Sidney, 1974, 'The Caribbean Region', *Daedalus* 103 (Spring), pp. 45–71.

Monteiro, Armindo, 1935, *Da governação de Angola*. Lisbon: Agência Geral das Colónias.

——, n.d., *Para uma política imperial*. Lisbon: Agência Geral das Colónias.

——, 1936, 'The Portuguese in Modern Colonization', speech delivered to the 22nd meeting of the International Colonial Institute, 18 April 1933 and published by the Agência Geral das Colónias (Lisbon).

Monteiro, Joachim J., 1875, *Angola and the River Congo*, 2 vols. London: Macmillan.

Monteiro, José Alberto Pereira, 1961, 'Considerações acerca da revogação do Estatuto de Indigenato', *Estudos Ultramarinos* 4, pp. 23–40.

Monteiro, Ramiro Ladeiro, n.d., 'Breves considerações sobre alguns aspectos focados no Plano de Contra-Subversão do G. C. I., no. 1', submitted to the Symposium on Counter-Subversion.

——, 1968, 'As profissões liberais e o problema do povoamento em Angola', presented to the Council on Counter-Subversion, 27 June.

——, 1973a, *A família nos musseques de Luanda*. Luanda: Fundo de Acção Social no Trabalho em Angola.

——, 1973b, 'From Extended to Residual Family: Aspects of Social Change in the Musseques of Luanda', in *Social Change in Angola*, pp. 211–33, ed. Franz-Wilhelm Heimer. Munich: Weltforum.

Morais, Carlos Alexandre de, n.d., 'Controlo das populaçoes nos reagrupamentos', presented to the Symposium on Counter-Subversion.

Morais, João David de, 1972, 'Quando o mar bate na areia', *Notícia*, no. 662 (12 August), pp. 40–5.

Moreira, Adriano, 1951, 'A revogação do Acto Colonial', *Estudos Ultramarinos* 1, (July–September), pp. 3–38.

——, 1954, *O problema prisional do ultramar*. Coimbra: Coimbra Editora.

——, 1955, *Administração da Justiça aos indígenas*. Lisbon: Agência Geral do Ultramar.

——, 1956, 'The "Elites" of the Portuguese "Tribal" Provinces (Guinea, Angola, Mozambique)', *International Social Science Bulletin* 8, 458–81.

——, 1961a, *Ensaios*. 2nd ed. Lisbon: Edições Panorama.

——, 1961b, 'Política de integração', *Estudos Ultramarinos* 4, 7–21.

——, 1961c, *Política ultramarina*. Lisbon: Junta de Investigaçoes do Ultramar.

——, 1962, *Batalha da esperança*, 2nd ed. Livraria Bertrand.

Morgado, Nuno Alves, 1958, 'Crónicas demográficas—III: População branca das províncias de Angola e Moçambique', *Boletim geral do ultramar* 34 (December), pp. 247–53.

——, 1960a, 'Perspectivas demo-económicas do povoamento', *Coloquios sobre problemas de povoamento*, Estudos de Ciencias Políticas e Sociais, no. 33, pp. 105–23. Lisbon: Junta de Investigações do Ultramar.

——, 1960b, 'Povoamento em África', speech presented at the Institute of Advanced Military Studies, 11 March 1960 and reprinted in *Estudos Ultramarinos* 2, pp. 101–18.

Morner, Magnus, ed., 1970, *Race and Class in Latin America*. New York: Columbia University Press.

Morris, Richard, ed., 1953, *Encyclopedia of American History*. New York: Harper and Brothers.

Moura, Horacio de, 1968, *Reflexões sobre os discursos de Salazar*, 2nd ed., vol. 2. Coimbra: Edição da Communidade Distrital de Combra.

Mouzinho, Fernando Borges *et al.*, 1969, *Parâmetros actuais do povoamento em Angola*. Luanda: n.p.

O mundo português, 1935, 2 (editorial) (July–August), pp. 217–19.

Murdock, George Peter, *Africa: Its Peoples and Their Culture History*. New York: McGraw-Hill.

Nascimento, Abdias do, 1968, *O negro revoltado*. Rio de Janeiro: Ediçoes GDR.

Nascimento, J. Pereira and Mattos, A. Alexandre de, 1912, *A colonização de Angola*. Lisbon: Typographia Mendonça.

Neto, João Pereira, 1962, 'Política de integração em Angola e Moçambique', *Estudos Ultramarinos* 2, pp. 100–3.

——, 1964, *Angola, meio século de integração*. Lisbon: Instituto Superior de Ciências Sociais e Política Ultramarina.

——, 1971, *Qualificação Sociale Profissional dos Alienigenas*. Lisbon: by the Author.

Nevinson, Henry, 1906, *A Modern Slavery*. London: Harpers.

Newitt, M.D.D., 1973, *Portuguese Settlement on the Zambesi*. New York: Africana Publishing Co.

Niddrie, David, L., 1969, 'The Role of Ground Transport in the Economic Development of Angola', *Journal of the American-Portuguese Cultural Society* 3 (Winter–Spring), pp. 1–13.

——, 1970, 'The Cunene River: Angola's River of Life', *Journal of the American-Portuguese Cultural Society* 6 (Winter–Spring), pp. 1–17.

Nogueira, António Francisco, 1963, *A Ilha de São Tomé*, cited by Douglas L. Wheeler, *The Portuguese in Angola, 1836–1891: A Study in Expansion and Administration*, pp. 37–8, Ph.D. dissertation, Boston University.

Nogueira, Franco, 1963, *The United Nations and Portugal: A Study in Anti-Colonialism*. London: Sidgwick and Jackson.

——, 1967, *The Third World*. London: Johnson.

Nogueira, Jofre Amaral, 1955, 'Perspectiva histórica e aspectos actuais do povoamento Europeu de Angola', in *I? Congresso dos economistas Portugueses: Problemas das economias ultramarinas; IV Secção—Colonização Étnica*. Lisbon: Centrode Estudos Economicos, pp. 83–123.

Nogueira, Oracy, 1959, 'Skin Color and Social Class', in *Plantation Systems of the New World*, pp. 166–75. Social Science Monographs 7. Washington, D.C.: Pan American Union.

Norton de Matos, José Mendes Ribeiro, 1926, *A província de Angola*. Porto: Edição de Marânus.

——, 1933, 'Como pretendi povoar Angola', *Boletim geral das colónias* 9 (October), pp. 90–9.

——, 1944, *Memórias e trabalhos da minha vida*, 4 vols. Lisbon: Editora Marítimo Colonial.

——, 1953, *African nossa*. Porto: Edições Marânus.

Nowell, Charles E., 1973, *Portugal*. Englewood Cliffs, N. J.: Prentice-Hall.

Nunes, Horácio Lusitano and Morao, Virgílio Gil Pires, n.d., 'Necessidade de enquadramento das populações rurais com elementos evoluídos', paper presented to the Symposium on Counter-Subversion.

Nunes, José Pereira, n.d., 'Reagrupamento das populações e saude'. Luanda: Inspecção Provincial de Saude e Assistência de Angola.

O'Brien, Rita Cruise, 1972, *White Society in Black Africa: The French of Senegal.* Evanston: Northwestern University Press.

Oliveira, Mário António Fernandes de, 1964, 'Aspectos sociais de Luanda inferidos dos anuncios públicados na sua imprensa', *Boletim do Instituto de Angola* 19, (May–August), pp. 45–53.

———, 1968, annotator, *Angolana: documentação sobre Angola,* vol. 1. Luanda: Instituto de Investigação Científica de Angola.

Oliveira, Mario António Fernandes de and Couto, Carlos Alberto Mendes do, annotators, 1971, *Angolana,* vol. 2. Luanda: Instituto de Investigação Científica de Angola.

Oliveira, Osório de, 1934, 'A mestiçagem: esboço duma opinião favoravel', *O mundo português,* November, pp. 367–9.

Oliveira, Waldir Freitas, 1965, 'Brancos e pretos em Angola', *Afro-Asia,* no. 1 (December), pp. 33–9.

Oliveira Martins, Joaquim Pedro, 1887, *O Brazil e as colónias portuguesas,* 3rd ed. Lisbon: Guimaraes.

Oliveira Monteiro, 1968, 'Relatório focando os aspectos que me foram dados observar através dos inquéritos que fiz contactando directamente com os colonos no colonato da Matala', internal report prepared for M.I.A.A., Luanda.

Oliver, Roland and Fage, J. D., 1962, *A Short History of Africa.* Baltimore: Penguin Books.

Osório, João de Castro, 1940, 'Aspectos económicos do problema da colonização branca nas colónias portuguesas', presented to the Ninth Colonial Congress and reprinted in *Congresso do Mundo Português,* vol. 15, part 2, pp. 249–68. Lisbon: Comissão Executiva dos Centenários.

Overseas Companies of Portugal, n.d., *The Cunene Development Plan.* Lisbon.

Padua, Mario Moutinho de, 1963, *Guerra em Angola: diário de um médico em campanha.* São Paulo: Editora Brasiliense.

Passos Guerra, A. J. and Veiga, Jorge Bonucci, 1970, 'Revisão do III Plano de Fomento: promoção social', unpublished government document (Luanda).

Passos Guerra, A. J., Diogo da Silva, F. and Martins da Silva, A. S., 1969, 'Relatório e Conclusões: Estudo da Secção VI ("Promoção Social-Reordenamento Rural")', paper presented to the Symposium on Counter-Subversion, 24 January.

Patch, Richard W., 1960, 'Bolivia: U.S. Assistance in a Revolutionary Setting', in *Social Change in Latin America Today,* pp. 108–76, ed. Richard N. Adams. New York: Vintage Books.

Patraquim, José Gonçalves Pereira, 1966, 'Colonização penal: algumas experiências em Angola (1870–1900)', Master's thesis, Instituto Superior de Ciências Sociais e Política Ultramarina, Lisbon.

Paxeco, Fran, 1916, *Angola e os alemais.* Maranhão: by the Author.

Pedriras, Horácio Reis and Pinto, Franklim de Jesus, 1968, 'Considerações gerais: povoamento versus subversão', paper presented to the Council on Counter-Subversion, 27 August.

Pelissier, René, 1974, 'Conséquences demographiques des revoltes en Afrique portugaise (1961–1970)'. *Revue française d'histoire d'outre-mer* 61 (222), pp. 34–64.

Pelissier, René, 1975, 'Resistance et revoltes en Angola 1845–1961', 3 vols., Ph.D. thesis, Paris, Sorbonne.

Pereira, Gil, 1963, 'Alguns elementos estatísticos sobre a emigração portuguesa', *Estudos políticos e sociais* 1, pp. 961–96.

Pery, Geraldo A., 1875, *Geographia e estatística geral de Portugal e colónias*. Lisbon: Imprensa Nacional.

Pettigrew, Thomas F., 1964, *A Profile of the Negro American*. Princeton: D. Van Nostrand.

Pierson, Donald, 1953, 'The Educational Process and the Brazilian Negro', in *Readings in Latin American Social Organization and Institutions*, pp. 101–8, eds. Olen E. Leonard and Charles P. Loomis. East Lansing: Michigan State College Press.

——, 1967, *Negroes in Brazil: A Study of Race Contact*, 2nd ed. Carbondale: Southern Illinois University Press.

Pigafetta, Filippo, 1970, *A Report of the Kingdom of the Congo and Surrounding Countries*, trans. Margarite Hutchinson. London: Frank Cass.

Pina, Luís Maria da Câmara, 1968, 'O valor da presença militar na difusão da cultura portuguesa em África', parts I and II, *Revista Militar* 120 (August–September), pp. 533–48 and 120 (October), pp. 636–61.

Pinheiro Chagas, Manuel, 1890, *As colónias portuguezas no século XIX*. Lisbon.

Pinto, Eduardo, 1968, 'Preconceito de classe atinge negros 80 anos apos abolição', *Jornal do Brasil* (Rio de Janeiro), 12 May.

Pinto, Julio Ferreira, 1926, *Angola: notas e comentários de um colono*. Lisbon: J. Rodrigues.

Pitt-Rivers, Julian, 1967, 'Race, Color and Class in Central America and the Andes', *Daedalus* 96 (Spring), pp. 542–59.

Plano de Fomento para 1959–64: programa geral de execução de investimentos inscritos e estimativa de repartição dos encargos nos seis anos de vigência, 1959. Lisbon: Imprensa Nacional.

Polanah, Luis, 1972, 'Resistência e adesão a mudança', *Reordenamento* (Luanda), no. 25 (July–September), pp. 7–16.

Ponce, Joaquim A. Montes Fialho, 1960, 'O Cuanza-Sul: considerações sobre povoamento europeu', Master's thesis, Instituto Superior de Ciências Sociais e Política Ultramarina, Lisbon.

Poppino, Rollie E., 1968, *Brazil: The Land and People*. New York: Oxford University Press.

Possinger, Hermann, 1970, 'Congresso de povoamento e promoção social', speech delivered 9 October, Andulo, Angola. Mimeographed.

——, 1973, 'Interrelations Between Economic and Social Change in Rural Africa: The Case of the Ovimbundu of Angola', in *Social Change in Angola*, pp. 31–52, ed. Franz-Wilhelm Heimer. Munich: Weltforum Verlag.

Prego, João de Madureira Fialho, 1969, 'Reagrupamento e controlo das populações: relatório e conclusões', paper presented to the Symposium on Counter-Subversion, 30 January.

Província da Guiné, 1959, *Censo da população, 1950*. Lisbon: Junta de Investigações do Ultramar.

Província de Angola, Direcção dos Serviços de Estatísticas, 1953, *II recenseamento geral do população, 1950*, vol. 1. Luanda: Imprensa Nacional.

——, 1955, *II recenseamento geral da população, 1950*, vol. 3. Luanda: Imprensa Nacional.

Província de Angola, *et al.*, 1964, *III recenseamento geral da população, 1960*, vol. 1. Luanda: Imprensa Nacional.

——, 1967, *III recenseamento geral da população, 1960*, vol. 2. Luanda: Imprensa Nacional.

——, 1968, *Anuário estatístico 1966*. Lisbon: Imprensa Nacional.

Quarenta e cinco dias em Angola: apontamentos de viagem, 1862, Porto: Pereira.

Rama, Carlos, 1970, 'The Passing of the Afro-Uruguayans from Caste Society into Class Society', in *Race and Class in Latin America*, pp. 28–50, ed. Magnus Morner. New York: Columbia University Press.

Ramos, Artur, 1952, *Las poblaciones del Brasil*, Mexico City, 1944, cited by Charles Wagley, *Race and Class in Rural Brazil*. Paris: UNESCO.

Ramos, Manuel da Silveira, 1952, 'Segregação—privilégio branco', *Estudos Ultramarinos* 2 (July–December), pp. 62–70.

Ranger, T. O., ed., 1968, *Aspects of Central African History*. London: Heinemann.

Raposo, Louisa Maria Simões, 1972, 'Angola: ocupação e posse de terras', *Prisma*, May, pp. 35–43.

Reade, W. Winwood, 1864, *Savage Africa*, 2nd ed. London: Smith, Elder and Co.

Rebelo, Horácio de Sá Viana, 1961, *Angola na África deste tempo*. Lisbon: by the Author.

Redinha, José, 1967, *Distribuição étnica da província de Angola*, 4th ed. Luanda: C.I.T.A.

'Relatório da Associação Comercial de Luanda', 1960, *Boletim oficial da colónia de Angola* 33 (suplemento), 1887, in Ilídio do Amaral, *Aspectos do povoamento branco de Angola*. Lisbon: Junta de Investigações do Ultramar.

'Relatório de conclusões: comissão de estudo da secção VI ("Promoção Social-Reordenamento Rural")', 1969, presented to the Symposium on Counter-Subversion, Luanda, 24 January.

Rella, José Manuel Zenha, 1974, 'A distribuição espacial da população e o planeamento regional', *Reordenamento* (Luanda), no. 32 (March–April), pp. 3–8 and no. 33 (May–June), pp. 37–40.

Renseignements coloniaux et documents publiés par le Comité de l'Afrique française et le Comité du Maroc. Supplement de l'Afrique française de Mars 1925.

Republic of South Africa, 1966, *Statistical Yearbook*. Pretoria: Bureau of Statistics.

Ribeiro, Orlando, 1961, 'Problemas humanos de Africa', in *Colóquios sobre problemas humanos em regiões tropicais*. Lisbon: Junta de Investigações do Ultramar.

——, 1975, *Destinos do ultramar*. Lisbon: Livros Horizonte.

Rios, José Arthur, 1971, 'The Growth of Cities and Urban Development', in *Modern Brazil: New Patterns and Development*, pp. 269–88, ed. John Saunders. Gainesville: University of Florida Press.

Rivers, Bernard, 1974, 'Angola: Massacre and Oppression', *Africa Today* 21 (Winter), pp. 41–5.

Roberts, R. D. *et al.*, 1963, *Area Handbook for Senegal*. Washington D.C.: U.S. Government Printing Office.

Robson, L. L., 1965, *The Convict Settlers of Australia*. London and New York: Cambridge University Press.

Rodney, Walter, 1968, 'European Activity and African Reaction in Angola', in *Aspects of Central African History*, pp. 49–70, ed. T. O. Ranger. London: Heinemann.

Rodrigues, José Honório, 1965, *Brazil and Africa*. Berkeley: University of California Press.

Rogers, Cyril A. and Frantz, C., 1962, *Racial Themes in Southern Rhodesia: The Attitudes and Behavior of the White Population*. New Haven: Yale University Press.

Rogers, William, 1971, Report of the Secretary of State, *United States Foreign Policy, 1969–1970*. Washington D.C.: U.S. Government Printing Office.

Rosa, Manuel Ferreira, 1961, *Indicações didácticas: Para professores primários, regentes escolares e professores da fase de adaptação*, 3rd ed. Luanda: n.p.

Rosental, Eric, 1934, 'Os Boers de Angola e o seu destino', *Boletim da Sociedade de Geografia de Lisboa* 52 (January–February), pp. 1–14.

Rotberg, Robert I. and Mazrui, Ali, 1970, *Protest and Power in Black Africa*. New York: Oxford University Press.

Ruddle, Kenneth and Hamour, Mukhtar, 1971, *Statistical Abstract of Latin America, 1970*. Los Angeles: Latin American Center, University of California, Los Angeles.

Sá da Bandeira, Marques de, 1873, *O trabalho rural africano e a administração colonial*. Lisbon: Imprensa Nacional.

Sá Carneiro, Ruy de, 1949, 'A política colonial do Estado Novo', *Boletim geral das colónias* 25 (February), pp. 24–5.

Sá Pereira, Jose Matos, 1968, 'O problema do povoamento', paper presented to the Council on Counter-Subversion, 25 May.

Salazar, António de Oliveira, 1939, *Doctrine and Action: Internal and Foreign Policy of the New Portugal, 1928–1939*, trans. Robert Edgar Broughton. London: Faber and Faber.

——, 1963, Speech broadcast on Portuguese radio, 1 November 1957 and cited by Anders Ehnmark and Per Wastberg, *Angola and Mozambique: The Case Against Portugal*. London: Pall Mall Press.

——, 1966, 'The Decision to Stay', speech delivered 13 April 1966 in 'reply to the tribute paid to him by the Province of Angola'. Lisbon: Secretariado Nacional da Informação.

——, 1968, 'Portugal e a companha anticolonialista', reprinted in *Reflexões sobre os discursos de Salazar*, vol. 2, 2nd ed., ed. Horácio de Moura. Coimbra: Edição da Comunidade Distrital de Coimbra.

Salazar, Sigurd von Willer, n.d., 'A alimentação nos agregados africanos do Distrito de Malange', paper presented to the Symposium on Counter-Subversion.

Samuels, Michael Anthony, 1967, 'The New Look in Angolan Education', *Africa Report* 12 (November), pp. 63–6.

——, 1970, *Education in Angola, 1878–1914: A History of Culture Transfer and Administration*. New York: Teachers College Press.

——, 1972, 'A Failure of Hope: Education and Changing Opportunities in Angola Under the Portuguese Republic', in *Protest and Resistance in Angola and Mozambique*, pp. 53–65, ed. Ronald H. Chilcote. Berkeley: University of California Press.

Samuels, Michael A. and Bailey, Norman A., 1969, 'Education, Health, and Social Welfare', in *Portuguese Africa: A Handbook*, pp. 178–201, eds. David M. Abshire and Michael A. Samuels. New York: Praeger.

Santa Rita, José Godinho de Matos, 1940, 'Da emigração portuguesa nos últimos 50 anos: como se deve preparar o emigrante para ser um bom colono', *Congresso do Mundo Português*, vol. 15, part 2, pp. 135–72. Lisbon: Comissão Executiva dos Centenários.

Santa Rita, José Gonçalo de, 1940, 'O contacto das raças nas colónias. Seus efeitos políticos e sociais. Legislação portuguesa', in *Congresso do Mundo Português*, vol. 15, part 2, pp. 11–70. Lisbon: Comissão Executiva dos Centenários.

——, 1952, 'Oliveira Martins e a política colonial', *Estudos Ultramarinos* 2 (January–June).

Santos, Beleza dos, 1930–1, 'O degrêdo e sua execução em Angola', *Boletim da Faculdade de Direito, Universidade de Coimbra* 12, pp. 161–201.

Santos, Eduardo dos, 1965, *Maza*. Lisbon: by the Author.

Santos, José de Almeida, 1966, 'Migrações e povoamento', in *Migrações e povoamento*, pp. 45–77. Luanda: Instituto de Angola.

Santos, Oliveira, 1957–58, 'O problema das terras em Angola', *Estudos Ultramarinos* 7, pp. 61–81.

Saraiva, António José, 1963, *História da literatura portuguesa*, 7th ed. Lisbon: Publicações Europa-América.

——, 1969, *Inquisição e Cristões-Nova*. Porto: Editora Inova.

Sarsfield, Alexandre, 1897, 'Questões coloniais', *Revista militar* (Lisbon) 49.

Saunders, John, ed., 1971, *Modern Brazil: New Patterns and Development*. Gainesville: University of Florida Press.

Schwartz, Stuart, 1973, 'Free Labor in a Slave Economy: The Lavradores de Cana of Colonial Bahia', in *Colonial Roots of Modern Brazil*, pp. 147–97, ed. Dauril Alden. Berkeley: University of California Press.

——, 1974, 'The Manumission of Slaves in Colonial Brazil: Bahia, 1684–1745', *Hispanic American Historical Review* 54, (November), pp. 603–35.

Selvagem, Carlos, 1952, *Imperio ultramarino português*. Lisbon: Imprensa Nacional de Publicidade.

Serpa, Eduardo, 1972, 'De degredado a governador', *Boletim Cultural* (Luanda) 37 (October–December).

Sharman, T. C., 1954, *Overseas Economic Surveys. Portuguese West Africa: Economic and Social Conditions in Portuguese West Africa (Angola)*. London: Her Majesty's Stationery Office.

Shaw, A. G. L., 1966, *Convicts and the Colonies*. London: Faber and Faber.

Silberfein, Marilyn, 1969, 'Selected Bibliography on African Rural Geography', in *Research in Rural Africa*, pp. 311–18, ed. Norman N. Miller. East Lansing, Michigan: Michigan State University, African Studies Center.

Silva, Elisete Marques da, 1973, 'Social Conditions of School Attendance and Achievement of Minors in Suburban Luanda', in *Social Change in Angola*, pp. 193–210, ed. Franz-Wilhelm Heimer. Munich: Weltforum Verlag.

Silva, Fernando Diogo da, n.d., *O Huambo, mão-de-obra rural no mercado do trabalho*. Luanda: Fundo de Acção Social no Trabalho de Angola.

Silva Cunha, J. M. da, 1949, 'Temas coloniais', *Boletim das colónias* 25 (April), pp. 9–20.

——, 1953, *O sistema português de política indígena, subsídios para o seu estudo*. Coimbra: Coimbra Editora.

——, 1955, *O trabalho indígena*, 2nd ed. Lisbon: Agência Geral do Ultramar.

——, 1963, *Problemas actuais de África negra*. Lisbon: Agência Geral do Ultramar.

Silva Rego, António da, 1957, 'História da colonização moderna', unpublished manuscript, Lisbon.

——, 1961, *Lições de missionologia*. Lisbon: Junta de Investigações do Ultramar.

——, 1967, 'Reflexões da história Caboverdiana (1460–1580)', in *Curso de Extensão Universitária—Cabo Verde, Guiné, São Tomé e Principe*. Lisbon: Instituto Superior de Ciências Sociais e Política Ultramarina.

Silva Rego, António da, 1969, *O ultramar português no século XIX*, 2nd ed. Lisbon: Agência Geral do Ultramar.

———, 1970, *O ultramar português no século XVIII*, 2nd ed. Lisbon: Agência Geral do Ultramar.

Silva Rego, António da and Santos, Eduardo dos, 1964, *Atlas missionário português*. Lisbon: Junta de Investigações do Ultramar.

Silva Telles, Francisco Xavier da, 1903, *A transportação penal e a colonisação*. Lisbon: Livraria Ferin.

Simons, H. J. and Simons, R. E., 1969, *Class and Colour in South Africa 1850–1950*. Baltimore: Penguin Books.

Simonsen, Roberto C., 1937, *História económica do Brasil, 1500–1820*, 4 vols. São Paulo: Companhia Editora Nacional, Biblioteca Pedagógica Brasileira.

Skidmore, Thomas E., 1964, 'Gilberto Freyre and the Early Brazilian Republic: Some Notes on Methodology', *Comparative Studies in Society and History* 6 (July), pp. 490–505.

———, 1974, *Black into White: Race and Nationality in Brazilian Thought*. New York: Oxford University Press.

Smith, Harvey *et al.*, 1967, *Area Handbook for South Vietnam*. Washington D.C.: U.S. Government Printing Office.

Smith, T. Lynn, 1971, 'The People of Brazil and Their Characteristics', in *Modern Brazil: New Patterns and Development*, pp. 51–70, ed. John Saunders. Gainesville: University of Florida Press.

———, 1972, *Brazil: People and Institutions*, 4th ed. Baton Rouge: Louisiana State University Press.

Soares, Amadeu Castilho, 1960, 'Povoamento e justaposição de grupos humanos no Ultramar', in *Colóquios Sobre Problemas de Povoamento*. Lisbon: Estudos de Ciências Políticas e Sociais, no. 33.

Soares, Vicente Henriques Varela, 1935, 'Um homen. Um chefe', *O mundo português* 2 (December), pp. 385–93.

Sodré, Nelson Werneck, 1942, *Orientações do pensamento brasileiro*. Rio de Janeiro: Casa Editora Vecchi.

Sorrensen, M. P. K., 1967, *Land Reform in the Kikuyu Country*. Nairobi: Oxford University Press.

———, 1968, *Origins of European Settlement in Kenya*. Nairobi: Oxford University Press.

Sousa Ferreira, Eduardo de, 1974a, *Aspectos do colonialismo português*. Lisbon: Seara Nova.

———, 1974b, *Portuguese Colonialism in Africa: The End of an Era*. Paris: UNESCO.

Southall, Aidan, 1971, 'Imperialism and Economic Development', in *Colonialism in Tropical Africa*, vol. 3, *Profiles of Change: African Society and Colonial Rule*, pp. 216–55, ed. Victor Turner. Cambridge: Cambridge University Press.

Soveral, Carlos Eduardo de, 1952, 'Introdução a um estudo sociológico de Angola', *Boletim da Sociedade de Geografia de Lisboa* 70 (April–June), pp. 127–46.

Spinola, António de, 1974, *Portugal e o futuro*. Lisbon: Arcádia.

Stampp, Kenneth, 1956, *The Peculiar Institution: Slavery in the Ante-Bellum South*. New York: Vintage Books.

Steward, Julian H. and Faron, Louis C., 1959, *Native Peoples of South America*. New York: McGraw-Hill.

Stillman, Edmond, 1969, 'Development in Angola, Some Remarks on the

Economic and Political Dimension', in *Angola: Some Views on Development Prospects*, vol. 1, pp. 153–74.

Tams, G., 1969, *Visit to the Portuguese Possessions in Southwestern Africa*, Introduction by H. Evans Lloyd, trans. H. Evans Lloyd. New York: Negro Universities Press.

Tannenbaum, Frank, 1964, *Ten Keys to Latin America*. New York: Alfred A. Knopf.

Tenreiro, Francisco José, 1953, 'Descrição da Ilha de São Tomé no século XVI', *Garcia de Orta* 1, pp. 219–28.

——, 1961, *A Ilha de São Tomé*, Lisbon: Junta de Investigaçoes do Ultramar.

——, 1964, 'Angola: problemas de geografia humana', in *Angola: curso de extensão universitária, ano lectivo de 1963–64*, pp. 35–60. Lisbon: Instituto Superior de Ciências Sociais e Política Ultramarina.

Thompson, Leonard, M., 1966, *Politics in the Republic of South Africa*. Boston: Little, Brown and Co.

Tillman, James A., Jr., 1963, 'Exiles No More', unpublished manuscript.

Torres Garcia, António Alberto, 1934, 'A tenatativa de colonização oficial de 1928', speech presented at the 1934 Congress on Colonization and reprinted in the *Proceedings of the Primeira Exposição Colonial*. Coimbra: n.p.

Trabalhos Preparatórios do IV Plano de Fomento (1974–79): Educação, Serviços de Planeamento e Integração Economica, 1974, cited in Eduardo de Sousa Ferreira, *Portuguese Colonialism in Africa: The End of an Era*. Paris: UNESCO.

Trancoso, Francisco, 1920, *Angola*. Lisbon: Instituto Superior de Comércio de Lisboa.

Tumin, Melvin M., ed., 1969, *Comparative Perspectives on Race Relations*. Boston: Little, Brown and Co.

Turner, Victor, ed., 1971, *Colonialism in Africa, 1870–1960. Profiles of Change: African Society and Colonial Rule*. Cambridge: Cambridge University Press.

Union of South Africa, Union Office of Census and Statistics, 1923, *Official Yearbook of the Union*. Pretoria: Government Printing and Stationery Office.

United Nations, 1962, *Report of the Sub-Committee on the Situation in Angola*, (A/4978).

——, 1965, Document A/6000/Add. 3 (Part 2), Appendix 2, 18 November.

——, 1968, Document A/7200/Add. 3, 17 October.

——, 1969, Document A/7752/Add. 1, 22 July.

——, 1970a, Document A/AC.109/L.625/Add. 1, 8 May.

——, 1970b, Document A/8023/Add. 3, 5 October.

——, 1971a, Document SCI/71/4, 14 July.

——, 1971b, Document A/8398/Add. 1, 6 December.

——, 1972, Document A/8723/Add. 3, 1 September.

——, 1973a, Document A/AC.109/L.865, 9 May.

——, 1973b, Document A/9023(Part III), 11 October.

——, 1974, Document A/AC.109/L.918, 4 February.

——, 1975, Document A/10023/Add. 1, 20 November.

United Nations Monthly Chronicle, 1973, 10 (November), p. 145.

U.S. Congress House Committee on Foreign Affairs, 1972, *The Faces of Africa: Diversity and Progress, Repression and Struggle*. Report of Special Study Missions to Africa, ninety-second Congress, second session, 1972. Washington D.C.: Government Printing Office.

U.S. Congress House Sub-Committee on Foreign Affairs, 1970, *Policy Toward Africa for the Seventies*. Washington D.C.: Government Printing Office.

Urquhart, Alvin W., 1963, *Patterns of Subsistence and Settlement in Southwestern Angola*. Washington D.C.: National Academy of Sciences.

Valahu, Mugur, 1968, *Angola, chave de Africa*, trans. Maria Joaquina Roquette. Lisbon: Parceria A. M. Pereira.

Valentim, Jorge Alicerces, 1969, *Qui Libere l'Angola?* Brussels: Michele Copans.

Vansina, Jan, 1966, *Kingdoms of the Savanna*. Madison: University of Wisconsin Press.

Vasconcellos Pereira de Mello, J. Leite, 1936–41, *Etnografia portuguesa*, 3 vols. Lisbon: Imprensa Nacional de Lisboa.

Venter, Al, 1969, *The Terror Fighters: A Profile of Guerrilla Warfare in Southern Africa*. Cape Town: Purnell.

Ventura, Reis, 1955, 'O caso de Cela e a colonização étnica de Angola', in *I.º Congresso dos Economistas Portugueses (Problemas das economias ultramarinas); IV Secção—colonização étnica (Comunicações e debates)*. Lisbon: Instituto Nacional de Estatística.

Verrière, Louis, 1963, *Où en est, où va la population du Sénégal*. Dakar: Institut de Science Economique Appliquée.

Vianna, F. J. Oliveira, 1922, 'O povo brasileiro e sua evolução', in Ministério da Agricultura, Indústria e Comércio. *Recenseamento do Brasil, 1920*, vol. 1, pp. 281–400. Rio de Janeiro: Directória Geral de Estatística.

Vieira, Renato Parestrelo, n.d., 'Crítica e aspectos que necessitem revisão ou ajustamento', paper presented to the Symposium on Counter-Subversion.

Vieira da Silva, Jorge and Morais, Julio Artur de, 1973, 'Ecological Conditions of Social Change in the Central Highlands of Angola', in *Social Change in Angola*, pp. 93–110, ed. Franz-Wilhelm Heimer. Munich: Weltforum Verlag.

Villard, André, 1972, *Histoire du Senegal*, Dakar: Imprimerie Viale, 1943, cited by Rita Cruise O'Brien, *White Society in Black Africa, The French of Senegal*. Evanston: Northwestern University Press.

Villas, Gaspar do Couto Ribeiro, 1929, *Os portugueses na colonização*. Lisbon: by the Author.

von Hapsburg, Otto and Marjay, Frederic P., 1965, *Portugal: Pioneer of New Horizons*. Lisbon: Livraria Bertrand.

Wagley, Charles, ed., 1952, *Race and Class in Rural Brazil*. Paris: UNESCO.

——, 1963, *An Introduction to Brazil*. New York: Columbia University Press.

——, 1965, 'On the Concept of Social Race in the Americas', in *Contemporary Cultures and Societies of Latin America*, pp. 531–45, eds. Dwight B. Heath and Richard N. Adams. New York: Random House.

Wagley, Charles and Harris, Marvin, 1958, *Minorities in the New World*. New York: Columbia University Press.

Wheeler, Douglas L., 1963, *The Portuguese in Angola, 1836–1891: A Study in Expansion and Administration*, Ph.D. dissertation, Boston University.

——, 1964, 'A Note on Smallpox in Angola, 1670–1875', *Studia* (Lisbon) 13–14 (January–July), pp. 351–62.

——, 1967, 'Reflections on Angola', *Africa Report* 12 (November), pp. 58–62.

——, 1968, 'Nineteenth-Century African Protest in Angola: Prince Nicolas of Kongo (1830?–1860)', *African Historical Studies* 1, pp. 40–59.

——, 1969, 'The Portuguese Army in Angola', *Journal of Modern African Studies* 7 (October), pp. 425–39.

——, 1970, 'An Early Angolan Protest: The Radical Journalism of José de Fontes Pereira (1823–1891)', in *Protest and Power in Black Africa*, pp. 854–74, eds. Robert I. Rotberg and Ali Mazrui. New York: Oxford University Press.

——, 1972a, 'Origins of African Nationalism in Angola: Assimilado Protest

Writings, 1859–1929', in *Protest and Resistance in Angola and Brazil*, pp. 67–87, ed. Ronald H. Chilcote. Berkeley: University of California Press.

——, 1972b, 'Portugal in Angola: a Living Colonialism?', in *Southern Africa in Perspective*, pp. 172–82, eds. Christian P. Potholm and Richard Dale. New York: The Free Press.

——, 1972c, 'The Portuguese Revolution of 1910', *Journal of Modern History* 44 (June), pp. 172–94.

——, 1975, 'Africans in the Military Forces of Portuguese African States', paper presented to colloquium, 'Political Change in Portuguese-Speaking Africa', African Studies Center, University of California, Los Angeles, 20 February.

Wheeler, Douglas L. and Pelissier, René, 1971, *Angola*. New York: Praeger.

Whitaker, C. S., Jr., 1967, 'A Dysrhythmic Process of Political Change', *World Politics* 19 (January), pp. 190–217.

——, 1970, *The Politics of Tradition: Continuity and Change in Northern Nigeria, 1946–1966*. Princeton: Princeton University Press.

de Wilde, J., 1967, *Experiences with Agricultural Development in Tropical Africa*, vol. 2. Baltimore: Johns Hopkins Press.

Wilensky, Alfredo Hector, 1968, *Tendencias de legislación ultramarina portuguesa en África*. Braga: Editora Pax.

Willems, Emilio, 1953, 'Racial Attitudes in Brazil', in *Readings in Latin American Social Organization and Institutions*, pp. 240–4, eds. Olen E. Leonard and Charles P. Loomis. East Lansing: Michigan State College.

Wilson, Monica, 1969a, 'Co-operation and Conflict: The Eastern Cape Frontier', in *The Oxford History of South Africa: I—South Africa to 1870*, pp. 233–71, eds. Monica Wilson and Leonard Thompson. New York: Oxford University Press.

——, 1969b, 'The Hunters and Herders', in *The Oxford History of South Africa: I—South Africa to 1870*, pp. 40–74, eds. Monica Wilson and Leonard Thompson. New York: Oxford University Press.

Wirth, L. and Goldhamer, H., 1964, 'Passing', in *Characteristics of the American Negro*, pp. 301–19, ed. O. Klineberg, New York: Harper, 1944, cited by Thomas F. Pettigrew, *A Profile of the Negro American*, pp. 68, 214, 234. Princeton, N.J.: D. Van Nostrand.

Wohlgemuth, Patricia, 1963, *The Portuguese Territories and the United Nations*. New York: Carnegie Endowment for International Peace.

Zeiger, Henry A., 1961, *The Seizing of the Santa Maria*. New York: Popular Library.

Newspapers, Magazines and Miscellaneous Publications

African Confidential (London).
African Development (London).
BBC Summary of World Broadcasts.
Christian Science Monitor (Boston).
A Cidade (Luanda).
O Comércio (Luanda).
Comércio do Funchal (Madeira).
The Daily News (Dar es Salaam).
Daily Telegraph (London).
Diário de Luanda.
Diário de Notícias (Lisbon).

The Economist (London).
Expresso (Lisbon).
Facts and Reports (Amsterdam).
Guardian (London).
Intelligence Report (Lisbon).
Jornal do Brasil (Rio de Janeiro).
Jornal do Comércio (Lisbon).
Jornal do Congo (Carmona).
Los Angeles Times.
The Natal Mercury (Durban).
New Statesman (London).

Newsweek.
The New York Review of Books.
New York Times.
Notícia (Luanda).
Notícias de Portugal (Lisbon).
Portugal Hoje (Lisbon).
A Província de Angola (Luanda).
Realidade (Rio de Janeiro).
Republica (Lisbon).
Revista de Angola (Luanda).

Seara Nova (Lisbon).
Southern Africa (New York).
Southern African Information Service (London).
The Star (Johannesburg).
Star Weekly (Johannesburg).
The Times (London).
Times of Zambia (Lusaka).
Tribuna dos Musseques (Luanda).
Vida Mundial (Lisbon).
Washington Post.

Index

Index